Foundations
of Information
Literacy

ALA Neal-Schuman purchases fund advocacy, awareness, and accreditation programs for library professionals worldwide.

Foundations of Information Literacy

Natalie Greene Taylor
Paul T. Jaeger

ALA
Neal-Schuman

CHICAGO :: 2022

ISBNs
978-0-8389-4970-2 (paper)
978-0-8389-3812-6 (PDF)
978-0-8389-3810-2 (ePub)

Library of Congress Cataloging-in-Publication Data
Names: Taylor, Natalie Greene, 1987– author. | Jaeger, Paul T., 1974– author.
Title: Foundations of information literacy / Natalie Greene Taylor and Paul T. Jaeger.
Description: Chicago : ALA Neal-Schuman, 2022. | Includes bibliographical references and index. |
    Summary: "Drawing upon both the latest research and best practices, the authors address information
    literacy in ways relevant for all types of libraries, providing both the broader context and a range
    of applied strategies and programs for promoting and teaching information literacy"—Provided by
    publisher.
Identifiers: LCCN 2021034871 (print) | LCCN 2021034872 (ebook) | ISBN 9780838949702 (paperback) |
    ISBN 9780838938126 (pdf) | ISBN 9780838938102 (epub)
Subjects: LCSH: Information literacy.
Classification: LCC ZA3088 .T39 2022 (print) | LCC ZA3088 (ebook) | DDC 028.7—dc23
LC record available at https://lccn.loc.gov/2021034871
LC ebook record available at https://lccn.loc.gov/2021034872

Cover design by Kimberly Hudgins. Cover images © Adobe Stock.
Text design and composition by Karen Sheets de Gracia in the Cardea and Acumin Pro typefaces.

⊗ This paper meets the requirements of ANSI/NISO Z39.48-1992 (Permanence of Paper).

Printed in the United States of America
26 25 24 23 22   5 4 3 2 1

For Oliver—who, as of this writing, is still waiting to enter the world but still reminds us that a better, more educated world is worth the fight.

And for the librarians around the world whose innovation and persistence have made it possible for libraries to continue serving their communities in new and extraordinary ways throughout the global pandemic caused by the novel coronavirus. In taking good care of those in their care, librarians have torn up their lawns to make room for vegetable gardens to feed hungry community members, turned their buildings into food pantries and virus testing and inoculation centers, and figured out how to deliver books to elementary and secondary students using drones.
We've never been more proud to be librarians,
which is really saying something.

CONTENTS

ACKNOWLEDGMENTS AND SANCTUARY *ix*

LIST OF ACRONYMS *xi*

1 Searching for Information (Literacy) *1*

2 Defining Information Literacy *11*

3 Information Literacy in the Context of Information Behavior
   and Everyday Life *29*

4 The Operationalization of Information Literacy, Part I
   Academic and School Libraries 43

5 The Operationalization of Information Literacy, Part II
   Public Libraries, Special Libraries, and Archives 61

6 Information Literacy Is a Human Right *77*

7 Controlling Information Literacy *85*

8 Literacy Politics and Literacy Policies *95*

9 Why Libraries? *101*

10 The Field Guide to Incorrect Information *115*

11 A Brief History of Advertising, Propaganda, and Other Delights *131*

12 Pandemic-Style Disinformation, Misinformation, and Illiteracy *137*

13 Toward Lifelong Information Literacy *147*

14 Advocacy, Activism, and Self-Reflection for Information (Literacy) Professionals *153*

15 The Social Infrastructure for Information Literacy *163*

16 The Lifelong Information Literacy Society *173*

REFERENCES *181*

ABOUT THE AUTHORS *215*

INDEX *217*

ACKNOWLEDGMENTS
AND SANCTUARY

WHEN WE WERE thinking about a book to follow up *Foundations of Information Policy*, a book on information literacy was the most obvious choice because we have long been writing about the connections of policy and literacy, as well as the opportunities for the field to think and act more broadly about literacy. In fact, the genesis of this book can be traced to a decade before its writing, when we cocreated and cotaught a course at the University of Maryland dedicated to preparing students to be teachers of and advocates for information literacy.

We proposed writing this book to the publisher in mid-2019. The timing to write a comprehensive text about information literacy turned out to be either amazing or terrifying, depending on your perspective. Disinformation-fueled political events around the globe had certainly made information literacy a more familiar concept to many, but that turned out to be nothing compared to the events of 2020. We suppose the best way to look at it is this: there has never been a better time to find examples of information literacy problems and a greater need to write a book to help people educate others about information literacy.

If 2020 has given us any gifts, it may be that we have all been emphatically reminded of the importance of interconnectedness and that humans really do rely on one another. Often, acknowledgment sections are long lists of people, tangentially related in one way or another to the author, the book, or the topic. We've certainly written long lists like that in some previous books. Under the current circumstances, however, we want to express more detailed gratitude to a smaller number of people who have been absolutely necessary for this book to exist, whether through providing encouragement or sanctuary.

The people we work with at ALA Neal-Schuman are simply extraordinary. Between us, we have produced quite a few books—we mention this not to be obnoxious but to provide context—and we have not previously experienced the boundless enthusiasm and irrepressible support that we have been graced with by this publisher. In particular, our editor Rachel Chance, along with Robert Christopher, Angela Gwizdala, and Jill Hillemeyer in marketing, design, and production, have been an absolute joy to work with and unfailing in their support across multiple books. We have once again been extremely fortunate to work with Carolyn Crabtree as our copyeditor, who has the ability to make our work as clear and accessible as possible while supporting our admittedly quirky approach to writing books, as well as Samantha Kundert, our managing editor, who had the unfortunate job of having to encourage us to cut our wordiness down to a manageable length. It is a wonderful, and unusual, sensation in the world of academic publishing for an author to feel like they have found a home publisher. And we certainly do. We owe this relationship to Rachel's reaching out to us, and we are immensely grateful.

The other group of colleagues that we absolutely have to mention are our collaborators in producing the journal *Library Quarterly*. It is the oldest scholarly journal in the field of librarianship, and we have had the honor to serve as editors there for a number of years. We have had the privilege of working for many years with Karen Kettnich of Clemson University and Ursula Gorham of the University of Maryland as fellow editors, and Shannon Oltmann of the University of Kentucky has recently joined us. Working on the contents of the journal and collaborating on editorials are extremely productive ways to workshop ideas and get new perspectives; through this process, our fellow editors have helped us work through and refine many of the major ideas that you will find in this book. They are also delightful to work with and as good friends as one could hope to have. While writing this book we also coedited a book with Karen and Ursula entitled *Libraries and the Global Retreat of Democracy: Confronting Polarization, Misinformation, and Suppression.* As the peerless Jim Henson once stated, "We should all be so lucky as we go through life working only with friends" (quoted in Jones, 2013, p. 385).

Writing a book takes bunches of time, surprisingly enough. Time when you need to be alone somewhere fitfully typing and muttering to yourself. So, a heartfelt thanks to our family members, who have had to take on extra responsibilities while we write (or stare sadly at a blinking cursor). In particular, Natalie would like to express her gratitude to her daughter (for enduring the occasional early bedtime so that mom could write and for the inspiration to keep working for a better future), her husband (for dealing with a cranky toddler when she inevitably ignored the early bedtime and for his constant support), Taylor baby number 2 (who is still gestating, but very much along for the ride), her brother (for offering the never-Trump conservative perspective and his astute political humor), and her parents (for the relief of nonpolitical conversations and their endless encouragement). Paul would like to express his gratitude to his mother, a veteran of the civil rights movement of the 1950s and 1960s (and who is always happy to provide feedback on his writings and to emphasize the need to make the world a more just place) and to his ever-present cats (who are terrible at giving feedback but are always willing to listen and ever-ready to prove that the earth is not flat).

We, sadly, would also be remiss if we did not acknowledge—"thank" would definitely be the wrong word here—social media for giving us so, so many awful examples to talk about in this book. Information online may be destroying democracy and enabling the global pandemic, but it sure provides a bounty of examples to anyone writing about information literacy.

The pandemic provided extraordinary examples of information and misinformation that we would have been remiss in not addressing in the book. But because it has defined so much of existence for everyone who has lived through it, and taken such an incomprehensible number of lives, simply writing this book during the pandemic would have made it an unavoidable presence. Our deepest sympathies go to those of you reading this book who have lost loved ones in the pandemic and to the souls of the departed.

Any mistakes in the text are the responsibility of the authors, not any of the kindly people thanked above. We hope you enjoy the book. Well, truthfully, we hope that you and heaps of other people enjoy the book. And, if we are ever fortunate enough to be asked to write an updated edition of the book, we sincerely hope that the world is at least slightly less interesting by then. We would be ecstatic beyond description if the number of times we have to talk about global pandemics and alien lizard people in any subsequent edition is zero.

Hopefully, the pandemic is over when you are reading this. If not, please remember to be kind and compassionate, get vaccinated, wear your mask, keep your distance, and keep yourself alive. And, if you are indeed reading this after the pandemic is over—lucky you!—please still be kind and compassionate.

ACRONYMS

AALL American Association of Law Libraries

AASL American Association of School Librarians

ACRL Association of College and Research Libraries

AECT Association for Educational Communications and Technology

AI artificial intelligence

AIPAC American Israel Public Affairs Committee

ALA American Library Association

AOL America Online

ASGCLA Association of Specialized, Government and Cooperative Library Agencies

BIPOC Black, Indigenous, and people of color

CAUL Council of Australian University Librarians

CDC Centers for Disease Control and Prevention

CFCS chlorofluorocarbons

CIPA Children's Internet Protection Act

CORA Critical Online Reasoning Assessment

CRAAP Currency, Relevance, Authority, Accuracy, and Purpose

CRS Congressional Research Service

CTC community technology center

DOE Department of Education

EBP evidence-based practice

EBSS Education and Behavioral Sciences Section

E-RATE educational rate

ETS Educational Testing Service

EU European Union

FAFLRT Federal and Armed Forces Libraries Round Table

FBI Federal Bureau of Investigation

HHS Department of Health and Human Services

IAL Innovative Approaches to Literacy

ICT information and communications technology

ICT4D information and communications technology for development

IFLA International Federation of Library Associations and Institutions

IIA Information Industry Association

IL information literacy

IMLS Institute of Museum and Library Services

IOM Institute of Medicine

IOT Internet of things

ISTE International Society for Technology in Education

IT information technology

KACST King Abdulaziz City for Science and Technology

LGBTQ lesbian, gay, bisexual, transgender, and questioning

LIS library and information science

LOC Library of Congress

MLA Medical Library Association

MLIS Master of Library and Information Science

MLS Master of Library Science

NAAL National Assessment of Adult Literacy

NCES National Center for Education Statistics

NCLIS National Commission on Libraries and Information Science

NCTE National Council of Teachers of English

NFIL National Forum on Information Literacy

NGO nongovernmental organization

NILAM National Information Literacy Awareness Month

NLM National Library of Medicine

NPR National Public Radio

NTIA National Telecommunications and Information Administration

OECD Organisation for Economic Co-operation and Development

PIAAC Program for the International Assessment of Adult Competencies

PLA Public Library Association

PLAIN Plain Language Action and Information Network

PLG Progressive Librarians Guild

REALM Rapid Estimate of Adult Literacy in Medicine

RUSA Reference and User Services Association

SAA Society of American Archivists

SAILS Standardized Assessment of Information Literacy Skills

SCONUL Society of College, National and University Libraries

SLA Special Libraries Association

SSHRC Social Sciences and Humanities Research Council

STEM science, technology, engineering, and mathematics

TATIL Threshold Achievement Test for Information Literacy

TMIA Tripartite Model of Information Access

TRAILS Tool for Real-Time Assessment of Information Literacy Skills

UDHR Universal Declaration of Human Rights

UK United Kingdom

UN United Nations

UNESCO United Nations Educational, Scientific and Cultural Organization

US United States

USPS United States Postal Service

WHO World Health Organization

WMDS weapons of mass destruction

WPA Works Progress Administration

Searching for Information (Literacy)

HERE, THERE, AND EVERYWHERE BE DRAGONS

A dragon was sunning itself at the edge of some woods in a rural corner of Essex in southeast England, startling awake as a country gentleman[1] rode toward it. The dragon, nine feet in length from nose to tail, raised itself in the air and fled on a pair of small, leathery wings. From that morning of May 27, 1668, until three months later, the villagers of Saffron Walden spotted the dragon every day around that wood, but it always escaped by ascending into the air or diving into the underbrush.[2] Soon after the dragon moved on to another wood, the events were recorded in a pamphlet entitled *The Flying Serpent, or Strange News Out of Essex* (Winstanley, 1669).

In 1669, of course, dragons were very real. If not real in a reality sense, at least real in the sense that everyone believed in them—even scientists. These beliefs were rather long-standing by 1669. Depictions of dragons in Asia, where they lived in clouds and water, date back to 5000 BCE, while the earliest depictions of dragons in Europe and the Mideast, where they lived in woods and caves, date to 800 BCE in Sumerian reliefs and 500 BCE in Greek artifacts. Pliny the Elder's *Natural History* from the first century CE, the world's first encyclopedia, detailed the epic battles in India that regularly occurred between dragons and their mortal enemies, elephants. Apparently, the reason for their epic feud was in the blood—dragons had hot blood and elephants had cold blood, which for some reason meant they were out to destroy one another.

In the 1700s, the first inklings of modern science—and the lack of tangible dragons to point to—began to chase away very common belief in dragons, sea dragons, satyrs, krakens, manticores, mermaids, goblins, and other fearsome mythical creatures. In a world that actually has the platypus, the mantis shrimp, the okapi, and the horseshoe crab, it is really amazing that people ever felt the need to invent strange animals rather than just noticing the real world. Figuring out the boundaries between imaginary and real, however, was not a perfect line for science. The earlier editions of Linnaeus's *Systema Natura* in the 1700s, which established taxonomies of plants and animals, included a cataloging of mythical beasts that listed pelicans among the animals of legend. Similarly, maps for many, many years were prone to include nonexistent places—sometimes nonexistent places that were sizeable on the map—the most famous probably being Atlantis (Tallack, 2017).

Human history is littered with dragons of many sorts, metaphorically speaking. Humans have believed, and continue to believe, an unimaginably vast array of truly ridiculous things. Francesco Redi, one of the first people to really deserve the title of "scientist," was the scientific advisor to the Duke of Tuscany in the mid-1600s. It was a prestigious job; Galileo Galilei had held the same post earlier in that century. The writings Redi left showed that the man spent much of his life valiantly, if usually unsuccessfully, trying to disabuse people from believing misinformation by performing scientific tests of unquestionable beliefs.

In one notable case, some religious pilgrims brought back from India stones that they claimed would remove poison. Not inclined to believe in such fancies, Redi gathered some hapless chickens and a poison made from tobacco leaves. One by one the chickens were poisoned, the stones were placed over the wound, the chickens expired, and the priests refused to believe the results. Confronted with a heap of dead chickens, the priests were adamant that the chickens were spontaneously dying for some reason unrelated to the poison. Of this episode, Redi wrote, "Doubt often wants to grow the foundation of truth like a blooming sprout" (1687, p. 7).

Sometimes those believing misinformation were quite a bit more than simply incredulous. Hypatia, a prominent Egyptian mathematician, was stoned to death with tiles by a mob of Christians in 415. Egyptians had invented the process for making tiles, so they were murdering a scholar with one of their most durable inventions, ironically enough. This event has been described, if a bit understatedly, as "a turning point when people in the Western world began to question the wisdom and learning of the Greeks" (Mesler & Cleaves, 2016, p. 11). The mob was troubled by her astrolabes and other scientific instruments, as well as the belief that the mathematics that she taught was some form of magic from the devil.[3]

Isn't this book supposed to be about information literacy?, you might be asking. So far we've discussed dragons, poisoned chickens, and a mathematician being stoned (tiled?) to death. Yet each of these stories is ultimately about information literacy—each involved the need to assess information and attempts to teach ways of assessing information, albeit not always successfully. Humans have uniquely distinguished themselves from other animals by their ability to record information and convey it across great distance and time. Human history can be seen as a rolling conflict between information and misinformation, with pieces of information often sliding from one category to the other.

Consider the dragon.[4] It really is not far-fetched in relation to many of the megalith species that humans once shared the earth with, in some cases only centuries before stories of mythical creatures arose—*Castoroides*, a seven-foot-long, 250-pound beaver; *Glyptodon*, an armadillo the size of a small car; *Megalonyx*, a ten-foot-tall sloth; and *Gigantopithecus*, a ten-foot-tall, one-thousand-pound, fruit-eating ape (LaPlante, 2019). Is a flying, fire-breathing lizard really that much weirder than a beaver the size of Shaquille O'Neal?

If you were living in England in the sixteenth century, the idea that dragons lived in Asia was hardly more implausible than that elephants lived there. You wouldn't be traveling there (or probably anywhere), and educated people said dragons lived there. And you probably also would not be going on a long sea voyage to ascertain the truth about sea dragons. In that case, widespread misinformation about dragons existing somewhere was hard to refute, but readily believing that they lived in the English countryside may have generated just a bit more reflection. A thoughtful person of the time might have accepted the existence of dragons far away as information and the existence of them in England as misinformation.

Charity is harder to muster in the other two examples. It is very easy to understand Redi's frustration with the priests' refusing to believe the information in front of them—in the very real form of a pile of chickens dead from the poison the priests witnessed being injected into the chickens—in favor of the misinformation about magical healing stones. Equating science to sorcery is clearly information illiteracy, but that is a trap that humans seem determined to fall into.

Recent years have also emphatically shown the social consequences of widespread misinformation and information illiteracy, heavily shaping the outcomes of the 2016 United States (US) presidential election and the 2016 Brexit vote in the United Kingdom (UK), nearly causing a 2018 war between Macedonia and Greece, and leading to outbreaks of diseases that vaccines had previously eradicated. Lest you feel too clever about people no longer believing that magical stones can draw out poison, keep in mind the myriad really terrible medical cures—ingesting bleach, snorting cocaine, smoking marijuana, imbibing lots of elderberry juice, and even drinking camel urine, among them—that were suggested as remedies for the pandemic caused by the novel coronavirus (COVID-19). People across Europe were blaming 5G wireless signals for spreading the virus. Also, Donald Trump, president of the US from 2017 to 2021, repeatedly claimed that the sound of windmills causes cancer. And that's just the tip of the impreciseberg.

THE MEANING OF LITERACY, PART 1

Exploring the meaning of information literacy is, of course, the point of this entire book. In an information age, information is literally everywhere. Every electronic device in your life requires information literacy for successful use, and further literacy is needed to deal with all the different kinds and sources of information you can find through the devices. Long before the age of information, however, humans lived in a world of information; the main difference now is the omnipresence of electronic information. The temperature, the colors of leaves on the trees, the plants currently in bloom, the smells on the breeze, and the position of the sun in the sky—all are vital pieces of information literacy required for survival throughout most of human history.

Over the course of thousands of years, information literacy has slowly spread from being a privilege of elites—confined to spaces like religion, academia, and governance—to being a basic human right, universally seen as a responsibility that societies must provide to their members (Jaeger, Taylor, & Gorham, 2015). Even for modern people in technologically rich environments, information literacy is not a monolithic concept. Types of information each require their own literacies, such as health, law, accounting, and governance. If you lack the appropriate information literacies to repair your car, it is best that you leave it to someone who does have such literacies. The same holds true for information technologies. Knowing how to use one form of technology does not guarantee that you know how to use another. Being a TikTok influencer does not necessarily make one a cybersecurity expert.

Simply put, information literacy is now a survival skill for individuals and for democratic societies. Libraries, as the socially designated providers of access to information and accompanying literacy, are better positioned than any other institution to equip people with the evolving skills required to remain information literate throughout the life course. Although schools have emphasized education related to foundational literacies, libraries—all types of libraries—stand as the only institution in society that is devoted to promoting comprehensive information literacy, encompassing foundational literacies through digital and media literacies to critical information literacy. This arc is clearly visible in public libraries that may very well be holding children's storytime in one part of the building while also teaching an Internet skills course in the computer lab and holding a science, technology, engineering, and mathematics (STEM) education session in the makerspace.

Information literacy is a fundamental contribution of libraries to their patrons and to their communities for education, employment, engagement, and enjoyment. It is also a contribution that supports the health and robustness of democratic societies, which could justify the title of *arsenals of democracy* if we took the role as seriously as it deserves. The promotion of information literacy is perhaps "the longest-running and most socially significant contribution of information professionals. As technologies and methods of communication have evolved, our focus has expanded from literacy in a print world to literacy in an online world and critical literacy to assess the quality of information found" (Jaeger & Taylor, 2019, pp. 158–159).

It is important to admit from the outset that the starting point for this discussion is not a pithy and easy-to-remember definition of information literacy. The field is swimming in information literacy articles, book chapters, conference papers, and books; entire journals and conferences are devoted to information literacy. Each professional organization in the field seems to have its own definition and standards for information literacy as well.

Plunking a term like *digital literacy,* which is one facet of information literacy, into a search engine returns thousands of statements, conferences, reports, news reports, and articles from an array of professions, governments, and organizations around the world; a similar search in any academic database provides an equally overwhelming number of results from seemingly every academic discipline, news organization, government agency, and more. And that's just one slice of information literacy.

The book will discuss this mess of information literacy stuff in subsequent chapters, and we will be offering our own definition of information literacy that we hope bridges the disharmonious definitions, but it is really important to know that information literacy is not an easily defined single thing or even necessarily an agreed-upon broad concept in the field. It is also extremely important to remember that information literacy is not an end point that anyone can reach. The relentless march of technological innovation means that information literacy is always in motion. People are just at different points in terms of the amount of information literacy skills that they have acquired and their capacities to deploy those skills.

Before the omnipresence of the Internet, literacy was a more constrainable concept. For many years, the US Department of Education (DOE) defined information literacy as comprising three foundational literacies: prose literacy (the ability to understand and summarize text), document literacy (the ability to complete forms), and quantitative literacy (the ability to read and apply practical math skills). Basically, all the things needed to complete paper tax forms every year. However, these foundational literacies now seem quaint in the world of the browsable web and wearable devices and smart home appliances.

Since at least 2014, the average person in the US and the UK has spent more time each day engaging electronic media in some fashion than sleeping (J. Miller, 2014; Petronzio, 2014).[5] As information and technology have infiltrated virtually every aspect of life, information literacy has become increasingly essential for survival and success. However, it also has become a far more all-encompassing set of skills, advancing beyond foundational literacy (reading, writing, and numeracy) to now include a wide array of information sources, types of media and technology, and online platforms, as well as new skills necessary for search, knowledge assembly, and validity assessment.

The global numbers related to information production and usage make the brain ache. In 2020, the number of Internet users was 4.6 billion out of a world population of 7.8 billion, and growing 6 percent a year, while the number of Internet devices and connections was 29.3 billion and estimated to grow to 40 billion in 2025 (Cisco Systems, 2020). You will note that there are currently about six devices and connections per user at this point. In 2020, 44 zettabytes of data were produced, and 50 zettabytes of data were stored—clearly people are making multiple backups of some things—and both of those numbers are estimated to more than triple in five years (Mauldin, 2019; NodeGraph, 2020; Petrov, 2019).[6] With this much information flowing about—and that amount always increasing—information literacy really is a comprehensive and lifelong pursuit.

With all this in mind, we want to introduce our definition of *information literacy*:

> **Information literacy** is a constantly refined practice of processing, accessing, understanding, critically evaluating, and using information in ways that are relevant to one's life. Information literacy relies on a social structure that promotes the agency of individuals in their communities and in the legal, political, educational, communication, and economic structures in their lives. Practicing information literacy is an iterative learning process that occurs throughout an individual's lifetime.
>
> Information literacy encompasses not only foundational literacies (reading/prose, writing/document, numeracy/quantitative) but also aspects of digital literacy (technology skills and ethics) and media literacy (critical analysis of nontextual content). In many cases, information literacy is closely associated with data, scientific, health, civic, and other context-specific literacies.

Chapters 2 and 3 build to and explain in detail how we arrived at this definition. So, the definition will have much greater nuance after you get through those chapters, but we hope having our definition at the outset will help you navigate the chunkiness of those chapters. We aren't kidding when we tell you that there are a ton of different ways of looking at information literacy.

THE STRUCTURE OF THE BOOK

Although this book engages with key aspects of the large body of literature on information literacy, it is not our goal to provide a summary of the entire corpus. Most of the literature about information literacy narrowly discusses it in terms of one part of the field—in school libraries or first-year courses for college students or digital literacy in computer courses at public libraries—and explains one type of information literacy program or practice. However, this book, by framing information literacy as a field-wide and field-unifying concept, differs from that narrow approach in a few major ways.

First, this book examines information literacy across types of institutions and interactions. It presents information literacy as a lifelong concept, one that people start developing from birth and that, hopefully, continues to be updated and reinforced throughout life (Jaeger & Taylor, 2021a). All information institutions have roles to play in instilling and supporting lifelong information literacy, so understanding the totality of efforts of information institutions and professions is necessary for understanding information literacy as a lifelong pursuit.

Second, this book does not treat information literacy as an isolated concept. Information literacy exists not only in information and technological contexts but in social, cultural, and political ones as well. This book approaches information literacy as making sense only in relation to its arch enemies—misinformation, disinformation, and information illiteracy.[7] Disinformation, misinformation, and illiteracy are signs of a disease, and information literacy is the cure. We will not be able to figure out how best to make the cure work if we do not consider it in the context of the disease it is meant to remedy. And if we too readily forgive people for falling for disinformation and for spreading misinformation, we are giving up on finding the most effective ways to teach information literacy as a lifelong skill before we even start. When millions of adults worldwide are embracing as fact misinformation that one would be disappointed in a ten-year-old for believing, it is not the time to tread lightly. Millions have died and tens of millions have been sickened by the pandemic, with disinformation and misinformation accounting for risky behavior that caused many of those illnesses.

Third, this book argues that information literacy is the big unifying concept that underlies the how and why of the information professions. Many questions have been raised—usually outside the profession—about the continuing value of libraries when everyone is carrying or wearing the Internet at all times. Events have emphatically demonstrated that having access to unlimited amounts of information does not result in comprehensive knowledge or widespread understanding of issues. Instead, people tend to encounter less breadth of information as filter bubbles and algorithms send them to information with which they already agree. Information institutions and information professionals, on the other hand, have the knowledge and training to teach lifelong information literacy. And actively working in a coordinated manner to improve information literacy would be a hugely important societal contribution at this point.

Finally, this book argues that information literacy has become a fundamental, if not *the* fundamental, human right. By making information and technology available and accessible, as well as by providing the education to use the information and technology, libraries are powerful engines of human rights and social justice in communities around the world (Jaeger, Taylor, & Gorham, 2015). Within a broad spectrum of human rights and social justice issues related to information, the ability to be active and successful in a world defined and constantly intermediated by information technologies is foundational for education, employment, health, civic engagement, and most other functions and is entirely dependent on information literacy. Information literacy is not just a human right; rather, it is one on which other human rights now depend.

As a whole, this book explores information literacy as a cross-national, cross-cultural, and cross-institutional topic, examining related issues of technology, rights and justice, public policy, community engagement, advocacy, and democratic self-governance, as well as threats to information literacy and the societal consequences of a lack of information literacy. Drawing upon the latest research and best practices, the book addresses information literacy in ways relevant for all types of libraries, providing both the broader context and a range of applied strategies and programs for promoting information literacy in practice. To help give the most comprehensive and instructive context for information literacy possible, we draw upon insights from a wide range of fields beyond library and information science (LIS), including education, psychology, sociology, computer science, and history, as well as relevant examples from many different places, times, and even works of art. As a result, the book works as a text for students and as a reference work for current professionals.

The book is divided into four sections that follow this chapter. The first section (chapters 2 through 5) provides readers a basic understanding of information literacy—the myriad definitions, the development of the concept, and the different contexts and programs in which information literacy can be an issue. Information literacy is introduced as an issue that directly impacts the individual, communities, institutions, and social interactions. We explore the myriad definitions of information literacy and consider information literacy in contexts of various other forms of literacy. The first section introduces the ways in which information literacy is fundamental to information access and behavior, as well as the ways in which information institutions and associations have sought to provide educational programs for information literacy, including core skills, standards, and a wide range of approaches to conceptualizing and teaching information literacy.

The second section of the book (chapters 6 through 9) examines information literacy as being shaped by legal, policy, governmental, and supranational structures. It is considered the core aspect of the idea of human rights—without information literacy, other rights are inaccessible. We also examine the differing ways in which information literacy is defined in policies, laws, and agreements, exploring the ways in which different definitions can lead to very different societal outcomes. This section includes examples of public policy interventions that have been attempted to promote information literacy and the results of those programs. The section concludes by delving into the unique responsibilities of information institutions—most especially libraries—in relation to information literacy.

The third section (chapters 10 through 12) examines the consequences of a lack of information literacy at the individual, community, and societal levels. The concepts of information illiteracy, misinformation, and disinformation are introduced, defined, and considered as long-running problems. Prominent examples from politics and government, as well as many examples from the Internet and social media, illustrate the prevalence and consequences of illiteracy, misinformation, and disinformation. Special attention is given to the social, technological, and psychological reasons that people are drawn to incorrect information and the ways in which communication can reinforce incorrect information, as well as the ways that bad actors gain power and make money from spreading misinformation. The disinformation swirling throughout the pandemic usefully and horrifically provides a massive, depressing example by which to examine these issues.

The final section (chapters 13 through 16) focuses on the unique and essential roles of librarians as community-based educators, including a discussion of strategies that librarians can employ to be effective information literacy educators for their patrons and their communities. These chapters include a detailed exploration of the concept of lifelong information literacy education, which we believe is the best process for librarians and other information professionals to conceptualize information literacy education (both for themselves and for others). This section considers the advocacy and activism that information professionals need to bring to policy discussions of information literacy at the local, state, national, and international levels, emphasizing information literacy as a social good and a human right. The social infrastructure necessary to support information literacy—building the empowerment, education, and agency in communities essential to promoting and sustaining lifelong information literacy—is the focus of the penultimate chapter. Finally, bringing it all back home, the book closes with a summation of why a lack of information literacy may present the biggest societal and human rights problems of our age, and why librarians and other information professionals may be better suited than anyone else to lead the way in addressing these problems.

Throughout the book, we use many examples of disinformation, misinformation, and other failings of literacy. Many are drawn from the novel coronavirus pandemic because that is something everybody can relate to. We also use quite a few examples from political leaders, especially ones who are prone to intentionally misleading others or embracing information illiteracy themselves. Some examples are from further back in time but continue to serve as historical markers in the march of misinformation.

LITERACY AND THE SINGLE LIBRARIAN

Information literacy is the responsibility of every information professional and every information institution. It is the center of a career as an information professional, hopefully becoming both a high-end practitioner of information literacy yourself and a skilled teacher of information literacy skills to patrons. "The prime function of education to create knowledge and truth and learning to read texts, images, media, and other documents is fundamentally about learning to understand the meaning of such things in order to develop knowledge and find truth" (Downey, 2016, p. 39). No matter what kind of institution you choose to work in, information literacy will heavily define what you do, even if your work is not spoken of as being about information literacy.

Information literacy also stands as perhaps the most outstanding contribution of our field to the communities that we serve. Providing banks of computers, limitless databases, troves of one-of-a-kind archival materials, and mountains of books and periodicals would mean very little if the people they were intended to help could not use them. The greatest contribution of libraries is to teach community members how to use those computers, databases, archival materials, books, and periodicals. Information is "our most precious resource. In such a world, education should empower everyone, not the few. . . . The challenge of educators is to help students make sense of a world described by some as 'information overload'" (Boyer, 1997, p. 140). Libraries, archives, and museums, each in its own way, are engines of information literacy in their communities.

When you entered the field, you may not have been thinking that you had chosen a career in information literacy, much less a career in teaching information literacy to others. Well, you have. That's okay, though, because it's a wonderful career. We generally don't talk about ourselves and what we do in education terms, but teaching information literacy skills—from how to read children's books to how to use email to how to write a cover letter and résumé to how to conduct Boolean searches in expensive databases—is the framework for information careers. In some cases, a career may focus on teaching such skills to coworkers, and in other cases, it will be on teaching such skills to members of the community.

Each person currently working in a library or preparing for a career in libraries—or in any other kind of information institution—will be promoting information literacy as a core part of their career. Every information professional is an information literacy professional. So, with that in mind, we hope that this book will be a great help as you consider the roles of information literacy in your career and will provide you ideas and resources for implementing information literacy activities in your institution.

To literacy, and beyond!

💬 CHAPTER 1 GUIDING QUESTIONS

1. As you begin this book, think about how you would define information literacy. Does your definition align with the definition we've offered here?
2. In what ways does information literacy contribute to the information society?
3. If information literacy is such a critical practice, why is the term so ambiguous?
4. In what ways do you consider librarianship to be an education career? Has your conception changed after reading this chapter?
5. Is information literacy the bedrock of librarianship? If not, why not? If so, how would you explain this concept to those not in the field?

NOTES

1. The Earl with the Dragon Tattoo?
2. Apparently, this was the dragon who lived by the sea and frolicked in the autumn mist.
3. Were that the case, she seemingly would have been better described as a mathemagician.
4. The title of Bruce Lee's most philosophical movie.
5. We're not sure which way these studies count smart beds.
6. Yes, we admit that *zettabytes* sounds like a term that we made up to see if you are paying attention. Rest assured that it is a real term, meaning, not to be overly technical, a whole honking lot of data.
7. And elephants?

Defining Information Literacy

TRYING TO DEFINE information literacy can feel like wading through metaphorical mud, with heavy boots on, wearing an overstuffed pack, during a downpour. Much of the confusion about defining information literacy stems from the struggle to define information itself. We have looked to Marcia Bates's (2010) *Encyclopedia of Library and Information Sciences* entry on *information* as a resource to condense the long history of the debate in information science about the definition of the word, but we should be clear that there is a robust collection of scholarship on the subject beyond what the constraints of this textbook can accommodate (see Webster, 2014).[1] By summarizing Bates, we have attempted to call out the major areas of research on information as a concept while not losing our focus on where this concept fits into the idea of information literacy.

Bates (2010) first underlies our modern understanding of information with the work of Claude Shannon, in which he articulates a "fundamental clarification of the relationship between messages and the amount of information they convey" (para. 27). Bates notes that Shannon's conception separated information from meaning, a differentiation that had not been made before. This separation led to conflicting understandings of information that still exist; is information a neutral entity, or does it only exist within the context of human understanding?

Bates discusses the communicatory understanding of information (one type of seven she outlines) through the work of Robert Losee. Losee (1997) understood information to be "the value attached or instantiated to a characteristic or variable returned by a function or produced by a process" (p. 267).[2] Losee explains:

> A good definition or theory of information both describes factually what occurs or what exists, as well as provides an explanation of events. In addition, it should bear some resemblance to the natural language notion of information but need not adhere to it when the natural language definition loses its generality and explanatory power. This happens when the common language definition of information, for example, becomes conflated with the notion of useful information. (p. 257)

Losee is describing information as an entity outside the construction of meaning. This concept is probably quite foreign to many in the library field specifically because our field is so human-focused. As a field, the focus tends to be on how information is used, understood, and accessed—in other words, the human element. Bates (2010, para. 37) offers the follow-ing critique (or perhaps clarification) of this definition:

> Losee says that examining the cake [an example provided in his explanation of the definition] provides information both about process and original ingredients. But, in fact, the person who had never seen a cake before almost certainly would not know enough to be able to figure out from the output alone all that went into making it, both in ingredients and processes. This is true with many processes. . . . Thus, in the expe-rience of human observers, information can be limited and distorted coming out of a process, and it can be also be [*sic*] quite unambiguous and complete, as when we know of the process.

You can see the relevance of the last sentence to our understanding of information literacy.

Other types of information conceptions that Bates describes include (a) Pratt's (1977) understanding of information as an event (or process), and (b) propositional conceptions, including those of Dretske (1981), who concludes that "information is that commodity capable of yielding knowledge . . . . If everything I say to you is false, then I have given you no information" (p. 44), and of Fox (1983), who argues that "we *inform* people of things that may or may not be true, but when we *misinform* someone, it necessarily involves telling the person something that is not true" (paraphrased by Bates, p. 154). Bates cites F. B. Thompson (1968) as an example of a structural concept, defining information as "a product that results from applying the processes of organization to the raw material of experience . . . . It is the organization that is the information" (pp. 305–306). One will see elements of these interpretations in the definitions of information literacy as well, particularly the notions that information literacy is a process, that misinformation is an enemy of informa-tion literacy, and that organizing information is a key skill in understanding information. But we're getting ahead of ourselves.

The two conceptions of Bates's (2010) concept groupings that are most relevant to our work are the socially constructed and multi-type definitions of information. Bates cites Cornelius (1996) as one of the major scholars in the social construction concept. Cornelius writes that information is "not . . . an objective independent entity as part of a 'real world,' but . . . a human artefact, constructed and reconstructed within social situations. As in law, every bit of information is only information when understood within its own cultural pack-aging which allows us to interpret it" (p. 19). Bates also cites Goguen (1997) as representing the socially constructed concept with his definition of information: "an item of information is an interpretation of a configuration of signs for which members of some social group are accountable" (p. 31). Here, context is king.

The multi-type definition of information conceives that "all types and forms of infor-mation need to be incorporated in our thinking in doing information behavior research" (Bates, 2010, para. 104). As an example, Bates describes Dervin's (1977) definition in which information is represented by three parts: external reality, internal reality, and the ways an individual makes sense of or reconciles these realities. Bates also cites her own concept in which she articulates several types of information, divided into four groupings: genetic information; experienced, enacted, and expressed information; embedded and recorded information; and trace information. Further definitions of all these types of information are thoroughly explained in her work (Bates, 2006, p. 1036), but for our purposes, it is really important only to consider that there can be a marriage between conceptions that informa-tion merely exists and conceptions that information must be constructed.

Bates (2010) also offers a few examples of deconstructionism, or general critiques of the concept of information itself. Perhaps most notably she cites the work of Jonathan Furner (2004) who argues that information is not needed as a word at all. Rather, he says, "[o]nce the concepts of interest have been labeled with conventional names such as 'data,' 'meaning,' 'communication,' 'relevance,' etc., nothing is left . . . to which to apply the term 'information'" (p. 428). Though a little extreme in our view, this standpoint gives an early glimpse into the many overlaps between different types of literacies and information literacy as well as the question of whether all are really necessary.

Bates ends her overview with this conclusion:

> The understanding of the core concept of "information" in information science remains a highly contested area. Information is seen as a proposition, a structure, a message, or an event; as requiring truth or indifferent to truth; as socially embedded and under perpetual re-interpretation, or as measurable in bits; as a worn-out idea deserving of dispatch, or as an exciting conception understandable in terms of evolutionary forces. (final para.)

Beyond those that Bates discusses, other works that attempt to define information focus on what it is not, such as Brown and Duguid's influential 2002 book *The Social Life of Information,* which defines "information" entirely as being inferior to "knowledge," or Michael Buckland's (1991, 1997) works, which distinguish between information and the entity that contains it as a way to define information. Other major works of information studies tie information to specific structures, as defining information in terms of required attributes (Svenonius, 2000) or in terms of the engineering required to deliver it (Shannon & Weaver, 1964). Entire books devoted to the difficulty of defining information in the Internet age were written when the Internet was just getting going (Borgmann, 1999; Nunberg, 1996).

Whitworth (2014) argues that, although information can be considered technical and a "property of biological systems," when considering information literacy, "it is necessary to focus on information as a human property. . . . It is by contextualizing, through active cognitive work at a particular place and time, that raw data becomes information and, in turn, develops into knowledge" (p. 11). He posits that "information is not some mystical 'out-there' phenomenon. It is created by us, exists within us, but is also encoded into the tangible world in bodies, acts, texts, technologies, and social relations" (p. 13). The rest of this book focuses on this idea of information. We discuss information with the intent to capture "the sum total of the content," including text, symbols, video, graphics, and other means of conveying messages through any physical or virtual medium (Jaeger & Burnett, 2010, p. 14).

With all the roles that information plays in everyday life and the fact that virtually every field is now invested in information in some fashion, the range of definitions of information sprawls far beyond what Bates (2010) covers and what we have added as further details. The confluence of text, numbers, symbols, emojis, colors, graphics, sounds, and videos that constitutes information flowing through seemingly innumerable platforms and devices makes defining information continually more challenging. We have spent so much time describing these different concepts of information—and, in turn, different scholarly definitions of the term—because the breadth of meaning in the word is important to our understanding of what it means to be information literate. In general, the tension that we see most clearly in the area of information literacy education is that of information as a neutral entity, viewed in terms of bits and technical transmissions, versus that in which meaning is essential—and socially constructed.

With all this talk about information, we have neglected the term *literacy*. No more! We touched on this in chapter 1, but literacy as it was first considered meant simply that one could read and write, and sometimes an understanding of numbers was included as well. This is the dictionary definition today. When we talk about foundational literacies later on, we are referencing this definition. Just as information literacy has complexities, however, so does this so-called basic or foundational literacy. Campbell (1990) defines literacy as

> the integration of listening, speaking, reading, writing, and critical thinking; it incorporates numeracy. It includes a cultural knowledge which enables a speaker, writer, or reader to recognize and use language appropriate to different social situations. For an advanced technological society . . . the goal is an active literacy which allows people to use language to enhance their capacity to think, create, and question, in order to participate effectively in society. (cited from Bawden, 2001, p. 221)

Although we won't explore all the ways that foundational literacy has been considered by scholars and institutions,[3] we do find it useful to look at a few of the more prominent modern understandings of the term. If you want to read further, Bawden (2001) lists a variety of resources, including W. S. Grey (1956) who emphasizes culture as an important criterion of literacy: "the knowledge and skills in reading and writing which enable him to engage in all those activities in which literacy is normally assumed in his culture or group" (cited from Bawden, 2001, p. 222). Bawden also cites Meek (1991), Kintgen et al., (1988), Street (1984), and Oxenham (1980) as useful discussions of the concept. We found Keefe and Copeland (2011) to be a more recent, thorough, and still succinct overview. For a longer collection of recent perspectives on the history of literacy, see Graff (2017).

We will spend our time in this chapter focusing on institutional conceptions of literacy both in the US and abroad in the last few years. In the US, we can look to the National Council of Teachers of English (NCTE) (2019) as an example from the education context. In its *Framework for Literacy in a Digital Age,* the council defines *literacy* as "a collection of communicative and sociocultural practices shared among communities" (n.p.). Someone who is literate "possess[es] and intentionally appl[ies] a wide range of skills, competencies, and dispositions . . . [that] are interconnected, dynamic, and malleable. As in the past, they are inextricably linked with histories, narratives, life possibilities, and social trajectories of all individuals and groups" (n.p.). These skills, competencies, and dispositions include the ability to

- Participate effectively and critically in a networked world;
- Explore and engage critically, thoughtfully, and across a wide variety of inclusive texts and tools/modalities;
- Consume, curate, and create actively across contexts;
- Advocate for equitable access to and accessibility of texts, tools, and information;
- Build and sustain intentional global and cross-cultural connections and relationships with others so as to pose and solve problems collaboratively and strengthen independent thought;
- Promote culturally sustaining communication and recognize the bias and privilege present in the interactions;
- Examine the rights, responsibilities, and ethical implications of the use and creation of information;

- Determine how and to what extent texts and tools amplify one's own and others' narratives as well as counter unproductive narratives;
- Recognize and honor the multilingual literacy identities and culture experiences individuals bring to learning environments, and provide opportunities to promote, amplify, and encourage these differing variations of language (e.g., dialect, jargon, register). (n.p.)

Interestingly, there does not seem to be much difference between this and many general understandings of information literacy.

In its seminal 2003 *National Assessment of Adult Literacy* (NAAL), the National Center for Education Statistics (NCES) describes literacy in both a task-based sense—"the ability to use printed and written information to function in society, to achieve one's goals, and to develop one's knowledge and potential" (White & Dillow, 2005, p. 4)—and in a way that is based on skills. For the latter, the NCES describes the three types of literacies it includes in the assessment—prose, document, and quantitative—and the six types of literacy skills that are tested: text search skills, basic reading skills, inferential skills, language skills, computation identification skills, and computation performance skills ("Framework," n.d.). This all goes slightly beyond the traditional definition of just reading, writing, and arithmetic. In the 2005 document *Key Concepts and Features of the 2003 National Assessment of Adult Literacy*, White and Dillow explain that

> [l]iteracy is not a single skill or quality that one either possesses or lacks. Rather, it encompasses various types of skills that different individuals possess to varying degrees. There are different levels and types of literacy, which reflect the ability to perform a wide variety of tasks using written materials that differ in nature and complexity. A common thread across all literacy tasks is that each has a purpose—whether that purpose is to pay the telephone bill or to understand a piece of poetry. All US adults must successfully perform literacy tasks in order to adequately function—that is, to meet personal and employment goals as well as contribute to the community. (p. 3)

That said, the NAAL fails to really background these tasks in any kind of sociocultural understanding of literacy. Still, there is a remarkable overlap between the skills called for in this "basic" literacy and those articulated by those teaching information literacy.

Internationally, three organizations demonstrate more skills-based approaches to defining literacy. The United Nations Educational, Scientific, and Cultural Organization (UNESCO) states that "[b]eyond its conventional concept as a set of reading, writing and counting skills, literacy is now understood as a means of identification, understanding, interpretation, creation, and communication in an increasingly digital, text-mediated, information-rich and fast-changing world" ("Literacy," n.d.). The European Literacy Policy Network's *European Declaration of the Right to Literacy*, funded with support from the European Commission, defines literacy as "the ability to read and write at a level whereby individuals can effectively understand and use written communication in all media (print or electronic), including digital literacy" (Valtin et al., 2016). Finally, in its Program for the International Assessment of Adult Competencies (PIAAC), the Organisation for Economic Co-operation and Development (OECD) defines literacy as "understanding, evaluating, using and engaging with written text to participate in the society, to achieve one's goals and to develop one's knowledge and potential" ("What Is PIACC?", n.d.). PIAAC is a cyclical, large-scale study that assesses four areas of adult competencies (literacy, numeracy, problem solving in technology-rich environments, and reading components).

Keeping these definitions in mind, we think Knoblauch insightfully notes that "literacy is one of those mischievous concepts, like virtuousness and craftsmanship, that appear to denote capacities but that actually convey value judgments" (Knoblauch, 1990, p. 74), an observation that also could be made about our next area of inquiry—definitions of information literacy.

BRINGING "INFORMATION" AND "LITERACY" TOGETHER

Before we get to our understanding of the combination of information and literacy as a concept, we will explore a brief history of the term, along with an overview of some of the more popular scholarly and professional definitions.[4] The conception of *information literacy* as a term has its origins in the mid-1970s emergence of a new "information society" (Bawden, 2001; Behrens, 1994; Doyle, 1994; Eisenberg et al., 2004; Whitworth, 2014). It is worth mentioning that although we are attempting to paint a broad picture of how information literacy developed, particularly in the United States, a more detailed examination can be found in Andrew Whitworth's *Radical Information Literacy* (2014), particularly chapters 2 and 3, as well as Bawden (2001) and Behrens (1994), both of whom also cite many of the literature reviews available on the topic.

Three seminal scholars—Zurkowski (1974), Burchinal (1976), and Hamelink (1976)—laid much of the groundwork for different perceptions of information literacy. Zurkowski, the most well-known of the three, outlined his understanding of information literacy in a 1974 report to the National Commission on Libraries and Information Science (NCLIS). He began the report by explaining that "information is not knowledge; it is concepts or ideas which enter a person's field of perception, are evaluated and assimilated reinforcing or changing the individual's concept of reality and/or ability to act" (p. 1). Recalling our discussion of the meaning of *information,* it is clear that Zurkowski was most concerned with the interaction between information and an information user. Beyond that consideration, he was concerned about value: "Information has value [for a user] in direct proportion to the control it provides him over what he is and what he can become" (p. 6). Those who can be described as "information literates . . . have learned techniques and skills for utilizing the wide range of information tools as well as primary sources in molding information solutions to their problems" (p. 6).

Conversely, people whom Zurkowski described as "information illiterates" are "literate in the sense that they can read and write, [but] do not have a measure for the value of information [and] do not have an ability to mold information to their needs" (p. 6). These definitions are embedded in a report that is largely focused on the value of information (and "information literates") to the economy. He lamented the potential for libraries and government-supported institutions to interfere with the free marketplace of information products (competition is heavily emphasized as the idealized outcome of publishing and new information systems) and issued an urgent call for the need for information literacy to service a competitive workforce. More on the results of this call to arms is described in chapters 4 and 5, but most important for the information professions is the influence of this view on the development of information literacy education in the 1980s and 1990s.

The prescience of Zurkowski's report was clear as the 1980s and 1990s demonstrated a rapidly changing educational, technological, and political landscape that had incredible import for the way information was accessed. The concept of the digital divide first rose to prominance during this period; in 1982 the Information Industry Association's (IIA) four-volume survey of the information infrastructure of the United States referenced information literacy and defined it as the "gap which . . . divides the information sophisticate who knows how and when to use the technology and does so easily and efficiently from the information naive who cannot use the technologies and hence has limited access to knowledge resources" (Horton, 1982, as cited in Behrens, 1994, p. 311). This divide or gap idea would permeate US, and global, information policy for the next two decades. It also had tremendous impact on the way libraries presented education; information literacy lessons could bridge a skills gap if information literacy was a set of skills that some people had and others did not.

Whitworth (2014) identified that "the most significant trend of the 1980s and 1990s to which information literacy responded was that use of a computer (or terminal) to access information moved from specialist locations (libraries, universities, or information providers like those listed by Zurkowski), and came into the home" (p. 48). Despite this fact, during this period the library and information science (LIS) field almost exclusively viewed information literacy through the lens of educational environments, in particular K-12 schools and higher education. The neoliberal shrinking of social institutions and the threat to libraries' existence undoubtedly played into this approach. As academic librarians lamented the fact that libraries were not mentioned in seminal education reports of the era, they found in information literacy a topic of which they could claim ownership (Whitworth, 2014). Breivik and Gee (2006) cited the 1987 publication *Libraries and the Search for Academic Excellence*, the proceedings of a symposium featuring nine papers discussing academic libraries and their impact on students, the economy, and the university, as "the initial attempt by leaders in higher education and librarianship . . . [to] consider a greater institutional role for libraries" (cited in Whitworth, 2014, p. 49).

At the same time, the American Association of School Librarians (AASL), in conjunction with the Association for Educational Communications and Technology (AECT), was also reconceiving the role of the school librarian in its 1988 guidelines, *Information Power: Guidelines for School Media Programs*. In a 1988 discussion guide published about the guidelines, the associations described several goals connected to the changing information environment, including "the reshaping of library media program outputs and environments to accommodate: changing and diversifying populations; challenges to intellectual freedom; equity of access to all formats of information including new and emerging technologies," as well as the "evaluation, management, and integration of emerging technologies" and "networks of information resources extending beyond the school library media center" (p. 9). Although information literacy is not clearly spelled out, there are certainly seeds of the concept in these evolving roles.

By the end of the 1980s, the American Library Association (ALA) had formed a Presidential Committee on Information Literacy. The committee's report, issued in 1989, offered the professional organization's first definition of information literacy: "To be information literate, a person must be able to recognize when information is needed and have the ability to locate, evaluate, and use effectively the needed information" (American Library Association, n.p.). The report further explained that students practicing information literacy would "know when they have a need for information; identify information needed to address a given problem or issue; find needed information and evaluate the information; organize the information; and use the information effectively to address the problem or issue at hand" (n.p.).

The report was remarkably forward-thinking in many respects. It specifically dissuaded the LIS profession from considering a narrow view of information literacy education:

> What is called for is not a new information studies curriculum but, rather, a restructuring of the learning process. Textbooks, workbooks, and lectures must yield to a learning process based on the information resources available for learning and problem solving throughout people's lifetimes—to learning experiences that build a lifelong habit of library use . . . [which] not only [will] enhance the critical thinking skills of students but will also empower them for lifelong learning and the effective performance of professional and civic responsibilities. (n.p.)

Given the thirty years preceding the report, it seems the major error was not that the authors of the report were narrow in their thinking. Rather, the mistake was that the report's authors believed that "the major obstacle to promoting information literacy is a lack of public awareness of the problems created by information illiteracy" (n.p.). Time has proven this belief untrue; in the three decades that have followed, many have recognized the lack of practice of information literacy in the population. What has failed to emerge is a social structure to support this practice.

The report called for a new education paradigm wherein "there would be more reading of original sources and more extended writing. Both students and teachers would be familiar with the intellectual and emotional demands of asking productive questions, gathering data of all kinds, reducing and synthesizing information, and analyzing, interpreting, and evaluating information in all its forms" (n.p.). And indeed there have been echoes of this paradigm in an education policy sense, such as the Common Core's emphasis on writing and primary resources. That said, the major education policy of the past three decades, 2001's No Child Left Behind Act, heavily emphasized standardized testing of all K–12 students, the legacy of which remains two decades later. This approach to education and evaluation makes it exceedingly difficult to emphasize context-specific critical thinking required to practice information literacy. Perhaps as a result (and certainly because of the neoliberal, economy-focused political environment that produced the act), the LIS interpretations of information literacy have tended to operationalize the concept as lists of skills that one either has or doesn't have. The education and social paradigms have not been amenable to the nuance required by a lifelong, situationally dependent information literacy.

Even in the initial work of the National Forum on Information Literacy (NFIL), a coalition of education, civic, and economic groups interested in information literacy and created as a response to recommendations from the 1989 report, there emerged a tension between an idealistic view of information literacy as an empowering concept and the nation's formal education goals (designed much more with the goal in mind of a productive workforce). An early study produced for the NFIL was conducted in 1992. Experts suggested by NFIL members took part in a Delphi study (a research methodology that uses iterative communication techniques to help reach consensus) that proposed to formally define and develop outcome measures for information literacy. From that study, the group defined information literacy as "the ability to access, evaluate, and use information from a variety of sources" and described an information literate person as one who

- Recognizes the need for information
- Recognizes that accurate and complete information is the basis for intelligent decision making
- Formulates questions based on information needs

- Identifies potential sources of information
- Develops successful search strategies
- Accesses sources of information including computer-based and other technologies
- Evaluates information
- Organizes information for practical application
- Integrates new information into an existing body of knowledge
- Uses information in critical thinking and problem solving (Doyle, 1992, p. 2)

The report emphasized the process element of information literacy as well as its lifelong nature—connections were made to the National Education Goals of 1990 for preschool and elementary students as well as adults.

Although the report asserted that "with these skills comes empowerment because the ability to use information is necessary to making informed decisions throughout a lifetime," one of the National Education Goals with which the authors attempted to connect these skills was that "by the year 2000, every adult will be literate and will possess the knowledge and skills necessary to compete in a global economy and exercise the rights and responsibilities of citizenship" (Doyle, 1992, pp. 2, 3). The emphasis is clearly on information literacy in the pursuit of economic gain.

Nevertheless, even as social structures became more neoliberal in orientation, the library profession was slowly assuming ownership of the concept of information literacy. This growing import to the profession wasn't without its critics. Some felt information literacy was a gimmick; Foster (1993) described information literacy as "an exercise in public relations" and "an effort to deny the ancillary status of librarianship by inventing a social malady with which librarians as 'information professionals' are uniquely qualified to deal" (p. 346).[5] Others viewed information literacy merely as an unnecessary term, that information literacy was already represented by existing concepts in the field (these arguments are summarized in Snavely & Cooper, 1997). But despite these scholarly arguments about the role of information literacy in librarianship, information literacy has become a hugely influential term and concept within the LIS field. In the 1990s, much of the information literacy scholarship began focusing on identifying ways to operationalize the term through skills-based standards and within the context of formal education environments.

Probably the most influential result of this scholarship was the *Information Literacy Competency Standards for Higher Education* developed by the Association of College and Research Libraries (ACRL, 2000). The *Standards* defined an information literate person as one who is able to

- determine the extent of information needed;
- access the needed information effectively and efficiently;
- evaluate information and its sources critically;
- incorporate selected information into one's knowledge base;
- use information effectively to accomplish a specific purpose; and
- understand the economic, legal, and social issues surrounding the use of information, and access and use information ethically and legally. (pp. 2-3)

Five standards were given for the information literate student and within these standards were twenty-two performance indicators. The standards "also list[ed] a range of outcomes for assessing student progress toward information literacy. These outcomes serve as guidelines for faculty, librarians, and others in developing local methods for measuring student learning in the context of an institution's unique mission" (p. 7). These outcomes are characterized by both higher and lower order thinking skills.

The influence of these standards cannot be overstated. Whitworth (2014) notes that "within the [higher education] library, much work outside the US and UK continues to reflect the same concerns, namely training in skills and competencies, developing rubrics or criteria for assessment, and trying to secure collaborations between libraries and academics" (p. 55). He goes on to cite Lin et al. (2012) and Babalhavaeji et al. (2009) as examples of the global influence of ACRL's information literacy definition, in these cases in Taiwan and Iran, respectively.

Alongside these developments in higher education librarianship, two major developments in the K–12 information literacy landscape can be seen in Eisenberg and Berkowitz's Big6™6 approach to information seeking (Eisenberg, 2008) and in the AASL *Information Literacy Standards for Student Learning* (American Association of School Librarians & Association for Educational Communications and Technology, 1998a). The Big6 model is not a set of information literacy standards per se but, rather, "an approach that can be used whenever people are faced with an information problem or with making a decision that is based on information . . . [and that] comprise[s] a unified set of information and technology skills [that] taken together . . . form a process" (Eisenberg, 2008, p. 40). The Big6 model has six stages, each with specific related tasks:

- Task Definition (Define the problem; Identify the information needed)
- Information Seeking Strategies (Determine all possible sources; Select the best sources)
- Location and Access (Locate sources; Find information within sources)
- Use of Information (Engage [read, hear, view]; Extract relevant information)
- Synthesis (Organize information from multiple sources; Present information)
- Evaluation (Judge the result [effectiveness]; Judge the process [efficiency]) (p. 42)

This approach has had tremendous influence on the way that the research process is taught to K–12 students in school libraries and thus has influenced the ways in which many people conceive the practice of information literacy.

When the *Information Power* guidelines were revised in 1998, AASL highlighted a new focus on information literacy; the guidelines (renamed *Information Power: Building Partnerships for Learning*) included new *Information Literacy Standards for Student Learning*, which outlined three categories of information literacy standards: general information literacy, independent learning, and social responsibility. These three categories comprised nine standards for which there were twenty-nine indicators. According to these guidelines, the student who is information literate (1) accesses information efficiently and effectively, (2) evaluates information critically and competently, and (3) uses information accurately and creatively. The student who is an independent learner is both information literate and (1) pursues information related to personal interests, (2) appreciates literature and other creative expressions of information, and (3) strives for excellence in information seeking and knowledge generation. The student who contributes positively to the learning community and to society is both information literate and (1) recognizes the importance of information to a democratic society, (2) practices ethical behavior in regard to information and information technology (IT), and (3) participates effectively in groups to pursue and generate information.

Also in 1998 ALA published a report detailing the progress made in the decade since the initial 1989 call to action for information literacy promotion in the United States. Although the report noted some progress, including a growth of the NFIL, it also noted that "there needs to be a national re-evaluation of the seemingly exclusive emphasis on and enormous investments in computers and networks," offering the belief "that the technology alone will never allow America to reach the potential inherent in the Information Age in not only its schools but also in its businesses. In fact, [NFIL members] believe that the dreams of a new and better tomorrow will only begin to be realized when all young people graduate into the workforce with strong information literacy skills" (n.p.). The emphasis on schools and businesses as the location of information literacy application returns again to an economic purpose for the information literacy agenda, but simultaneously the report noted the danger in this focus: by targeting only the increase in physical access to technology, policy is in danger of neglecting the perhaps more important need to ensure that people are empowered to use that technology. Regardless, the various standards and definitions of information literacy in the LIS field to this point largely cede to a neoliberal worldview of information (Seale, 2013).

It should be noted that the preceding history demonstrates our Western and particularly US bias. Whitworth (2014) fills in some of the gaps in *Radical Information Literacy,* as does Behrens (1994) to a lesser extent, with discussions of international literature on information literacy, but Whitworth also notes the tremendous influence of the American standards developed during this period on other countries' information literacy programs. It is best to consider this chapter a history of information literacy development in the United States. At the same time, we believe that this account represents many trends present in other places around the world. For example, in 1999 the United Kingdom and Ireland's Society of College, National and University Libraries (SCONUL) produced the position paper *Information Skills in Higher Education,* which describes "both information skills and information technology skills . . . as essential parts of a wider concept of information literacy" and suggests that this model is "based on seven sets of skills developing from a basic competence in library and IT skills" intended "[f]or the development of the information literate person" (p. 1). (We should note that this paper was updated in 2011 to become *The SCONUL Seven Pillars of Information Literacy: Core Model for Higher Education,* which will be discussed in more detail in chapter 3). Whitworth (2014) also asserts that "much work outside the US and UK continues to reflect . . . training in skills and competencies, developing rubrics or criteria for assessment, and trying to secure collaborations between libraries and academics" (p. 55).

The economic foundation of so many of these information literacy conceptions is often the main underpinning of international conceptualizations; as an example, in the mid-2000s the participants in the High-Level Colloquium on Information Literacy and Lifelong Learning released the *Alexandria Proclamation on Information Literacy and Lifelong Learning,* which declared that information literacy

- comprises the competencies to recognize information needs and to locate, evaluate, apply and create information within cultural and social contexts;
- is crucial to the competitive advantage of individuals, enterprises (especially small and medium enterprises), regions and nations;
- provides the key to effective access, use and creation of content to support economic development, education, health and human services, and all other

aspects of contemporary societies, and thereby provides the vital foundation for fulfilling the goals of the Millennium Declaration and the World Summit on the Information Society; and

■ extends beyond current technologies to encompass learning, critical thinking and interpretative skills across professional boundaries and empowers individuals and communities. (UNESCO/IFLA/NFIL, 2006, n.p.)

CRITICAL INFORMATION LITERACY

Around the turn of the century, professional organizations and scholars alike began to focus on a more sociocultural, critical view of information literacy. "Critical theory brings new dimensions to academic thinking about education and literacy, and these theories have made teaching and learning more interesting, complex, and in some ways, problematic processes than past education models have implied" (Elmborg, 2006, p. 193). This viewpoint wasn't entirely new. We mentioned earlier two scholars in addition to Zurkowski who influenced the early perceptions of information literacy. Perhaps the best introduction to Burchinal (1976) and Hamelink (1976) is to mention what some scholars found lacking in the viewpoint of Zurkowski. Whitforth (2014) believes that the main missing element was agency: "no particular mention is made of learning . . . there are no references to specific educational institutions, whether universities, schools or training companies, nor to pedagogy" (p. 32). He also highlights the limited nature of what Zurkowski describes as necessary "information banks" (basically large databases of information) in an optional "Information Service Environment," explaining that this approach "obscures the broader nature of information landscapes, and the recognition that information literacy skills can, and should, be applicable to stocks of information held . . . in oral, embodied, or cultural forms" (p. 32).

The first omission—the explicit reference to learning—was a major element of Burchinal's (1976) conception of information literacy. He states that information literacy "requires a new set of skills . . . how to efficiently and effectively locate and use information needed for problem solving and decision-making" (p. 11). Burchinal's skills-based approach argued that given the increased importance of information in society, people needed to be trained and educated in how to manage information in new ways. Hamelink's (1976) conception of information literacy departed from the skills-based definitions ("acquired so a person can be fitted into a technology- and information-rich system that is currently being designed by others"; Whitworth, 2014, p. 36). Instead, Hamelink believed that information is largely filtered through those with dominant positions in society (this point of view recalls Gramsci's [1971] concept of hegemony). Whitworth (2014) explains that

> Zurkowski and Burchinal see information literacy as something that needs to be developed *in* populations in order to assimilate them into the emerging ICT- [information and communications technology-] and information-rich society. Hamelink sees information literacy as something that has to be developed *by* populations so they can defend themselves against the *cognitive costs* of that society. (p. 36)

Hamelink sees information literacy as the capacity for liberation and empowerment.

As for where this information literacy development would occur, Hamelink described the ideal location for information literacy education as community centers which give access to a set of information resources with which the user can interact, i.e., ask for and receive information at his own initiative and in his own perceived self-interest. To avoid sophisticated forms of well-intended paternalism, such centers would have to be designed and developed with a major input from those who are supposed to benefit from them. (Whitworth, 2014, p. 37)

Hamelink was writing from a Dutch perspective, so the American system of public libraries may not have been considered; from our own perspective, it is easy to see the possibility of public (and other types of) libraries as this type of institution. However, the warning against paternalism is critical to consider. Indeed, the top-down establishment and development of information literacy conceptions, standards, and assessments in all areas of librarianship demonstrates this paternalism perfectly. (For a good discussion of how this paternalism can manifest as imperialism, particularly evidenced in international policy statements and recommendations about information literacy, see Pilerot and Lindberg, 2011). The emergence of a critical conception of information literacy within the past two decades of library scholarship allows for the possibility of the field of LIS evolving information literacy into a more community-based conception.

Pawley (2003) articulates the questions driving much of the critical information literacy scholarship:

Rather than focusing only on negotiating some essentialist concept of [information literacy] and on the best techniques for transmitting the agreed-upon skills, we should also be debating the issue of what, fundamentally, we are trying to do when we engage in information literacy practices, however defined. Such a challenge requires us to ask why as well as how, and to draw on scholarship not only in LIS but also in education, epistemology, ethics, politics, and social theory, to ask questions like: "What is information literacy for and who is it for?" "In what social and institutional circumstances does it take place?" "What consequences does information literacy have for the distribution of social and cultural goods in society as a whole?" Furthermore, the analysis should recognize that socially and historically constituted power relations based on, for example, class, race, gender, and age mediate thought and definitions of knowledge. (p. 445)

She invites the field to highlight the

importance of learning about context and content in understanding how information 'works' . . . to be both explicit about the moral and political commitment to flattening rather than reinforcing current information and literacy hierarchies, . . . to recognize that information 'access' is not just about information consumerism, . . . [and] to come to terms with the fact that freedom and control perpetually vie with one another in LIS. (p. 448)

The last point—that librarianship has its roots in a hierarchical view of knowledge—is particularly important.

Tewell (2018) defines critical information literacy "as an approach to education in library settings that strives to recognize education's potential for social change and empower learners to identify and act upon oppressive power structures" (p. 11). Gregory and Higgins (2013) note that this definition "differs from standard definitions of information literacy (ex: the ability to find, use, and analyze information) in that it takes into consideration the social, political, economic, and corporate systems that have power and influence over information production, dissemination, access, and consumption" (p. 4). Altogether, the critical information literacy lens views the practice as

- **Holistic**—"information skills cannot be taught independently of the knowledge domains, organizations, and practical tasks in which these skills are used" (Tuominen et al., 2005, p. 329)
- **Socially bound**—"an understanding of society and its textual mediation" (J. Andersen, 2005, p. 213; see also Lloyd, 2010a, 2012)
- **Interrogative**—"developing a critical consciousness about information, learning to ask questions about the library's (and the academy's) role in structuring and presenting a single, knowable reality" (Elmborg, 2006, p. 198)
- **Transformative**—"We should not only be inviting our students to be part of the 'culture of ideas and arguments' in our field and to engage in the problem-posing of digital literary history, but also to participate collectively and creatively in transformative actions that will help us work through the problems of selection, classification, preservation, and access" (Jacobs, 2014)

For more, see Tewell's 2015 article, "A Decade of Critical Information Literacy: A Review of the Literature." The critical view echoes much of what we will discuss in chapter 3, including the ways that information behaviors shape information literacy practices, how other types of literacies impact information literacy, and how information literacy might be best considered a metaliteracy.

CRITICAL INFORMATION LITERACY, AGAIN[7]

This section turns to some of the practical implications of this growing consciousness of a more community-driven information literacy. In 2011 the International Federation of Library Associations and Institutions (IFLA) released a set of media and information literacy recommendations to governments in which the organization declared information literacy

> a basic human right in an increasingly digital, interdependent, and global world, and [it] promotes greater social inclusion. It can bridge the gap between the information rich and the information poor. Media and Information Literacy empowers and endows individuals with knowledge of the functions of the media and information systems and the conditions under which these functions are performed. (n.p.)

Despite the reassertion of the "gap" between those with information and those without (implicitly placing some forms of information as better than others, because of course those who are "information poor" are obviously lacking a certain type of information, not information entirely), the emphases on empowerment and on an education in how media and information are created recall a more holistic understanding of the information life cycle (though again, Pilerot and Lindberg's 2011 critique of international information literacy conceptualizations as too generalized is worth noting). Likewise, the Prague Declaration's six principles of information literacy, prepared at the 2003 Information Literacy Meeting of Experts organized by UNESCO, NCLIS, and NFIL, emphasized understanding that information has cultural contexts: "Information Literacy, in conjunction with access to essential information and effective use of information and communication technologies, plays a leading role in reducing the inequities within and among countries and peoples, and in promoting tolerance and mutual understanding through information use in multicultural and multilingual contexts," although this appears alongside the assertion that "governments should develop strong interdisciplinary programs to promote Information Literacy nationwide as a necessary step in closing the digital divide through the creation of an information literate citizenry, an effective civil society and a competitive workforce," betraying the continued neoliberal thread of understanding in information literacy conceptions (UNESCO/NCLIS/NFIL, 2003, n.p.).

More recently, the culmination of scholarly emphasis on critical information literacy can be seen in the adaptation of professional organizations' frameworks for learning. Perhaps the most significant change based on the scholarship in critical information literacy in the American context is the development of the 2015 ACRL *Framework for Information Literacy for Higher Education*. In the *Framework*, the ACRL offers a new definition of information literacy: "the set of integrated abilities encompassing the reflective discovery of information, the understanding of how information is produced and valued, and the use of information in creating new knowledge and participating ethically in communities of learning" (p. 8).

The ACRL *Framework* "is based on a cluster of interconnected core concepts, with flexible options for implementation, rather than on a set of standards or learning outcomes, or any prescriptive enumeration of skills" (p. 7). Within the six frames included are enumerated knowledge practices, or "demonstrations of ways in which learners can increase their understanding of these information literacy concepts," as well as dispositions, "which describe ways in which to address the affective, attitudinal, or valuing dimension of learning" (pp. 7–8). Key to the *Framework* is the idea of threshold concepts, "which are those ideas in any discipline that are passageways or portals to enlarged understanding or ways of thinking and practicing within that discipline" (p. 7).

This approach is at least seemingly a great departure from the skills-based *Standards* that came before. Foasberg (2015) notes that

> the Framework's more conceptual approach does not as easily lend itself to listing a similar set of steps. Rather, its constructivist understanding of information and information literacy allows us to consider how the value of information artifacts may differ from one context to another. The Framework better recognizes the complexities of information and information behavior, and explicitly makes space for students as participants in the process of knowledge production. (p. 703)

Conversely, Hicks (2018) argues that the definition of information literacy remains largely unchanged between the 2000 *Standards* and the 2015 *Framework*, suggesting an adjustment rather than a sea change in how information literacy is conceptualized. Both the *Standards* and the *Framework* discuss information literacy as a set of abilities, for example.

Our own comparison of these definitions is more generous than Hicks's. The 2000 *Standards* merely mention "locate" as an action of information literacy, whereas the *Framework* describes an act of "reflective discovery of information." "Evaluate" becomes "the understanding of how information is produced and valued," and "use effectively the needed information" becomes "the use of information in creating new knowledge." Furthermore, the *Framework* adds "participating ethically in communities of learning" (cited in Hicks, 2018, p. 72). Although we see definite progress in the expansion of the concept of information literacy, Hicks seems to believe that the words are dressed up but the ultimate actions are the same. The *Framework* still situates information literacy as a distinct concept defined in librarianship and accessed through an understanding of specific, prescriptive knowledge. Indeed, Hicks asserts that "information work may look very different when it is explored ethnographically rather than measured in relation to pre-established models" (p. 72). Emphasizing the need for a new perspective on information literacy, Hicks believes that "if information literacy is understood as a social practice that emerges from a community's information interactions, a sociocultural perspective helps us to question and explore the values and assumptions that are being obscured when we define information literacy in homogenous or uniform terms" (p. 74).

Hicks is not alone in her criticism. Beilin (2015) notes that

> from a critical information literacy perspective . . . it appears that the specific type of information literacy advocated by the *Framework* is one which accepts the existence of a particular regime of knowledge, and demands that we as librarians focus our energies on making students and faculty competent citizens of that regime, even if dynamic, critical, and progressive ones. (n.p.)

Bombaro (2016) seems to largely object to the concept for exactly the opposite reason—the *Framework* is too esoteric, is too vague, and does not have enough practical applications to be used in a library instructional session. In chapters 4 and 5, we will return to the ongoing tension between philosophy and practical skills-based instruction.

By and large there doesn't seem to be nearly as much discussion about or influence of critical information literacy in the K–12 context, but the echoes of its scholarship have imprinted on the profession's most recent guiding documents. The AASL *Standards Framework for Learners*, part of the *National School Library Standards*, was published in 2017. Neither this *Framework* nor its 2007 predecessor, *Standards for the 21st Century Learner*, places as much emphasis on information literacy per se as do the 1998 *Information Power* standards. That said, inherent in the new *Framework* are concepts we find closely related to information literacy.

The *Framework*'s Shared Foundations and Key Commitments include the call for learners to

- **Inquire:** Build new knowledge by inquiring, thinking critically, identifying problems, and developing strategies for solving problems
- **Include:** Demonstrate an understanding of and commitment to inclusiveness and respect for diversity in the learning community
- **Collaborate:** Work effectively with others to broaden perspectives and work toward common goals
- **Curate:** Make meaning for oneself and others by collecting, organizing, and sharing resources of personal relevance
- **Explore:** Discover and innovate in a growth mindset developed through experience and reflection
- **Engage:** Demonstrate safe, legal, and ethical creating and sharing of knowledge products independently while engaging in a community of practice and an interconnected world (pp. 4–5)

Berg et al. (2018) note that the AASL *Framework*, though not fully nonlinear like ACRL's guide, echoes many of the same assumptions about information literacy, including the concepts of questioning authority, developing an open mind, and coming at information from a skeptical stance. Berg et al. relate these concepts to the AASL calls for learners to adjust their awareness of the global learning community by interacting with other learners who reflect a range of perspectives, evaluate a variety of perspectives during learning activities, and represent diverse perspectives during learning activities (n.p.).

Naturally, there have been critiques of the AASL standards as well. Loertscher (2018) has many, many quibbles with the *National School Library Standards*, but important to our discussion of critical information literacy is his concern about the dominating force of information literacy in the document to the detriment of other roles of the school library (interesting considering that in the actual *Framework for Learners* the term doesn't appear to have been used). Despite this, he believes the document presupposes a conception of information literacy that is defined by a course or grade-level curriculum. Indeed, he also laments the fact that AASL didn't take the opportunity to get beyond the imposed nature of the typical standards document; he imagines, what if students "helped write [the *Standards*] and then were encouraged to create their own personal set of standards? Talk about personalized learning!" (p. 48). These criticisms do not seem to be explicitly related to critical information literacy, but you can see how a scholar in that field might agree with his assertions in at least these areas.

In the years following the release of the revised standards/framework, many scholars interested in academic and school librarianship have turned their focus to what instruction looks like in critical information literacy instruction. Much more about pedagogical approaches to practicing information literacy will be discussed later in the book.

Now we need to turn to the place of information literacy in everyday life. We recognize that we've teased professional standards and frameworks—indeed, if you're more interested in the operationalization of information literacy definitions, you should skip ahead to later chapters. We would encourage you, however, to allow us to explain the foundation of information literacy because we think these later chapters will make much more sense if you do. That said—if you have a pressing need to review the ACRL *Framework for Information Literacy*, don't let us stop you.[8] If not, onward to chapter 3 where we will frame information literacy as the basis of power in the twenty-first century.[9] Or, at a minimum, try to explain what metaliteracy is.[10]

💬 CHAPTER 2 GUIDING QUESTIONS

1. What is information? Why is it so important to consider this definition in order to conceptualize information literacy?
2. In this chapter, we quote Knoblauch (1990): "Literacy is one of those mischievous concepts . . . that appear to denote capacities but that actually convey value judgments." How do you think this comment relates to the concept of information literacy? What value judgments does information literacy education carry?
3. How did the origins of information literacy shape what it has become today?
4. Is information literacy a uniquely LIS concept? If not, how does it apply to other fields?
5. In what ways does critical information literacy expand on the original understanding of the term?

NOTES

1. A chronicle of the debates about the meaning of the word *information* would also make for a really good book. But we definitely do not want to write that one.
2. This article also delightfully mentions the definition of information offered by *Sesame Street*'s Cookie Monster more than once. This recognition has led us to consider the woeful lack of Muppets in this book so far . . .
3. That's yet another book.
4. We emphasize "some"—a lot of definitions of information literacy are floating around, though, interestingly, there is not one in the *Encyclopedia of Library and Information Science*.
5. Seems like a fun guy to have at a party.
6. Yes, Big6 is actually trademarked.
7. This time with feeling!
8. Although, please do let us know what the pressing need is. We're curious . . .
9. Muwahaha!!!
10. Hint: it is not a dietary supplement.

Information Literacy in the Context of Information Behavior and Everyday Life

WE SPENT MUCH of chapter 1 of this book discussing all the ways that information rules our lives. This chapter returns to that concept by exploring the role of information literacy. In other words, the practice of information literacy—or a lack of practice—has direct impact on you, your community, the political institutions that guide the laws you live under, and the media you consume.[1] The practice of information literacy—or again, a lack thereof; we'll let you assume that this is always a possibility as we move forward in this chapter—is fundamental to information access and guides information behavior. It is dependent on education, socioeconomic status, geography, language, ability, and infrastructure. All this points to its inherent power—and much of the reason why those fighting for or currently in power might be disinclined to promote information literacy to others. The political nature of information literacy will be discussed much more in later chapters, but you will see the groundwork for this consideration as we discuss the different contexts of information literacy here.

First, we will return briefly to our definition of information literacy:

> **Information literacy** is a constantly refined practice of processing, accessing, understanding, critically evaluating, and using information in ways that are relevant to one's life. Information literacy relies on a social structure that promotes the agency of individuals in their communities and in the legal, political, educational, communication, and economic structures in their lives. Practicing information literacy is an iterative learning process that occurs throughout an individual's lifetime.
>
> Information literacy encompasses not only foundational literacies (reading/prose, writing/document, numeracy/quantitative) but also aspects of digital literacy (technology skills and ethics) and media literacy (critical analysis of nontextual content). In many cases, information literacy is closely associated with data, scientific, health, civic, and other context-specific literacies.

Inherent in our definition of information literacy are some principles of information behavior. Depending on where you are in your LIS journey, you will likely be familiar with some or all of these concepts. Nevertheless, we feel it is useful to reflect on some key terminology that is important both to an individual's process of information literacy and to the way we teach, promote, and discuss information literacy as information professionals. Indeed, Julien and Williamson (2011) call for increased research on the overlap between information seeking and information literacy because the former is more often the domain of the academic and the latter, the practitioner (this echoes a similar, earlier call by Limberg and Sundin in a 2006 research article). The intention of this book is to make information literacy accessible and useful to both researchers and practitioners.

Carol Kuhlthau's (1991) information search process, a seminal information-seeking model in our field, acknowledges that certain feelings are regularly associated with various stages of information acquisition. Additionally, in her 2018 book *Fake News and Alternative Facts: Information Literacy in a Post-Truth Era*, Nicole Cooke gives a succinct overview of the research on affective (or emotional) information behaviors. One example particularly useful to our discussion here is her explanation of Knud Illeris's work. Illeris (2002) describes learning as "two distinct processes: an internal psychological process in which new information is acquired and added to existing knowledge, and an external process in which the individual's information acquisition is shaped and influenced by interactions with their environment" (Cooke, 2018, p. 5). This environmental or social element is emphasized; "the learning that occurs during these internal and external processes encompasses three socially situated contexts: the cognitive domain of knowledge acquisition, the psychological dimensions of emotion and motivation, and the social domains of communication and cooperation" (Cooke, 2018, p. 5). This connection between theories of learning and information acquisition is critical because so much of the work of librarians is education. The practice of information literacy *is* learning. Cooke further describes five examples of affective (or emotional) information behavior: confirmation bias, filter bubbles (also known as an echo chamber), information overload, satisficing, and information avoidance (p. 7). We will explore the definitions of these concepts, among others, next.

Confirmation bias is "the seeking or interpreting of evidence in ways that are partial to existing beliefs, expectations, or a hypothesis" (Nickerson, 1998, p. 175). In his review of a number of studies on the phenomenon, Nickerson concludes that

> our natural tendency seems to be to look for evidence that is directly supportive of hypotheses we favor and even, in some instances, of those we are entertaining but about which are indifferent. We may look for evidence that is embarrassing to hypotheses we disbelieve or especially dislike, but this can be seen as looking for evidence that is supportive of the complementary hypotheses. (p. 211)

Given that the practice of information literacy is in the pursuit of knowledge, it would seem that confirmation bias is a psychological hurdle that must be overcome in our search for and acquisition of accurate information.

The perpetuation of confirmation bias is aided by the existence of filter bubbles and echo chambers. In 2011 Internet activist Eli Pariser described what was then a revolutionary concept to Internet users—the actions Google was taking to personalize searches to your activity. In order to provide search results more likely to align with those you would click, according to the algorithm's predictions, Google was in essence creating a "filter bubble" in which you could be fed only information that you liked to see. This practice has extended across the web but particularly to social media, where your newsfeed or the equivalent is informed by complex algorithms that rely on your search history—not just on that site but throughout the rest of your Internet activity as well. An echo chamber, according to the *Cambridge Dictionary*, is the more general concept of "a situation in which people only hear opinions of one type, or opinions that are similar to their own." It is often referenced in terms of political debate, perhaps because of the way that influential political scientist V. O. Key (1966) framed the electorate:

> For a glaringly obvious reason, electoral victory cannot be regarded as necessarily a popular ratification of a candidate's outlook. The voice of the people is but an echo. The output of an echo chamber bears an inevitable and invariable relation to the input. As candidates and parties clamor for attention and vie for popular support, the people's verdict can be no more than a selective reflection from among the alternatives and outlooks presented to them. Even the most discriminating popular judgment can reflect only ambiguity, uncertainty, or even foolishness if those are the qualities of the input into the echo chamber. (pp. 2–3)

In other words, garbage in, garbage out. The information circulating within a given society will necessarily determine the outcomes decided based on that information. This is why Habermas made "the free flow and debate on matters of public, civic concern" so essential to his concept of the public sphere, or "the space within a society, independent both of state power and of corporate influence, within which information can freely flow" (Corner, 1995, p. 42).

Additionally, it is essential not only that people can interact freely but also that "accessible, authoritative and reliable information resources" are available (Burnett & Jaeger, 2008, p. 3). The American electorate, described by V. O. Key, combined with the public officials they vote into office, is one example of a lifeworld, or "the intricate universe of political and social information and communication that comprises the diverse and myriad voices and perspectives of the members of an entire society that the members participate in and transmit to others" (Burnett & Jaeger, 2008, p. 4).

Within a lifeworld are a number of small worlds or "social group[s] in which 'mutual opinions and concerns are reflected by its members' and in which the interests and activities of individual members are largely determined by the normative influences of the small world as a whole" (Chatman, 1999, p. 213). The origin of the information transmitted to and within these small worlds depends on the in-world information practices. Information might come from official access points, channels of the public sphere, and interpersonal connections (Case, 2002; Williamson, 1998). Schutz (1964) determines that within an information community, "the power of socially approved knowledge is so extended that what the whole in-group approves—ways of thinking and acting, such as mores, folkways, habits—is simply taken for granted . . . although the source of such knowledge remains entirely hidden in its anonymity" (p. 133, cited in Whitworth, 2014, p. 17). A concept similar to information worlds is information landscapes, or "the communicative spaces that are created by people who co-participate in a field of practice" (Lloyd, 2010b, p. 2).

All these worlds, communities, and landscapes are essential to people's understanding of the world. People often exist in multiple small worlds or landscapes, and these communities change, making the flow of information to and from each individual a dynamic process. Not only is the information transfer often invisible, it is also a moving target. This feature makes Lloyd's (2010b) assertion that "the process of becoming information literate requires the whole person to be aware of themselves within the world . . . to experience information through the opportunities that are furnished by the landscape or context; to recognize these experiences as contributing to learning; and, to take into account how the context and its sanctioned practices, sayings and doings enable and constrain information use" (p. 2) an extremely complicated practice and one that necessitates constant attention. That attention, of course, requires time and resources, often unavailable to many (including the entirety of some small worlds), leading us to the concept of information poverty.

Information poverty is often characterized as a gap between those who can access information and those who cannot (Goulding, 2001). Some conceptions focus on the changing information environment—of mass media and later the Internet—as the cause of this divide. Coleman (1972), for example, describes the information environment of one hundred years ago as "information-poor" in comparison to today's "information-rich" society (p. 72). We could just as easily say the same about the information environment of 1972 compared to that of 2021. Childers and Post (1975) describe the information poor as those people in society with low information processing, as "harboring an inordinate amount of unawareness and misinformation (myth, rumour, folklore)," and with negative personal attitudes; "report after report portrays the various disadvantaged populations as despairing, fatalistic people with a pervasive sense of helplessness" (pp. 32 and 34). (We should note that this conception of information poverty can certainly be construed as elitist; should you be interested in exploring these definitions more, K. M. Thompson, 2007, offers a more in-depth look at the history of the term *information poverty* and all the ways in which it has been defined.)

Other conceptions of information poverty focus on the power structures that contribute to differences in information access. For example, Foucault's studies in the 1970s demonstrate that "coercive, legitimate, and competent authorities assert power to define discourses, and create information landscapes, backed up by institutions, that coerce people to conform" (Whitworth, 2020, p. 38). Even those with information privilege or power may be confronted with impediments to information given the modern information environment. The sheer volume of information has led to a variety of practices necessary to find information and use it in a reasonable amount of time. One such practice is satisficing, or stopping a search before all the possible information has been found, thereby potentially missing the best or most relevant information. In their study of this phenomenon, Caplin et al. (2011) found that most participants stopped their search when they had reached "an environmentally determined level of . . . utility," again suggesting the need to consider context in information seeking (p. 2899).

Beyond making environmental judgments, one might engage in satisficing behavior because of information overload. Goulding (2001), in fact, compares those suffering from too much information to the information poor. She describes the information poor as "unable to take action because they do not have necessary data and facts that would enable them to take control," whereas "those with too much information, or the inability to cope with the amount of information they encounter in their work and daily lives, are similarly paralyzed into inaction because of an inability to order the sea of information washing over them and thus make judgements about what is important and what is not" (p. 111). People also differ in their orientation on the spectrum of a "Need for Cognition (the tendency to engage in and enjoy cognitive efforts) and Need for Cognitive [C]losure (the desire for unambiguous information, as opposed to uncertainty or ambiguity)" (Fortier & Burkell, 2014, p. 2).

All these theories of information behavior have profound importance for our study of information literacy. In the process of understanding someone's practice of information literacy, there must be an effort to understand the lifeworld and small world(s) that underlay their practice. Their biases; access to information; approach to media figures, politicians, and other authority figures; and other emotional responses to information will all be influenced by societal factors. Even the choice not to practice information literacy is impacted by these factors. The practice of information literacy hinges on motivation; if someone does not want information or wants to continue to believe wrong information, there's not usually much to do to stop them. This situation is often known as information avoidance, or "any behavior intended to prevent or delay the acquisition of available but potentially unwanted information. Information avoidance can entail asking someone not to reveal information, physically leaving a situation to avoid learning information, or simply failing to take the necessary steps to reveal the content of information" (Sweeny et al., 2010, p. 341). The information might be against their community's norms or belief systems; the information might come from an authority that has previously caused distrust; and the information might simply be unrelated to that person's needs or desires. Given the multitude of information behaviors and psychological components of information, is it any wonder that information literacy is a difficult practice to engage in?

THE WIDE WORLD OF LITERACIES

Because of information literacy's role in information behavior, it has critical importance to so many contexts that are essential to well-being. In their discussion of defining information literacy, Snavely and Cooper (1997) list examples of the use of the term *literacy* to denote basic knowledge of a subject or field and find more than thirty examples in their search of book titles.[2] We haven't included all these examples in our own definition of related literacies—hence, the addition of other field-related literacies.[3] However, we did find six—digital literacy, media literacy, data literacy, scientific literacy, health literacy, and civic literacy—important enough to call out and describe because of how often they are needed in and presented at libraries.

Digital Literacy

Digital literacy "encompasses the skills and abilities necessary for access once . . . technology is available, including a necessary understanding of the language and component hardware and software required to successfully navigate the technology" (Jaeger, Bertot, Thompson et al., 2012, p. 3). *Digital literacy* as a term was popularized by Paul Gilster (1997) when he defined it as "the ability to understand and use information in multiple formats from a wide range of sources when it is presented via computers" (p. 33). This conception does resemble information literacy though, in the sense that Gilster also associates "being able to understand a problem . . . develop a set of questions that will solve that information need . . . using search methods that allow you to access information sources on the Internet and evaluate them" with the practice of digital literacy (p. 33).

Some argue that *digital literacy* serves "as an 'umbrella' term for a range of distinct educational practices which seek to equip the user to function in digitally rich societies" (Leaning, 2019). We would argue that most definitions of digital literacy, however, rely on the practice of information literacy, such as Bawden's (2008) summary of four essential components of digital literacy from relevant scholarly literature: basic and ICT literacy, background knowledge ("the world of information" and "the nature of information resources"), competencies such as information and media literacies, and certain attitudes and perspectives (including "independent learning" and "moral/social literacy") (p. 29). Ultimately the key difference between information literacy and digital literacy, for our purposes at least, is that the practice of digital literacy always necessitates the use of some technology, whereas information literacy does not. Still, in the modern era, the vast majority of information needs are likely to have at least a small digital component.

Media Literacy

A. Rubin (1998), in an amalgamation of several scholarly and policy definitions, defines media literacy as "understanding the sources and technologies of communication, the codes that are used, the messages that are produced, and the selection, interpretation, and impact of those messages" (p. 3). According to Aufderheide (1992), "media literacy, the movement to expand notions of literacy to include the powerful post-print media that dominate our informational landscape, helps people understand, produce, and negotiate meanings in a culture made up of powerful images, words, and sounds" and ensures that people have "a critical autonomy relationship to all media" (p. 9). J. A. Brown (1998) adds that media literacy education must consider that "meaning is situated in what audiences bring to their media experience (selective perception), the context in which they use media (accommodation), and how and why they use the medium (uses and gratifications)" (p. 44). A growing trend in media literacy education is the inclusion of media production in the definition—in other words, ensuring that the practice of media literacy includes producing media in addition to critical consumption (Hobbs & Jensen, 2009).

From these definitions, and the discussion of media literacy education, the parallels to information literacy are obvious. There are really only a couple of key differences. One is the emphasis on the production of media. Although information literacy does encourage those practicing information literacy to contribute to the information landscape, it is not specifically in the realm of media production. The second difference, somewhat less certain, is Koltay's (2011) argument that one distinctive element of media literacy is its emphasis on being aware and critical of advertising or commercial messages. Information literacy arguably does this as well, though maybe not quite as centrally situated. On the whole, though, media literacy probably has the most overlap with information literacy as any others we discuss.

Data and Scientific Literacies

We have grouped data and scientific literacies together because they both have some connection to field-specific knowledge. In other words, certain numerical and scientific thought processes are essential to understanding most information that is associated with these areas. Schield (2005) argues "that information literacy, statistical literacy, and data literacy are tied together by a common set of problems and a similar level of approach. All three are more general than specific, they each involve interdisciplinary study and they deal with fundamentals" (pp. 8–9). Data literacy is "a suite of data acquisition-, evaluation-, handling-, analysis- and interpretation-related competencies that lie outside the scope of statistical competencies" (Prado & Marzal, 2013, p. 124). Modern legislative and economic decisions increasingly are made as a result of big data or "the collection, processing, analysis, and visualization associated with very large data sets" (Emmanuel & Stanier, 2016, p. 1). Additionally, more and more, scientists are making available to the public the large data sets that they use in their work.

The argument that a basic understanding of data (and statistics) is of growing importance to everyday life echoes the first calls for increased scientific literacy. In 1958 Hurd called for increased science education in general because "[a]ttempts to define human values, to understand the social, economic, and political problems of our times, or to validate educational objectives without a consideration of modern science are unrealistic" (p. 13). In a 2016 review of the scholarship on scientific literacy, the National Academies of Sciences, Engineering, and Medicine's Committee on Science Literacy and Public Perception of Science reported that there are generally four rationales for scientific literacy: economic, personal, democratic, and cultural. (Sound familiar?) Feinstein (2011) takes a more socially constructed point of view and defines people with scientific literacy as those who are

> *competent outsiders* with respect to science: people who have learned to recognize the moments when science has some bearing on their needs and interests and to interact with sources of scientific expertise in ways that help them achieve their own goals. It follows from this definition that the pursuit of science literacy is not *incidentally* but *fundamentally* about identifying relevance: learning to see how science is or could be significant to the things you care about most. (p. 180)

Health Literacy

Though health literacy could be seen as a subset of scientific literacy, given the fact that we are writing this book as the global pandemic caused by the novel coronavirus plagues the entire world, even while a significant portion of American society derides it as a fake phenomenon, it seems important to call out health literacy specifically. The US Institute of Medicine (IOM) described health literacy as "the degree to which individuals have the capacity to obtain, process and understand basic health information and services needed to make appropriate health decisions" (Kindig et al., 2004, n.p.). Nutbeam (2008) describes the IOM definition

> as a set of individual capabilities in the four domains of cultural and conceptual knowledge, speaking and listening skills, writing and reading skills, and numeracy. . . . It also emphasizes that health literacy is context specific and subject to influence by health care interactions and structures such as the way in which services are organized and delivered. (p. 2074)

Perhaps because the concept is often applied to clinical environments, health literacy is often measured systematically by validated tests in various domains thought to be associated with health literacy, including basic literacy and numeracy. These tests, such as the Rapid Estimate of Adult Literacy in Medicine (REALM), are necessarily limited because of time constraints in clinical situations. They also clearly approach the concept of health literacy as a set of skills, the knowledge of which, or lack of knowledge of, results in better or worse health outcomes. Nutbeam (2008) identifies an alternative conceptualization—health literacy as the outcome itself, as opposed to better health decisions. He explains that

> the purpose of the health education [is] directed towards the development of relevant personal knowledge and capability . . . and interpersonal and social skills. . . . People

who have better-developed health literacy will thus have skills and capabilities that enable them to engage in a range of health enhancing actions . . . . The results are not only improved health outcomes but also a wider range of options and opportunities for health. (p. 2075)

Nutbeam also notes that what constitutes health literacy will change depending on the person's age and context (again, similar to information literacy).

Civic Literacy

Civic literacy is "an approach to learning that emphasizes the knowledge, skills, and dispositions necessary for active and engaged citizenship" (Masyada & Washington, 2019). Some of this required knowledge concerns how the government information system works. We said in chapter 1 that traditional literacy was concerned with those skills you need to fill out your tax forms, but in a glaring example of how times have changed, these traditional skills are often now not enough. With the US government's shift toward electronic government (often at the expense of human-staffed government offices), technological skills and knowledge of the organization of government are increasingly necessary to accomplish such acts as filing your taxes, registering your child for school, and completing requests for government assistance (Bertot, Jaeger et al., 2006).

Beyond the everyday connection to government, however, is the essential connection of civic literacy to democracy. This book was being written as the 2020 election and its strange aftermath of conspiracies and denials by the losing candidate and some of his supporters were unfolding. Civic literacy thus presently seems like the most pressing of all the associated literacies. We have already discussed the ways in which information literacy is so carefully tied to democratic society. Scholarly studies demonstrate how closely information literacy is tied to civic literacy as well.

L. N. Smith (2016) notes that in her study of teenagers' political knowledge and self-efficacy, "when they actively seek information, they report feeling unsure about where to find reliable and trustworthy information" (p. 18). In another recent study of middle-school-age youth, young people were found to have critical gaps in their knowledge of government, were quick to question authority, and often believed conspiracy theories about the government (Taylor, 2015). A national survey of civics teachers found that less than half of respondents, despite believing that information literacy is critical, were confident in their skills in teaching it (Kawashima-Ginsberg, 2014).

Whitworth (2020) sums up the reason to be concerned about this neglect: "Informed political judgements are not just a factor of the amount or availability of information; nor of the delegation of decision making to 'professional' politicians. They depend also on an ability to discern . . . understand where information is relevant, make connections and evaluate impacts" (p. 27). In other words, efficient, effective, and democratic political society is dependent on both information and civic literacy.

METALITERACY

We hope that it is becoming clear how information literacy intersects with so many disciplines. We want to return briefly to how information literacy is conceived in both the LIS field and in scholarship.[4] You might have noticed that information literacy seems to be itself embedded in the adjacent literacies we mentioned previously. Some scholars have posited that information literacy is not just related to these other literacies; rather, it foregrounds them. Shapiro and Hughes (1996) believed that information literacy does have components of a skills-based education ("Information and computer literacy, in the conventional sense, are functionally valuable technical skills"), but they also conceived it much more broadly than these skills alone:

> Information literacy should in fact be conceived more broadly as a new liberal art that extends from knowing how to use computers and access information to critical reflection on the nature of information itself, its technical infrastructure, and its social, cultural and even philosophical context and impact—as essential to the mental framework of the educated information-age citizen as the trivium of basic liberal arts (grammar, logic and rhetoric) was to the educated person in medieval society. (n.p.)

This viewpoint is strongly related to the concept of information literacy as a metaliteracy. Mackey and Jacobson (2011) assert that

> metaliteracy provides a conceptual framework for information literacy that diminishes theoretical differences, builds practical connections, and reinforces central lifelong learning goals among different literacy types. Rather than envision these methods as unrelated or disconnected, we see information literacy as the essential framework that informs and unifies additional literacy types. (p. 76)

Because of this connection, they see information literacy education as a process of learning how to learn and share information in a new media environment. In some ways, this returns to the idea of critical information literacy in which reflection is a key part of the iterative process of practicing information literacy.

Ultimately, for our own study of information literacy, it is not essential that you decide whether you think it is the basis of other literacies or merely a natural companion. The key takeaway from this discussion of different but related literacies is to consider that library education needs to encompass skills present in all these literacies (and more) that we have discussed. Teaching people how to use a library may be important, but it is not the entirety of information literacy education that belongs in a library. And you may find yourself reconceptualizing programs you are already running in your library as information literacy education.

WHERE IN THE WORLD IS INFORMATION LITERACY?[5]

Now that we have convinced you of the connection of information literacy to virtually every area of your life (we have convinced you, right?), you might be wondering why we as people seem to be suffering such a deficit. The unfortunate reality of the modern world is that as the importance of information literacy has grown, the more a half-baked, confused, and ineffectual form of the practice of information literacy has permeated our societies (at least those of the Western world's liberal democracies). We believe that the ultimate result of a population that fails to practice information literacy—for whatever reason—is a society that is more unequal, more authoritarian, and more partisan. Ray Bradbury famously said,

"You don't have to burn books to destroy a culture. Just get people to stop reading them." It's not hard to see parallels between this admonition and the gobs of information we take in every day. You don't have to censor news if people can't find it or don't trust it.

The rest of our book focuses on some of the reasons for the confused information literacy soup we are currently experiencing. From legal and political decisions to operationalizations of information literacy in information institutions, it is clear there is much work to be done. And if 2020 is any sign of the future, the need for this work is both critical and urgent.

A LITTLE CLARITY

If you've grown tired of the oodles of definitions, conceptualizations, and historical approaches to information literacy,[6] we can offer a bit of a reprieve and an explanation for why we've put you through that ordeal.[7] The simplest reason there are so many different definitions of information literacy in the LIS field is that we are a diverse profession made up of many types of information institutions, and different audiences of users create a need to focus on different outcomes. We are, or at least we aim to be, also a reflective field that builds on prior research in the tradition of proper scholarship; with new information and understandings, new definitions are formed.

Perhaps a more cynical take is that academics tend to have a fair amount of ego, as well as a seemingly unending need to create models, definitions, and frameworks.[8] But regardless of the reasons why, it is hard to argue that the field is lacking in definitions. Thankfully, you probably have already noticed some common themes over the course of the book thus far. In creating our own definition of information literacy to guide this book, we found two of these common elements particularly compelling: (1) information literacy is an iterative lifelong learning practice, and (2) information literacy requires a surrounding social structure that actively encourages agency.

Information Literacy Is an Iterative Lifelong Learning Practice

Despite the common refrain (even in the preceding information literacy definitions) of the digital divide as the "haves and have nots," many if not most descriptions of information literacy emphasize that skills are acquired across the lifetime rather than in a one-and-done shot. For example, in the 2011 update of SCONUL's information literacy guidelines, *The SCONUL Seven Pillars of Information Literacy: Core Model for Higher Education*, the authors state that "an individual can develop from 'novice' to 'expert' as they progress through their learning life, although, as the information world itself is constantly changing and developing, it is possible to move down a pillar as well as progress up it" (p. 3). There is an obvious need for a growing and changing practice of information literacy as one's information environment and needs change.

Harkening back to the argument that information literacy is not a new concept but, rather, a relabeled library or bibliographic instruction, Rader and Coons (1992) use the lifelong nature of information literacy to justify a distinction in the concepts: "bibliographic instruction is more often a situation-specific response, whereas information literacy contributes towards life-long learning by educating individuals to effectively utilize and evaluate information" (cited in Bawden, 2001, p. 236). The scholarly arguments against information literacy as a library-dependent concept frequently note the importance of information literacy skills outside a formal research environment. O'Sullivan (2002), for example, notes that the concept of information literacy hasn't really permeated the corporate work environment. Lloyd (2005) argues that an information literacy practice largely driven by the educational context and a connection to textual information "produces a deficit model of information literacy which does not take into account the importance of informal learning or other sources of information which are accessed through communication or action. This reduces the power of information literacy and . . . the ability to transfer skills and practices between contexts" (p. 87). We agree that although libraries may be particularly well-suited environments for information literacy learning and practice, neither should information literacy be confined to one field or institution. (In many practical ways, public libraries have already embraced this notion. The trouble seems to be that the expanded practices of information literacy promoted by public libraries, such as the activities in makerspaces and the communication in book clubs, aren't really identified as information literacy).

Information Literacy Requires a Surrounding Social Structure That Actively Encourages Agency

As we took in the plethora of meanings (excess of explanations? surfeit of specifications?) previously discussed, what we found particularly important for this particular study and introduction of information literacy are the apparent social structures that must be present in order for an individual to be able to practice information literacy. These structures include an economy that rewards intellectual contributions (textual, creative, and scholarly work) but that also ensures equitable distribution of these works. Day (2017) notes that

> in the light of all sorts of fake news, illegitimate knowledge, our addiction to our electronic devices, etc., we need to come to terms with a fundamental fact: knowledge is hard to create and come by. It requires education, methods, institutions, the preservation, organization and access to valid and reliable documents and data (the information domain traditionally given to libraries), good faith dialogue and continuous traditions . . . To put it succinctly: knowledge requires institutions and institutional parameters for its production; it is hard, and in all senses of the term, costly work for individuals and for society. Information may or may not want to be free, but knowledge is not. We shouldn't be fooled otherwise. (p. 59)

What these social structures enable is agency. One early objection to the term *information literacy* even suggested that it be renamed *information empowerment* (H. S. White, 1992, p. 76, cited in Bawden, 2001, p. 245).

Knowing your context, the structures that make up your place in the world, is necessary to practice information literacy. J. Andersen (2005) concludes, through a sociopolitical perspective, that information literacy is

> the ability to read society and its textually and genre-mediated structures. Information literacy represents an understanding of society and its textual mediation. We might go as far as to say that information literacy implies a critique of society insofar it includes a particular use and reading of particular information sources and use of particular forms of communication. (p. 226)

You will note that much of the content of chapters 4–6 describes an American society that distressingly offers limited support for the practice of information literacy.

One final note on the social structures than enable information literacy practices. The open access to information is a critical piece to the puzzle. Beatty (2014) notes that much of the content of higher education literacy education is predicated on

> the continuance of the current system of walled gardens. Its conception of information literacy is about knowing not how but where to find gold untainted by dross. It redefines expertise as little more than knowing how to find one's way around these walled gardens, and to identify when one has stepped outside. In short, the "information ecosystem" and "information marketplace" metaphors naturalize the enclosure of what might instead have been a commons. (n.p.)

The problem with the notion of a completely free information commons is that social media demonstrates natural consequences to a sea of information without regard for systematic organization. The fact that it is difficult to conduct the organization of information without imposing authority doesn't negate the fact that such organization is incredibly helpful in the practice of information literacy. This fact lies at the heart of the dilemma of information literacy instruction—how much control should authoritative institutions have over information?

BRINGING IT ALL TOGETHER

Beyond these two commonalities in the literature, we have three final points to make before turning again to the definition of information literacy that will guide this book. One point regards the nature of information retrieval. Although we acknowledge the important steps in the formal information-seeking process, we also want to emphasize that information literacy is critical to more informal means of acquiring information. A specific information need isn't a prerequisite to receiving information (P. J. McKenzie, 2003; Wilson, 1977). Consider a conversation between friends in which one brings up a popular conspiracy theory. You wouldn't have to seek out the misinformation in order to receive it.

Several of the major information-seeking models of the past three decades have import on the defined actions affected by information literacy. We have already mentioned the Eisenberg Big6 approach and Kuhlthau's 1991 information search process, the latter of which "incorporates three realms: the affective (feelings), the cognitive (thoughts), and the physical (actions) common to each stage," which are information initiation, selection, exploration, formulation, collection, and presentation (pp. 366–367). The tasks related to each stage are recognition (initiation), identification (selection), investigation (exploration), formulation, gathering (collection), and completion (presentation; p. 367). In many of the definitions of information literacy previously discussed, these are the actions that are explicitly called out. The limitation of this model and the Big6 model, however, is that both were at least initially conceived as formal research models within the context of education. We can point to Kundu (2017) for an explanation of the many other information-seeking models developed in LIS.

We want to focus, though, on a more recent concept gaining popularity in the field—that of everyday-life information seeking. P. J. McKenzie (2003) not only describes the research in this area but also develops a model that includes several ways in which participants made connections with information sources (through active seeking of sources, through active scanning, through nondirected monitoring, and by proxy) and interacted with information sources (through active seeking in information encounters, through active scanning, by nondirected monitoring, and by proxy or being told). She concludes "that a focus on the social concept of information practices is more appropriate to everyday life information seeking than the psychological concept of information behaviour" (p. 19). We believe that information literacy is a practice essential to formal information seeking, such as in the identification of information needs, information use, and reflection on the process of acquiring information, but that it is equally important in the informal transfer of information that occurs throughout one's everyday life.

A second important point is the recognition that the practice of information literacy doesn't mean that people will never believe misinformation. Whitworth (2014) notes that Kuhlthau's (1993) concept of information seeking indeed considers this "a natural part of the human condition" and that "information literacy must allow for personal constructs, which contribute to the possible rejection of information, even specifically relevant information" (p. 59). Practicing information literacy involves purposefully choosing which information to accept and reject. In other words, if you want to believe something that is scientifically wrong, fine, but you should understand the consequences of those beliefs and truly why you hold them. You will have the knowledge, access, and ability to be able to interrogate the information presented to you. Some might call this critical thinking and, in a way, it is. However, information literacy also encompasses so many other skills and processes, and relies on so many external factors, that it goes beyond critical thinking. It is having the means (time, ability, and access) to question sources, to seek out relevant information, and to use the information once found. It extends beyond an understanding of search, retrieval, and use because information literacy relies on other types of literacy—foundational, civic, data, science, and many more—for need identification and use. The consistent practice of information literacy is reliant on access to societal structures that support education, economic and social equity, intellectual freedom, and political agency.

Finally, we have used the word *practice* throughout chapters 2 and 3 and in our definition in the vein of Whitworth (2020):

> Practice has an innately *affective* element and our reactions and judgements made in context can never be reduced entirely to 'rational' or 'objective' judgements. Practice is also innately *social* and this reveals a tension with how IL [information literacy], as an educational endeavour, has defined itself more as an individual cognitive capacity rather than a characteristic of groups and communities. (p. xvii)

With the importance of information actions, learning, social conditions, and agency at the forefront of our minds, along with all the understandings of information literacy discussed earlier, we reached the definition of information literacy that we are using in this book:

> **Information literacy** is a constantly refined practice of processing, accessing, understanding, critically evaluating, and using information in ways that are relevant to one's life. Information literacy relies on a social structure that promotes the agency of individuals in their communities and in the legal, political, educational, communication, and economic structures in their lives. Practicing information literacy is an iterative learning process that occurs throughout an individual's lifetime.

Information literacy encompasses not only foundational literacies (reading/prose, writing/document, numeracy/quantitative) but also aspects of digital literacy (technology skills and ethics) and media literacy (critical analysis of nontextual content). In many cases, information literacy is closely associated with data, scientific, health, civic, and other context-specific literacies.

We don't think this is a definitive definition, but we hope both the definition and how we arrived at it now make sense. This definition at least offers a guide as you engage with the rest of this book. Perhaps after engaging in a study of this topic, you will be the one to finally unite the understandings of information literacy![9]

🗨 CHAPTER 3 GUIDING QUESTIONS

1. Have you noticed a tendency toward confirmation bias or the use of filter bubbles in your own information practices? Can you think of examples?
2. How does the "lifeworld" in which you live impact the type of information you consume? What about the various "small worlds" that you inhabit?
3. Why do you think we chose these six literacies—digital literacy, media literacy, data literacy, scientific literacy, health literacy, and civic literacy—as literacies to highlight in this chapter? Do you agree with these choices, or are others more relevant?
4. Is information literacy a metaliteracy? What are the benefits and drawbacks to defining it this way?
5. After reading chapter 3, are there changes you would make to our definition of IL? What might those be?

NOTES

1. Or that consumes you . . . one could remake *Little Shop of Horrors* by replacing Audrey II with Facebook and have a prescient hit on their hands. The musical version, of course. Featuring songs like "Mean Green Mother from Cyberspace" and "Suddenly Seymour Is Liking a Photo" and "You'll Be on Pinterest."
2. One imagines an Oprah-esque giveaway: "This field gets a literacy! That field gets a literacy! Everyone gets a literacy!"
3. Understanding them all requires literacy literacy. Or maybe metaliteracy.
4. As if you didn't get enough of that in chapter 2.
5. We hope you caught the Carmen Sandiego reference; if not, Google Rockapella stat.
6. If you're not, check out H. B. Rader (2002) and Sample (2020) for even more definitions! Fun times!
7. Other than simply to torment you, of course.
8. Admittedly, we say this as academics who have offered you a new definition and who have collectively created several models and frameworks . . .
9. One definition to rule them all!

The Operationalization of Information Literacy, Part I

Academic and School Libraries

REALLY EARLY INFORMATION LITERACY

When infants are born, they have no concept of how to make music. A baby might first bang a spoon on a pan or ring a bell, but no one would mistake them for a percussionist. The baby would, however, be practicing their rhythm. As the child gets older, a mischievous uncle or grandparent might purchase them their first toy drum set. Again, the sounds that come from this instrument would in no way resemble music.[1] It is likely, however, that this noise would be more akin to actual songs than would the early efforts. Gradually, with practice, better tools, and instruction, the child might learn to read music, play in a school band, and perhaps even become a professional musician. At some point along the way, they might even begin to consider themselves a drummer. But even the most expert musician will say they still have much to learn. And certainly the context of the playing matters—a child playing in a school band is not expected to be as good as someone playing in a concert that others have paid to hear. A professional musician riffing with their friends would not need to have the same precision as they would in their work environment.

If you've spent any time at all studying library scholarship related to digital literacy, you are bound to have come across references to the digital divide. This phrase, especially popular in the early part of the twenty-first century, describes a state in which one group of people has digital access (both physical and intellectual—though heavily emphasizing physical) and one group does not. In previous chapters, we have explained the fact that we find the idea of either having or not having literacy skills, access, or information overly simplistic. Rather, we mention in our definition that we prefer the terminology of the "practice of information literacy" rather than speaking of people having, and conversely not having, information literacy skills.

Consider our musical metaphor and imagine information literacy is a practice akin to playing music. Like playing music, information literacy is something that is often developed as a person gets older, is dependent on context, and requires appropriate tools and instruction to improve. It is also a practice that different individuals might consider more or less important. In other words, some might find that for their purposes, stopping at the school band stage is okay.[2] Others might find that their situation requires more professional expertise. Perhaps they even need to expand beyond the drum set to another instrument. It wouldn't necessarily be appropriate to describe the school band player as lacking musical talent, just like it wouldn't be appropriate to consider someone with elementary practice at information literacy as being information illiterate. Rather, it would be more accurate to consider that both just need more practice, better instruction, or more appropriate tools (again, if their context requires it).

When we discuss information literacy in the context of practicing, it is both a current action (as in the school band player who is playing at a football game is practicing the art of drumming) and a progressive one (as the player practices the music, it is likely they see an improvement in their skill—or at least a better version of what they know to do now). Now, consider the practice of teaching music (and information literacy). The education will be dependent on context (a school band director is different from an orchestra leader; an academic librarian is different from a public librarian), will be tailored to the specific learner need (learning the flute or understanding a government website is different from learning the drums or understanding an academic database), and will require tools (an instrument or an information resource).

In this chapter and its companion that immediately follows, we will attempt to explain the various ways that information literacy education and programming have been operationalized in different types of libraries. This chapter is devoted to academic and school libraries, whereas chapter 5 focuses on public libraries, special libraries, and archives. Each of these contexts has different populations of users, different available resources, and different historical practices. What you'll find in common, however, is a keen desire to ensure that users have the tools and knowledge to meet their information needs. That is, after all, what a library is all about.

A LITTLE MORE ON CHAPTER 4 AND MORE[3]

People practice information literacy every day, from the moment they wake up and check the news on their phones to their bedtime routine of obsessively monitoring Twitter; for those Luddites reading this, even you practice information literacy when you read a paper newspaper or decide whether to ignore your neighbor's warning to stay away from unfiltered water. Librarians likewise practice information literacy constantly in their professional role. It is present when you evaluate a new book to add to the collection or consider whether to sign a licensing agreement with a new digital vendor, and perhaps most prominently, in the education you provide to your users. Even that last role can be a little murky, though. Is information literacy education a one-off academic library instruction session on how to search the catalog and access databases? Is it a public library session that teaches people how to search for their family history using genealogical tools? Is it a school librarian's lesson on reliable and useful resources for students to use in the third-grade science fair? The answer, of course, is all the above. This chapter is going to focus on this category of information literacy in libraries—how do libraries educate their users about information literacy?

This chapter and the next will demonstrate the ways that all types of libraries (public, school, academic, and others) currently promote information literacy. We will reiterate the core information literacy skills that have been identified by the professional organizations representing each type of library and the most recent standards or frameworks in use. Examples of the types of programming and lessons used in different libraries will be highlighted. We should mention three things before starting, though. First, we will be focusing on the modern era, which we are conceiving as being the last two decades of programming.[4]

Second, as we discuss the ways that each type of library has structured its information literacy approach, it is important to keep in mind that, at least in the US context, these libraries are situated within a neoliberal economic structure. This positioning strongly influences the type of programming that librarians feel they can do. Finally, although we have made an effort to include international programming in these examples, we clearly have a US bias simply because of where we live, our prior research in these areas, and our knowledge of the scholars in this area of practice. Even with the international examples we use, there is an obvious Western bias in our portrayal of instructional methods.

With that out of the way, onward! We think these two particular chapters are so important because they demonstrate the ways in which the definitions we discussed in chapters 2 and 3 are actually put into practice.

ACADEMIC LIBRARIES

We begin with academic libraries for two reasons.[5] First, scholarship on information literacy in higher education makes up the bulk of published literature on the subject. You'll note that the academic library section in these two chapters is the longest by a fair bit and the most citation-intensive and quotacular. Second, the development of standards on information literacy across types of libraries and around the world is heavily influenced by the work of the ACRL. For better or worse, ALA has almost entirely ceded its definitional approach to information literacy to those in colleges and universities. Thus, a look at the context for these standards and this education seems prudent.

One metric of context is to look at the user group to which higher education libraries are speaking. Although of course faculty is one such constituency, college and university students are the typical recipients of information literacy outreach and education. These students are not the same audience as those who made up the academy two decades ago. Almost every minority group has seen growing attendance in higher education, changing both the racial makeup of student bodies and the cultural contexts the students bring with them (Espinosa et al., 2019). The economic and information environments for higher education are different as well. Shelby Foote, a prominent twentieth-century historian and writer, is widely credited across the Internet as saying, "A university is just a group of buildings gathered around a library," in a 1993 issue of *North Carolina Libraries*. This idea is quaint but very outdated. For one thing, the library's main contributions to student learning often occur online—a student can easily go all four years of their university career without once stepping foot in the library. Those taking online classes may not be located within a hundred miles of the actual library building. Additionally, the prominent trend in higher education over the past fifty years has been a gradual move to a more business-oriented model of administration (P. Davis, 2012; McKenna, 2018; L. McKenzie, 2020). Even as libraries' budgets are cut, costs have increased, specifically for digital scholarship housed in proprietary databases (Enis, 2018).

Of course, the economy of education has always had a tremendous impact on how information literacy education is constructed and assessed. As we mentioned in chapter 2, one of the major reasons libraries first began their push to define information literacy was the way that education funding ignored libraries' contributions to student learning. What also hasn't changed is the need for students to practice information literacy. It is perhaps more important now than ever. Academic librarian Barbara Fister (2019) notes that she believes we may be at the beginning of information literacy's "third wave," the first wave being bibliographic instruction, or empowerment to ask questions of library resources, and the second a reconfiguration of what students needed to know based on the changes to information sharing caused by the Internet. She believes we are "just beginning to respond to the commercialization and portability of networked information" (n.p.). Barclay (2017) also notes the changing scholarly thinking regarding truth and fact:

> Further complicating the situation is the relativism of the postmodern philosophy underpinning much of postmodern scholarly thinking. . . . While postmodernism has had positive effects, it has simultaneously undermined the concept of authority. If, as postmodernist philosophy contends, truth is constructed rather than given, what gives anyone the right to say one source of information is credible and another is not?" (n.p.)

There are solutions to this dilemma, but it makes information literacy a more complicated prospect than just understanding that information in an academic journal equals fact.

Beyond the understanding of expertise, reliable information, and contextual truth, the rise of social media and an increase in online research also lend themselves to an increased need for information literacy practice and instruction. A study conducted by Johannes Gutenberg University Mainz and Goethe University Frankfurt found that, despite a preference for online information when doing research, college students taking part in their Critical Online Reasoning Assessment (CORA) struggled to find reliable and relevant information to answer CORA's questions ("CORA study examines", 2020). Other, earlier studies found similar results—college students struggle with online information assessment (Head, 2007; Metzger et al., 2003). That said, this inability isn't unique to college students. As C. H. Becker (2012) states, "the abundance and convergence of new media . . . is changing the structure of libraries and library service. However, adherence to generational differences as an underlying cause hinders educational pedagogy principally because we are all part of the current consumer-driven technology bubble" (p. 360). We focus a lot, rightly so, on the context of the user when designing instruction, but it would be negligent to not also address the changing information environment itself. The evolution of the ACRL *Information Literacy Competency Standards for Higher Education* (2000) to the *Framework for Information Literacy for Higher Education* (2015) demonstrates these technological and environmental conditions, as well as the nature of information literacy instruction.

The Years of the Standards

Briefly step back in time with us to the dawn of the new millennium. In the year 2000, the ACRL *Information Literacy Competency Standards for Higher Education* were officially unveiled. The creation of the *Standards* was heavily influenced by the proliferation of research on information literacy brought on by the 1989 ALA Presidential Committee on Information Literacy report, the work of the National Forum on Information Literacy, and the 1998 school library standards, *Information Power: Building Partnerships for Learning* (Juskiewicz & Cote, 2015). The *Standards* included both performance indicators and learning outcomes, emphasized working with faculty, aimed to institutionalize information literacy, and highlighted assessment (Juskiewicz & Cote, 2015). In the *Standards* (2000), the committee states that the document

> provides a framework for assessing the information literate individual. It also extends the work of the American Association of School Librarians Task Force on Information

Literacy Standards, thereby providing higher education an opportunity to articulate its information literacy competencies with those of K–12 so that a continuum of expectations develops for students at all levels. The competencies presented here outline the process by which faculty, librarians, and others pinpoint specific indicators that identify a student as information literate. (n.p.)

This period saw a flurry of new official guidelines and standards for academic libraries internationally as well. The Canadian Social Sciences and Humanities Research Council (SSHRC) conducted a national information literacy project in 2000 to study instructional outcomes at three Canadian universities (Mokhtar & Majid, 2008). The Australian benchmarks, the *Information Literacy Standards*, developed by the Council of Australian University Librarians (CAUL), were based on the ACRL *Information Literacy Competency Standards for Higher Education* and adapted for the region. They were revised and renamed the *Australian and New Zealand Information Literacy Framework* in 2003, following input from those who had used the first version of the standards (Mokhtar & Majid, 2008). In the United Kingdom, the Society of College, National and University Libraries (SCONUL) Working Group on Information Literacy (1999) produced a position paper on information skills in higher education, and Sweden and South Africa had active research programs on information literacy in higher education (Bruce et al., 2000).

Almost as soon as all these standards and the results of the research were released, scholars were discussing how they should influence instruction. For example, UK scholars Webber and Johnston (2000) concluded that "the top pillars of the SCONUL model need to be addressed by a learning and teaching strategy which incorporates evaluation, comparison, reflection and exchange of views . . . If the student is to be able to reflect on and sustain his or her progress, and appreciate the linkages between the various pillars, then he or she will need time to develop" (p. 392). They go on to argue for information literacy as its own discipline. At the same time, scholars were situating information literacy within the context of other professions; Bradley (2013) examined the place of information literacy in the accreditation standards of nursing, social work, and engineering, noting the usefulness of mapping the ACRL standards to the expected outcomes in these fields.

Other research during this period describes potential topics for instructional sessions (Swanson, 2005b), the need to consider freely available research tools alongside traditional library databases in instruction (Ettinger, 2008; Jacobs, 2010), the introduction of Web 2.0 into information literacy instruction (Luo, 2010), and the urgent imperative for librarians to advocate for more instructional time than the traditional fifty-minute information literacy session allows (Macklin & Culp, 2008). Julien (2005) describes instruction as a new core role of librarianship, particularly in the context of information literacy, while at the same time lamenting the lack of emphasis placed on instruction in the education of librarians.

Several publications focused on assessing information literacy instruction. Some discussed ways of evaluating students during sessions (McCulley, 2009; Oakleaf, 2008), while others focused on evaluating programs themselves (Oakleaf & Kaske, 2009). Evidence of both standardized and more authentic assessments was present in professional and scholarly literature. Blevens (2012) studied both computer-based, standardized tests developed to test understanding of the information literacy standards and more authentic assessments. One popular test during this period was Project SAILS (Standardized Assessment of Information Literacy Skills), an online, multiple-choice test based on the ACRL *Information Literacy Competency Standards for Higher Education*, developed in 2002 by Kent State University researchers. (In 2012 the test was licensed to Carrick Enterprises, a corporation that recently developed a new assessment tool for the ACRL *Framework*, the Threshold

Achievement Test for Information Literacy [TATIL], discussed more in Clarke & Radcliffe, 2018—but that's getting ahead of ourselves.) Outside standardized testing, H. Davis (2010) outlined the need for the development of rubric-based assessment.

Using the results of these assessments for advocacy was commonly suggested. Gratch-Lindauer (2002), for example, discussed the place of information literacy outcomes in regional higher education accreditation standards—and how it might boost the status of the academic library in the academy. In a University of Illinois at Urbana-Champaign (UIUC) case study, Searing (2007) described how "sharing assessment results . . . [could] generate good will between the library and the academic program" (p. 1). Oakleaf and Kaske (2009) explained the importance of information literacy program assessment: "First, information literacy assessment data can be directly applied to increase student learning. *Second, librarians need to use information literacy assessment data to respond to calls for accountability* [emphasis added]. Finally, information literacy assessment results can be used to improve library instruction programs" (p. 273). In an earlier work, Oakleaf (2008) also situated assessment within the realities of higher education's need for evidence of outcomes. Weiner (2012) described ways that academic librarians could work within four different models of higher education, explaining that knowing how your institution works—"how effective communication occurs, which campus relationships should be developed and how, what institutional knowledge should be invoked, whether incentives and awards are helpful, what publicity is important, how power should be used, and what processes are important" (p. 291)—is essential to institutionalizing information literacy.

Whether this advocacy was practiced or effective, however, is unclear. In 2011 Badke still articulated plenty of gaps in support for information literacy to be seen as a true necessity in higher education:

> Information literacy is invisible to academia because it is misunderstood, academic administrators have not put it on their institutions' agendas, the literature of information literacy remains in the library silo, there is a false belief that information literacy is acquired only by experience, there is a false assumption that technological ability is the same as information literacy, faculty culture makes information literacy less significant than other educational pursuits, faculty have a limited perception of the ability of librarians, and accrediting bodies have not yet advanced information literacy to a viable position in higher education. (p. 129)

DaCosta (2010) similarly found in a study of faculty in England and the United States that although faculty frequently stated the importance of information literacy skills, this standpoint was not often reflected in their curricula.

Attempting to sum up the various ways that information literacy was approached in higher education instruction during the early 2000s is a daunting prospect; there was no one method that librarians used for teaching. In perhaps the most comprehensive framework for information literacy instruction for the time, Bruce (1997) outlined three approaches—skill-based, constructivist, and relational—believing that instruction should take into account the various ways that students experience information literacy and their world. She and her coauthors would later expand these three approaches into six frames:

- **Content Frame** (using a discipline orientation)
- **Competency Frame** (a skills-based, performance orientation)
- **Learning to Learn Frame** (the constructivist approach)

- **Personal Relevance Frame** (IL is learned in context and differs from person to person)
- **Social Impact Frame** (how information literacy is used by society)
- **Relational Frame** (interacting with information is experienced in multiple ways) (Bruce et al., 2006)

Bruce et al. (2006) argued that "each frame brings with it a particular view of IL, information, curriculum focus, learning and teaching, content, and assessment" (p. 3). In their 2013 reflection on this period of information literacy, Addison and Meyers provided a three-part framework of information literacy instruction that is remarkably similar, including instruction that focuses on information literacy as a set of skills (including an emphasis on formal information seeking and the framing of research as a linear process), instruction that conceives of information literacy as a way of thinking (including process models such as Kuhlthau's work), and instruction that teaches information literacy as a social practice (the way information literacy impacts and is impacted by the way we live).

Sample (2020) traces definitions of information literacy in research during this period (2000–2015) using the Addison and Meyers framework and finds that, though examples of all types of definitions were found during all years of this period, there did seem to be an evolution from a majority of definitions with a skills-based focus to more definitions with a focus on cognitive processes and then finally to definitions with an increasing focus on using a social lens for information literacy. It is indeed the lens of experienced, contextual, and relational information literacy that most resembles the direction of information literacy research and learning as the second decade of the twenty-first century began.

Moving Toward a Framework

Seeds of what would later become woven into the 2015 *Framework for Information Literacy for Higher Education* were present even in the years immediately following the 2000 *Standards'* release. Grafstein (2002), for example, foretells the approach that ACRL would later take in talking about discipline-specific ideas, what would come to be known as threshold concepts, when she asserts that her "approach to teaching IL . . . assumes that being information literate crucially involves being literate about something" (p. 202). In 2008 Harris highlights the importance of community to the practice of information literacy: "the ability to recognize and comprehend the values of communities, and apply those values in the creation, transmission, or receipt of information, is a core activity in the development of 'common knowledge' between community members" (p. 254).

We have already mentioned some of the new lenses of information literacy—constructivist, relational, social—that were appearing in select models of learning. Martin (2013) reflects on many of the criticisms of the *Standards*, including the inauthentic skills-based nature of the document in light of how information literacy is used in real life, the use of rote behaviors to analyze information at the expense of encouragement for true learning, and the focus only on siloed research and information, and finds encouraging progress in new (at the time) frameworks offered by UK organizations. Seale (2013) criticizes wholesale the conception of information literacy up to that point, describing it as firmly situated within a neoliberal context and as extending power imbalances.

It was within this context of scholarship that the new ACRL *Framework for Information Literacy for Higher Education* (2015) was developed. Bell (2013) describes the origins of the

Framework's development: the 2011 ACRL task force that was directed to consider potential changes to the *Standards* unanimously recommended revision based on "emerging models of information literacy, . . . the development of multiple new literacies and the need to provide a stronger continuum of literacy from K–16" (n.p.). This recommendation led the ACRL board of directors to issue a charge to the newly created ACRL Information Literacy Competency Standards for Higher Education Task Force:

> Update the information literacy competency standards for higher education so that they reflect the current thinking on such things as the creation and dissemination of knowledge, the changing global higher education and learning environment, the shift from information literacy to information fluency, and the expanding definition of information literacy to include multiple literacies, e.g., transliteracy, media literacy, digital literacy, etc. (Bell, 2013, n.p.)

After input from the organization's membership, this task force ultimately produced the *Framework for Information Literacy for Higher Education*, which was formally adopted by the ACRL board in 2016. Though we briefly introduced the *Framework* (and its approach to critical literacy) earlier, it's worth returning to now in the context of academic libraries specifically. As a reminder, the *Framework* (Association of College and Research Libraries, 2015) "is organized into six frames, each consisting of a concept central to information literacy, a set of knowledge practices, and a set of dispositions" (n.p.). The six frames are:

- Authority Is Constructed and Contextual
- Information Creation as a Process
- Information Has Value
- Research as Inquiry
- Scholarship as Conversation
- Searching as Strategic Exploration

The *Framework* introduces its new definition for information literacy: "the set of integrated abilities encompassing the reflective discovery of information, the understanding of how information is produced and valued, and the use of information in creating new knowledge and participating ethically in communities of learning" (Association of College and Research Libraries, 2015, n.p.). The *Framework* also set out two concepts as underlying this revision of information literacy—metaliteracy ("a renewed vision of information literacy as an overarching set of abilities in which students are consumers and creators of information who can participate successfully in collaborative space") and threshold concepts ("those ideas in any discipline that are passageways or portals to enlarged understanding or ways of thinking and practicing within that discipline") (n.p.).

The *Framework* has been met with mixed reactions, as mentioned in chapter 2. We return to this discussion of how well the *Framework* engages with critical literacy to reiterate the tension in the academic library field. Jacobson and Gibson (2015) seem to find the *Framework* an opportunity to infuse more authentic learning into information literacy instruction. They describe some ways to weave the *Framework* into different types of programs, including the one-shot session:

> The *Framework* encourages us to shift our emphasis, away from guiding students to follow set steps to find the product, and towards understanding the creation processes

that result in mutable information sources and reflecting upon what implications this holds for the researcher. (p. 107)

Others are less positive. Beatty (2014) extends the arguments that Seale (2013) made about the *Standards* and suggests that the *Framework* is similarly situated in the neoliberal agenda—for example, using crisis rhetoric of "uncertain information ecosystem" to justify resources. Beilin (2015) expresses concern for the *Framework*'s threshold concepts:

> While the framework does an admirable job of showing how threshold concepts can help shift information literacy toward a pedagogy that stresses the development of self-critical and self-conscious learning in the student, it does not state as its goal the formation of possible solidarities for the student to help change the information system itself, nor the hierarchies of knowledge and status within academia. Furthermore, by continuing to stress the individual learner, it obscures the fact that any real change would actually require collective understanding and action rather than individualized learning. (n.p.)

Seale (2016) also extended her 2013 critique to assert that the *Framework*'s argument for situated and contextual information literacy is undercut by its "universality, narrative of progress, and uninterest in power" (p. 89). Morgan (2015) likewise believes that "the developing *Framework* treat[s] threshold concepts as immanent entities, unique to specific disciplines, and not as essentially contingent phenomena" (pp. 186–187), potentially exacerbating existing inequities in scholarship.

In spite of these criticisms, the field as a whole seems to struggle more with how to operationalize the *Framework* than with its underlying ideas. In their interviews with fifteen US academic librarians, Gross et al. (2018) found that participants believed that the *Framework* made it easy to articulate the definition of information literacy and to work with faculty but, conversely, was difficult to fit into the traditional methods of information literacy instruction, particularly the short, one-shot session. In a separate survey of 622 librarians wherein participants (most of whom were academic librarians) were asked questions about the current state of information literacy instruction in the American higher education context, these same researchers found that though "the vast majority of respondents see connections between the concepts presented in the *Framework* and their responsibility to raise the level of information literacy among students," most instruction still focuses on traditional database, search, and library skills (Julien et al., 2018, p. 189). Additionally, the researchers found that most assessment is informal and that many of the instructional sessions lack clear objectives. In deployments of the survey in two other countries, Israel and Canada, the researchers found similar results (Aharony et al., 2020; Polkinghorne & Julien, 2019).

During this period, ACRL also revised its *Characteristics of Programs of Information Literacy That Illustrate Best Practices: A Guideline* (Association of College and Research Libraries, 2019b). This revision was designed to "bring the document in alignment with current practices, approaches, and guidelines; and . . . update the language and syntax to ensure uniformity and clarity" (n.p.). The document provides a framework to

- categorize details of a given program;
- analyze how different program elements contribute to attaining excellence in information literacy;

- benchmark program status;
- implement program improvement; and
- map out long-term development.

The document covers topics such as determining a mission, goals, and objectives; proper planning; the need for and guidance on administrative and institutional support; how to sequence a program; pedagogy; communication and advocacy; and assessment and evaluation.

We'll use this "best practices" guideline as a segue to discussing some of the recent trends in academic library instruction. In 2015 E. Ford et al. incorporated badging in their collaborative work with faculty and as a way for students to track IL-related competencies. Guo and Goh (2016) also used gamification techniques in their creation of an information literacy game, "Library Escape," which also incorporated user-centered design. Contextual instruction became more common: Peter et al. (2017) discuss strategies of blended learning that emphasizes personalized instruction, while Feekery and Jeffrey (2019) introduce a context-specific information evaluation guide, the *Rauru Whakarare Evaluation Framework*, "which offers a kaupapa Māori-informed perspective designed to foster deeper engagement with the information evaluation process in secondary and tertiary institutions within Aotearoa New Zealand" (p. 3).

In terms of content, there have been examples of increased interest in data literacy (S. Scott, 2020a, 2020b) and issues of privacy and surveillance in information literacy education (Hicks, 2020). Academic librarians are responding to calls to address the issue du jour of fake news, though Lim's (2020) study of twenty-one institutional guides on fake news found that many of the definitions didn't incorporate bias, the checklists failed to suggest demonstrated strategies as lateral reading, and psychological factors were often ignored. Similarly, M. C. Sullivan (2019c) asserts that the library's response ignores work in related fields and that the information literacy–related evaluation skills that librarians teach are mostly related to fact-checking (which in itself is often superficially described in instruction). Sullivan argues that technological solutions show the best promise of negating misinformation (see more about this in chapter 9). Still, fake news is reviving many academic librarians' drive to lead in the information literacy landscape (Banks, 2016; Dollinger, 2017).

Perhaps the defining characteristic, so far at least, of the *Framework* years of information literacy scholarship and practice is the trend toward critical views of information literacy. In addition to the critiques of information literacy—and the associated standards and frameworks—discussed earlier, Ellenwood (2020) has engaged with the "information has value" strand of the ACRL *Framework*, discussing the political economy of information capitalism "so that through our teaching we can use this understanding to mount credible, comprehensive challenges to the system itself" (n.p.). Hare and Evanson (2018) encourage academic librarians to work with their students on understanding information privilege—how they have privileged access to certain types of information and the impact of their scholarship. Saunders (2017) proposes a new frame to the ACRL *Framework*—information social justice—which purports that "information is created within existing power structures, and those power structures can impact the production and dissemination of information, as well as distort, suppress, or misrepresent information" (p. 67).

All things considered, the expansion of information literacy to include sociocultural perspectives is positive—it just remains to be seen how well these perspectives will be implemented in a higher education environment suffering from library budget cuts, online instructional trends, and a precedent for one-off information literacy sessions.

SCHOOL LIBRARIES

In many ways, the context of school libraries mirrors that of academic libraries. The state of education is certainly similar, at least in the American context. Just as higher education has slowly adapted to businesslike models of administration, there has been a steady corporatization of K–12 education as well (see, for example, the discussion of personalized learning programs developed by for-profit companies in Roberts-Mahoney et al., 2016). Many schools now rely in part on corporate funding through sponsorships and vending contracts for basic operations (Buschman, 2012).

School libraries have been funded haphazardly, with some districts eliminating them entirely (American Library Association, 2020; Golden, 2019), and the federal government has alternated between pulling back on funding and granting assistance (see chapter 8 of Jaeger & Taylor, 2019). In terms of the information environment for youth, there is an odd mix of assuming them capable of using technology because they have grown up with it as "digital natives" (Prensky, 2001)[6] but also policymaking that is based on fear of what children may encounter online, such as the Children's Internet Protection Act (CIPA; 2001) and the Protecting Children in the 21st Century Act (2008). The media and official guidelines endlessly warn parents of the dangers of too much technology use (Hawkey, 2019), while realistically, children spend much of their days in front of screens (Council on Communications and Media, 2016). And though too much screen time is probably a bad idea, this isn't totally clear in research and is likely not as terrible as many argue (Gottschalk, 2019). There seems to be a clear need to teach young people about the context of information online, but keeping them from social media or adult topics online does not appear realistic or helpful to this learning (Kranich, 2004). Kids do have some skill in navigating devices due to their early exposure (Oliemat et al., 2018), but they have no more innate ability to discern truth from misinformation than any of the rest of us (Breakstone et al., 2019; Julien & Barker, 2009; Varlejs & Stec, 2014).

There may be some differences in how younger generations view issues related to information literacy. Privacy, for example, seems to be a mixed bag in terms of concern. Although many find little to be concerned about when warned of the practice of businesses collecting their personal information (Crocco et al., 2020), other studies demonstrate that young people may actually care quite a bit, just perhaps about different aspects of privacy than adults are concerned about (Madden et al., 2013). But on many issues, young people are not that different from the general populace. Again in the US context, young people reflect the general growth of mistrust among all Americans. They often embrace conspiracy theories (Barnett, 2020; Taylor, 2015) and distrust institutions (Rainie et al., 2019).

Information Power (1998–2007)

The general context just described would seem to produce an audience ripe for formal practice in information literacy and a natural environment for this practice in school libraries. Although we won't go too much into the history of school libraries' relationship with information literacy prior to the late 1990s (see Loertscher & Woolls, 2002, for a broader history), we can certainly see evidence of the influence of information literacy in the school library profession with the advent of 1998's *Information Power: Building Partnerships for Learning* (you'll recall our earlier discussion in chapter 2). This collection of guidelines for the school library field included the *Information Literacy Standards for Student Learning*, which provided

> a conceptual framework and broad guidelines for describing the information-literate student. The standards consist of three categories, nine standards, and twenty-nine indicators . . . . Taken together, the categories, standards, and indicators describe the content and processes related to information that students must master to be considered information literate. (American Association of School Librarians & Association for Educational Communications and Technology, 1998b, p. 1)

These guidelines reflect the skills-based approach to information literacy of the time. That said, there were pushes to extend the concept of information literacy to something beyond just checking a skill off a list. Abilock (2004) called for a transformational definition of information literacy:

> to teach our students the rigorous, analytical, sweaty work of closely examining an argument, questioning our thinking patterns, ferreting out inconsistencies—fundamentals of critical thinking. Rather than teach the skill, if we teach to transfer that skill—in using a library, recognizing bias, or analyzing an argument—from one setting or task to another, students recognize that information literacy is not a school task but a lifetime habit of mind—of evaluating and using information for personal, social, or global purposes. (pp. 9–10)

Internationally, this period also saw the development of K–12 literacy standards. One example was Singapore's *Information Literacy Guidelines* produced by the Languages and Library Branch of the Curriculum Planning and Development Division in the Ministry of Education. The 1997 guidelines "listed eleven learner outcomes and framed two areas in the information literacy curriculum, namely the skills domain and the attitudes domain" (Mokhtar & Majid, 2008, p. 7). From a meeting convened by IFLA and UNESCO, seven countries in Southeast Asia—Cambodia, Indonesia, Lao PDR, Malaysia, the Philippines, Thailand, and Vietnam—met and began to implement programs to increase information literacy in their countries' schools. A survey sent out in each country found that "only half of the respondents indicated that their school had a policy statement on IL, although it was rarely explicitly stated" (Mokhtar & Majid, 2008, p. 8). Ultimately, the attempt did kickstart an effort to tailor information literacy standards to Asian contexts, but "the distinct characteristics and different socio-economic status of each Asian nation throughout the region makes it a challenge to adopt an overarching standard for the region" (Mokhtar & Majid, 2008, p. 8). Although South Africa's outcome-based education policies during this time included several information literacy-related practices, such as research skills and the collection, evaluation, and organization of information, they didn't have explicit information literacy standards (Moore, 2005).

Three particular trends in this era of school library information literacy instruction were the use of research models, the development of evaluation acronyms, and the development of online assessment tools. And it is important to note that most of these are still used today. The previously discussed Eisenberg and Berkowitz Big6 is probably the most well-known of the research models introduced for use in school libraries. Although this certainly isn't the only model used in schools (see also, for example, iLEARN developed by Neuman, 2011, and revised by Neuman et al., 2019), the Big6 is a useful example for grasping the general idea behind these models—simplified sets of steps to guide young researchers. First developed in 1988, the model was created in a seminal school library text authored by Eisenberg and Berkowitz that aimed to provide a conceptual framework along with practical guidelines for school librarians to properly integrate their services with the school curriculum. The Big6 is a process model that, according to its website (https://thebig6.org), demonstrates "how people of all ages solve an information problem." As we mentioned in chapter 2, the six steps are task definition, information-seeking strategies, location and access, use of information, synthesis, and evaluation. The model has been used internationally and has been featured in commercial tie-ins, books, resources, and videos. The name is trademarked, and, in his review of the model, Carey (2003) notes that part of the model's popularity is "due to entrepreneurial efforts by Eisenberg and Berkowitz," though Carey also stresses that the model "has face validity; that is, it makes good common sense and matches our experience with reality" (n.p.).

Although the earliest iterations of the model were tied to Bloom's Taxonomy, these connections were removed by the authors in later publications and replaced with the "little twelve" substeps within each of the six process steps. As Carey notes, this change meant that "an important anchor to instructional theory disappeared, and the prospect of misleading users was raised by oversimplifying very complex processes . . . . [H]owever, [he] understand[s] the allure of a simple model for grabbing users, and without users there is no impact on information literacy in the field" (n.p.). Some researchers are updating the research model approach by presenting the inquiry process through an online learning platform, walking students through the steps (Wade et al., 2020). Although these models only aim to target information literacy in the form of formal research, that research is still an important part of the educational information literacy landscape.

One of the more generally accepted ways to teach research and information literacy to young people is through the use of easy-to-remember acronyms. One of the more popular, and perhaps aptly named, acronyms is the CRAAP test—which stands for Currency, Relevance, Authority, Accuracy, and Purpose—developed by academic librarian Sarah Blakeslee (2004) after a training session for information literacy instructors of first-year students when she was trying to remember a list of criteria for evaluating a website off the top of her head. Despite her experience, she found it was difficult to list from memory all the criteria to check. She took a list from the library's existing information literacy handout and developed CRAAP: "Not only . . . memorable due to its associative powers, it also meant something in the context in which it would be used. For every source of information we would now have a handy frame of reference to inquire, 'Is this CRAAP?'" (pp. 6-7). Although developed for academic libraries, such acronyms are used extensively across K-12 libraries. A more recent adaptation includes Lisa Nowlain's (2020) information literacy–related instructional comic intended for parents of young patrons during the novel coronavirus pandemic, "Give Information the CRAAP Test."

Finally, many K-12 libraries embraced the use of online standardized tests for information literacy skills during this period. One such test is TRAILS (Tool for Real-Time Assessment of Information Literacy Skills), developed by the Kent State University Libraries in 2004. The initial version of TRAILS was created as part of a grant from the Institute of Museum and Library Services (IMLS) and the US Department of Education to evaluate a one-time view of the level of information literacy skills held by the high school students participating in a high school outreach program run by the library. The test was later expanded into an open access online tool available for grades 3 to 12. In a history of the assessment, one of the founders explains that

> the vision for TRAILS was to create a standards-based tool for measuring information literacy competencies. . . . Developed as a self-service tool, TRAILS provided the capability for users to create and administer assessments and immediately generate reports. TRAILS-9 went live in January 2006. Over its fourteen-year history, 31,000 librarians registered and administered more than 126,000 assessments to nearly 2.5 million students. (Schloman, 2019, n.p.)

The tool was taken offline in 2019 due to lack of maintenance funds, and the content was archived on the website of Carrick Enterprises, the aforementioned developer of the higher education information literacy assessment tool, TATIL. Another example of a standardized test is the Educational Testing Service (ETS) iSkills assessment, particularly the core version that is targeted to high school students to test their readiness for college. This computer test "measures students' abilities to research, organize, and communicate information using technology" and purports to focus on problem-solving and critical thinking rather than the ability to use technology (Katz, 2007, p. 4).

The Next Two Waves of Standards (2007–2020)

In 2007 AASL adopted a new set of standards, the *Standards for the 21st Century Learner*. In the introduction to these standards, information literacy was professed to have "progressed from the simple definition of using reference resources to find information. Multiple literacies, including digital, visual, textual, and technological, have now joined information literacy as crucial skills for this century" (p. 3). The *Standards* state that "learners use skills, resources, and tools to:

1. Inquire, think critically, and gain knowledge;
2. Draw conclusions, make informed decisions, apply knowledge to new situations, and create new knowledge;
3. Share knowledge and participate ethically and productively as members of our democratic society; and
4. Pursue personal and aesthetic growth." (p. 4)

Within these four points, the *Standards* outlined various skills, dispositions, responsibilities, and self-assessment strategies that students should practice in pursuit of these goals. The *Information Literacy Standards for Student Learning* that were part of the second iteration of *Information Power* (1998) were retired. Farmer (2013) notes the confusion about the term *information literacy* within LIS generally and that, in the 2007 standards, "the American Association of School Librarians cleverly sidestepped the problematic term 'information literacy' when it used learners as its linchpin" (p. 172).

As AASL was working on implementation of these standards, Loertscher (2008) recognized that there was a tension in the field about whether information literacy "is the research process a la the Big Six™ . . . [or a] broader mission to teach other literacies such as media literacy, technology literacy, critical thinking, creativity, and reading skill in addition to other emerging literacies" (p. 43). He also noted that there were questions concerning the role of standardized tests in library information literacy instruction, how content-related instruction tied in, and how much information literacy should be "owned" by school librarians. He concluded, "It is unclear whether given a room full of library educators and/or district library media educators a consensus on the answers to the above questions could be produced" (p. 43). It was a tension that would continue as these *Standards* were put into use.

In 2015 AASL began the process of revising the school library standards again. Mary Keeling (2017), the chair of AASL's standards implementation task force, describes the process of revision and what librarians wanted to see changed:

> In 2015 AASL assembled an editorial board of expert practitioners and researchers to examine its existing standards, assess them for relevance and validity, and compare them with those of comparable groups. More than 1,100 school librarians were surveyed and another 200 participated in focus groups. Users liked the standards but thought they should be streamlined. They wanted an easy-to-follow presentation and materials for different audiences, including the solo librarian who lacks access to professional development opportunities. (n.p.)

It's unclear whether that goal was accomplished. In 2018 the *National School Library Standards* were officially adopted and are now the guiding principles of the AASL. In its online guide, "How Do I Read the Standards?," AASL (2018) explains that

> the *National School Library Standards for Learners, School Librarians, and School Libraries* are anchored by six Shared Foundations—Inquire, Include, Collaborate, Curate, Explore, and Engage—which highlight the standards' core educational concepts. Think of these as the big ideas that provide a compass for teaching and learning with students, teachers, and communities. A one-sentence Key Commitment then describes the essential understandings for each of the six Shared Foundations. Each Shared Foundation is broken down into three to five Competencies for each learning category or Domain: Think (cognitive), Create (psychomotor), Share (affective), and Grow (developmental). The Competencies are measurable statements describing the knowledge, skills, and dispositions essential for learners and school librarians. The Competencies are expressed as Alignments for school libraries.

Initial reviews and studies on implementation aren't promising. Interestingly, one of Loertscher's (2018) critiques, of which there are many, seems to be that information literacy is too much a focus of the new *Standards*. He directly equates the Shared Foundation of Inquire with information literacy and states that "one soon recognizes that [inquiry] is the umbrella under which every other program element must fit. If asked by teachers, administrators, boards, and parents, the simple and simplistic elevator speech is: 'My role as a librarian is to teach inquiry (information literacy)'" (p. 38). He believes that this has been an unsuccessful practice to this point, demonstrated in the rapidly dwindling number of school librarians, and that it neglects such important topics as technology and free reading.

In their evaluation of the links between the *Standards* and ACRL's *Framework*, Burns et al. (2019) found that "while there is significant overlap between the two documents, there is not a clear bridge between the two to scaffold a learner's development toward the independent scholar to which the ACRL Framework speaks" (p. 11). In her examination of the implementation of the *Standards* in Virginia school libraries two years after their introduction, Burns (2020) concluded that most of the practitioners studied were still in an "awareness" stage of practice and that "the need to reflect the goals and values of a school library program remained a challenge as resources and training did not immediately align with other efforts within the school or district that were perceived to be a priority for the school librarians" (p. 10).

A potential problem with implementation of any AASL standards is that school librarians generally find themselves with an abundance of guidelines and frameworks relevant to their roles and also must work within the context of school and state curricula (Church et al., 2012). Other standards relevant to K–12 literacy instruction include the *Standards for Students* developed by the International Society for Technology in Education (ISTE), which include such information literacy-related goals as being a "digital citizen" (e.g., "Students manage their personal data to maintain digital privacy and security and are aware of data-collection technology used to track their navigation online") and "knowledge constructor" (e.g., "Students plan and employ effective research strategies to locate information and other resources for their intellectual or creative pursuits" and "Students evaluate the accuracy, perspective, credibility and relevance of information, media, data or other resources"; ISTE, 2016, n.p.). School librarians also must be aware of the Common Core, particularly the English Language Arts Standards, as well as the Next Generation Science Standards, among others. A number of these complementary standards have been "crosswalked" or aligned with the *National School Library Standards*.

Regardless of the standards used by the field, students will continue to need information literacy practice. Berg et al. (2018) describe the many types of questions that school librarians help young people address. Their elementary list, for example, includes such essential questions as the following:

- What are your interests and how can you find out more about them?
- How can you ask questions that help lead you to what you need? Once you know your questions, how do you decide who to ask?
- What is information and where can you go to safely look for it? What technology is available to help you?
- When you find information that is helpful, how can you use it? (n.p.)

School libraries are ideal places for young people to practice information literacy and to receive instruction. Without them, it is unclear how explicitly information literacy skills will be tied into students' everyday learning experiences.

Whereas this chapter has focused on information literacy in the information institutions most directly tied to traditional educational settings, the next chapter explores information literacy in the broader contexts of public libraries, archives, and a range of special libraries, including medical libraries, law libraries, news libraries, and government libraries.

💬 CHAPTER 4 GUIDING QUESTIONS

1. Can you think of other examples (like the music one we offer in this chapter) that might help explain the practice of information literacy and information literacy education to others (both LIS professionals and those outside the field)?
2. How have academic libraries' standards and frameworks for information literacy shaped the entire LIS field's understanding of the term? In what ways has this been beneficial and detrimental to the development of information literacy education?
3. How does your own experience with information literacy in higher education echo the trends discussed in this chapter?
4. How do the K–12 and higher education environments impact these libraries' definitions and operationalizations of information literacy?
5. How does the practice of information literacy look different in formal education environments than in everyday life?

NOTES

1. Perhaps you can tell that one of us is a parent to a small child.
2. Though they would need to continue to practice lest they revert to banging with a spoon.
3. See the aforementioned reference to Natalie's toddler—after a few too many board books, it is easy to start speaking in rhyme. We will attempt to refrain in later chapter headings, at least in this chapter, this time. Stop it, I meant it. Anybody want a peanut?
4. If it is from the 21st Century, it has to be modern, right?
5. And alphabetization, of course.
6. Although the youth to which this particular study referred are now in their thirties . . .

The Operationalization of Information Literacy, Part II

Public Libraries, Special Libraries, and Archives

PUBLIC LIBRARIES

When we teach concepts of information literacy in our graduate courses, our students are often surprised by the relative lack of professional standards for information literacy in public libraries. The Public Library Association (PLA) places a great deal of emphasis on digital literacy—for example, the website digitallearn.org with the tagline, "Use a computer to do almost anything!"—but doesn't really directly reference information literacy. This isn't a recent phenomenon either. A decade ago, in her search for information literacy references on PLA's website, Hall (2010) found just two—a presentation about partnering with schools and as a note in a strategic plan from 2005 about developing a literate nation. Harding (2008) similarly reviewed the literature and notes a lack of mention of the public library in many core information literacy texts in the field, in a number of published articles, in formal studies, and in reports on practice, though she does say that the latter search is somewhat mitigated when the terms *lifelong learning* and *user education* are substituted for *information literacy*.

There are notable exceptions. Studies have been conducted to explicitly understand the information literacy role of public librarians, such as Julien and Hoffman's (2008) examination of the roles of Canadian public librarians in information literacy; in interviews, library staff participants noted the significance of information literacy in their work and considered themselves both "teachers/agents of empowerment" and "public parents" (p. 32). Nielsen and Borlund's (2013) small-sample study of information literacy in the Dutch public library context found that "the public librarians consider the public library an important place for learning, but also that they do not share a common understanding of the concepts of information literacy and lifelong learning" (p. 632). In an Australian study of twenty public librarians, researchers found that in these public libraries, information literacy was conceived as "intellectual process, technical skills, navigating the social world and gaining the desired result" (Demasson et al., 2019, p. 473).

There are also reports of information literacy in specific types of programs. Jacobsen (2017) describes the strong connections between his program on fantasy football decision making and information literacy: "Librarians help and teach our patrons to find the best information possible in order to make the best decisions possible. . . . My main goal in having [a fantasy football expert] give this talk was to teach information literacy skills and connect the library to the idea of information literacy for an audience that doesn't usually see us in that light" (n.p.). In perhaps a more life-changing example, De Jager and Nassimbeni (2007) describe a research project with public library workers in rural South Africa. The researchers found that, though the participants didn't practice information literacy as the researchers had initially defined it in a skills-based model, like the Big6, they nevertheless developed a contextualized practice that met their patrons' needs, such as finding information related to establishing a garden and teaching community members how to grow their own vegetables. As the researchers state, participants

> foregrounded the social contexts of their interventions by portraying their understanding of the power of information literacy to impact on their own social problems. . . . In our presentation, we had privileged a particular conception of information literacy which was resisted by the participants who generated alternative conceptions which were socially situated in their communities rather than an idealized and normative vision of the library as classroom. (p. 320)

Most of these studies show that public librarians' information literacy-related work is often defined by differing conceptualizations of information literacy. Whether that's good or bad likely depends on how well their information literacy practice aligns with the needs of the library's community.

The relative dearth of scholarship and professional guidance is certainly not because of a lack of place for information literacy in public libraries. As the preceding examples demonstrate, librarians have found a number of ways to practice information literacy with their users. Matteson and Gersch (2020) make clear the ways that information literacy research connects to the larger mission of the public library as well, specifically through the public library's role in aiding lifelong learning, developing an engaged citizenry, and enhancing users' social capital. And though it was designed for an academic and school librarian audience, the introduction to the IFLA *Guidelines on Information Literacy for Lifelong Learning*—a guide to creating information literacy programs—states that "most of the concepts, principles and procedures can be applied with minimal adaptation to any library setting" and lays out the importance of information literacy instruction in all types of library spaces:

> Information professionals working in all types of libraries should have as one of their main institutional goals the facilitation of users' efforts to acquire information competencies. Information skills are vital to the success of lifelong learning, employment, and daily interpersonal communication of any citizen, such as when a person needs information about health services for someone in his/her care, or a student requires specific information to complete an assessment. (Lau, 2006, p. 1)

There are many different areas in non-work and non-school contexts in which information literacy practice is needed, and, aside from public libraries, there are almost no places left to provide this practice. For those who are no longer in school and whose work doesn't provide training, where can these skills be learned?

Given this context, why is there a relative lack of emphasis on information literacy in public library professional associations and research? In looking at current programming and roles of public librarians, it may be that public libraries are in fact practicing information literacy with their users, but the connections to information literacy are made within larger programs or actions that do not necessarily readily identify as such. Matteson and

Gersch (2020) note that the concept of time is different for academic, school, and public libraries—in other words, those in formal settings can often tie classes to a set academic schedule and have built-in collaborative partners. It's possible that public library information literacy is practiced more informally than in structured courses. In their study of how reference interactions with patrons fulfill information literacy goals, the researchers note that though

> the librarians in this study operate with a perhaps broader definition of what consti-
> tutes information literacy instruction than might be traditionally held in academic set-
> tings . . . the public librarians still saw their work as instructional in service to a notion
> of information literacy perhaps best characterized as maximum utility to the user in
> the moment; a just-in-time-and-place information literacy to address an information
> need at the time and without a need or mandate to connect information literacy to a
> larger educational context. (p. 85)

For example, public libraries fill vital roles in providing access to government information, including providing "access to and assistance with understanding government websites, programs, and services . . . [and] assistance to patrons applying for or accessing e-government services, such as taxes or Medicare applications," services that encompass information (and government and technology) literacy (Jaeger & Bertot, 2009, p. 43). In terms of formal programs, public libraries also often embed information literacy into instruction as opposed to specifically calling it out as the purpose of the session. For example, the introduction to a Reference and User Services Association (RUSA) guide to financial literacy programming in public libraries offered an explicit reference to the incorporation of information literacy, but the program itself was more likely classified as a financial literacy session than as one specifically focused on information literacy:

> Management of personal finances requires information. Different kinds of informa-
> tion are needed to safely and successfully earn, borrow, save, invest, spend, and protect
> against risk. A multitude of sources provide financial information, and these sources
> can vary widely in their opinions, reliability and objectivity. Principles of informa-
> tion literacy should be integrated at each level of the financial literacy guidelines. As
> with other literacies, libraries are uniquely qualified to address this information need.
> (Keller et al., 2014, p. 2)

The issue with these examples is not how well the programs incorporate information literacy but, rather, that the larger field doesn't make clearer that information literacy is a major function of public libraries (both now and in the future) and that there is a clear, overarching understanding of information literacy in the public library context. There are attempts. For example, Kathleen de la Peña McCook and Jenny Bossaller's textbook *Introduction to Public Librarianship* (2018), a popular resource in LIS graduate programs, directly references the public library role in information literacy instruction (along with emphasizing the role of the librarian as teacher more generally). Some LIS schools also include courses on teaching information literacy in contexts beyond the academic and school libraries (as it happens, both authors of this book teach such courses). But in terms of scholarly work and professional guidelines, information literacy is still largely viewed through the lenses of academic and school libraries. Not clearly and fully explaining the role of public librarians in providing practice and instruction in information literacy is doing a disservice to both the library field in general and to users in particular. We shouldn't consider information literacy the province only of formal education. To do so discredits the vital information actions we perform in our daily lives and creates a perception of elitism regarding the concept of information literacy. It dilutes the term.

Though written from the academic library perspective, Ward's (2006) description of opening up the conception of information literacy beyond just critical thinking is particularly appropriate for the public library's role in information literacy practice:

> Perhaps our emphasis on critical thinking about information is not an adequate response to the complex information universe in which we live. Our relationship to information is much more complicated than that. We understand our selves and the world in other ways as well. Information comes to us in many forms, including metaphor, poetry, literature, and myth. We use psychological processes of intuition and imagination as much as critical thinking to mediate our relationship to the world. Personal, interior experiences of information are fundamental to a vital information literacy that can make a difference in our lives and in the world. (p. 397)

If libraries are to use information literacy to aid in lifelong learning and the development of a more engaged, empowered, and, yes, critical populace, we must emphasize our current practices and expand our thinking about the place of information literacy in the public library.

SPECIAL LIBRARIES AND ARCHIVES

It's easy to overlook special libraries and archives in the context of information literacy education. The major reason for this neglect is that special libraries are often quite connected to their related discipline—law libraries and the legal profession; medical libraries and the medical field—so their focus on information literacy often is couched in the language of that profession. We have attempted to solve this dilemma by breaking down special libraries into several types: government libraries, news libraries, law libraries, medical libraries, and finally archives. In each case, we'll start first with the context of this type of special library and then discuss the related standards and instruction used therein, if they exist.

Before jumping in, we do want to note that the Special Libraries Association (SLA) in 2016 developed and revised its *Competencies for Information Professionals*, which according to the association's then president, "describes the skills and knowledge that special librarians need to be effective in their role of helping organizations succeed" (Hales, 2016, n.p.). SLA's competencies

> are divided into two groups: core competencies, which are intrinsic to the information profession, and enabling competencies, which are used by professionals in other fields as well as special librarians. The core competencies, such as information and data retrieval and analysis, essentially define what information professionals do and how they work; the enabling competencies, which include effective communication, project management, and innovation, support overall professional success and development. (Hales, 2016, n.p.)

Information literacy is specifically mentioned in the elements of the first core competency, Information and Knowledge Services, as "Teaching, training, and developing information literacy and associated skills for stakeholders." The other core competencies mostly focus on the organization and management of information. It's unclear whether these competencies are used by the professionals in all the various types of libraries outlined in the following sections, but it makes for a good starting point to understand how information literacy might be reflected in non-public, -school, or -academic library contexts.

Government Libraries

For this particular section, in the interest of space, we will focus on US federal libraries, the ALA federal libraries membership, and IFLA's government libraries section. The Federal Library and Information Center Committee Education Working Group's (2014) third edition of the *Handbook of Federal Librarianship* describes federal libraries as being as "diverse as those in the non-federal realm are" (p. 9). The document goes on to say that these libraries

> range from well-known, national libraries and repositories to one-person units for a specific subject. They include organizations specializing in science, technology, medicine, transportation, law, intelligence, culture, and in the environment, monetary and financial systems, national defense, education, and much more.
>
> The variety in federal libraries also includes the populations served. Most support federal agencies and their employees while some libraries assist academic communities or provide for military members and their families. Many also serve the public. Federal libraries also vary in the ways they perform their missions. Some hold vast collections of physical objects and interact with many of their users in person. On the opposite end are digital libraries, which communicate exclusively with their customers by phone or electronically. The majority of federal libraries and information centers fall somewhere in the middle.
>
> Despite their multiplicity, federal libraries hold several commonalities. They each support one branch of the federal government—legislative, judicial, or executive, and receive federal funds. (p. 9)

In this document, there is no mention of information literacy. The introduction states that "because the *Handbook of Federal Librarianship* is a guide written for professional librarians, it [is] not intended to be a manual on how to be a librarian. Instead, it focuses on the federal angle of otherwise standard practices and procedures of good librarianship. This edition omitted topics if it did not contain any uniquely federal characteristics" (p. 2). Thus, we can assume that the authors at least believe that the information literacy instruction that professionals receive in their general LIS education is generalizable enough to fit specific government-related needs.

Information from ALA's membership representing government libraries is difficult to find. The ALA Federal and Armed Forces Libraries Round Table (FAFLRT) was absorbed into a new division in 2019—the Association of Specialized, Government and Cooperative Library Agencies (ASGCLA; Hughes, 2018)—and that new division was itself disbanded in 2020.[1] Members from the former FAFLRT group were directed to form an interest group within ASGCLA (Association of Specialized, Government and Cooperative Library Agencies, 2020). It is unclear whether this dissolution was merely part of ALA's general push to consolidate its organizational structure or due to low membership numbers.

In 2011 IFLA's Government Libraries Section produced a document of examples of mission and vision statements of government libraries worldwide, a search of which yielded no references to information literacy or to literacy at all. The website for this section had no documents related to information literacy that we could find and, indeed, sadly seems quite out of date at the writing of this book. Ultimately, it's unclear whether information literacy just isn't explicitly stated as a goal of government library professional associations or those associations are just not highly active.

The following are examples of the types of information literacy that government libraries might practice:

- The **National Library of Medicine**'s (NLM) partnership program with the Public Library Association and Wisconsin Health Literacy demonstrates the government library role in providing information for other librarians to disseminate to the public. "We're calling on you to partner with us to offer virtual digital health literacy training and citizen science programming to your community and we'll help you promote it to All of Us program participants" (National Library of Medicine, n.d., n.p.).
- The **Library of Congress** (LOC) offers an example of professional development for public and school librarians with an online training targeted to teachers and librarians in how to use primary sources with their students. "Information literacy involves multiple skills, including examining information sources in a variety of media; evaluating claims and evidence; identifying bias; and researching for additional information. In this interactive webinar, participants will apply these information literacy skills to historical primary sources from the Library of Congress and reflect on how these strategies may be used with their students" (2020, n.p.).
- In terms of service to government elected officials, the **Congressional Research Service** (CRS) is a good example. However, though the agency's professed duties—"to marshal interdisciplinary resources, encourage critical thinking and create innovative frameworks to help legislators form sound policies, reach decisions on a host of difficult issues and address their constituents' concerns and needs"—certainly sound like IL-related actions, they aren't expressed as such (Congressional Research Service, n.d., n.p.).

None of these services are part of any connected government strategy for information literacy instruction, however. Maybe the best government-wide action in the service of information literacy is the plain language movement (www.plainlanguage.gov), which is surprisingly unconnected to any official library. The Plain Language Action and Information Network (PLAIN) is a group of unfunded government employees who promote training, a website, and a community of practice related to the idea of clear communication to the relevant audience of a government resource.

News Libraries

There are two ways of looking at news libraries—one concerns the ways in which information literacy is considered within the context of a library situated within a media environment, such as a newspaper or a cable network, and the other concerns the ways in which information literacy is considered within the training of journalism students in higher education. We'll take each in turn.

First, a brief overview of the purpose of news libraries and their constituencies. Although in pre-Internet days, news libraries were physical repositories of the publication's archives, Paul (1997) describes the role of the news librarian in an age of automation with several steps of an information strategy in then modern newsrooms:

1. **Information Needs Assessment** (who in the newsroom needs what in terms of help with information-seeking)
2. **Information Task Definition** (before adopting a tool for news collection, determine how it will be used)
3. **Information Evaluation** (choosing and understanding different tools for news gathering and explaining them to users)
4. **Information Acquisition** (the actual logistics of getting non-public information into the newsroom)
5. **Information Access** (who has access and what do they need to know to be able to use it)
6. **Information-Seeking Skills/Training** (teaching people how to use the tools you select)
7. **Information Maintenance** (keeping resources and data up to date and preserved)

Elements of information literacy are certainly woven into this strategy, but it is in a quote from step 3, Information Evaluation, that we see most clearly how much the news environment (and indeed the information-gathering environment) has changed since 1997. Paul asserts that

> in the information age, the information professional will be the key player in evaluating and selecting resources. "Test driving" different resources and doing detailed comparisons, and knowing how to use the resources well enough to be able to teach their use to others will take time in the short run, but will save hours for the end-user searcher. (n.p.)

In fact, today's information professional is often left out of the process of information gathering entirely because people more and more can find information freely for themselves faster than waiting for a librarian's help, if they have access to a librarian at all. The physical news library is, of course, now online. Assisting others in learning how to evaluate and select resources seems to be the increasingly important role of the modern information professional—and, if we take that view, we're basically describing the practice of information literacy instruction.

There is little in the way of scholarly and professional literature available about how news libraries work with journalists and use information literacy practices and instruction. A major reason for this scarcity may be the rapidly declining existence of such libraries. The current state of the news library field is not particularly grand. As newspapers have been hit hard by changing media consumption, staffing for news libraries has fallen (Hansen & Paul, 2015; Paul & Hansen, 2002). So in modern times, what role do news libraries have in information literacy instruction and other information literacy-related tasks? Or what role should they have? One way to look at this issue is to investigate some of the gaps in information practices noted in newsrooms. A 2003 survey of newspapers with circulation over one hundred thousand found that in six areas of information practice—access, training, quality control, archiving, revenue, and alerts—newsrooms were well situated in only one, access to information through tools and services (Hansen et al., 2003). In terms of training in the tools made available to journalists for search, budgets have been shrinking, and there is little consistency in who is overseeing the training. The researchers assert that "news researchers/librarians should be proactive in shifting their role from information gatekeeper and server to information trainer" (p. 44).

Archival practices, traditionally the purview of the news librarian, are still important; as newspapers have taken on more types of content, "the need to manage text and image assets, and audio, video and animated graphics" within legacy archival systems is a growing problem (Hansen et al., 2003, p. 45). A more recent study (Hansen & Paul, 2015) recalls this dilemma and notes that the current state of newspaper archives is appallingly disorganized, with not one of the nine legacy newspapers studied possessing a complete archive of its website. Indeed, in Boyles and Meisinger's (2020) interviews with sixteen newsroom librarians, the participants said they often skipped their publication's digital archive because they knew it was missing content and had sensitive search parameters. In this study, many of the participants resorted to using the hard copy version of the archive, and, indeed, serving as the publication's archivist was seen by these participants as their primary role. That said, in order to "institutionalize research knowledge across the organization, newsroom librarians provided training sessions for the publication's journalists. Other newsroom librarians reported developing internal wikis that explain how and where to access the paper's artifacts" (p. 186). Again—information literacy practices, though not identified as such.

In general, though it seems that news libraries would have much to do in terms of information literacy instruction, there just isn't much to go on in terms of a professional identity in this area or a convergence of best practices. It is possible that much of the related work is being categorized as media literacy, fact-checking, and verification of sources (Courtney, 2017). In her study of an Irish university journalism faculty, Courtney notes that

> there was a limited understanding of information literacy and the role of the librarian. . . . Many of the journalists were unaware that librarians were trained in teaching and some even had a limited understanding of information literacy. Journalists mainly considered the role of the librarian as one of procurers of books and databases. (p. 27)

Courtney's interviews with these journalism faculty members, as well as academic librarians, revealed that "when asked to compare each other's core values, both librarians and journalists were surprised at the correlations and most had not, in the past, considered the commonalities of both professions" (p. 30). It's possible that there is more convergence in the US context. In 2011 the ACRL issued the *Information Literacy Competency Standards for Journalism Students and Professionals,* and the ACRL has recently released a draft of the *Framework for Information Literacy in Journalism for Higher Education,* aligned with the current Framework.

In the UK, MacMillan (2014) studied 215 journalism students over the course of five years and found through a thematic analysis of their information use, as understood through statements made by the participants, that there is value in "reconfiguring information literacy (IL) instruction to align with the professional needs and practices in their discipline. Deliberate scaffolding encouraged students to transfer ways of understanding and using information between personal, academic, and journalistic contexts" (p. 3). She makes a number of recommendations, including the following, among others:

- Understand IL as a means to solving information problems, not an end in itself.
- Understand professional information requirements and behaviours to develop authentic activities and assignments . . . .
- Ensure students understand how to use freely available and open access resources as well as proprietary databases. (p. 17)

These recommendations are, of course, also applicable to the education of professionals in many of the other special libraries contexts.

Ultimately, there are obvious connections for information literacy in news environments, and a clear role for librarians in newsrooms, but it doesn't seem that there is a strong will toward encouraging more information literacy training and practices in this space. An emphasis on the connection between the work of journalists and librarians seems to be a fruitful direction.

Law Libraries

Perhaps the best place to start when looking at information literacy practices in law libraries is to discuss the vision of the American Association of Law Libraries (AALL), the pre-eminent professional organization for the field. AALL's (2019) vision is to "position [its] members as the recognized authority and experts in all aspects of legal information" (n.p.). In pursuit of this mission, AALL has adopted the *Principles and Standards for Legal Research Competency*. Revised in 2020, the document states:

> The Principles are broad statements of foundational, enduring values related to skilled legal research, as endorsed by the American Association of Law Libraries. The Standards provide a set of more specific applications of those norms or habits that demonstrate one's commitment to and attainment of the principles. The Competencies are activities that demonstrate knowledge and skill. Competencies provide concrete measures or indicators of successful achievement of the abilities required to meet the standards. (p. 1)

Each of the standards, of which there are seventeen within five principles, begins with the phrase "an information-literate legal professional" and includes such skills as considering the "full range" of information sources, understanding the legal system, constructing "efficient, cost-effective search strategies," and evaluating "legal information through cost-benefit analyses." It is very obvious that though the field places a strong emphasis on information literacy, practitioners are very context-dependent in interpreting common information literacy practices, such as knowing how to evaluate sources and finding relevant information. There is almost a complete absence of user education—law librarians are seen as the researchers and lawyers as the recipients of the information.

There is an interesting relationship to information literacy at the heart of the original development of the competencies (the first iteration of which was formally adopted in 2013). In the 2011 report of the AALL Law Student Research Competency Standards Task Force developed for the review of the AALL Executive Board, the task force describes the background to the standards as originating from a draft of a document entitled "Law Student Information Literacy Standards" developed by a self-formed group of AALL members chaired by Dennis C. Kim-Prieto. This document was submitted to the AALL board for approval. The board directed the then AALL president to form the task force, of which Kim-Prieto would be a member, to study the standards and make revisions as necessary. In the process of revising the report, the task force changed the phrase "information literacy" to "research competency" because it "would resonate most with the legal community, which is [AALL's] primary focus" (p. 1).

Kim-Prieto attached a separate minority report to the main task force report in which it was argued that "allowing the concept of IL to remain at the heart of these standards not only brings instructional law librarianship into the wider community of IL librarians and their scholarship, it also allows us to more easily apply and adopt theories and techniques of IL-focused instruction into our own legal research curricula" (p. 7). Obviously the research competency votes prevailed, but this history makes it easier to see the divide between law librarianship's conception of information literacy and that of academic libraries. More on the development of the initial standards can be found in scholarly work by Kim-Prieto, specifically a 2011 article on information literacy's relationship with legal research education.

In a discussion of law librarians who serve law students in academic libraries, Gire (2010) notes that

> today's law librarians are teachers. As teachers, law librarians must determine the education needs of their patrons, design curricula and methods to meet those needs, evaluate the education process for effectiveness, educate patrons in the methodologies of legal research, and provide training in the organization and use of legal resources in various formats. (p. 31)

Written in the context of a higher education environment, and specifically in the context of the development of an information literacy plan for the library, it's clear that there are different functions of law librarians serving lawyers and of those serving law students (as there probably should be!).[2] Overall, it seems that all communities of law librarians have embraced the concept of information literacy, just some in more explicit terms and in different flavors than others.

Medical Libraries

Medical libraries, like government libraries, can take many forms. Unlike government libraries, however, the Medical Library Association (MLA; 2017) has developed a common set of competencies for the field. The introduction to the *MLA Competencies for Lifelong Learning and Professional Success* outlines the core values of medical librarians:

> the use of scientific evidence in making health care decisions; public awareness of, access to, and use of high-quality health information; lifelong learning and professional development; advancement of health information research and evidence-based practice; community and collaboration within and outside the profession; and irreproachable ethical standards. (p. 1)

Of the six competencies outlined in the document, one explicitly mentions information literacy—"Competency 3, Instruction and Instructional Design: A health information professional educates others in the skills of bioscience, clinical, and health information literacy" (p. 5)—though concepts related to the practice of information literacy are woven throughout. In this section, we'll take the particular focus of medical librarians as consumer health advocates and librarians working within the context of higher education to train future health professionals. Both are common topics in research and have numerous instances of information literacy instruction and models to discuss.

Just as in other special libraries closely related to other professions, medical libraries use the common parlance of the medical field. Woven throughout discussions of information literacy's role in medical library work is the connection to evidence-based practice (EBP). Adams (2014) compares and contrasts the two, using the 2000 ACRL *Standards* to represent information literacy and the Guyatt et al. (2011) definition of evidence-based practice: "the conscientious, explicit, and judicious use of current best evidence in making decisions about the care of individual patients" (p. 314). Adams concludes that

> the outcomes described in the ACRL *Standards* provide a foundation for evidence-based practice. These two frameworks mirror each other in many ways, and IL skills are highly valued by evidence-based practitioners. The skills and attitudes that academic librarians can inculcate through IL instruction are those that will prepare students to be successful in EBP-influenced professions. (p. 243)

As a practical example, Bingham et al. (2016) emphasize that information literacy was represented in their evidence-based practice instruction to social work students in the New Zealand context, and Schardt (2011) connects health information literacy with EBP in her call to improve consumer health literacy; she describes evidence-based practice as the consideration that values and preferences are critical to health decisions and the determination that these decisions are improved by better research. She asserts that health literacy is tied to the first aspect of evidence-based practice (preference and values) and essential to the second.

Speaking of health literacy,[3] in an earlier chapter, we mentioned it as one of the associated literacies to information literacy. We are reminded of that here when looking at the significant similarities between the two terms. The National Library of Medicine's (2021) web introduction to health literacy cites the US Department of Health and Human Services' (HHS) Healthy People 2030 initiative in defining health literacy as "the information and services that people need to make well-informed health decisions," including personal health literacy ("the degree to which individuals have the ability to find, understand, and use information and services to inform health-related decisions and actions for themselves and others"; HHS, 2021), organizational health literacy, digital health literacy, and numeracy.

A comparison of the terms in the context of nursing and library/information science found that "health and information literacy share common antecedents and attributes: literacy, health or information need, comprehension, decision-making and degree of technological competency. Unique to health literacy is an emphasis on interactive communication and unique to information literacy is a focus on discovery and search skills" (Lawless et al., 2016, p. 144). Indeed, this type of comparison between health competencies and information literacy has been common in the higher education context. Many of these crosswalks were developed under the old ACRL *Standards*. For example, the *Information Literacy Competency Standards for Nursing*, approved by ACRL in 2013, purported to provide a framework for faculty and students of nursing . . . in the development of information literacy skills for evidence-based nursing practice; encourage the use of a common language for nursing faculty and librarians to discuss student information seeking skills; guide librarians and nursing faculty in creating learning activities that will support the growth of information literacy skills over the course of a program of nursing education and for lifelong learning; provide administration and curriculum committees a shared understanding of student competencies and need; and provide a framework for continuing education in the area of information literacy for the field of nursing practice and research. (n.p.)

Bradley (2013) mapped "the connections between requirements outlined in nursing, social work, and engineering accreditation standards of four countries: Canada, the US, the UK, and Australia" to the *Standards* (p. 46).

More recently, nursing professional standards have been mapped to the *Framework* on an assessment rubric (Willson & Angell, 2017), Brennan et al. (2020) have created a health information literacy competencies map that connects the Association of American Medical Colleges' *Core Entrustable Professional Activities* and the Accreditation Council for Graduate Medical Education's *Common Program Requirements* to the ACRL *Framework*, and the ACRL Education and Behavioral Sciences Section (EBSS) Social Work Committee (2020) was charged with "demonstrating where the ACRL *Framework* and social work educational competencies and standards, as well as professional ethics and values, intersect," a process that resulted in the document *Social Work: Companion Document to the ACRL Framework.* The ACRL Health Sciences Interest Group has completed research into nursing faculty information literacy practices to inform a revision (currently in progress) of the 2013 *Information Literacy Competency Standards for Nursing* in light of the adoption of the ACRL *Framework* (McGowan et al., 2020). Young and Hinton's (2019) literacy handbook for the health sciences offers overviews of the ACRL *Framework*, maps accreditation standards of health professions to the *Framework*, and describes case studies of how information literacy was taught to students in health-related fields.

Perhaps because of the general understanding of health literacy in the medical field and the great overlap between health and information literacies, the health sciences seem the most well-situated of the special library audiences to expand on information literacy instruction and understandings.

Archives

We will end our exploration of the operationalization of information literacy with a discussion of information literacy instruction in archives. Just as with specialized libraries, archival institutions have particular audiences and missions. The Society of American Archivists (SAA; 2020) leads its Core Values Statement with an articulation of the work of archivists, including the following:

- Identifying and preserving essential records that document the cultural heritage of society.
- Organizing and maintaining the documentary record of institutions, groups, communities, and individuals.
- Assisting in the process of interpreting documentation of past events through the use of primary source materials.

■ Serving a broad range of people who seek to locate and use the information found in evidentiary records. (n.p.)

The four values described include access and use, accountability, advocacy, and diversity. Through these values runs a strong thread of amplifying underrepresented voices, preserving history, and ensuring that records are used. The statement asserts that

> the goal of use should be considered during every phase of acquisition, description, and access. Even individuals who do not directly use archival materials still benefit indirectly from research, public programs, and other forms of archival work, including an increased awareness that records exist, are being cared for, and can be accessed when needed. (n.p.)

Underlying many of these principles is the expectation that both archivists and those who use archives will have practice at using the information literacy skills needed to access archival records.

One model that further demonstrates the interconnection of archives and information literacy is the work of Yakel and Torres (2003) who, using interview research, concluded that there are

> three distinct forms of knowledge required to work effectively with primary sources: domain (subject) knowledge, artifactual literacy [the ability to interpret and analyze primary sources], and the authors' own concept of archival intelligence . . . [which] is a researcher's knowledge of archival principles, practices, and institutions, such as the reason underlying archival rules and procedures, the means for developing search strategies to explore research questions, and an understanding of the relationship between primary sources and their surrogates. (p. 51)

Carini (2016) extended this work with a set of skills and outcomes that could be used to build instructional programs and assessment in these areas. These included six standards—know, interpret, evaluate, use, access, and follow ethical principles—with associated outcomes outlined. Baker's (2013) model for lifelong learning places cultural heritage in the context of information literacy. A review of the book describes the model's five parts as "the catalysts, components (carrier, content and context), core process and tasks, generic learning outcomes, and contextual fluidity as applied to an information literacy cultural heritage framework" (Wellington, 2013, pp. 619–620). These lists and models are evidence of what Wellington (2013) describes as "the increasing amount of interest in GLAM (gallery, library, archive, museum) integrative ideology in both the academic and professional cultural heritage milieu" (p. 620).

The SAA online *Dictionary of Archives Terminology* (n.d.) defines information literacy as "the ability to recognize when sources of knowledge or data are needed to address a situation or problem and to identify, locate, evaluate, and use the sources" and notes that "terms such as *archival literacy, primary source literacy, digital literacy, visual literacy*, and *artifactual literacy* are often considered aspects or conceptualizations of information literacy" (n.p.). In terms of primary source literacy, a joint task force between the ACRL Rare Book and Manuscript Section and SAA created guidelines that

> articulate the range of knowledge, skills, and abilities required to effectively use primary sources. While the primary audience for this document is librarians, archivists,

teaching faculty, and others working with college and university students, the guidelines have been written to be sufficiently flexible for use in K–12 and in general public settings as well. The guidelines articulate crucial skills for navigating the complexity of primary sources and codify best practices for utilizing these materials. (ACRL RBMS-SAA Joint Task Force, 2018, p. 1)

Intended to be "flexible rather than prescriptive," the *Guidelines* "were developed in the spirit of the ACRL *Information Literacy Framework*" (p. 2). Information literacy is explicitly mentioned as one of the literacies that primary source literacy intersects, and the *Guidelines* note that

users of primary sources, and those who seek to guide them in the process, are not working in isolation from other skills and disciplines. To create order in this complex landscape, these *Primary Source Literacy Guidelines* identify core ideas that undergird successful work with primary sources, as well as more specific learning objectives to guide those who teach the use of primary sources. (p. 2)

There is a strong connection to the way that information literacy has been developed in the academic library field.

Overall, the trends toward digitized collections, community-based archives, and the use of archives in K–12 and university education all create new ways for information literacy to be centered in archival practices, which to this point have been mainly focused on primary source literacy.

CONCLUSION

The various types of information institutions discussed in chapters 4 and 5 represent the diversity of the library profession. We did not even cover every possible type of library; business and corporate libraries, historical associations, and museums all certainly have unique information literacy needs and practices. Given our space limitations, we have hoped to demonstrate that the commonality among all these libraries and information organizations is the question of how to sell a context-dependent, fluid view of information literacy in environments that frequently demand outcomes and quantitative results.

In the case of information literacy, scholars have recognized a gap between research and practice in LIS. Pilerot (2016), for example, notes three distinct strands in information literacy discourse: practitioner reports of best practices, policy texts describing population-level requirements of information literacy skills, and LIS empirical and theoretical research studies. We think that bridging this gap is necessary for achieving the goal of creating spaces in all types of libraries for information literacy practice—one purpose of this textbook.

We have covered only a small percentage of the reports, research, presentations, and personal stories about the practice of information literacy in real libraries for real people, so as a conclusion to these two chapters, we will encourage you to seek out the professional organization to which your type of library—either current or prospective—belongs and examine its practices related to information literacy. You will want to pay particularly close attention to reports from the field of the ways in which information literacy is being implemented, as well as any attempts to revise existing standards. Both of these areas will tell you much about the direction of information literacy in your everyday practice.

Of course, often the best ideas come from talking to the patrons of your institution. It is important to know the historical path that information literacy has taken in your particular area of librarianship and imperative to understand the current frameworks guiding the profession, but it is truly critical to know your own users, your own institution, and your own understandings of information literacy.

🗩 CHAPTER 5 GUIDING QUESTIONS

1. Why do you think public libraries tend to use language alternative to the term *information literacy*?
2. In what ways does the general lack of professional guidance on information literacy in the news and government library sectors impact the work they do in this area?
3. How do law libraries conceptualize information literacy differently than other types of libraries?
4. In what ways are health and information literacies similar?
5. Is primary source literacy a key part of information literacy or vice versa (or both)?

NOTES

1. If only to do away with the displeasing acronyms?
2. We thought we might work a kraken reference in here somewhere but decided it was just too soon.
3. Thanks to the pandemic, now the title of a game show.

Information Literacy Is a Human Right

LITERACY AS LIVING

In 1984 two small clay tablets, first made about 4000 BCE, were discovered in Tell Brak, Syria. Through line-drawn pictographs in the clay, one tablet indicates ten sheep; the other, ten goats. The tablets are quite possibly the oldest surviving examples of human writing. They also mean that people were demonstrably reading and writing more than six thousand years ago. They were using writing for a range of purposes very early on; some stone tablets have survived, recording Babylonian weather forecasts that are nearly six thousand years old (Milham, 1918). Other surviving examples of very early writing include carvings in bones from China; even earlier writing may have occurred but not survived if less sturdy materials were used (Lerner, 2009). The ability to write has long been associated with freedom or maturity in many cultures. For many of the most influential civilizations and belief systems through history—ancient Mayas, Buddhist cultures, Abrahamic religions, as a few prominent examples—learning to read was the rite of passage into adulthood or into society. Literature is filled with stories both fictional and nonfictional built on the idea that literacy is freedom.

The quest for literacy as essential to the quest for freedom is the central story of Fredrick Douglass's autobiography, *Narrative of the Life of Fredrick Douglass, An American Slave*, written in 1845 after his escape from enslavement. In Virginia Woolf's *A Room of One's Own* (1929), literacy and the privilege of access to books are presented as feminist emancipation—gaining access to a space from which academic libraries traditionally restricted women, with the narrator being thwarted in her quest to conduct research by the university rules that permitted women in the library only if accompanied by or with a note of reference from a male faculty member.

Information literacy is tied to surviving and navigating the contemporary world of information and technology superabundance. However, being literate about information is as old as complex life itself. Plants make decisions based on information around them. Even the smallest plants rely on information, assessing temperature, air composition, light, and water to make decisions about how to invest their energies to promote long-term survival, such as when to bloom and how many seeds to make and the best time to drop leaves.

So, reading, in the sense of understanding signs in nature or the feelings of others, is an ancient social skill that predates humans (Battles, 2015). It is a part of most lived experiences; we all read ourselves and the world around us in order to glimpse what and where we are. "We read to understand, or begin to understand. We cannot do but read. Reading, almost as much as breathing, is our essential function" (Manguel, 1996, p. 7). The languages that humans have subsequently developed from reading the world around them and wanting to communicate about it act as a "symbolic shorthand" that was originally developed through—and continues to work as a result of—shared experiences, attributes, and environments (Berns, 2017, p. 14).

Information, communication, and reading connect humans to other living things; the written word separates humans from every other living thing. Words serve to conjure symbolic images, such as "flower," which may give each listener an image of a different type of flower, but all speakers of the language will get the general concept. The jump from understanding information and verbal and physical communication to the written word, however, was an enormous evolutionary leap. Focusing all one's concentration on printing or reading print, rather than focusing on the normal skills of survival, does not seem like a good choice when one does not wish to be eaten by large predators. Writing was as radical a change as humans have ever experienced (N. Carr, 2011). The ability to write and read the written word was not a natural, foregone evolution, but one that people had to actively choose to do given the other sacrifices involved (Wolf, 2007).

The modern world in which information literacy is now far more vital to survival for most people than avoiding packs of wild dogs may be as shattering an evolution as the first inklings of the written word. In 2018 it was estimated that the average person was consuming roughly 34 terabytes of information each day across various devices and in various formats, which is the equivalent of one hundred thousand words or a decent-length book every day (Wolf, 2018). We are not built to absorb that volume of information, and yet that amount keeps spiraling upward.

We are also having to rapidly change our understandings of what we interact with in terms of information. For the vast majority of human history, like all but the last few dozen years of it, we interacted with other living beings and reacted to nonliving things. As a result of advanced computing power, super high-speed connectivity, artificial intelligence (AI), and synthesized voices, we now have to adapt to interacting with all kinds of inanimate objects—vacuums, watches, refrigerators, thermostats, cars, phones, personal assistants—pretending to be like living beings. The brilliant Allie Brosh (2020) explains this evolutionary problem pithily in an essay about her smart car stereo trying to take over her life: "It isn't alive. I don't need to get mad at it. But this is confusing for me . . . Gone are the days that inanimate objects acted like inanimate objects. Hardly any of them do anymore" (pp. 278–279). So, most of us are getting way more information than we can ever hope to handle from way too many sources, quite a few of which are rather unexpected from an evolutionary standpoint.

At the other end of concerns in the information age, the lack of access results in being cut off from key elements of society. Inequities in access result from numerous problems—ability, age, income, geography, and language, among others—and impact wide ranges of the population (K. M. Thompson et al., 2014). But these problems were widely ignored by much of the population until the pandemic, when online learning relied on the access that people had at home. For example, when schools went online in spring 2020 because of the pandemic, many students lacked sufficient—or any—computers or connectivity at home to participate fully or at all; in Washington, D.C., 30 percent of elementary and secondary students lacked Internet access or computers at home (Stein, 2020). Students of color, students with disabilities, English learners, and students with lower socioeconomic status have suffered especially in gaps in access and resulting gaps in achievement (Meckler & Natanson, 2020). This problem also impacts higher education. The pandemic forced the overwhelming majority of higher education courses online, leading to very large declines in college applicants and enrollment among the poor and rural, who often lack sufficient computers and access to participate in courses (Long & Douglas-Gabriel, 2020; Lumpkin, 2020).

If written literacy is uniquely human, then information literacy is central to being human. As a result, literacy, equity of access, and other dimensions of information literacy are now elemental considerations of human rights. Given the ways in which all other central human rights—communication, education, employment, civic engagement—are becoming heavily or entirely dependent on information literacy, one could argue that information literacy is now the most important human right. Coincidentally, that is exactly what we are going to do next.

FOUNDATIONS OF HUMAN RIGHTS

Information, quite simply, is "our most precious resource" (Boyer, 1997, p. 140). To understand the centrality of information literacy to the entire scheme of human rights, we need to begin with a general understanding of human rights. The foundations for modern conceptualizations of human rights were articulated and developed during the Enlightenment and first expressed in governance through the American and French Revolutions (Sellars, 2002). However, human rights, ironically enough, were not originally intended for everyone.

The Magna Carta in the UK, the foundational documents of the original French Republic, and the Declaration of Independence and Constitution of the United States include many rights that were initially intended for the moneyed, white, Christian, and male classes of those nations. Wollstonecraft's 1792 *A Vindication of the Rights of Woman* proposed that women be given opportunities equal to those of men in education, employment, and politics. Although launching feminism, the book did not result in social change, unfortunately. At about the same time, French playwright Olympe de Gouges published pamphlets arguing that as long as the French Revolution was saying that it would recognize all men as equal, the new government should give all the same guaranteed rights to all women as well. The reception of her early argument for universal rights was less than positive—she was executed by the French government soon after her ideas were published.

Moreover, the founding documents of the United States contain broad—and ambiguous—rights, such as the pursuit of happiness, as well as more specific rights to activities such as assembly and expression. By no means were these documents written to create universal rights, as evidenced by the Constitution's original limitations on political participation and the inclusion of the, umm, "right" to enslave others.[1] Despite these limitations of the founding documents, the international structures of human rights rely heavily on the Declaration of Independence in creating the notion of the state as the protector of individual rights, an idea heavily influenced by the writings of John Locke (Calhoun, 2007). Although modern states generally have much more robust and broad guarantees of human rights, the practical results vary rather widely.

The first major proposals for what we would now think of as an international human rights structure began circulating in the 1920s as a reaction to the First World War, intended not only to ensure universal human rights but to provide consistency to the rights being protected across national boundaries. The modern idea of universal human rights, and what such rights might be, derives heavily from the welfare programs and social protections articulated in the United States during the Franklin Delano Roosevelt administration (Woodiwiss, 2005). The new social programs to protect the disadvantaged and ensure that basic needs were met, together with the broader ideals expressed as goals of President Roosevelt, created a nascent human rights program within the United States, though it was known as the "New Deal." Roosevelt's 1941 speech advocating for an international social contract of "Four Freedoms"—to speech and expression, to religion, from want, and from fear—was the key inspiration for the development of international human rights structures (Woodiwiss, 2005). In his 1944 State of the Union address, Roosevelt used the fact that the Second World War was winding down to expand the idea of the Four Freedoms into what he hoped would be a centerpiece of his postwar legislative agenda—what he dubbed "a Second Bill of Rights" (Sunstein, 2004).

The creation and adoption of the Universal Declaration of Human Rights (UDHR; United Nations, 1948) represents the symbolic arrival of rights to the world stage in 1948 (Ignatieff, 2005; Raphael, 1967). The UDHR is the cornerstone of the entire modern human rights movement globally (Glendon, 2002).

Perhaps the greatest asset for promoting human rights internationally was the fact that the fight for the creation of an international structure for universal human rights was led by Eleanor Roosevelt, one of the most important social justice activists in human history, who also happened to be married to Franklin. Eleanor, as US ambassador to the United Nations (UN), led the group that wrote the UDHR and got it approved. After the final vote, she received the first—and so far only—standing ovation by UN delegates for another delegate. In her own words from 1944:

> Freedom for our peoples is not only right, but also a tool. Freedom of speech, freedom of press, freedom of information, freedom of assembly—these are not just abstract ideals to us; they are tools with which we create a way of life, a way of life in which we can enjoy freedom (Roosevelt, 2019).

Note that one of the freedoms that she specifies is freedom of information, and the other three all depend on information to have any meaning or value.

INFORMATION AND HUMAN RIGHTS

The UDHR and its two later accompanying covenants—the International Covenant on Civil and Political Rights and the International Covenant on Economic, Social, and Cultural Rights—are known as the International Bill of Human Rights. The UDHR is now seen as customary international law (Sellars, 2002), and the internationally accepted human rights contained therein "include freedom of expression, freedom of association, freedom from fear and persecution, freedom of religion, as well as a right to shelter, education, health and work" (Halpin et al., 2000, p. 5).

Mostly influentially, the International Bill of Human Rights places people as the agents of their own rights rather than as the objects of rights bestowed by the nation-state (Blau & Moncada, 2006). Unlike the US Constitution, which focuses on sovereignty and personal autonomy, the UDHR links individual rights with rights of community, focusing on society. The UDHR contains twenty-four specific rights. Eighteen of these rights are civil and political rights, such as expression, cultural heritage, and mobility. The remaining six are economic rights, focusing on concepts of property, employment, and social services. The UN now views these articulated human rights as being "indivisible, interdependent, and interrelated"—though none of these terms are in the UDHR—meaning that the rights must be provided and protected as a complete set (Whelan, 2010). The UN has engaged in many further steps to encourage the adoption of, as well as to elaborate on, the International Bill of Human Rights. The 1993 Vienna World Conference on Human Rights, as one example, reaffirmed the intentional commitment to UDHR and the subsequent conventions.

As information and ICTs have become a central aspect of daily life, increasing attention has been paid to information as a central aspect of human rights. "Everyone is a consumer of information, and everyone should have the skills necessary to be critical consumers and creators of information" (Cooke, 2017, p. 219). As information and related technologies have become increasingly essential to communication, education, employment, social interaction, and civic participation, greater focus has been placed on the idea that information can be seen as a necessary human right. Information intersects with human rights in several major ways, including the following:

- The wide range of social, cultural, economic, legal, and political forces shaping information and rights;
- Impacts of rights on information professions, practices, standards, and cultural institutions; and
- Considerations of rights in the information behavior of different populations (Jaeger, Taylor, & Gorham, 2015).

Although early antecedents of current information technologies were still fairly new when the UN adopted the UDHR in 1948, the idea of human rights has been evolving and adapting to social, cultural, and technological change. Though the desktop computer, the Internet, and mobile devices were developed long after the UDHR was originally drafted, many of the principles articulated in the UDHR are directly related to information, communication, and technology. Most items directly stated as rights are now either entirely dependent on or greatly enabled by information access and digital literacy, including such major activities as education, employment, and civic participation. As examples, the freedoms of speech, press, assembly, and expression are far more practicable when involving a literate populace with access to information technologies. Human rights to education and development are possible without access to and use of information technologies, but they are much more effective with the technologies.

Article 19 of the UDHR most explicitly deals with issues of information, enshrining rights to "freedom of opinion and expression" and to "seek, receive and impart information and ideas through any media," as well as freedom from "interference" in seeking and exchanging information and ideas. ALA, IFLA, UNESCO, and other information professional and governmental organizations have adopted Article 19 and the principles of information access as a human right into their bylaws and policies. The Progressive Librarians Guild (PLG) in particular has advocated on human rights issues for several decades. The 2003 and 2005 World Summits on the Information Society, for instance, yielded assertions of the importance of technology for rights to exist in the age of the Internet.

A number of these organizations have held two global information literacy summits. The 2003 *Prague Declaration*, from a joint meeting of UNESCO, NFIL, and NCLIS, stated that information literacy is a "key to social, cultural, and economic development of nations and communities, institutions and individuals in the 21st century" and is "part of the basic human right of lifelong learning" (p. 1). The subsequent *Alexandria Proclamation* from UNESCO, IFLA, and NFIL extended the argument to hold that information literacy is a basic human right that "promotes social inclusion in all nations" (2006, p. 1).

Also, in 2011 a UN report explicitly discussed Internet access as being central to supporting Article 19 of the UDHR and enabling many other aspects of the UDHR (UN Human Rights Council, 2011). Although the report never explicitly labels Internet access as a human right, many media outlets interpreted the report as doing so (Olivarez-Giles, 2011). In 2016, the UN finally declared Internet access to be a human right. The IFLA-led *Lyons Declaration on Access to Information and Development* (2014) called on the UN to make information literacy and digital inclusion central to the organization's human rights and development agendas, building on the assertions made in the *Alexandria Proclamation* for the UN and individual nations to make information literacy a central part of their goals. Such statements reflect the ideas that have come to be known as information and communications technology for development (ICT4D), which encourages the use of ICTs to promote community development and the growth of education, health care, and general welfare (Zelenika & Pierce, 2013).

INFORMATION LITERACY AS A FOUNDATIONAL HUMAN RIGHT

As these various declarations and statements make clear, increasing attention has been paid to the role of information in human rights in recent years, and many clear articulations have been made for the central role of educational and cultural heritage institutions—including libraries, archives, and museums—in ensuring human rights related to information in an age so dependent on information and technology. Libraries, archives, museums, and other educational and cultural heritage institutions are engaged in many activities at the intersection of human rights and information and often are finding new ways to foster and promote rights to information in the communities they serve (Gorham et al., 2016). Further, given their unique understanding of information issues, the information professions have the potential to be a societal leader in areas such as privacy, intellectual property, and other key topics at this intersection of human rights and information (Mathiesen, 2015; Zimmer, 2014).

From within the field of library and information science, specific arguments have been made that information as an entity or that various aspects of information, such as information access, intellectual freedom, freedom of expression, Internet access, digital literacy, and information behavior, among others, all should be viewed as falling under the category of human rights (Duffy, 2001; Hoffman, 2001; Jaeger, Bertot, & Gorham, 2013; Jaeger, Bertot, Thompson et al., 2012; Mathiesen, 2013; McCook & Phenix, 2006; Phenix & McCook, 2005; Stinnett, 2009; Suarez, 2007; K. M. Thompson et al., 2014). When you combine these arguments with those from other fields focused on access to the Internet and related technologies as a human right, as well as Ms. Roosevelt's 1944 assertion of freedom of information as a foundational human right, it seems that virtually every facet of information and related technologies has been claimed as a human right. So, why then the focus specifically on information literacy as the central human right?

Information literacy is necessary as a right for all the other facets of information to be successfully guaranteed as rights. All the other facets of information and technology that have been argued for as human rights are unified by being dependent on information literacy. What good is access to information if one doesn't have the skills to assess the information? What good is availability of a computer if one doesn't know how to use it? How much can one do with the Internet without knowing how it works? Information literacy is the connective tissue that binds together all other facets of information and technology rights. If human rights were imagined as a tree, information literacy would be the roots because the growth in other areas depends on information literacy.

The role of information literacy as the foundational human right can be understood in two prongs, both absolutely essential. First, one needs information literacy to be able to use the technologies of the Internet; one needs to be able to use the technologies of the Internet to successfully gain access to education, employment, civic engagement, and other forms of interaction. Second, one needs information literacy to be able to make sense of the masses of information online; one needs to be able to make sense of the masses of information online to successfully participate in education, employment, civic engagement, and other forms of interaction. Simply put, because most other human rights are dependent on information literacy partly or wholly at this point, information literacy is as foundational as a human right can be.

Along with all its importance in social, economic, educational, and civic participation, information literacy also acts as a human right of self-empowerment. Information literacy is the basis of making informed, reasonable decisions. It is the greatest tool that an individual has for navigating a world of too much information and inescapable ICTs. In this kind of information environment, information literacy becomes an information-age version of Occam's razor. Medieval philosopher William of Occam articulated the logical assertion that the truth is most likely to be closest to the simplest explanation of observable facts. In a less modern world, Occam's razor would be the process of determining the explanation of a situation in which the kitchen garbage can is on its side and a dog is rolling around in the garbage. The simplest explanation—the dog knocked over the garbage can in order to have the opportunity to roll deliriously in the garbage—is the most likely. On the flipside, deciding that the lizard people were paid by Bill Gates to break into the house, spill the garbage, and brainwash the dog to roll in it would not qualify as the simplest explanation. Information literacy serves that role in the world of the Internet. When there is so much information to sort through, information literacy allows for sense-making of information and disregarding of misinformation.

For all its centrality to human rights and to general participation in existence, information literacy is often overlooked in policymaking and politics. In the very early 2000s, Internet access and digital government were seen as great innovations that could bring civic engagement to everyone. Governments around the world tried projects to promote engagement online, some of which failed spectacularly due to lack of an understanding of information literacy on the part of policymakers (Jaeger, 2003; Jaeger & Thompson, 2003). Perhaps none was more impressive than the government of India's decision to put public computer kiosks on streets in communities that had the lowest levels of employment and technology access. Without any guidance or training materials, people tried these kiosks but couldn't make much use of them, other than figuring out how to use the painting and drawing programs.

The next two chapters include other examples of government programs that made similar mistakes. Access to information and availability of technology are of very limited use if the literacy is not there. If this seems too abstract, find a video of someone speaking a language that you do not know and that lacks captions in a language you do know; even under the best of circumstances, you really won't be able to figure out very much about what is going on. It is the same with an unknown language or an unknown technology—the literacy is absolutely necessary for it to make sense.

As discussed at the beginning of this chapter, information literacy is the element of being human that most enables us to be different than all other animals. Not only is it essential for all other human rights related to information to work, it may also be the most uniquely human of human rights. Unfortunately, along with information literacy being the building block of all other human rights related to information—and thereby all human rights dependent on information, which is almost all of them—there is another, darker reason to view information literacy as the essential human right. As long as there has been written information, people with power have sought to control information literacy in others. As the next chapter will explore, control of information literacy has heavily shaped much of human history.

💬 CHAPTER 6 GUIDING QUESTIONS

1. Is the ability to practice information literacy a human right? Why or why not?
2. How has the volume of information present in our lives changed our capacity for practicing information literacy?
3. How have national and international crises illuminated the importance of information literacy to humans' basic needs?
4. In this chapter, we quote Boyer (1997, p. 140) as saying that information is "our most precious resource." Do you agree? Why or why not?
5. How can the practice of information literacy be a source of freedom?

NOTE

1. Who could vote was also super limited: "If particular care and attention is not paid to the Ladies we are determined to foment a Rebellion, and will not hold ourselves bound by any Laws in which we have no voice, or Representation." From a breathtakingly insightful March 31, 1776, letter that Abigail Adams wrote to her husband, John, arguing for equal rights for women in the new government. Alas, her admonitions were ignored.

Controlling
Information Literacy

INFORMATION LITERACY FOR SOME

Information literacy has power. It is power. It has been used as a means of social control and of revolution. As long as writing has existed, the powerful have tried to control access to it. The majority of the earliest extant texts are not epic romantic poems; they are lists of outstanding debts, primarily what we would now think of as government tax rolls (J. C. Scott, 2017). For much of human history, access to literacy was held in the hands of rulers, religious leaders, and academics who controlled the production and dissemination of the written word.

The pre-modern world was one of restricted literacy—it was not very common and avenues to learning it were extremely limited (Lyons, 2010). Enslavers throughout history have been especially concerned about preventing enslaved peoples from accessing information or achieving literacy. The oppressors understood that command of information was one of their greatest mechanisms of power. Sadly, the control of information literacy has been one of the primary ways that people have tried to control one another throughout history (Manguel, 1996).

More than five hundred years ago,[1] the creation and spread of the printing press made information far more available than had previously been possible, opening up considerable opportunities for education and sharing of knowledge and increasing literacy in the overall population. Although history tends to focus on editions of the Bible driving the early success of the printing press, it was the mass produced, affordable playing cards that actually excited both the masses and the aristocrats, as well as driving profits for printers (Azzarito, 2020; Beal, 1975). By 1500 there were 260 cities in which printing presses were in operation, with about half of the publications being religious and the other half not religious (Lerner, 2009).

Before the printing press, much of the knowledge that humans gained was either recorded in handwritten texts that did not survive long or not recorded at all, leaving the corpus of recorded knowledge stuck in a small number of religious and canonical texts (Eisenstein, 1993). The creation of the printing press allowed the recorded body of human knowledge to expand exponentially, a great benefit to our understandings of history and science and arts. For all the great contributions of the printing press, however, it also caused really big immediate problems. That religious half of the materials coming off printing presses heightened feelings of tribalism and isolation along national and religious lines because people suddenly had access to widely distributed printed materials saying that their views were correct and the views of others were wrong. The immediate result was the bloodiest 150-year period in human history, with dozens of overlapping major religion-fueled wars including the English Civil War, the Scottish Civil War, the German Peasants' War, the French Wars of Religion, the Irish Confederate Wars, the Smalkaldic War, the War of the Holy League, the Thirty Years' War, the Eighty Years' War, and the Spanish Inquisition, among much else (Pinker, 2011).

Many of these conflicts rank among the greatest disasters in human history in terms of population loss—the Thirty Years' War killed one-third of the German population, for example. The mass production of books created the first period in human history in which it was possible to be overwhelmed by the amount of information, and the results were somewhat less than ideal. "The amount of information was increasing much more rapidly than our understanding of what to do with it, or our ability to differentiate between the useful information and the mistruths" (Silver, 2012, p. 3). The birth of the printing press launched the struggle between the amount of information produced by technological advancements and the ability of people to make sense of the information being produced. It is worth remembering that the printing presses were producing information equivalent to a few drops of rain in contrast to the daily tsunami of information churned out by the Internet today.

The more widespread availability of printed materials also inspired many rulers to increase limitations on printed materials and literacy as a means of maintaining their power (Berlin, 1996). Increased access to printed information undermined one of the primary means of power and control that governments had at the time, and the outbreak of so many wars was an indication of that erosion of central government control. Governments saw dramatically increased control over information—what could be produced, who could produce it, who could have access to it—as a necessary reaction to the printing press. Long before, the creation of city-states and the establishment of agriculture and commerce and trading helped make governments the focus of people through the control of information necessary for interaction between different cities (Sunstein, 2005). These reasons spurred government secrecy and censorship efforts and continue to inspire them to this day (Pool, 1990).

Though the printing press did make printed materials—books, newspapers, pamphlets, and playing cards—more affordable, it did not immediately lead to dramatic increases in overall literacy. Literacy remained so highly limited that books were often read aloud for entertainment at social gatherings or paid performances for centuries after the development of the printing press. In medieval Europe, troubadours provided high-art programs, reciting classic literature and their own writings (and contrary to historical imaginings, about a quarter of these troubadours were women), though joglars, who recited popular texts and songs, were far more common and far more popular (Manguel, 1996).

The limited scope of literacy was reflected in the limited nature of early dictionaries. The first English language dictionary was *Cawdrey's Table Alphabeticall* in 1604; it contained a mere three thousand words, ran to barely one hundred pages, and contained cases of failings in alphabetization and even included one word twice. That effort was followed by a half dozen equally sloppy and abbreviated dictionaries over the next century.[2] The first comprehensive English dictionary arrived in 1721, Nathaniel Bailey's *Universal Etymological English Dictionary*.

The biggest advancements in overall literacy began with the rise of the middle class and then the subsequent mechanization of printing, cutting, and folding of paper in the mid-1800s that greatly reduced the cost of printed materials (Burnett & Jaeger, 2008; Hanson, 2008; Jaeger & Burnett, 2010). Literacy became increasingly essential to widening business activities, and the lower cost of materials provided newspapers and other materials to the increasingly literate class, fueling interest in reading, especially about business and current events (Corner, 1995; Habermas, 1989). In the mid-1600s, books began to become a common middle- and upper-class gift between social equals in England and France; in the next century, books became the go-to gifts for children in middle- and upper-class families, helping significantly to encourage the spread of literacy (Flanders, 2017).

The modern public library movement coalesced in the mid-1800s as a way to advance literacy and learning among the general population. Public libraries and their capacity to promote education became linked to all the major social reform and uplift movements—suffrage, temperance, assistance to the poor, better working conditions, abolition of child labor—of the late 1800s and early 1900s (Ditzion, 1939; Stauffer, 2005; Watson, 1994).

With massive transfusions of more than $41,000,000 in cash from Andrew Carnegie to 1,420 towns to establish public libraries between 1886 and 1919, free public libraries truly became commonplace in the US (Davies, 1974).[3] In a vast majority of these small communities, the new public libraries were the first places that citizens had free access to books (Wiegand, 2011). The development of public libraries as a social instrument of literacy moved at a similar pace in the UK, even bringing a Western approach to libraries in Africa and Australasia, though those libraries were, of course, for the colonizers rather than the colonized (R. Harvey, 2015; Olden, 2015). And, of course, increases in literacy were not always popular among those in charge.

BOOK BURNINGS AND OTHER WAYS TO KEEP WARM WHILE CURTAILING LITERACY

The notion of democratizing literacy was not the norm; many nations did not place a priority on literacy among the populace until well into the twentieth century. As a result, the history of public libraries in Europe is far different from that in the English-speaking world. In nineteenth-century Europe, educational opportunities were limited, and those that existed focused on preparing people for work rather than creating a literate and informed citizenry. The public libraries that did exist primarily offered scholarly, theological, and high literature, none of which was intended for the masses. Communists and fascists expanded the role of libraries in Europe in the 1930s and 1940s, however, as means to reinforce state ideology and nationalism in the populace (Lerner, 2009).

Overall, limiting who had access to literacy and written materials has not been enough for most governments through history. In a contemporary sense, censorship seems antithetical to freedom and an idea that would commonly be rejected. But historically, censorship has been not only common but popular. Governments have regularly banned the printing of the "wrong" kind of materials for public consumption, whether it be to protect delicate public sensibilities, such as the works of Sinclair Lewis or James Joyce, or to limit exposure of ideas the government opposes, such as communist materials for much of the twentieth century in the US.

In the US, censorship was not just accepted by the public, it was absolutely popular with the public (Jaeger & Sarin, 2016b). For several decades, the US even had a chief national censor named Anthony Comstock, who was terribly effective at his job, and simply a terrible person—he liked to brag about the number of people he had driven to suicide

(Beisel, 1997). Mercifully his position did not survive his death.[4] The Soviets, as another example, actively supported libraries as a means to further party messages and nationalism, engaging in widespread censorship in collections and cutting off access to knowledge of the rest of the world (Hoare, 2015).

Sadly, censorship as a means of controlling access to information is as venerable as writing things down. The earliest known examples all date from before the Common Era in ancient places like Rome, Jerusalem, Greece, and China where book banning and book burning started with papyrus scrolls (Manguel, 1996). The first recorded program of book burning was in 213 BCE: Chinese emperor Qin Shi Huang had all the books that contradicted his version of preferred history burned, along with more than four hundred historians, just to be thorough. These efforts were often formalized into government offices. The Roman Empire had an official Office of the Censor to promote public morality. The Catholic Church managed to maintain an official banned books list, *The Index of Forbidden Books,* for more than four hundred years from 1559 to 1966.

Forcibly limiting literacy and access to written materials reached its apex in World War II, in which more books and works of art and libraries and archives and museums were destroyed than during any other event in human history, with the destruction primarily being direct and intentional (Knuth, 2003). Destroying the information and the information institutions of a culture or a nation is nothing new, but World War II was its zenith. Not surprisingly, the Nazis in particular did book burning with great enthusiasm, holding what they called *Feuerspruche,* "fire incantations," to burn books written by authors from cultures and perspectives they intended to annihilate. After that, they systematically pillaged and destroyed every library, archive, and museum in the very large amount of territory that they conquered, obliterating a large, irreplaceable portion of recorded human history, experience, and expression in the process.

In the US, libraries also actively engaged in censorship of their own materials by removing all kinds of German-language, pacifist, and labor-associated materials during the First World War (Wiegand, 1989). Similarly, during the Cold War, the collections of many libraries were directly and indirectly influenced by the politics of the McCarthy era, often leading to the silencing of unpopular viewpoints in many library collections (Richards, 2001). And although the Library Bill of Rights underwent a major revision in 1948 in response to McCarthyism, the relationship between the library profession, social responsibility, social justice, censorship, and democratic responsibility would remain controversial (Robbins, 1996). In the 1960s, the Library Bill of Rights would be revised once more in response to concerns that the directive in the existing document that only materials in the library of "sound, factual authority" should not be removed for partisan reasons might be used as a subtle way to censor resources the selecting librarians disagreed with (Samek, 1996). This is the classic problem of censorship versus selection (Asheim, 1953).

Though book burnings may sound like a thing of the past,[5] they continue today in manners both big and small. In 2020 a regional library in China hosted a huge book burning—and posted pictures of it online and filed a report on it with the Library Society of China—of materials that were deemed insufficiently acceptable to the political ideology of the government; government education and culture officials were honored guests at the event. And in the US, students at Georgia Southern University held a burning of the books of Jennine Capó Crucet, who had been invited on campus to talk about racial discrimination in higher education (Balingit, 2019).

During World War II and its epic destruction of cultural materials, President Franklin Roosevelt asserted, "Books cannot be killed by fire. People die, but books never die." While clearly an admirable sentiment, limiting literacy and access to the written word has long been seen as a key tool in asserting and maintaining power. "Attacks upon libraries are recognition that someone recognizes their importance" (Lerner, 2009, p. 154). In Senegal, a commonly used metaphor for death is that someone's library has burned down, which may be the most poetic way of expressing the essential nature of literacy and access to information to life itself.

ONLY WHAT THE REFRIGERATOR WANTS YOU TO KNOW

As literacy has evolved into information literacy, it is no longer just governments that seek to control information literacy. In fact, as many of the world's educational, commercial, entertainment, and interpersonal interactions have moved into the online environment, the companies that control communication on the Internet and Internet of things (IoT) connected devices now significantly shape the information literacy of individuals and even entire societies. Subsequent chapters will explore the ways in which this dynamic spreads and amplifies misinformation, disinformation, and illiteracy, so the discussion herein focuses simply on the mechanics of corporate control of information literacy.

Corporations were interested in information literacy prior to the Internet. Literacy education has been encouraged by corporate entities for many years as an important part of creating viable future employees; from a purely economic perspective, literacy has been seen by some corporations as a kind of capital (Barber, 2003; Brandt, 2001). To a company, the more information literate that someone is when they graduate from college, the better prepared they will be to use technology in the workplace immediately when they arrive, thus saving money on training.

There were many reasons to be optimistic about the Internet as a tool for democratizing information access and information literacy. Access and literacy were no longer limited by the scarcity, reproduction, or distribution of physical things—"it is easy to copy anything these days, and most books exist in endless multiples; a single book no longer has the preciousness it had when books came to life through a cumbersome, labored process" (Orlean, 2018, p. 56). The democratization of the production and dissemination of information from the realm of specialists to the general public brought both intended and significant unforeseen consequences (Bousquet & Wills, 2003). Initially, the biggest challenges were the lack of even distribution of access and inequities in the means to afford the technologies and connectivity (K. M. Thompson et al., 2014), and these gaps persist to this day. However, the centralization of control of information exchange has instead proven to be the biggest concern for information literacy.

The early optimistic view of the Internet was that "the power to inform and persuade was no longer the sole province of those who owned or controlled printing presses, radio stations, or television networks. Every machine connected to the Internet is potentially a printing press, a broadcasting station, or a place of assembly" (M. Conway, 2002, n.p.). This assertion was indeed correct, but it failed to anticipate that information exchange and information seeking would become centralized in the control of a very small number of large corporations—notably Facebook, Google, Twitter, Microsoft, Amazon, and Apple. As people have become even more reliant on digital home assistants and wearable technologies, the corporate influence on information literacy continues to expand. As an executive at a major media conglomerate explained in 2018, "I want more hours of engagement. Why are more hours of engagement important? Because you get more data and information about a customer that then allows you to monetize through alternate models of advertising as well as subscriptions" (quoted in Hornaday, 2018, p. C1).

The more information that users give to digital assistants, social media platforms, or online retailers, the better those resources are at providing services to users, but the increased information about users allows the companies to continually tailor and strategically limit the information available to the user (Lanier, 2018; Vaidhyanathan, 2018). As the companies continue to gather data and to run new experiments on it, the knowledge about the user and the ability to anticipate and direct user interests continue to increase. All those great recommendations from an Alexa only work because of the amount of data that the company has about each user to analyze.

Most users do not have a clear sense of what happens to information about them, whether they provide it intentionally or not (Jaeger & Taylor, 2019). Social media companies have business models built on people happily sharing their personal information. The explosion of Internet-enabled devices into homes has escalated the ability of companies to collect information from smart TVs, personal assistants, health devices, security systems, cars, doorbell cameras, vacuums, watches, glasses, picture frames, thermostats, refrigerators, toilets, and numerous other IoT devices that people have welcomed into their homes. "The information society is like a tree that has been growing its far-reaching branches much more widely, hastily, and chaotically, than its conceptual, ethical, and cultural roots" (Floridi, 2010, p. 7). Hence, the ability of companies to hoover up personal information of users.

Most of these platforms and devices collecting information not only report it back to the parent company, but often the information is shared with many other companies with which the parent company has data-sharing agreements. Although terms of service agreements for online activities exist for users to review, the agreements have been written primarily to obscure the data practices of the companies since the advent of online businesses (Grimes et al., 2008). Lots of users never even read these agreements—which are written to be as user-unfriendly as possible—so are not even aware of the types of data being collected.

As a result, mountains of information get collected in forms that the user cannot control. Simply by using innumerable programs, apps, and devices, a user automatically consents to have information collected by the company. The decision not to allow such collection is a decision not to use the product or service; one does not have a choice as the consumer. Opting out of all the companies that require users to agree to data collection would leave one disconnected from most aspects of society and daily life.

In most cases, thanks to all these data being collected and shared about each user by online entities, the user now sees what the algorithm thinks the user would like to see, based on all the information that the algorithm has about the user, derived from the use of that particular product and other information shared between products. "The people behind Facebook, Twitter and Google know you well. They know what shocks and horrifies you, they know what makes you click. They know how to grab your attention and hold it so they can serve you the most lucrative helping of personalized ads" (Bregman, 2019, p. 15).

This cycle commercializes confirmation bias—that is, believing only the information that confirms existing beliefs—drastically increasing the challenge to the user of being information literate about any topic for which they search. As a result, the user continually receives reinforcing messages that further limit the range of information that is presented to the user. In contexts related to policy, the political and current events information is not designed or intended to educate, but it is instead tailored to perpetuate any existing beliefs with one-sided results that conform to those beliefs.

AUTHORITARIANISM ONLINE, OR NOT QUITE WHAT AOL ORIGINALLY STOOD FOR

New ICTs have often been used by governments to increase "the powers of the ruler over the ruled" (Hanson, 2008, p. 19). The telegraph and the telephone not only made people more connected as individuals, they made governments more connected to all parts of their territories and better able to maintain control; the telegraph in particular was especially useful for maintaining far-flung empires. The power of the telegraph was obvious from the outset; an initial test run used the message "Everything worked well," but, for the public unveiling, the message sent was the thundering Biblical quote "What hath God wrought" (Howe, 2007). The Internet, from the perspective of governments, was a far more monumental step in the ability to control information access and information literacy among their populations.

Efforts by governments to limit the information available online for their citizens began almost as soon as the web went worldwide. Dozens of nations around the world filter all Internet access for their populations, with China, Saudi Arabia, and Malaysia all launching their government filtering policies in 1999, just as the browsable web was taking off (Zittrain & Palfrey, 2008). Within a few more years, Turkey had a law against "airing pessimism" online, China had closed most of the Internet cafés in the country, and Saudi Arabia had a purpose-built city—King Abdulaziz City for Science and Technology (KACST)—to monitor, screen, and censor Internet usage in the country (Klotz, 2004). In 2001 the US enacted the Children's Internet Protection Act (CIPA), which required public libraries and public schools to filter their computers for certain kinds of information if they wished to receive federal government technology funding, and almost all public schools and most public libraries complied (Jaeger & Yan, 2009). Cuba, not to be left out, mass arrested the country's librarians in 2003 (Vaidhyanathan, 2004).

Authoritarian states have never been better able to repress dissent and monitor citizens, thanks to Internet technologies (Foa, 2018). Perhaps the most internationally well-known effort is the Great Firewall of China, which blocks countless foreign websites—and the information that they contain—from being accessible in the country. Simultaneously, government censors constantly monitor Internet traffic inside China, greatly limiting the ability to create new content, including anything seen as negative about the government or any of its policies. AI is especially useful for authoritarians because they can merge collected big data, machine learning, algorithms, and advanced processing capacity to merge data, video feeds, facial recognition, voice recognition, and social media to monitor and control citizens—especially China (Feldstein, 2019; Qiang, 2019). The Chinese government even has an AI product that scans video of crowds to estimate age, sex, and ethnicity of crowd members, with the specific purpose of identifying people from dissident minority groups, particularly members of the Uighur population who have been brutally detained en masse (Harwell & Dou, 2020). The company that manufactured the products even had advertisements for it on its website among other available products (Dou & Harwell, 2020).

The Chinese government is now using AI to automate patrolling for dissidents online and eliminating any unwanted information, combining what is found to identify and limit opposition preemptively. In fewer than twenty years, China has moved from simply blocking outside ideas with the Great Firewall to compiling files on the ideas of every citizen (Deibert, 2015). These files are used not only to track people and monitor their expressions but to assign citizenship scores through China's Office of Creditworthiness, scores that impact everything from the ability to take public transit to get a loan (Strittmatter, 2020). State surveillance through phones and apps also increased significantly in many countries that made available or required citizens to use novel coronavirus tracking and alerts (Fahim et al., 2020).

All these efforts not only suppress the citizens, they ensure that the information literacy of citizens and the ideas that they can access are carefully controlled. The less costly, but far more common, approach is for a government is just have the Internet turned off. When Congo had a disputed election in 2019, the government simply turned off the Internet by ordering all telecommunications companies to shut down all types of Internet connections and text messaging for twenty days (Bearak, 2019). Kashmir, a disputed border region between India and Pakistan, has repeatedly had its Internet access cut off for long stretches as part of the disputes about its fate.

Cutting public funding for structures supporting information literacy is a more nuanced approach to limiting access for at least some. When newly elected president Donald Trump released his first proposed budget in 2017, the budget called for the reduction and, in many cases, the elimination of federal funding for many government-funded programs that disseminated information or provided public access to the Internet, such as funding for public libraries and the Innovative Approaches to Literacy (IAL) program, which helps schools in high-poverty areas (C. L. Douglass et al., 2017).

Limiting access is not the only way in which governments can use the Internet to shape information literacy in their own populace or more broadly. Through surveillance and digital methods of manipulating elections and political discourse, social media quickly moved away from being a potentially liberating technology to becoming a tool of control by governments (Shahbaz & Funk, 2019). States and intelligence agencies swamp social media to sway opinions and electoral results at home and abroad, as well as promote general confusion about and distrust of all information sources (Waisbord, 2018). Authoritarian governments often place conspiracy theories at the heart of their policies and actions, in no small part to make them more viable online. "The emotional appeal of a conspiracy theory is in its simplicity. It explains away complex phenomena, accounts for chance and accidents, offers the believer the satisfying sense of having special privileged access to the truth" (Applebaum, 2018, n.p.).

Some conspiracy theories are so effective that the same idea gets applied to different contexts through time. Do you think that the so-called War on Christmas—that is, people saying the nonreligious "happy holidays" instead of the clearly religious "merry Christmas"— is a product of twenty-first-century cultural politics? Well, the funny thing is that the phrase first appeared a century ago in the wretched book *The International Jew* (1921), written by Olympic-level anti-Semite and car industry tycoon Henry Ford, who claimed that an international cabal of Jewish leaders were going to ban Christmas. In the 1950s, the far, far right-wing anti-Communist, anti-reality organization, the John Birch Society, used the same phraseology and ideas, but this time it was an international Communist cabal that was going to destroy Christmas.[6] Although mostly forgotten now, the John Birch Society had millions of active members in the 1950s, so apparently there were lots of believers in the War on Christmas then. Some of the claims that the pandemic was fake asserted that it was just made up as a part of the War on Christmas. Similarly, the twenty-first-century opponents of legal rights for lesbian, gay, bisexual, transgender, and questioning (LGBTQ) people recycled the odd invented menace of unisex public bathrooms that was created by opponents of women's rights a half century before.

Other conspiracy theories that are held by a small number of very enthusiastic adherents exist in a continuity. Some people cling to the idea of the earth being flat—this belief is easily disproved by many scientific means as well as many kinds of visual proof, such as photos of the earth from a spacecraft or of the horizon from an airplane. The Flat Earth Wiki is an actual thing, so somebody is using it as a, umm, reference tool. The persistence of this belief in any media is astounding; the Greeks figured out Earth was round more than 2,500 years ago. In the 1800s, astronomer Fredrich von Struve spent forty years of travel and geometry to definitely determine the circumference of the round planet—he came up with 40,008,696 miles as his figure, whereas NASA's current satellite-measured figure is 40,007,017 miles, barely different at all (Winchester, 2021).

If the flat earth theory seems way too "mainstream" to you, then you might be interested in the theory that the earth is expanding and that the continents fit together not because of plate tectonics but because the earth used to be tiny and the surface smooth. Thanks to YouTube, this false theory is becoming more widespread. Another baffling theory is something called Phantom Time Theory, which is based on the idea that large parts of history did not actually happen, or something like that; it's so convoluted, it is really hard to figure what the followers are going for. And anti-Semitism is always popular in conspiracy theories, with a member of the Washington, D.C. city council being a prominent supporter of the idea that an international Jewish cabal is using weather control machines to take over cities (Jamison, 2018; Jamison & Straus, 2018). And so forth.

The rise of the World Wide Web was greeted with many optimistic claims that it would invigorate democratic governance around the world. Instead, democracy has been suffering net declines in terms of political rights and civil liberties around the world for a decade and a half, due in large part to the impacts of the Internet (Freedom House, 2019). The next chapter explores the politics and policies that have directly and indirectly shaped, improved, or reduced information literacy, and the ways that such policies have developed.

🗩 CHAPTER 7 GUIDING QUESTIONS

1. How has the control of information historically contributed to the subjugation of different groups of people?
2. In this chapter, we state, "Information literacy has power. It is power. It has been used as a means of social control and of revolution." What are some examples of this power?
3. What arguments might be made for censorship of information? How might you disagree with these arguments?
4. How does a lack of practice in information literacy contribute to corporate power?
5. How has social media aided government and corporate control of information?

NOTES

1. When England still had dragons.
2. Internet sources also credit the first English dictionary to Confucius, Mark Twain, Dorothy Parker, George Takei, Grumpy Cat, and Billie Eilish.

3. Way back when $41,000,000 was real money.
4. If you wish to know about Comstock and his impact on US society from the perspective of our field, he is one of the primary villains of our book *Foundations of Information Policy* (Jaeger & Taylor, 2019). We're not repeating his story here because we used up all our Comstock jokes in that book. Some of them are pretty good.
5. Yes, we can hear some of you muttering about physical books being a thing of the past. You're wrong.
6. Pro-tip: if the phrase "international cabal" factors into an idea, it may just be a conspiracy theory.

Literacy Politics and Literacy Policies

THE POLITICS OF INFORMATION LITERACY

Many aspects of the founding of the US were unique. For our purposes, the fact that the founding documents place significant emphasis on information issues is most notable. The Constitution and the Bill of Rights are full of information issues, from the creation of the United States Postal Service (USPS), the establishment of the census, the protection of intellectual property, and access to government information in the Constitution to the protections of freedom of expression, press, and assembly in the Bill of Rights. However, neither document directly addresses an issue that is pretty important to information literacy: the Constitution does not include the word *privacy*.[1]

In fact, if you were to read James Madison's notes from the Constitutional Convention, originally published in 1840, you would find that information issues are frequently key topics of discussion. Particularly, the founders worried about how much the new system of government that they were creating would rely on informed voters and leaders. Madison, the primary author of the Constitution as well as the notetaker,[2] was concerned about the majority trying to enforce its opinion on the rest of the nation and about individuals gaining too much power, which he memorably labeled "the tyranny of the majority." He was hardly alone in such fears among the people debating and crafting the Constitution; hence, the enormous number of checks and balances in the document, ambition counteracting ambition.

There would likely have not been a revolution if the colonies were not already uniquely literate for their time. Visitors to the colonies remarked on the reading culture, high levels of literacy for the time, and wealth of discussion of ideas (J. S. Brown & Duguid, 2002). Thomas Paine's *Common Sense* sold more than five hundred thousand copies just in 1776— it is the best-selling American book in terms of proportion of population. In the time of the Revolution and the founding of the US republic, documents—pamphlets, newspapers, declarations—served to create a new sense of community that replaced the foundation of sovereigns and subjects with self-governance around shared ideals, practices, and interests (B. Anderson, 1991).

Literacy, in its broadest sense, has been a political issue as long as education has been an issue of public discourse. Educational leaders, especially those at Ivy League schools, have been self-righteously decrying declines in literacy among Americans basically as long as America has been its own country and complaining about the declining skills of the students entering their hallowed halls since pretty much those halls were built (Daniels, 1983). General literacy skills have been tracked since the end of World War II, primarily using standardized tests that show very little about what a student knows or has learned (Berliner & Biddle, 1995). Public attention to literacy may have peaked in the 1950s, with the *Why Johnny Can't Read* (Flesch, 1955) phenomenon, which posited that the Soviet Union had put a satellite in space before the US because of poor science literacy skills resulting from an inept public education system.

In 1961 an interest group called the Council for Basic Education released a report cheerfully entitled *Tomorrow's Illiterates*, projecting that the average American student was quickly devolving into a slobbering heap capable of communicating only by throwing rocks. In 1983 *A Nation at Risk: The Imperative for Education Reform* (National Committee on Excellence in Education, 1983) warned of the threat of "the rising tide of mediocrity" (n.p.). The attacking of the literacy of American students soon had turned into a full-fledged industry of consultants, lobbyists, and public interest groups, despite the lack of any real evidence of such catastrophes.

From a policy perspective, it is far easier to attack the educational system or the literacy of the population for cheap political points than to produce actual legislation to improve information literacy, which the political history of the US reflects. It has become more difficult as the importance of information literacy has grown. Since the early twentieth century, literacy has become a skill to help children prepare for the uncertainty of being an adult in a world guaranteed to be very different than the one they were born into. As ICTs now shape every aspect of everyday life, information literacy has become exponentially more important as a policy problem, but also more all-encompassing, and therefore harder to address.

As a result, most politicians simply do not try to grapple with information literacy. When attempts to address some aspect of literacy are made, they primarily focus on physical access to technologies. Leaders tend to confuse possession of technologies as being interchangeable with the abilities to use and understand the technologies and the information to which they provide access (Jaeger, Paquette, & Simmons, 2010). Otherwise, the policy focus on information literacy by governments around the world has primarily been to encourage educational institutions to spend more time on literacy (McTavish, 2009).

As a result, policy discussions of information literacy generally occur among nongovernmental organizations (NGOs). As was discussed earlier, the ALA Presidential Commission on Information Literacy was created in 1987, issuing a report in 1989—with the shockingly creative title of *The Presidential Commission on Information Literacy: Final Report*—that emphasized the growing importance of information literacy, educational and economic opportunities derived from information literacy, and the need for information literacy to become a key focus of education. The report also prompted the creation of a coalition of the National Forum on Information Literacy, a network of professional and educational organizations, and some business organizations, collaborating on the promotion of greater attention to information literacy and the creation of policy about information literacy.

Such information literacy policy has not been forthcoming, sadly. In 2009 President Barack Obama proclaimed October 2009 as National Information Literacy Awareness Month (NILAM).[3] Although the proclamation said all the right things, such as "though we may know how to find the information we need, we must also know how to evaluate it" and "we now live in a world where anyone can publish an opinion or perspective, whether true or not, and have that opinion amplified within the information marketplace" (Obama,

2009, n.p.), that is where information literacy policy at the federal level in the US pretty much ends. And begins.

The US has instead attempted to address information literacy as a problem that would be solved by policies that increase the availability of technology. This philosophy predates the ideas of information literacy and digital inclusion and even the earliest version of the Internet (Jaeger, Bertot, Thompson et al., 2012). The Communications Act of 1934 (48 Stat. 1064) focused on increasing the availability of wire and radio communication technologies, without addressing issues of literacy related to the new technologies. The gaps between availability of and literacy about a new technology were made painfully apparent a few years later when an exquisitely produced radio play of H. G. Wells's story *The War of the Worlds,* masterminded by Orson Welles,[4] caused much concern because many listeners mistakenly assumed they were hearing real reporting of an actual invasion of the US.

The Telecommunications Act of 1996 (47 USC 225 et seq.) explicitly focused on promoting universal access to communications technology, which by then included the Internet, by making access more available and more affordable, though once again neglecting considerations of information literacy. The creation of the National Telecommunications and Information Administration (NTIA) gave operational capacity to the focus on availability and affordability. Soon after the passage of the 1996 law, broadband and mobile technologies became commonplace, increasing the importance of access and affordability, but even more so of literacy. Access was framed as "haves" and "have nots" rather than anything more nuanced, having access being made politically equivalent to understanding the necessary information and ICTs (Bertot, 2003).

Government programs that could have been focused on supporting information literacy have avoided the challenge and instead focused entirely on availability of ICTs as the solution to all problems (K. M. Thompson et al., 2014). The educational rate (E-rate) program was created out of the Telecommunications Act to assist schools and libraries in acquiring ICTs and paying for Internet connectivity. Though the program has distributed hundreds of millions of dollars since the year 2000 (Jaeger, McClure, & Bertot, 2005; Jaeger & Yan, 2009), it completely ignores issues of information literacy (K. M. Thompson et al., 2014).

The failure of one of NTIA's flagship programs in the early 2000s demonstrated the utter foolishness of ignoring information literacy. Community technology centers (CTCs) were established in many communities across the country where there were gaps in Internet access due to inequities of connectivity or financial barriers to access; these CTCs were basically rows of computers with a minder to make sure no one walked off with the computers (Strover, 2003; Strover et al., 2004). What CTCs lacked, however, were any attempts to provide training or instruction in using the computers, meaning that people who did not have access previously were left to their own devices to figure out how computers and the Internet worked. Not surprisingly, CTCs failed spectacularly; people without Internet access at home invariably chose to go to the local public library, which offered instruction and educational support along with the computers (Jaeger & Fleischmann, 2007).

A few years after CTCs, the federal government launched the website DigitalLiteracy. gov, which served the interesting dual purposes of providing resources and training materials to people who were teaching others to use the Internet and of providing self-teaching materials for people learning to use the Internet on their own. The majority of the content on the site when it launched, in fact, was directed at this latter audience, raising the obvious question of how on earth someone unfamiliar with the Internet would magically know about the site and have the skills to reach it, so that they could then learn how to use the Internet.

Lack of literacy about government is strongly connected to an overall lack of digital literacy (Jaeger & Thompson, 2003, 2004), so this leap is especially unrealistic.

Even policymaking entities within the government seem to be conspicuously ignoring information literacy. As an example, the DOE's Office of Educational Technology exists to establish policy and vision for the roles of ICTs in all levels of education in the US. The agency's 2017 *National Educational Technology Plan* mentions information literacy only once, with no exploration of what is meant by the term, as an element of the discussion of digital citizenship.

This large-scale ineptitude in terms of information literacy is perhaps not unrelated to the lack of interest in or awareness of these issues by the people making the policies. The most famous example is probably that of former Senator Ted Stevens, then serving as the chair of the committee overseeing telecommunications regulations, who awkwardly tried to explain the Internet as a "series of tubes" with little trucks delivering messages through the tubes (Series of tubes, n.d.).

On the other side of ignorance, the political leaders in the US who have been enthusiastic about the Internet have often been uncritically so, arguing against regulations of Internet-related businesses to maximize the competitiveness and profitability of such companies (Jaeger & Taylor, 2019). Vice President Al Gore's relationship to the Internet is best remembered for his inability to find the right words to explain his enthusiastic support of Internet policy and funding in the 1990s, leading many people to think that he somehow claimed to have invented the Internet in 2000. However, his leadership in that area really was extensive and was devoted to championing unfettered growth of Internet-related businesses and widespread adoption of Internet technologies by all sectors of society, including ushering government agencies online without a discernible strategy for being there (Jaeger & Bertot, 2011). He even considered charging citizens to visit government websites as a way for agencies to make money (Jaeger & Taylor, 2019).

The first US presidential campaign in which the Internet was addressed clearly as a political issue and employed effectively as a tool of politics was in 2008. Barack Obama's campaign emphasized information issues and heavily relied on Facebook, MySpace, YouTube, Twitter, and Flickr for campaign activities, sending more than one billion emails and organizing tens of thousands of campaign activities online (Jaeger, Paquette, & Simmons, 2010).

Once in office, Obama and his team embraced the Al Gore mode, cheerleading for the industry and uncritically adopting new technologies—most notably social media, open data, and big data—into government operations, seemingly without sufficient consideration of the implications (Bertot, Gorham, Jaeger, Sarin, & Choi, 2014; Bertot, Gorham, Jaeger, & Sarin, 2014). In his post-presidency memoir, Obama acknowledged the ramifications of his viewing the Internet in an entirely positive light rather than considering "how malleable this technology would prove to be; how quickly it would be absorbed by commercial interests and wielded by entrenched powers; how readily it could be used not to unify people but to distract or divide them" (Obama, 2020, p. 130). Thanks, Obama.

Society gives context to literacy because it is learned through social relationships and cultivated through social cues and framing (E. Long, 1992). Also, a great deal about literacy is valued in a society by the way it is addressed in policies and politics. And though we wish we could say that policy has become more attuned to and thoughtful about information literacy, we would be lying. With some friends, we once wrote, "Along with a muddled policy and economic approach that serves to hinder digital literacy and digital inclusion, the policy approach to actively promoting digital literacy and digital inclusion in the United States is also contradictory and problematic" (K. M. Thompson et al., 2014, pp. 62–63). Harsh, but accurate. Three fun things to consider with that quote: first, we were talking specifically about just digital literacy, not the bigger and mostly ignored concerns of information literacy; second, the president at the time—Barack Obama—was a skilled and enthusiastic supporter of new technologies; and third, things are now worse than when we wrote that sentence.

INFORMATION LITERACY MEETS POLITICIANS, 2020-STYLE

Information literacy itself is a sociopolitical construct, which arises "as a contested social construction, rather than as a naturally occurring phenomenon" (Elmborg, 2016, p. ix); 2020 demonstrated that fairly clearly. In the summer of 2020, with a global pandemic raging and the world's economy in free fall, accompanied by a burgeoning new social justice movement in the US, the Senate held a hearing to question the leaders of four of the most valuable, well-known, and influential companies in the world. Talking to Amazon, Microsoft, Apple, and Facebook about substantive business and regulation issues could be a very productive contribution to policymaking processes. For a frame of reference for the power and scope of these companies, at the time of the hearing, Amazon stock sold for the astounding rate of more than $3,100 a share (Macrotrends, 2020).

The hearing, however, was far less than productive. Whenever US legislators hold hearings of this type, several unhelpful and embarrassing things invariably occur. At least one legislator will ask the head of one company about the products or strategies of another company (for example, asking the head of Apple about Twitter's business model or the head of Facebook about how to use Fortnite), several will openly admit to not understanding the issues at hand, at least one other will inadvertently make evident that they have no idea what is going on, and several will incorrectly complain that the companies are biased against conservative viewpoints. What could—and should—be a valuable policymaking tool descends into haplessness. Instead, Internet policy in the US seems put together in the way that a group of sugar-addled toddlers might try to assemble a large, complex Lego set without instructions or even a picture. Sadly, this disheartening performance has been recurring in the US Congress since about the time that the web became browsable; in 2020, however, the occupant of the White House possessed an impressive level of technological incoherence, even for a politician.

Since starting his presidential campaign, Trump evidenced a strange duality to the Internet. He has mastered the use of social media as a political tool, employing Twitter as an extremely effective means of communicating directly with his supporters, pushing his agenda, and marginalizing his perceived enemies, such as the traditional media and politicians who do not agree with him. On the other hand, his statements about the functionality of the Internet and the nature of Internet policy have consistently demonstrated a thorough lack of understanding of even the most basic issues, including repeatedly pushing for widespread adoption of nonexistent 6G technologies (Jaeger & Taylor, 2019).

Without more consistent information literacy among US political leaders, Internet-related companies have been given, by default, wide discretion in the ways that they collect and handle personal information, the ways that they monitor and disseminate content in their systems, the roles of algorithms in their systems, and other key issues that significantly impact what information users are exposed to and what happens to information about the users themselves. One can look at this sad history of the past twenty-five or so years of leadership in information policy in the US simply as partisan politics in a highly polarized society, with one side overly enthused about new technologies and the other wary of them.

Such a reality becomes even sadder when one considers the opportunities that the technologies of this era offer. The Internet and related technologies now allow citizens to set political and social agendas and participate in politics at the local and global levels in previously unthinkable ways (Kaplan & Haenlein, 2010). If policy had adequately prioritized information literacy, the value of the Internet and the information it contains could have been far greater than what has resulted instead. A later section of this book will focus on the gigantic mess of online misinformation, disinformation, and information illiteracy that has been caused by policy failures and the extraordinary consequences in all aspects of human interaction.

🗨 CHAPTER 8 GUIDING QUESTIONS

1. What might a federal information literacy policy look like? Is it desirable? Why or why not?
2. What are some of the negative ramifications of governmental policy decisions that focus only on physical information access and not intellectual access?
3. We mention in this chapter that society gives context to literacy because it is learned through social relationships and cultivated through social cues and framing (E. Long, 1992). What does the Internet society contribute to literacy (and information literacy specifically)?
4. How does a lack of regulation of technology corporations contribute to information illiteracy?
5. What connections do you see between the attitudes that the writers of the US Declaration of Independence and the Constitution had about information and the attitudes reflected in federal information policy today?

NOTES

1. Other words missing from the Constitution that would make it more interesting if added: quokka, flapdoodle, anteater, fandangle, collywobbles, rapscallion, whelk, clowder, geranium, and appaloosa.
2. Perhaps not coincidental.
3. It was not significant enough for the government to even give it an acronym, but it makes us feel better to pretend that they did.
4. No relation. At least, we assume so, because they spelled their last names differently.

Why Libraries?

LIBRARIES? WHY?

"Tumblr Is Rolling Out an Internet Literacy Initiative to Help Combat Misinformation and Cyberbullying" (Alexander, 2020)

"Facebook to Label Posts about Voting from Political Candidates" (Mihalcik, 2020)

"Coronavirus: Twitter Will Label Covid-19 Fake News" (Sardarizadeh, 2020)

These are just a few of the headlines pronouncing technology-driven solutions to misinformation that have graced news stories during the past year. In case you didn't follow Donald Trump on Twitter when he was still allowed on Twitter, you could hardly come across a tweet that didn't have the label "Some or all of the content shared in this tweet is disputed and might be misleading about an election or other civic process." Google has added fact-checking to Google Image searches and YouTube (Cohen, 2020). It would be easy to think by reading these stories that we all just need to sit back and let social media and the Internet take care of the problem. Of course, as most of us can attest, false information still gets shared. At best, these are stopgap measures to address misinformation and disinformation; at worst, they are exacerbating the problem. Geoffrey Fowler (2020) characterizes the tags that were placed on Trump's tweets as "the equivalent of Big Tech slapping the 'PARENTAL ADVISORY' labels from album covers on the president of the United States"—and we all know how effective those warnings are.

So what are we to do? Should we study how previous crises of misinformation were handled by the media and look for solutions there? Should we look to technology and media companies to figure out best practices in slowing the spread of conspiracy theories? Should we attempt to address underlying systemic inequities that are driving the need to search for false news? Should we ban all social media and start training pigeons for our communication needs? The answer to all these questions is, well, probably.[1] But what of libraries? In many of the media- and technology-driven solutions to false information, information literacy is noticeably absent. What role do we, and should we, as information professionals have in addressing these problems? In this chapter, we will consider why libraries are well suited to work with the media, technology, and psychology fields to address the roots of much of the misinformation floating around today.

In earlier chapters, we have established the work that libraries are doing already, along with the political and economic environments within which they are working.[2] It's possible that this background is enough to convince you that libraries are uniquely well suited to empowering citizens to practice information literacy to address misinformation and disinformation. In case you're not convinced, though, or, more likely, you're tired of refuting constant refrains that libraries are dead because of Google, this chapter explores three main topics: the purpose of libraries in the modern era, the connection of libraries' purposes to information literacy, and the reasons that libraries are unique in the information literacy education space. Finally, we will conclude with how all this misinformation and disinformation signals the imminent collapse of society.[3]

THE RELATIONSHIP OF LIBRARIES' MISSIONS TO INFORMATION LITERACY

Maybe it's best to start this section with a grand question: what is a library? We'll answer this question by consulting prominent professional organizations' visions for libraries, as well as some key definitions in library scholarship.

ALA's (2017) strategic plan lists as one of its goals that the library should be "a hub of community engagement and continual learning: a place to form the critical thinking skills fundamental to learning in a technologically evolving world, to access information, and to create and share new knowledge" (p. 3). IFLA's (2019) current strategic plan lists the organization's values, two of which explain the perceived purpose of libraries: "The belief that people, communities and organisations need universal and equitable access to information, ideas and works of imagination for their social, educational, cultural, democratic and economic well-being" and "The conviction that delivery of high-quality library and information services helps guarantee that access" (n.p.). ACRL's (2019a) revised strategic plan describes academic libraries as playing

> a critical role in building diverse, welcoming, and equitable communities; developing inclusive organizations, spaces, and services; guarding against policies and practices that intentionally or unintentionally create racial inequalities; embodying diversity in the profession; and creating conditions so that all users are respected and supported in their intellectual dialogues and pursuits. Librarians and their colleagues design services that provide scholars and learners the unfettered ability to create, access, evaluate, and use knowledge. (n.p.)

In its 2016–2020 strategic plan, the LOC (2015) describes its central mission as "to provide Congress, and then the federal government, and the American people with a rich, diverse, and enduring source of knowledge that can be relied upon to inform, inspire, and engage them, and support their intellectual and creative endeavors" (p. 9).

Jacobs and Berg (2011) have performed a similar exercise in looking at libraries' founding documents; they find that

> ambitious goals of empowering people and enabling citizens, communities, and nations may seem out of scope for librarians who are perceived to be gatekeepers, tutors, or

helpers (Polger & Okamoto, 2010). The existence of the ALA Core Values statement, however, reminds us that part of our purview as professional librarians includes working toward values such as democracy, diversity, education and lifelong learning, the public good and social responsibility. (p. 385)

In library scholarship, one of the more famous articulations of library philosophy is Ranganathan's (1931) five laws of librarianship: (1) Books are for use. (2) Every reader his book. (3) Every book its reader. (4) Save the time of the reader. (5) The library is a growing organism.

Kuhlthau (1993) articulates that the objective of library and information services is

to increase access to resources and information. Basic access is provided through selection, acquisition and organization of resources . . . Increased or enhanced access is provided primarily through two services, reference and instruction. Enhanced access encompasses intellectual as well as physical access. Physical access addresses the location of resources and information. Intellectual access addresses interpretation of information and ideas within resources. (p. xvii; cf. Whitworth, 2014, pp. 28-29)

Lankes (2016a) describes the main raison d'être for libraries (both historically and today) as clustering around a few themes, specifically:

- Collective Buying Agent
- Economic Stimulus
- Center of Learning
- Safety Net
- Steward of Cultural Heritage
- Third Space
- Cradle of Democracy
- Symbol of Community Aspirations (p. 8)

In a separate text, Lankes (2016b) summarizes the roles of librarians: "Librarians are defined by three things: our mission to improve society through facilitating knowledge creation; our means of facilitation to achieve this mission; and the values we bring to our tasks. We share each of these things separately with professionals in other fields. It is in combining all three that librarianship is unique" (p. 19). What then is a library? Lankes (2019) describes the concept of a library as one changing from the notion of "a library as a set of resources for a community to access, to the library as a supporter of building knowledge locally" (n.p.).

As a collection, these definitions articulate a mission for libraries that encompasses transformational lifelong learning in the form of access to quality information and to instruction on how to use this information, the provision of equitable access to information, and access to resources and services under the auspices of building a more democratic society. A library is situated within its community and is of the community. Even in Ranganathan's almost century-old conception, and despite the text's focus on books, there is also an emphasis on serving the reader, on efficient transfer of information and access, and on the library as being in a state of constant change. We will spend the next few paragraphs looking at each of these goals in the context of information literacy.

In earlier chapters, we've already established that many public libraries use lifelong learning as a way to conceptualize their information literacy-related practices. We think three other studies might add to this evidence that opportunities for information literacy practice are important for all ages. Young children, even as young as age 3,

> are capable of planning and reflecting, key aspects of critical thinking. As planners, children begin with a goal and decide where to work, what materials to use, how to manipulate them, whether to work alone or with others, and so on. When reflecting, children do more than remember what they have done: They apply the lessons learned. (Epstein, 2008, p. 40; cf. Heider, 2009, p. 514)

These are critical first steps to practicing information literacy (Heider, 2009). School-age children practice different methods of information literacy both within and outside the classroom, but the non-school modes of information literacy are not typically acknowledged in formal school settings (McTavish, 2009). Older adults continue to practice information literacy, but the role of social interactions in information transfer and the need for assistive technologies, become more central to the practice (Williamson & Asla, 2009). All of these age-related information literacy practices point to the need for libraries (public, school, and others) to support lifelong learning.

Information literacy is a core element of equitable access to information—and existing inequities can also impact information literacy. At least one study revealed that in Florida, socioeconomic status, gender, and race were all correlated with lower scores on a standardized ICT assessment (Ritzhaupt et al., 2013). Library information literacy instruction and opportunities for practice can mitigate inequalities. Conversely, practice with information literacy in different contexts allows for greater educational, political, and economic opportunity. To be sure, some significant issues accompany such statements because of the ways in which these spaces are structured—the information literacy practices required of these spaces are tied up in historical racism and socioeconomic classism, so we want to be careful about placing certain information literacy practices in a hierarchy of importance; we will return to these issues in chapter 15.

Finally, numerous studies have established the link between information literacy and democracy. Kim and Yang's (2016) study of Korean high school students found that "an adolescent who can critically understand and effectively evaluate online information is more likely to become an active civic participant than one who lacks such skills" (p. 438). Lenker (2016) notes that much of the political polarization that currently plagues US society is due to the partisan news outlets that are increasingly the source of political information—and that partisan information literacy practices are to blame. Jacobs and Berg (2011) point to foundational international information literacy documents such as the *Alexandria Proclamation* as evidence of the connection between the practice of information literacy and the ability to be an informed citizen. All things considered, both the type of information consumed and the ability to engage with it seem to be essential aspects of making informed political decisions.

SO WHY NOT LIBRARIES?

Considering the ways that information literacy practice intersects with core aspects of libraries' missions, why would anyone not consider libraries central to the process of increasing information literacy practice in the general populace? There are those who believe that the ways libraries teach information literacy are ineffective (M. C. Sullivan, 2019b) or that librarians are not outspoken enough in providing education on information evaluation

(Dempsey, 2017). In his article "Information Literacy Is Dead: The Role of Librarians in a Post-Truth World," B. Johnson (2017) asserts that "analysis and critical thinking were a feeble defense, easily overrun by a torrent of opinion and raw emotion" (n.p.). Libraries have long "extoled the virtues of information literacy . . . [and] insisted that facts are important. We have insisted that it is critical to recognize where information is needed, to evaluate it, and to effectively use it. We failed" (n.p.).

Despite these arguments, "why not libraries" usually has very little to do with anything libraries are doing wrong or not enough. Outside the LIS field, in most abstract discussions of improving information literacy practices, neither the term *information literacy* nor libraries are mentioned at all. Webber and Johnston (2017) assert that "progress in the development of information literacy (IL) has been hindered by tendencies such as: denying that information literacy is even a subject, paying exclusive attention to forces outside the discipline and forming information literacy silos" (p. 156). At a 2017 media conference, Lowrie and Truslow "heard repeatedly from the journalists, both formally and informally, that they had never considered librarians as potential partners in addressing this [misinformation] issue" (p. 6; cf. M. C. Sullivan, 2019b, p. 98).

We can take the recent hubbub about fake news as a lens into this phenomenon. Fake news as a concept isn't new, though admittedly there are some new elements to its spread, including the role of social media. Regardless, the topic is suddenly everywhere; it is being blamed for everything from increased political polarization to the decline of democracy (and these accusations aren't without some merit, though we don't think they tell the whole story). Because of the surrounding fervor, suddenly everyone is talking about how to address misinformation and disinformation. Suggestions range from technological solutions to changes in the media environment to better understandings of cognition. We'll take some of these proposed solutions and dig a little deeper. First, the need for direct action by big technology companies.

Technology Companies

Technology companies are addressing their role in misinformation with several strategies. One strategy includes placing labels and warnings on posts deemed misleading or hate speech. Facebook and Twitter have experimented with labeling posts that discourage voting, promote hate speech, or cite false election results (Dwoskin & Romm, 2019; Lerman, 2020; Lerman & Timberg, 2020; Yurieff, 2020). Technology companies are also working to develop new tools that aim to assist fact-checking; CrowdTangle, for example, is "'increasing its focus on misinformation and the part we can play in helping prevent it. Our goal is to make it fast and easy to research public content'" (Macaraeg, 2019, n.p.). The tool, in beta and currently available only to Facebook's fact-checking partners, enables journalists to search by keyword, hashtag, or URL, filter by a number of measures—platform, time frame, and the like—and sort by such factors as number of interactions and followers. At least one media outlet (Rappler, a Philippine online news website that uses social media to distribute its content) is using the tool to "assess viral posts and see which channels amplify dubious posts" (Macaraeg, 2019, n.p.).

Some social media sites are banning ads that are associated with certain types of political information. In fall 2020, Facebook made the decision to stop running any new political ads on its site in the week preceding the 2020 presidential election (Isaac, 2020). To clarify, this policy applied only to new ads:

If you saw an ad yesterday, you could see that same ad again today. And in fact, campaigns running these ads can distribute them as far, as wide as they choose. They can change their spending. They can change their targeting. They just can't change the message. Facebook says it's doing this because there just may not be enough time in these final days of the election to contest any new claims that are made in ads. (Bond, 2020, n.p.)

This action might not seem like a big deal—and really, considering how close to the election Facebook made this decision, in the grand scheme of things, it's not—but considering the great lengths the company went to before this decision to argue that it wouldn't be pulling political ads, it seems like a significant change of heart (Hachman, 2020). Google (which owns YouTube) also allows political ads but not microtargeting (Rosoff, 2019). And, as of 2019, Twitter and TikTok don't allow political advertising at all (Conger, 2019; Perez, 2019).

In addition to their increasing proactivity in addressing pockets of misinformation, some tech companies have engaged in user education. Facebook has published a help guide, "Tips to Spot False News," and research suggests that viewing the tips may make people less likely to believe a false headline—though this effect on behavior isn't long-term (Guess, Lerner et al., 2020). Google recently invested $3 million in the Poynter Institute's MediaWise program, which will produce a media literacy classroom curriculum and an online teen fact-checking initiative (Poynter Institute, 2018). Twitter is partnering with UNESCO with money going to NGOs focusing on media literacy, to distribution of a "Teaching and Learning with Twitter" handbook in multiple languages, and to providing visibility on the company's network for media literacy campaigns (Costello, 2019). It's easy to be cynical about these efforts—social media got quite a bit of bad press after the 2016 election after all, and purporting to make more of an effort against false information can only help. That said, these are decisions being made ostensibly to improve public discourse.

Media

A second solution to the proliferation of false news, and one that is frequently bandied about in public discourse, is that we as a society need a new focus on media literacy. A 2019 Pew study found that the majority of Americans (68 percent) think "made-up news and information greatly impacts Americans' confidence in government institutions," while 54 percent say "it is having a major impact on our confidence in each other" (Mitchell et al., 2019, p. 3). In assigning blame, partisan differences are stark. The same Pew study found that "Republicans are nearly three times as likely as Democrats to say journalists create a lot of it (58% vs. 20%)" (p. 6). Republicans "also place more blame on activist groups, with about three-quarters (73%) saying these groups create a lot, close to twice the rate of Democrats (38%)" (p. 6). Partisanship aside, more than half of both Republicans and Democrats believe that politicians are to blame for a lot of misinformation and disinformation.

Members of both parties see the media as having a responsibility to find a solution, though this viewpoint is more common among Republicans (69 percent) than Democrats (42 percent) (Mitchell et al., 2019, p. 7). Despite this difference it's clear that Americans and the media see a role for journalists in lessening the incidence of misinformation. Some media companies are already addressing these issues. Most of these companies employ one of two methods: using their platform to talk about misinformation and provide tips for how to avoid it, or running programs specifically designed to educate the public about media literacy. The first method is exemplified by a *Wired Magazine* article that tells readers "how to spot phony images and online propaganda" (Grey Ellis, 2020); a piece in the *MIT Technology Review* that purports to help readers protect themselves from misinformation (Ohlheiser, 2020); and a *New York Times* article (Yee, 2020) that offers a guide with resources on fake news targeted to older adults.

The *Washington Post* blog *Answer Sheet* has been offering weekly "lessons from the nonprofit News Literacy Project, which aims to teach students how to distinguish between what's real and fake in the age of digital communication and a president who routinely denounces real news as 'fake'" (Strauss, 2020, n.p.). It's possible that media literacy education like this works. Though focused on a topic slightly different from fake news, research by Schmuck and von Sikorski (2020) found that news reports that mentioned the problem of social bots without also discussing ways of mitigating their effect made people feel an increased lack of control about their ability to protect themselves against negative impacts, but when the information was partnered with supporting literacy, people felt less threatened. Whether they were actually less likely to be deceived by these bots is unclear.

The second type of media-led literacy instruction is user education via games, standardized indicators of news quality, and programming. Examples include the following:

- **A game developed by the Finnish Public Broadcasting Company Yle** encourages users to think like a troll through a mock "messaging app style conversation on a virtual smartphone" (Lomas, 2019, n.p.). The game includes "'authentic social media content' that viewers may find disturbing . . . you'll see examples of Islamophobic slogans and memes that have actually been spread on social media" (Lomas, 2019, n.p.). The game then encourages users to take actions such as "seeding . . . conspiracy theory memes on social media; the exploitation of real news events to spread fake claims; microtargeting of hateful content at different demographics and platforms; and the use of paid bots to amplify propaganda so that hateful views appear more widely held than they really are" (Lomas, 2019, n.p.). At the conclusion of a week in game mode, you get rated on how well your troll tactics spread and then the game shows you "contextual information on the influencing methods demonstrated—putting the activity you've just participated in into wider context" (Lomas, 2019, n.p.).
- **The Trust Project,** led by journalist Sally Lehrman, has developed eight Trust Indicators through user input and with leaders of more than one hundred news outlets. These indicators work as "standardized disclosures about the news outlet, the journalist, and the commitments behind their work—to make it easy to identify trustworthy news" ("The Trust Project Explained," 2020, n.p.). The project has worked with social media, search, and news sites to integrate their indicators on news stories and websites. "When Facebook launched its process to index news Pages, they worked with the Trust Project to make it easy for any publisher to add optional information about their Page, such as links to fact-checking, ethics and corrections policies, which are all part of the 'Best Practices' Trust Indicator" (Trust Project, 2018, n.p.).
- **The Dallas Public Library (DPL)** and reporters at the *Dallas Morning News* collaborated to host an eight-week program, "Storytellers without Borders,"

designed to teach principles of community journalism to high school students (Banks, 2016).

Other Fields

Some seek solutions or explanations for misinformation by searching scholarship in fields as diverse as psychology, political science, and education. Indeed, there's certainly much to learn from interdisciplinarity. In a report summarizing presentations from academic institutions, technology companies, and fact-checking organizations, the authors discuss "developing multidisciplinary community-wide shared resources for conducting academic research on the presence and dissemination of misinformation on social media platforms" as one of three immediate steps that need to be taken in fighting false news (Lazer et al., 2017, p. 3). We can draw from the extensive research on psychological reasons for believing misinformation, including confirmation bias (Nickerson, 1998), motivated reasoning (Lenker, 2016), and cognitive dissonance (Festinger, 1962). M. C. Sullivan (2019b) notes the extensive literature in political science that might inform solutions to misinformation, including topics such as "levels of political knowledge and participation . . . well-known measures of polarization . . . and the extensive literature on the consequences of exposure to misinformation" (p. 95). Likewise, scholars from the field of education have much to teach us about the process of lateral reading—or engaging in fact-checking as you scan a news article, rather than reading information and investigating further only after finishing (Wineburg & McGrew, 2019; see also the Digital Polarization Initiative of the American Association of State Colleges and Universities' American Democracy Project, as described in Kamenetz, 2017).

WHAT'S WRONG WITH THIS PICTURE?

If the preceding were taken at face value, it would seem that a combination of media-driven education campaigns, social media algorithms and rules, and a little help from the academy should suffice for ensuring that people are able to effectively practice information literacy. This is pretty obviously not the case. For the most part, the efforts just described wouldn't hurt. (Though there is a case to be made that some of the social media labels have the opposite effect on certain users; see Christenson et al., 2020). But even if these solutions help, they are undoubtedly not the whole solution.

For one thing, there are disincentives for for-profit companies to engage in some of these efforts, so it's not entirely clear how long they will remain interested. There are actual costs related to developing tools and devoting staff time to these issues, but the real cost comes at the risk of alienating users and readers. The *Wall Street Journal*'s editorial page devoted an entire article to maligning the labeling of misinformation by tech companies ("The Social Media Fact-Check Farce," 2020). And Parler, a social media network under the auspices of limited content moderation, threatens Twitter's market of conservative users (Newhouse, 2020).

It's also unclear how well many of these solutions actually work. Although some studies do show initial promise that labeling social media posts leads to less trust of misinformation (Clayton et al., 2019; M. C. Sullivan, 2019b, 2019c), others, as mentioned, demonstrate otherwise. And while some people praise the restriction of political ads on social media, to put these actions in perspective, Stewart (2019) discusses the way that the relatively super-ficial ad policy change disguises the other negative actions on these sites:

> When Google is talking about political microtargeting, what it's not talking about is how YouTube's recommended and autoplay features push people toward more radicalized and extremist content. While we're debating whether or not Facebook should permit politicians to lie in ads, what we're not discussing is how fake news, memes, and dis-information spread organically on the platform. Twitter is banning political ads, but it has a much bigger challenge in addressing how the platform is used to spread hate, the president's use of his Twitter account, and the abuse and harassment that happens on its platform every day. (n.p.)

There is also the enormous problem of lack of trust in the media. In a 2018 survey, the majority of Americans thought that the news media favored one side or another when talking about political or social issues and don't believe the media will admit it when they make mistakes (Gottfried et al., 2018). The same survey showed sharp partisan divides in the role the media play in either critiquing politicians or interfering in their roles. One won-ders, when people doubt the messengers, is education about misinformation that comes from these same people really going to land? Finally, at least one study has shown that media literacy alone, without the support of other literacies, may not do much (Jones-Jang et al., 2021). According to boyd (2018), it is possible that crude versions of media literacy— this source is better than that source; mocking comments leveled at conservative media— may be doing more harm than good.

Research from other fields is enormously helpful to developing solutions to misinfor-mation. Issues like confirmation bias and other cognitive processes have informed library practices already (Cooke, 2017). The problem with these studies in isolation, though, is that many fields don't have the same practitioner infrastructure as library science with which to put their findings into use. Education does, of course, but classrooms are already politicized and overburdened with standards, so it seems that schools can't be the only solution. Addi-tionally, they don't reach people outside formal education, including adults, young children, and those educated at home.

Given these points, we will spend the rest of this chapter describing three primary attributes of libraries that place them in a unique position to address misinformation and disinformation: experience, trust of and relationships with the communities they serve, and physical spaces within the community.

Experience

Librarians have been providing resources and help with information seeking for many decades. Buschman (2003, 2009, 2012, 2017) notes the role of the library in disseminating "rational, reasoned, and organized discourse" (cf. Jaeger, Gorham, Bertot, & Sarin, 2013, p. 368). Berg et al. (2018) outline the critical role that school libraries play in helping young people learn how to "locate, process, sort, and apply . . . information, and perhaps more importantly, . . . impart that knowledge to others" (n.p.). In a 2016 Pew study of people's relationships with their public libraries, 37 percent of participants indicated that they think libraries "can help people [a lot] decide what information they can trust," which may seem low until you find that it is a 13-point increase from a survey deployed the previous year (Horrigan, 2016, p. 3). Overall, Geiger (2017) found that surveyed Americans of all races say that public libraries help them find information that is trustworthy and reliable (notably, 83 percent of Blacks and 87 percent of Hispanics). Libraries also have experience engaging with members of their community in decision making (Goulding, 2009). DelGuidice (2012)[4] provides a useful overview of the various roles of libraries of all types in helping patrons find information.

Trust and Relationship with Communities

Regardless of their community—which is, of course, different for academic, public, school, and special libraries—libraries are important. The 2016 Pew survey mentioned earlier found that people believe that public libraries "are a major contributor to their communities in providing a safe place to spend time, creating educational opportunities for people of all ages, and sparking creativity among young people" (Horrigan, 2016, p. 6). Vårheim (2014) describes the increase in trust of public libraries, librarians, and other library users that first-generation Mexican immigrants demonstrated after participating in public library programming. This increase occurred despite a generally low level of trust in outsiders. In the Danish context, Svendsen (2013) found that

> public libraries are not only breeding grounds for two well-known types of social capital—bonding and bridging—but also for a highly valuable third type, institutional social capital. It is argued that the closing down of more than half of branch libraries in rural Denmark since 1988 is partly due to politicians being ignorant of the great socioeconomic value of these "gracious spaces," which has a strong capacity to foster "full-scale" community social capital consisting of all three types of social capital. (p. 52)

Though in one study, M. C. Sullivan (2019a) found that public libraries were not able to leverage their trust into impacting people's decision making (indeed, social media corrections fared better in terms of changing people's behavior), he called for more concrete and tested information literacy interventions, "more aligned with contemporary misinformation research," and not that the trust that libraries have earned holds no promise for information literacy (p. 9).

There are also indications that other types of libraries hold this trust. Ramsey and Aagard (2018) discuss the role that academic libraries can play in promoting student wellness because of their reputation as safe places. In the UK context, research demonstrates that young people similarly find that their school libraries are friendly spaces that are likely to increase their academic success (Clark, 2010). All told, there seems to be a general perception that libraries are places to learn, are safe, and are trustworthy.

Physical Spaces

The state of public spaces in many countries has been on the decline for years (Buschman, 2003). Even online communities benefit from a space to connect in person. Koh et al. (2007) found that "offline interaction helps virtual community members understand, trust, and identify with one another, providing a stronger base for online community activity" (p.

71). In the United States, the quest for lowered costs has led many institutions to eliminate in-person help for information-related needs in favor of websites and automatic messages. Government services are increasingly being moved online, with local in-person assistance limited. For the average citizen, suddenly the public library has become one of the only locations left to seek help with government information (Jaeger & Bertot, 2011). In summarizing recent roles in the community that public libraries play, Cabello and Butler (2017) note that "in health care and other areas, libraries are combining the access and trust characteristics of a third place with a hub role in the community—using partnerships with other institutions to connect people with services and help" (n.p.).

Additionally, US public library buildings serve other essential democratic functions, such as their use as polling places in elections (this function was particularly critical in 2020 because in many states libraries provided secure ballot drop-off points to serve the needs of a society under quarantine (Klinenberg, 2020). In Canada, public libraries have become hubs for English language learners and those seeking a public place to gather and learn (Leckie & Hopkins, 2002), and in Norway, the federal law that governs libraries explicitly increased their role to be "more active disseminators as well as independent meeting places and arenas for public conversations and debate" (Golten, 2019, p. 1). In many respects, when taking into account school, public, academic, and special libraries, the infrastructure for and practice of information literacy already exists. A more holistic, lifelong, and better connection to interdisciplinary work can enhance what is there already.

WHY, LIBRARIES!

Ultimately, though these aspects of libraries make them essential in the practice and promotion of information literacy, libraries aren't perfect. Of the critics of libraries' roles that we have mentioned thus far in this book—Sullivan, Dempsey, and Johnson—none of them believes that libraries are extinct. Indeed, Johnson (2017) concludes his argument with the belief that "strong libraries build strong communities. We must insist that we provide quality information, even if our communities choose not to use it. And if false information wins the day, we can take comfort in knowing that we kept the option of truth available" (n.p.). M. C. Sullivan (2019b), perhaps the most ardent naysayer of librarians' current information literacy practices, has several useful suggestions for moving forward, including moving away from checklists that misrepresent the way that online information should be evaluated (the overall move of the field away from skills-based information literacy would suggest that librarians already know this is a priority, though certainly the checklist endures). A more long-term suggestion he describes is the need for LIS researchers and practitioners "to draw on and contribute to a larger body of research pertaining to misinformation, biases, and critical thinking" (p. 105). He's certainly not the first to suggest this approach, as he mentions in the essay.

Looking at these criticisms, though, it's clear to us that they can be overcome. Expanding our research to other professional theories is a huge need in the field, but as M. C. Sullivan (2019b) notes, many LIS scholars are already working in this area:

> In the context of fake news and misinformation, these include calls to address the roles that biases, prior beliefs, emotions, and social factors play in processing information and decision making (Baer, 2018; Bluemle, 2018; Boden, 2017; Lor, 2018), as well as the ways in which we process conflicting information (Becker, 2016). Ireland's (2018)

emphasis on visual or meme-based tutorials also anticipates a major change in the misinformation landscape, as seen in the French and UK elections, where visuals were more widely shared and more difficult to debunk than the type of fake news sites seen in the U.S. election (Wardle & Derakhshan, 2017). (p. 105)

Libraries are no more able to go it alone in providing places for and instruction in information literacy practice than are the other groups we mentioned earlier. Instead, we should view information literacy as a practice that we engage in across commercial and noncommercial entities, between communities and the information institutions that serve them, and between fields of study. Technology companies can partner with libraries to better understand effective ways of providing information literacy education. Media and information literacy efforts can be combined for a fuller picture of the practice of understanding and using information. Librarians can read up on concepts from cognitive science about bias, the adoption of new ideas, and the effort of getting information. We can use new methods of reading developed in the education field to teach users how to better understand information read in online spaces. We can research polarization from the perspective of political science in order to better work with all members of our communities. And perhaps most importantly, we can engage with community members to get a fuller picture of the practices they find effective in information literacy. Indeed, all the organizations and fields we've discussed would benefit from using a different lens for information literacy. Specifically, Jacobs and Berg (2011) consider that viewing information literacy as a problem that needs to be solved unnecessarily promotes a deficit model of access. Instead they suggest that we see information literacy as a "difficult or demanding question" (p. 387). This second conceptual understanding better enables us to work within the populace instead of treating information literacy as something that needs to be explained to nonexperts (which is both patronizing and elitist).

To get started with—and in some areas to continue—these practices, though, libraries must clarify their role in information literacy to those outside our field. Owusu-Ansah's (2005) article, aptly titled "Debating Definitions of Information Literacy: Enough Is Enough!," expresses the need for the field to move on from "continued debate over appropriate definitions and descriptors" and instead focus on "actually working to improve student capabilities, on exploring the role the library can play in that process, and on determining the legitimacy and desired extent of the library's participation in the education of information literate students" (p. 373). Although this point was made in the context of academic libraries, we think the idea of figuring out the place of library-related information literacy within the larger education, information, and societal landscape is definitely a direction that library research should go. We will return to this issue of communicating our role in society in later chapters.

Finally, we want to address one additional criticism that M. C. Sullivan (2019b) notes in his essay. (We should insert here, though, that we aren't trying to malign the article; it has a number of useful suggestions for areas of research to explore outside LIS, partners to reach out to, and strategies to try.) It is when Sullivan (2019b) suggests that a visionary model of lifelong information literacy infrastructure built with the help of librarians is not possible that we find fault. He discusses the fact that many LIS scholars

imagine a complex, scaffolded program that spans one's entire educational career, building up an incremental set of skills (e.g., Burkhardt, 2017). Others still paint a picture that is vast but vague, as when [C.] Gibson and Jacobson (2018) write of "critically reflective learners," "transformative learning," and "communities of inquiry." As ideal as this would be, it is doubtful that many librarians can implement the type of program they imagine. (p. 100)

We do indeed have faith that the library field and individual librarians can implement such programs. Although it will be enormously hard work and require a great deal of advocacy, this is the type of information literacy infrastructure that we should be intent on building in our communities. But we can only do so with awareness of mountains of disinformation, misinformation, and information illiteracy that stand in the way of such efforts.

There is no way to understand information literacy, how to promote it, how to advocate for it, and how to teach it to others without spending some time thinking about the barriers and challenges to information literacy and why people seem so ready to embrace demonstrably false ideas. Dishearteningly, one cannot discuss disinformation and misinformation in any depth without using some very soul-crushingly peculiar examples, which may sound like mad libs on steroids, but they are all real examples of disinformation and misinformation with their dedicated adherents. We're genuinely sorry to have to expose you to this mind-bending nonsense in the next few chapters, but we have to. This is what information literacy is up against.

💬 CHAPTER 9 GUIDING QUESTIONS

1. Why are libraries often ignored in media and government policies related to misinformation and literacy?
2. In what ways are libraries well suited to offering a place to practice information literacy? (And if you disagree that they are, why?)
3. How might libraries work with the media to help people increase their news (and information) literacy? What might be the drawbacks to this type of partnership?
4. What are some incentives and disincentives for technology corporations to offer information literacy education?
5. How can libraries better situate themselves in the landscape of information literacy education?

NOTES

1. Maybe not the pigeons. Especially if they are trying to drive a bus to deliver their messages.
2. Hopefully we've at least got that covered by now.
3. Well, not really; we just wanted to make sure you were still paying attention at this point.
4. Although the content of this article is what earned its place in this chapter, we would be remiss not to mention that the title goes a long way to making us pay attention . . . in case you haven't made it to the references yet, it is "Snooki, Whale Sperm, and Google: The Unfortunate Extinction of Librarians When They Are Needed Most." Delightful. Though we quibble with the extinction part. We're "not dead yet!"—cue the coconuts . . .

The Field Guide to Incorrect Information

THE MYTH OF CURRENCY (THE CURRENCY OF MYTH?)

As a part of existing in a society, there are certain fictions that we have collectively agreed upon for that society to function. States are one example. There is no boundary line on the ground that inevitably separates Mexico from the US or Spain from France. In both cases, the artificial boundaries that have been agreed upon have shifted more than a little since the states were created. The earliest evidence of demarcation of land appears in the Bronze Age. The first recorded peacefully settled, agreed-upon by both parties, national boundaries were between France and Andorra in 1278; there are 317 national borders across the globe today (Winchester, 2021). We decided to live in states as a way to order societies, mostly after giving up on ordering societies according to the inheritances of hereditary royalty.

Many of the states that tend to be thought of as historically old really are not, such as Italy and Germany, which are both far younger as actual states than the US, no matter what they try to tell you. The "Italian Renaissance" ended hundreds of years before the nation of Italy began; it actually occurred in predecessor states like Venice. The city of Warsaw uniquely gives a sense of how unstable nations and borders tend to be. In the time that the US has existed, Warsaw has been a key city of eight entirely different states: the Polish-Lithuanian Commonwealth, the Duchy of Warsaw of the Napoleonic Empire, Prussia, the Kingdom of Poland, Imperial Russia, Germany, the Soviet Union, and the present-day Republic of Poland.

The UK encompasses everything strange about states and borders in one convenient set of isles. The UK contains England, Scotland, Wales, and Northern Ireland, all readily identifiable as countries with their own histories and containing far more historical nations of people than just those four eponymous groups. Yet, none of those countries is a sovereign state; only the UK is. The isles are shared with the Republic of Ireland, which is its own nation and state, as well as the Crown Dependencies of the Isle of Man and the Channel Islands, which are not part of either the UK or the Republic of Ireland but belong directly to the British monarch. The Crown Dependencies are self-governing, with local parliaments, and are not part of the European Union (EU). Because the Crown Dependencies belong to the British monarch, the residents are given British residency.

The US, of course, is no better, even if it is older than most other current countries. We can readily turn to the founders of the US to find plenty of silly fictions about the origin of the nation. In 1806 Mason Locke Weems—known to history as Parson Weems, though he made that up, too—wrote the phenomenally successful *Life of George Washington: With Curious Anecdotes, Equally Honorable to Himself and Exemplary to His Young Countrymen*. It was almost entirely fictional—Weems did not know Washington or apparently anyone else who had ever met Washington, but that did not stop him from writing a detailed biography. If you've ever heard the story of young George Washington chopping down a cherry tree and his inability to tell a lie, Weems made it up, along with pretty much everything you have probably heard about George's personal life.

In the US, we also pave over issues of internal territorial inconsistency. We do not spend overmuch time celebrating states that have come into existence by seceding from other states, such as West Virginia, which seceded from Virginia at the outset of the Civil War in order to stay with the Union. Delaware has the unique status of declaring independence from both Britain and Pennsylvania on the same day, June 15, 1776; it had previously labored under the uninspiring name of the Assembly of the Lower Counties of Pennsylvania, which was reason enough to declare itself independent just to pick a better name.

And it is not just states and boundaries and founding myths that we accept as collective fictions. We rely on money, but it is entirely without value beyond what we agree to give it. Money is certainly easier than barter, especially if you have to figure out what to do with a bunch of chickens that you get paid with every week. But paper money really has no inherent value until we give it a fictional value. The fiction of money is perhaps best evidenced by the global reliance on the US dollar as the default international currency. Money from the US is backed by the world's largest economy and, perhaps more importantly, the world's largest military. The value of stocks and real estate is based solely on what people are willing to pay for them in the money that has a value only because we collectively agree that it does.

These are some of the major collective fictions that we agree to and adhere to in order for society to function. There are also fictions that we employ in an ad hoc way in interpersonal relations, the "your new haircut looks great" kind. Being overly optimistic about an acquaintance's new haircut, no matter how bad it actually looks, is not a threat to democracy, but a large number of fictions have the potential to be highly destructive. There are kinds of fictions—disinformation, misinformation, and information illiteracy—that can be extremely harmful, especially when they become pervasive.

MEET MISINFORMATION, DISINFORMATION, AND ILLITERACY

As the world has begun to pay greater attention to the impacts of information that is incorrect, the most commonly used term to describe this incorrect information has been *fake news*. Well, *lie* is actually the correct and venerable term, but people—especially journalists—seem oddly resistant to using that word. Fake news, however popular as a term, serves to obscure that incorrect information is not all of a single type with a single goal or uniform effect.

The term *fake news* was not invented by or about Donald Trump; before his embrace of the term, it had previously been used to describe political propaganda, press releases, photo manipulations, satire, and news parodies (Tandoc, Lim, & Ling, 2018). One of its earliest uses was by newspapers in Allied nations to identify Axis propaganda before and during World War II. Fake news in any format is often identifiable by its flaws—poor writing, misspellings, absolute language, flowery terminology, and obvious play on emotions (Cooke, 2018).

Once the term reentered the mainstream lexicon in 2016, however, it was embraced as a way to help capture how much incorrect information was being absorbed by people, especially about sociopolitical issues. Fake news online can serve a wide range of purposes: state propaganda, profitable business, weapon of war, type of media bias, attempt to undermine mainstream media, or individual pettiness or dishonesty, among others (Haigh & Haigh, 2020; Haigh et al., 2018). In the three months before the 2016 election, the top twenty false stories about the election—led by the one about Pope Francis endorsing the candidacy of Donald Trump—generated far more traffic than the top twenty actual news stories (Tandoc, Jenkins, & Craft, 2019). And people seem very prone to accepting false information; one study from the 2016 election year found that "fake news headlines fool American adults about 75% of the time" (Silverman & Singer-Vine, 2016, para. 1). Yikes.

These limitations are present not just in individuals of some particular demographic or level of technological engagement. A 2016 national study of middle school, high school, and college students described their online information literacy as "bleak" and noted that they are "easily duped" into believing fake content (Wineburg et al., 2016). Interestingly, and perhaps depressingly in light of the previous statement, a 2018 Pew Research Center study found that younger Americans (18- to 49-year-olds) were better at distinguishing factual news statements from opinions, although no age group did particularly well; well under half of those surveyed could distinguish all the factual and opinion statements correctly (Gottfried & Grieco, 2018).

The term *fake news* is generally meant to indicate one of two types of bad information: *disinformation*, which is incorrect information spread with malicious intent, or *misinformation*, which is incorrect information spread without malicious intent. When done with intent, these actions are often driven either by the desire to muddy political waters or make money off the gullible. In short, a bad actor spreads disinformation, whereas a poorly informed actor spreads misinformation. This general typology has been widely adopted by fields ranging from journalism to psychology, and it covers many of the problems with incorrect information. These problems are also quite venerable, as can be seen by the 1983 publication date of Fox's book *Information and Misinformation: An Investigation of the Notions of Information, Misinformation, Informing, and Misinforming*. Just like fake news, misinformation and disinformation were not invented by the Internet.

It did not take long after the advent of the browsable web for people to notice that "misinformation is pervasive on the Internet and disseminated through online communication media" (Zhou & Zang, 2007, p. 804). Misinformation can be examined without considering intent, seeing it as information that is incomplete, vague, uncertain, or ambiguous (Losee, 1997; Zhou & Zhang, 2007). Misinformation may also be seen as context-dependent, being "true, accurate, and informative" in one context and misleading in another (Karlova & Lee, 2011, p. 3). An example of such context was identified in the early days of government websites, with concerns that a user might misuse government information by "taking something publicly available, through a listserv or electronic journal or newsletter, without checking the original source" (Hernon, 1995, p. 136).

Disinformation is generally viewed through the lens of dishonest intent, ranging from maliciousness and clear intent to cause harm down to little white lies meant to spare hurt feelings (V. L. Rubin, 2010). Disinformation is often carefully planned, can be generated by individuals or coordinated groups, and frequently gets disseminated by entities—such as a news organization—other than the information creators (Cooke, 2018). There have been suggestions that the truly worst forms of disinformation may deserve their own designation. Wardle and Derakhshan (2018) suggested using the term *malinformation* for information that is based in reality but that has been decontextualized or otherwise twisted to intentionally inflict harm.

The kinds of misinformation and disinformation that one encounters are wide-ranging in nature, intent, and potential impacts:

- Satire and parody (humor, not intended to be taken seriously, but misinformation when taken seriously)
- Misleading/biased content (framing the issue using misleading or biased information)
- Imposter content (genuine sources used for other purposes)
- Fabricated content (made up, designed to deceive)
- False connections (headlines and visuals that do not connect to content)
- False context (genuine content but in false context)
- Manipulated content (visuals or videos) (Carillo, 2019; Wardle & Derakhshan, 2018; Zannettou et al., 2019)

There are also descriptors for different kinds of disinformation and misinformation, such as *cheap fakes,* which are visuals manipulated with little effort that significantly alters the impression of the visual, like slowing down video; or *deep fakes,* which are visuals manipulated by using high-end software to make very realistic but completely false videos (Harwell, 2019, 2020).[1] Although disinformation and misinformation are not new, the capacities of the Internet in general and social media in particular have given them "an alarming new patina" (Cooke, 2017, p. 211).

Disinformation and misinformation as content can be produced and spread by more than individuals as well; bots, filters, and algorithms can all generate—and incessantly do—disinformation and disseminate misinformation without human oversight. Bots, in particular, are responsible for a huge amount of online traffic; they are "fake accounts that are used to propagate false information in the wild" (Zannettou et al., 2019, p. 3). Botnets, basically an army of coordinated bots, are usually employed to diffuse false information to generate profit or sow chaos, or both if really successful.

The amount of disinformation and misinformation that users must navigate and assess has expanded as rapidly as the Internet has expanded, often being fed directly to users through search results and newsfeeds. In 1995, the first year that users were able to browse the web, there was already research showing that many websites were sources of misinformation, intentionally or unintentionally (Hernon, 1995). As more automation has taken over the dissemination of online information, the volume of misinformation and disinformation has skyrocketed. The disinformation and misinformation that users encounter even varies by country. In the US and the UK, disinformation about political actors is uniquely prominent, whereas in continental European nations, sensationalized stories of outside populations, especially immigrants, are notably prominent (Humprecht, 2019).

In practice, consider the result of a Russian government operative, Boris, who invents a false and scandalous story about a politician named Rocky in another country to benefit that politician's opponent, Natasha, who is curiously friendly to the Russian government. Hypothetically, of course. When Boris creates the false story about Rocky and sends it into the cyberverse, that is a deliberate act of disinformation. That's pretty clear. The bots and algorithms that pick up the disinformation spread it unwittingly because they have no sense of ethics or values. But what about the person who deliberately chooses to spread the lie?

If the actor knows the information is false but spreads it anyway because the actor is a fan of Natasha and wants to hurt support for Rocky, then it is still an act of disinformation. If the actor does not realize that the story is disinformation when they spread it, then the actor is engaging in misinformation. But is that really enough of an explanation? Should the actor have known better or done better research to ascertain the veracity of the misinformation? Should they be expected to?

When you ask those questions about misinformation, the disinformation/misinformation dyad seems insufficient from an information literacy perspective. Misinformation alone misses the element of whether the actor should have been able to assess the false nature of the disinformation or taken the time to try to ascertain the truth. There are plenty of ways to assess the truth of most information, with libraries having produced bounteous, easily findable guides to assessing the validity of information (Agosto, 2018). Examining information for author credibility, source credibility, and internal biases is a well-known strategy, and consulting authoritative fact-checking sites and employing reverse image searches are options available to anyone with access to the Internet. Even if one is familiar with those strategies and tools, employing them can take a certain amount of effort, but that feels like a poor excuse.

So what else is going on? Let's consider the unpleasantness of a false story that got lots of attention in 2016. The InfoWars company run by Alex Jones is a primary distributor of many of the most durable, far-out lies that have gained traction among at least some people in recent years. Jones is an example of someone who has monetized spreading false information because it generates traffic for his website and sells branded merchandise. He has made extensive claims that school shootings are faked, that Democrats plan to impose Sharia law, and that government is controlled by all kinds of different groups that he is bigoted against (Holan, 2016). His most famous role may be in popularizing the "Pizzagate" false story about Hillary Clinton running a child enslavement ring out of the basement of a Washington, D.C., hipster pizza parlor called Comet Ping Pong.

Shortly after being posted, Jones's Pizzagate video was watched more than five hundred thousand times and featured in more than 1.5 million tweets (Robb, 2017). One enthused user shared the Pizzagate story more than four thousand times in five weeks! Another, related conspiracy called "Frazzledrip" sprang out of Pizzagate and added vampirism to the story, with doctored YouTube videos showing Hillary Clinton, Katy Perry, and friends drinking children's blood (Timberg et al., 2018). A heavily armed man actually showed up to the restaurant to free the nonexistent child prisoners trapped in the nonexistent basement; fortunately, no one was injured, and he went to jail for a long time.

We hope that as you read this account, you are asking how and why anyone could possibly believe that a presidential candidate was using an overpriced pizza place to engage in vampirism on children. But it gets better. Even though the gun-toting individual who invaded Comet Ping Pong admitted that nothing was there but a pizza place, the vampirism on enslaved children concept became the foundational myth of the conspiracy theory group that is known as QAnon. QAnon is based on the false notion that Donald Trump was waging war with "the deep state" of satanic government officials who traffic children and engage in mass executions, with the messages coming through social media platforms from supposed government insider "Q."

Q claims to be a government insider with the highest level of security, and members of QAnon await "Q drops," in which Q leaves messages for the followers on far right social media platforms. The adherents of QAnon believe that Trump was recruited by military leaders to root out the cabal of Satan-worshipping predators who eat children and run the world, most of whom are Democrats and Hollywood elite, along with a few progressive-minded Republicans, like George H. W. Bush and John McCain, thrown in for good measure (Roose, 2020; Timberg & Dwoskin, 2020). QAnon's discourse is premised on racism, misogyny, homophobia, anti-Semitism, anti-vaccines, and other such awfulness.

Benefiting from the algorithms of social media platforms constantly pushing controversial topics, QAnon amassed more than three million followers of various QAnon-affiliated accounts on Facebook before Facebook and other social media companies took any action to remove QAnon content (Wong, 2020). By combining the reach of social media and the buffet-style approach to embracing basically every conspiracy while making up bunches of new ones, QAnon is able to appeal to a dizzying range of biases and illiteracy. "The choose-your-own-adventure nature of QAnon makes it compelling to vulnerable people desperate for a sense of security and difficult for Twitter and Facebook to control, despite their efforts" (Andrews, 2020, p. B2).

People still believe in QAnon even though every measurable prediction it has made has been totally, bizarrely wrong. In 2018 the entity known as Q claimed to have discovered and revealed a "16-Year Plan to Destroy America," which was supposedly written by the cabal.[2] Along with exposing and destroying the Satan-worshipping cabal, Q assured its followers that Trump would imprison Hillary Clinton, reveal the existence of the lizard people, and announce at the 2020 Republican convention that John F. Kennedy Jr.—son of former president John F. Kennedy—had faked his own death in a plane crash and was coming out of hiding to be Trump's vice president for his second term. Numerous times Q has indicated that "the storm" was about to happen, which is the day that Trump would declare martial law and have all registered Democrats in the country arrested. As you may have noticed, none of these predictions, or anything remotely similar to them, have happened. There are also claims that are much harder to disprove, primarily because they are so weird and impossible—for example, there are secret bunkers under Central Park to store children being trafficked, the Federal Reserve plants tracking microchips into everyone who goes inside a bank, the assassination of Osama bin Laden was faked, and the whole lizard people thing.

This mishmash of conspiracy theories for fans of disinformation is so compelling that it has large numbers of adherents in Australia, Canada, England, Ireland, New Zealand, Germany, and the Netherlands. The Canadian branch believes that Prime Minister Justin Trudeau was fraudulently elected and that he plans to invade the US; the German branch believes that Trump will liberate the entire world from the lizard people, not just the US; and the Australia/New Zealand branch believes that liberal politicians around the world created the novel coronavirus so that they could infect older adults and then use their identities to vote (Rahula & Morris, 2020). All these international groups are unified by faith in Donald Trump, unshakable anti-Semitism and other rabid bigotries, and a belief that governments around the world run Satanic child trafficking rings.

QAnon also offers an excellent example of those driven to create disinformation and spread misinformation for profit. Forums that promote QAnon conspiracies are full of links to e-commerce sites selling QAnon merchandise, through which one can buy QAnon stickers, t-shirts and other apparel, flags, phone cases, and mugs (Timberg & Stanley-Becker, 2020). On Amazon in December 2020, there were more than eight thousand different QAnon-branded products, including three dozen book titles promoting the conspiracy; on eBay, there were more than three thousand different QAnon-branded products. Not only have people figured out how to make money from the conspiracy, some of these people have figured out how to act as evangelists for the conspiracies and then direct those listening to their own products—spin lies about the mind control of drugs from pharmaceutical companies to sell their own alternative medicines, and tell tales of the impending social collapse to sell their doomsday prepper supplies.

Trump's post-2020 election loss offered a clinic in the monetization of disinformation. As he incessantly broadcast false claims about electoral fraud, he sent out a blitz of 498 fundraising emails in a month to raise money to challenge the nonexistent fraud (Lee & Narayanswamy, 2020). In just the first four weeks after the election, he raised more than $207.5 million from his supporters while spending only $9 million, with the remainder going into a fund that he could spend pretty much any way he wanted whenever he wanted. Others figured out this game because there was quickly a booming market in merchandise echoing the disinformation about the election, and Newsmax managed to increase its viewership by more than twenty times in that same four weeks by parroting all Trump's lies about the election. And numerous companies, probably many that were already selling QAnon merchandise, started profiting from "Fight the Fraud" and "Stop the Steal" bumper stickers, masks, headbands, hats, mugs, shirts, and whatnot.[3]

Although QAnon may be the current world leader in these types of disinformation-based and enthusiastically bigoted online movements, it is important to remember that it is just a prominent example of a worldwide problem. Disinformation + bigotry + social media is a potent combination everywhere, with the reasons for the bigotry producing varying results by nation. For example, in India, the world's most populous democracy, 2020 found state governments around the country—at the encouragement of the national government—passing laws to ban interfaith marriages. An online conspiracy theory called "love jihad" gained widespread belief among the Hindu majority in the nation. This conspiracy theory claimed that Muslim men were marrying Hindu women to force them to convert, playing into entrenched biases against Muslims in Indian culture (Slater, 2020). Although there is absolutely no evidence of this trend and the number of interfaith marriages of any sort in India is really small anyway, the conspiracy theory moved with alarming speed from online extremists to mainstream online platforms to protests against companies that depicted interfaith marriages in their advertising to legislation.

We can hear you hitting your head on a hard surface at this point, so we'll stop talking about ludicrous QAnon and other conspiracies and methods for profiting from them. But the sheer absurdity of these notions cannot be overlooked when considering misinformation and disinformation. The overwhelming focus on the dissemination of disinformation by media, academic, and political discussions has served to excuse those users who fall for—or enthusiastically embrace—and spread the misinformation (McDevitt & Ferrucci, 2018). The focus on the sources of disinformation fails to account for the strong embrace of misinformation by so many people.

To help fill this gap, we believe that another concept is needed in concert with misinformation and disinformation, which we are calling *information illiteracy*. You will recall from chapters 2 and 3 that the idea of being "information illiterate" is not new (American Library Association, 1989; Zurkowski, 1974). However, previous use of the term described people who simply needed to be taught to be information literate and would presumably be grateful for such education. Time and the Internet have revealed that belief to be rather quaint and painfully elitist. The real problem with information illiteracy is that it is often a chosen state—hence, our move from talking about information illiterates to positing a state of information illiteracy. If information literacy is good practice with information, then information illiteracy is bad practice with information.

This term is intended to invoke a willful, purposeful lack of literacy, the state of intentionally choosing to believe what is clearly false information that does not require any additional research to check its veracity. This stance entails the enthusiastic embrace—diving headfirst into the deep end—of false information. For example, when one encounters a preposterous story about lizard people secretly controlling the world and does not immediately dismiss it as completely ridiculous, one is actively choosing to be information illiterate. And sometimes ignorance is less blissful than advertised. Local and state elected officials have reported being accosted by Trump supporters who refused to accept the results of the popular vote and the Electoral College vote and argued that elected officials do not need to allow the Constitution to dictate what they can do (Gardner, 2020). That would be information illiteracy about civics proudly at work.

It should also be understood that the willful nature of information illiteracy is intended to distinguish it from simply not knowing something. There's an infinite amount of stuff that any person does not and cannot know. The authors of this book would hardly be a good choice to write a book about the history of bowling or new advances in theoretical physics. That's just stuff that we do not know, that we are fine with not knowing, and that has no impact on our lives. Were we to suddenly start writing that bowling was invented by the lizard people as part of their plan for world domination and that the sound of theoretical physics causes cancer, then we'd be off into the land of information illiteracy.

One exceptionally well-known example of information illiteracy involves the size of crowds. Photographic evidence clearly showed, in no uncertain terms, that the inauguration of Donald Trump in 2017 was less well attended than many preceding inaugurations, especially the two of his immediate predecessor, Barack Obama. Photos taken by the National Park Service from the same location and angle demonstrated unmistakably, significantly diminished crowd size. Trump claimed—contrary to irrefutable photographic evidence—that he had the largest inauguration crowd ever. This event gave us the unbeatable term *alternative facts,* which Trump officials used to describe the lies that they were repeating about the crowd size. Amazingly, many people chose to believe his disinformation instead of the readily available photographic evidence before their own eyes. Information illiteracy, ahoy.

Rather than just being a case of very confused or insufficiently credulous people, information illiteracy can have very real consequences. For example, if one does not know the ways to vote, plenty of sources of information can be clearly identified as valid, most obviously government agencies. However, some voters in the 2016 US presidential election fell for social media ads that were obvious disinformation, encouraging supporters of Democratic candidate Hillary Clinton to vote by text message to "save time, avoid the line" (Stapleton, 2016). Although the ads looked professionally produced and were labeled "Hillary for President 2016," anyone who had gone through the process of registering to vote should have been able to ascertain the falsity of these ads with minimal work. Aside from checking with your local government,[4] there are also prominent nonpartisan entities devoted entirely to identifying and debunking falsehoods, including PolitiFact, NewsGuard, the *Washington Post* Fact Checker, and Snopes. But hey, voting by text would be so simple, so why check? Unknown numbers of voters embraced information illiteracy and passed on the chance to actually vote by "text voting" for Clinton.

Though we've used political examples thus far, it is important to note that the concept of information illiteracy is not inherently tied to political information. Here's an example familiar to many people—the argument in which you are using every piece of evidence possible to show someone that they are getting the lyrics to a song wrong. You show them the lyrics on the LP jacket and then pull up the lyrics on the artist's official website, but the person sticks to their own incorrect lyrics. These kinds of things are less pernicious versions of information illiteracy than are the lizard people running the world kinds of things, but they still are examples of clearly and deliberately choosing to believe incorrect information when the correct information is findable.

Everyone is exposed to huge amounts of disinformation and misinformation, but only some people actively choose to spread it. Information illiteracy is not a phenomenon that happens to people; instead, when people willfully embrace clearly bad information, the results can be detrimental to themselves and others, especially when a global pandemic is occurring.

PSYCHOLOGY AND INFORMATION LITERACY

The next question—other than can I stop hitting my head on a hard surface now?[5]—is why are people susceptible to misinformation and disinformation and sometimes rush head-long into information illiteracy?[6] As long as there has been a spoken and written language, information could be manipulated and used to deceive, but it is ever so much easier now (Burkhardt, 2017).

Now, social media is one of the primary sources of political and election information for members of the public, and many social media accounts of individuals have a larger number of readers than major news organizations (Allcott & Gentzkow, 2017). During the 2016 election, 62 percent of Americans were getting news from social media (Gottfried & Shearer, 2016). The homogeneity of the beliefs of the members of social networks—often called an *echo chamber* or a *filter bubble* as we mentioned earlier—then gives the incorrect information a welcoming environment in which to take root (Del Vicario et al., 2016). And these bubbles can lead to violent action in some cases—a 2018 study found direct linkages between the intensity of anti-immigrant Facebook discussions in German cities and phys-ical violence against immigrants in those same cities (Muller & Schwartz, 2018).

Generally, people rely on the familiar when searching for and evaluating information, with social networks playing a large role. One is more likely to accept information from a known source—say, one's hairstylist—than an unfamiliar source, even on a matter that has nothing to do with hair care. Judgments of credibility are highly subjective assessment processes (Rieh, 2010). Fake news thrives on social networks, friends lists, filter bubbles, and echo chambers (Cooke, 2018). Ultimately, people frequently "cling to a system of belief, not because of its epistemic warrant, but because it serves some non-cognitive [socioeco-nomic or sociocultural] interest" (Shelby, 2003, p. 170).

Isolation into like-minded groups truly hampers the ability of people to understand one another, a truth that was well established long before the invention of the Internet. For nearly a century, contact between different groups has been known to be the best way to reduce and eliminate prejudice (Allport, 1954). During World War II, the members of white American military units that fought side-by-side with units comprised of Black Americans were nine times—nine times!—less likely to be prejudiced against Black Amer-icans because they had close contact with them. Mountains of evidence support the idea that getting to know the other makes it much harder to hate, but the converse is also true. Racial and ethnic isolation of whites at the zip code level was the strongest predictor of support for Donald Trump; support for the border wall with Mexico was highest in areas with the fewest immigrants (Pettigrew, 2017). And it's not just a US thing; Brexit support was highest among the least culturally diverse constituencies (Lawton & Ackrill, 2016; Meleady et al., 2017).

The extent to which people or the members of their social networks lack control of the information that they see is another new wrinkle in literacy. Users generally do not understand the role, or possibly even the existence, of algorithms in determining the information that they are exposed to and share with others through newsfeeds, search engines, and even advertising (Eslami et al., 2015; Proferes, 2017; E. Rader & Gray, 2015). In most cases, the user now sees what the algorithm thinks the user would like to see, based on all the information that the algorithm has about the user, continually reinforcing the messages the user gets and further limiting the range of information that is presented to the user. So, along with trying to identify what information is being generated by bots rather than people, users must try to be aware of the ways in which algorithms are shaping the information that they see.

There are very powerful tendencies among most people to want to find information that supports what they already believe (Burkhardt, 2016, 2017). Although the human propensity to believe information sources that reinforce what the reader already believes predates the Internet, the problem is greatly exacerbated by the overwhelming quantities of information online, the tenacity of algorithms to provide information that you will like, and the ease of staying in places where everyone shares the same opinion (Del Vicario et al, 2016; Proferes, 2017). The sheer vastness of the information online alone may be enough to steer people toward sensationalist things and misinformation as the result of being over-awed by the infinite options (Chatfield, 2019). Ultimately, a great deal of belief in disinformation and conspiracy theories comes down to "lazy thinking" in seeking simplicity and clarity (Haupt, 2020, p. 11).

A wide range of research across many academic fields has demonstrated that human brains are not especially good at dealing with this infinite abyss of online information, generally opting toward information that the user already agrees with and information that is sensationalist (for summaries of such research, see Bauman, 2020; N. Carr, 2011; and Levitin, 2017). Fortunately, social psychology and cognitive psychology give us some very helpful insights. Not happy insights, but certainly helpful ones.

The most primal of these factors is *pattern recognition*. To make up for a lack of claws, armor, speed, camouflage, stingers, wings, or any other physical adaptations that would have promoted survival, humans relied on their fast brains to quickly assess opportunities and dangers, finding the signal in the noise and creating patterns that promoted survival. The ability to make patterns became a key trait in the human gene pool, which worked great in the pre-modern world when the amount of information that people had to process was limited. Unfortunately, this extremely important feature in our brains that allowed furless, slow, squishy creatures to take over the planet also now leads us to find patterns where there are none when confronted with the vastly too much information that the Internet throws at us (Silver, 2012). Not only does that trait lead us to find patterns that do not exist and make conclusions that are really dopey, it greatly increases the likelihood that we will stick with those bad conclusions.

Psychologists began describing and naming the ability of people to actively embrace misinformation in the 1950s, with the identification of *cognitive dissonance*, the ability of people to maintain beliefs that are logically impossible (Cooper, 2007). The story most frequently used to explain cognitive dissonance is the well-known "The Emperor's New Clothes" written by Hans Christian Andersen (1847) one hundred years before the term was coined. In the story, swindlers convince a ruler that they can make him clothes that only the worthy can see; there are no such clothes, of course, but no one is willing to admit being unable to see the nonexistent clothing as the ruler cheerfully wanders around in his underclothes. This phenomenon might possibly be at work when someone decides to believe someone who claims that the sound of windmills causes cancer.

The concept that perhaps most explains why people are drawn to disinformation and misinformation is *confirmation bias.* It means that people seek and prioritize information that agrees with what they already believe and discount information that contradicts their existing beliefs. The phenomenon has been known since the early seventeenth century and became a central part of psychological discourse in the early twentieth century (Nickerson, 1998). Repetition of messages heightens the impact of confirmation bias.

Modeling further explains the dispiriting vitality of misinformation and disinformation. People are prone to admiring the behavior of others whom they see as successful and as being somehow similar to themselves. Observing a person perceived as a model embrace a piece of false or biased information makes that information appealing; this is how a phrase like "Build the Wall" spreads (Bauman, 2020).

Social norming is the desire of members of a population to behave in a way that is perceived as being expected by the rest of the population (Schultz et al., 2007). For most individuals, social approval is very important and sought after. If some members of a community generally adopt certain information, that increases the likelihood that other members of that community will also adopt that information.

Most insidious is the cognitive process of *moral disengagement,* in which the person justifies an immoral behavior (Bandura, 1999, 2002). It may be through convincing oneself that the act is small or is not as bad as the behavior of someone else or is excused by a higher purpose. Regardless of the justification, moral disengagement allows the individual to use false information without guilt.

Negativity bias also plays a strong role in information. The human mind spends far more time processing—and thereby has stronger reactions to—things that it views as negative rather than those that are positive or neutral (Baumeister et al., 2001). This focus on the negative is a carryover from when remembering which animals were predators was a very important bit of everyday information (e.g., saber-toothed cat = bad). When something has negative connotations, or is made to have negative connotations through association, it becomes very hard to shake. Taking advantage of negativity bias, disinformation can readily be presented in ways that get people to pay more attention and be more likely to believe the disinformation. People who hold conservative political views are far more influenced by negativity bias (Hibbing & Smith, 2013), which may help explain why the volume and impact of disinformation aimed at conservatives far outweigh those of disinformation aimed at liberals.

Some purveyors of disinformation have learned to use tricks from advertising to their advantage. *Social contagion* describes the human tendency for individuals to model their own behavior on the behavior that they see others engaging in (Christakis & Fowler, 2011; Gureckis & Goldstone, 2009). Humans are inherently copycats—think of the cyclical surges in popularity of baby names or clothing styles or breeds of dogs or blockbuster movies—and will often engage in behavior because everyone else is doing it or because they are told that everyone else is doing it. Adding a nonsmoker to a social group that includes a bunch of smokers greatly increases the odds of the nonsmoker becoming a smoker. So, while some creators of disinformation emphasize being outside the mainstream to draw interest, others rely on social contagion, presenting the claims as something everybody knows is true.

A burst of social contagion often begins with the phenomenon known as *pixie dust* in marketing (Lindstrom, 2011)—that is, everyone is doing it because that famous person did it. Think about the influence of the UK's royal family on baby names; if Kate and Will had named their kids McNugget Windsor and Spatula Windsor, there would be a huge spike in babies around the world named McNugget and Spatula. As a result, some disinformation creators try to gain acceptance by tying it to a famous person—through names or images or video, authentic or not—who might be an influencer in a particular community or more broadly. The pixie dust phenomenon partially explains why Donald Trump is so successful as a super-spreader of disinformation; his followers are heavily inclined to believe something because he believes it, a reaction that began even before he was a presidential candidate with the huge acceptance of his stream of racist lies that then president Obama was born outside the US and therefore not really president.

Thanks to social media, people have previously unthinkable opportunities to sequester themselves inside filter bubbles only with people who already share their beliefs. Like-minded individuals in a group have the tendency to keep agreeing with each other, which collectively heightens those shared beliefs, a process known as *group polarization* (Sunstein, 2005).

Once a large number of people, or perhaps more accurately a large number of communities, have decided to believe a clear falsehood, it becomes *counterknowledge* (D. Thompson, 2008). Much counterknowledge is harmless, such as giraffes having long necks to eat leaves at the top of trees, but it can have devastating consequences. The counterknowledge that vaccines are the cause of autism has resulted in a huge number of preventable deaths from and outbreaks of previously eradicated diseases around the world.

The sheer volume of information also plays a major role in the spread of disinformation and misinformation as well. The more information that people are exposed to and the more overwhelmed they become, the more likely they are to revert to previously established cognitive pathways and only be receptive to what seems very simple or that agrees with what they already believe, making confirmation bias far more likely (Deibert, 2019). Once all these processes begin intermingling with information, the pathways for spreading disinformation and misinformation—and choosing to be information illiterate—lead in every direction. Clearly, not all these elements are at work with each piece of misinformation, or at least how each individual responds to a piece of misinformation, but they collectively profoundly shape and greatly enable the spread of misinformation.

Being aware of these processes will not necessarily change the impacts of the processes. Take confirmation bias, which is a really serious impediment to information literacy, even when one is actively trying to avoid it. When faced with information that contradicts what they believe, or even demonstrably proves what they believe to be incorrect, people "tend to resist facts" (Kulinski et al., 2003, p. 792). Confirmation bias can color not only "how we see things, but how we reason, as well" (Jackson & Jamieson, 2007, p. 76). Strong believers in incorrect information will engage in "mental gymnastics" to avoid processing conflicting information (Gaines et al., 2007, p. 957).

Alarmingly, the more misinformed an individual is, the more likely that individual is to firmly hold that those beliefs are correct (Kulinski et al., 2003). Perhaps the most jarring example of this phenomenon was documented in a study in which participants read the final government report conclusively documenting that, contrary to assertions made before the invasion of Iraq in the early 2000s, there were no weapons of mass destruction (WMDs) in Iraq. The report demonstrates without question that the entire pretext for the invasion was a lie. The participants who incorrectly believed that WMDs were found in Iraq, and then read the report officially documenting the lack of WMDs, overwhelmingly were more convinced that there were WMDs after reading the report (Nyhan & Reifler, 2010). The same has been found true in terms of other major issues, such as climate change—the more misinformed a partisan is, the more likely they are to disagree with someone on the other side of the issue (Kahan et al., 2012). Overall, attempts to correct political misinformation have the unintended effect of reinforcing the incorrect beliefs (Sunstein, 2009).

Curiously, the spread of disinformation seems to be heavily driven by a small, but apparently very dedicated, number of people, such as the aforementioned Twitter user who shared the Pizzagate story four thousand times in five weeks. One study has estimated that 0.1 percent of Twitter users share 80 percent of the misinformation on that platform and that 1 percent of users account for almost all the misinformation being shared (Grinberg et al., 2019). Another study found that only 8.5 percent of Facebook users shared links to disinformation sites and that older users and more politically conservative users were the most likely to share misinformation; users over age 65 were seven times more likely than younger users to share misinformation, the "vast majority of which was pro-Trump" (Guess, Nagler, & Tucker, 2019). However, the number of spreaders is less important than the number of spreadees.

If one person with eighty-nine million followers on Twitter disseminates disinformation, eighty-nine million people are exposed to it even if none of them retweet it. Disinformation often appeals to those who feel powerless, so disinformation coming from someone seen as powerful grants believers a sense of power themselves. Believing the disinformation can equate to gaining power in the mind of the believer.

INFORMATION ACCESS AND MISINFORMATION ACCESS

The field of information studies has traditionally approached information access and exchange with the presumption that people would seek and want to find accurate information rather than just something that reinforces existing beliefs. Nevertheless, the approaches that our field has adopted can provide a frame for understanding the process of finding and spreading misinformation as a part of information behavior.

Say that you one day find yourself wondering what year the British burned down the first version of the White House. It was probably in 1812, since that was when we had another war with Britain because the Revolution had been such a popular success. So, you decide to look it up.

If you choose a reliable source of historical information, you find that the White House, the main government library, and much of the rest of the newly constructed District of Columbia were burned by the British army during the 1813-1814 campaign of the War of 1812. That war was an offshoot of the Napoleonic Wars, with most of the combat involving the US occurring at sea or in Canada. In one stupendous bit of incompetence on the part of the Americans, however, defending the nation's seat of governance was not given terribly high priority even after the British had landed in Maryland. To make up for this loss of the library, former president Thomas Jefferson offered his personal library—to which he had added an average of several books a week over the course of his then long life—to the nation "on whatever terms the Congress might think proper." The collection of 6,487 books was hardly all devoted to governance. The largest parts of the collection were focused on art, philosophy, architecture, cooking, gardening, and wine making; a quarter was in languages other than English. This new library for Congress became the LOC and utterly revolutionized the idea of a government library. Previously, they had been utilitarian collections entirely for reference purposes. Instead, the nascent American republic suddenly had the foundation of a comprehensive collection devoted to the whole range of human knowledge. Hooray, you know lots more!

Unless you distrust reliable historical sources and instead seek out sources that say there never was a War of 1812 nor the broader Napoleonic Wars, labeling them fake news created by the lizard people as a cover story for when they landed on Earth, which is flat, of course. Boo, you know less! But you can also share this misinformation just as easily as the correct information.

Information access occurs in three stages, which carry the snazzy name Tripartite Model of Information Access (TMIA):

1. **Physical access**—the information that you seek is available and accessible to you in some format
2. **Intellectual access**—the information is in a form that you can understand and make sense of
3. **Social access**—you are able to articulate and share the information with others (Burnett, Jaeger, & Thompson, 2008; Jaeger & Burnett, 2010)

Although this model is based on the notion that the information seeker will seek out, read, and share information, the same process works if the information is disinformation.

In one case, you seek the answer to when the White House burned down, find and believe a historically accurate account, and share this information anytime that anyone says anything related to the White House. In the other, you find and believe misinformation, and when anyone near you mentions the White House, you loudly explain that it never burned down because that's what the lizard people want you to believe.

In 1910 philosopher and reformer William James published an essay entitled "The Moral Equivalent of War." The essay focused on his epiphany about what had seemed an intractable problem to him—why, given the massive suffering, loss of life, economic waste, and ecological damage caused, do people still support and engage in wars? To his understandable dismay, James finally realized that the answer was that all those things that struck him and other pacifists as so horrifying were, in fact, keen incentives to those who supported and engaged in wars. Some people found ways to increase their power and their treasure through war, and some people enjoyed the destruction and suffering. The same challenge holds true with disinformation and its ilk. It will never be vanquished because some people have found it a means of gaining power and treasure, while other people simply enjoy the damage that it inflicts on individual lives and on society as a whole. The best that information professionals can hope to do is equip the greatest number of people to recognize and reject disinformation because some actors will always find incentives to continue to create it.

A subsequent chapter will focus more specifically on disinformation, misinformation, information illiteracy, and the information-seeking and psychological processes discussed in this chapter as they relate to one area in which they have played a most prominent role in society: the intersection of politics and social media in the middle of a pandemic. On the upside, the recent pandemic has given us plenty of examples to work with; on the downside, well, the pandemic. But, before we get to that, we should spend some time reminding ourselves that spreading disinformation did not begin when America Online (AOL) was founded.[7]

🗩 CHAPTER 10 GUIDING QUESTIONS

1. What are some facts that you take on faith in your own life (e.g., the existence of national borders; monetary value)? In what ways might information literacy contribute to or detract from these sorts of societally accepted norms?
2. How would you define fake news? Is it different from the popular definition in the media and among non-information professionals?
3. What are the primary differences between misinformation and disinformation?
4. How can the government, information professionals, and media companies counter the growing use of deep fakes online?
5. Could psychological tendencies toward modeling and social norming be used to counteract conspiracy theories? How or how not?

NOTES

1. Neither should be confused with *peep fakes*, which are poor imitations of distressing, gaudily colored marshmallow chickens.
2. Had this report been real, it at least would have deserved credit for having a much easier to understand title than most government reports.
3. And, in spite of our pointing out in the first chapter of the book that people stopped believing in krakens long ago, some members of Trump's post-2020 election legal team took to describing their case as "The Kraken." Apparently intended to make it sound imposing despite the lack of a shred of evidence or remotely coherent legal theory, it argued for disenfranchising tens of millions of people because they did not vote for Trump. The Supreme Court dismissed The Kraken without a hearing.
4. Astoundingly, the US government used to maintain its own nonpartisan fact-checking site, rumorcontrol.gov, but shut it down after determining that it was not needed.
5. Yes, if you wish. It will make reading easier.
6. We also would have accepted: "Why are there so many songs about rainbows and what's on the other side?"
7. You've got misinformation!

A Brief History of Advertising, Propaganda, and Other Delights

DIVINE RIGHTS AND WRONGS

Entire books have been written about the history of propaganda by governments and advertising by companies. They are big topics, but a small overview is necessary to give context to understanding misinformation, disinformation, and information illiteracy in the world of social media and the Internet of things. There's a lot more information now and a lot more venues by which to disseminate information, but the tools for spreading false information are quite venerable.

Though there is no historical marker for the first time a person discovered the value of disinformation, it seems likely that the practice really became useful only after the invention of language and took off after the invention of writing. The first monarch who articulated a divine right to rule was perhaps history's first great practitioner of disinformation—I was born to rule because the gods told me so; if you question my authority, they will punish you, and I've got a moat full of Nile crocodiles, too. Regardless who came up with the idea, dynastic monarchs ran with it until well into the twentieth century. That bit of disinformation helped some royal dynasties sprawl across much of the world for ridiculously long periods.

Of course, all other forms of government have also employed—or at least tried to employ—disinformation to their advantage. It is as old a tradition as government; the empires of ancient Greece, Egypt, and Rome were all enthusiastic practitioners of propaganda. When governments present disinformation to their benefit, it is called propaganda. When a politician presents disinformation for their own personal benefit, it's called spin. Many governments have formed entire agencies to make up and spread disinformation (Jeffreys-Jones, 1989), while those looking to replace or overthrow those governments have been equally devoted to the value of creating and disseminating disinformation (M. Carr, 2006). Shortly after coming to power in Germany, the Nazis created a Ministry of Propaganda with its own broadcasting division. At the same time, they steered industry into creating really affordable radio sets so that every German home would have the technology to receive the vile outputs of the Ministry of Propaganda (Bergmeier & Lotz, 1997). This is an extreme example, but one thing that is very clear from history is that governments will readily employ disinformation, as many examples scattered throughout this book demonstrate, so we will not belabor the point here.

ALL THE NEWS WE FEEL LIKE MAKING UP

Although we don't have a clear history of the invention of the divine right of kings, we do have a clear sense of the role of disinformation in newspapers. It is, in fact, more venerable than accurately chronicling what actually happened. "Deceitful information wrapped in news packages has a longer history than news conspicuously produced to represent real events. News that falsely portrayed or simply invented facts were common early forms of news and journalistic practice, particularly at times of high anxiety, crisis, conflict, and revolution" (Waisbord, 2018, p. 1867). So, basically, the avalanche of disinformation coming from dubious sources these days could be seen as upholding the earliest traditions of media.

The newspapers in the early years of the US republic were highly partisan and were often directly supported by political patronage, with the goal being to directly influence politics and public opinion. Most newspapers lined up with the Federalist Party or the Democratic-Republican Party or the Whig Party, portraying events of the day through whatever spin was best received by their patrons, "eschewing even the slightest pretense of neutrality or objectivity" (M. Harvey, 2020, p. 174). Some of their tactics were devious tricks. During the 1800 election, for example, Federalist papers repeatedly published stories of Jefferson's death to limit enthusiasm for his campaign. It did not work; he won the election.

The rampant disinformation in newspapers of the day served to drown out real reporting. During Jefferson's political career, a reporter had the scoop of the early eighteenth century—that Jefferson had fathered children with one of the enslaved women on his plantation. Although utterly shocking and disgusting, this practice was not uncommon in the American South. In Jefferson's case, it was also incestuous. Jefferson's wife, Martha Wayles, had brought some enslaved persons with her into the marriage, including Sally Hemings. Because Jefferson's father-in-law had engaged in these practices as well, Martha and Sally were half-sisters. Sally's mother was also the product of similar circumstances. When Martha died, Jefferson turned his attentions to the much younger Sally, who reportedly looked much like her half-sister. When this appalling super-scandal was reported in 1802, however, it was ignored as typical political disinformation of the day.

After mainstream newspapers became less tied to political parties, many still saw themselves as an entertainment medium. So, they moved into new kinds of disinformation as their source of profit. The penny press arose in the mid-1800s as a predecessor of tabloids. Such publications filled real stories with fabrications to make them more sensational and drive readership. Or they just fabricated stories entirely. In the 1830s, the *New York Sun* moved from being a struggling paper to being the paper with the highest circulation in the world by simply making stuff up, starting with a six-part series on the discovery of life on the Moon, told in great detail—bipedal beavers, bison, unicorns, and man-bats.[1] Rival newspapers ran stories pointing out the complete fabrications, but it did not hurt the circulation of the *Sun*.

This is not to say that all journalism of the time was garbage or partisan propaganda. The exceptions were pretty exceptional. William Lloyd Garrison, for example, founded, edited, and published the weekly *Boston Liberator* newspaper for thirty-five years, a pioneer of investigative journalism. Devoted to documenting injustices through its reporting, the paper contributed mightily toward abolition of enslavement and the expansion of suffrage; Fredrick Douglass, Henry David Thoreau, and Sojourner Truth were among the authors who contributed to the paper, and the first edition of Douglass's 1845 renowned autobiography, *Narrative of the Life of Fredrick Douglass, An American Slave*, was published by Garrison in the *Boston Liberator* offices (Mayer, 1998).

The rise of objective journalism did not end fabrications or exaggerations in newspapers; the idea of journalism as a public service profession was not widely embraced until the 1880s (Schudson, 1978). Editors such as Joseph Pulitzer at the *New York World* built major papers based on the idea that providing accurate information about what actually happened was a major public service. Prominent investigative journalists became influential international figures by providing in-depth reporting. For example, Ida B. Wells of the *Chicago Defender*—the largest Black American newspaper and one of the largest overall—brought international attention to lynching, race riots, and other white atrocities of the Jim Crow-era South through her investigative reporting. Utilizing the telegraph and the USPS to exchange information at previously unimaginable speed, national and international news agencies began to emphasize objectivity and accuracy, which was a big change from previous approaches to reporting, and the information that people could access became much more consistent and much less partisan (Barth, 2014; Bimber, 2003). Mostly.

On the other hand, William Randolph Hearst fought against integrity in journalism as long as he could. In the first few decades of the twentieth century, Hearst owned the largest print media empire in the world, and there was not very much other than print media at the time. Hearst was not a savory character, being a fan of Hitler and Mussolini before the US entered World War II. He used his papers, among other things, to encourage Americans to go to war with Spain by inventing Spanish atrocities, faking documents from both governments, and creating Spanish plans for conquest. Newspaper sales soared, and when war was declared, Hearst had rockets fired from the top of the *New York Journal* building. The next day, the top headline of the paper was: HOW DO YOU LIKE THE JOURNAL'S WAR? (Daly, 2012).

During the presidency of Theodore Roosevelt, who had risen to national prominence serving in the Spanish-American War, his political enemies tried to hurt his efforts for environmentalism, food safety, and worker protections by planting false stories in the newspapers to make him look hypocritical on these issues. One report claimed that he allowed his children to torture a live turkey delivered to the White House for the Thanksgiving dinner, though the turkey had in fact arrived dressed to be roasted (Shafer, 2019).

Newspapers often had help in these disinformation endeavors. Remembering how successful newspapers had been at getting the US to declare war on Spain, a group called the US Committee on Public Information engaged in a broad campaign to generate false stories to feed to the newspapers to encourage the US to enter World War I. They created pamphlets, posters, and film footage—at times credited to other, nonexistent organizations—to support the false stories that they were trying to get the newspapers to run (Howard, 2020). And the US did enter the war.

Newspapers, and later other types of media, have also proven adept at cementing other people's misinformation into common counterknowledge, sometimes in really strange ways. The popular belief that spinach helps make people strong was popularized by the *Popeye* comic strip in newspapers in the 1930s. It was based on a German research study from the 1870s about nutrients in vegetables. In 1937 it was discovered, rather belatedly, that the study had made some decimal errors, overstating the iron content of spinach by a mere 1,000 percent (LaPlante, 2019). However, the comic had already engrained the idea—which subsequent comics, cartoons, and movies continued to reinforce—into popular culture, where it still lives.

BUT AT LEAST CORPORATIONS HAVE OUR BEST INTERESTS IN MIND, RIGHT?

As William Randolph Hearst was bestriding the newspaper world, one of his former reporters invented the political consulting firm in 1933. It was officially named Campaigns, Inc.

and intended to provide persuasion campaigns for corporations and political organizations; it soon became known as the Lie Factory (Lepore, 2018). The big innovation of Campaigns, Inc. was to turn garden variety lies of advertising into organized, wide-scale publicity efforts for major corporations and monopolies.

Modern advertising campaigns—coordinated ads across media platforms, catchy messaging, radio jingles, and such—had only begun in the 1920s (Kelley, 1956). Thanks to Campaigns, Inc., advertising campaigns would use disinformation to sell not only the products of corporations but their political agendas as well. Corporations defeated many kinds of proposed regulations of corporate powers and many progressive and reform-minded candidates who scared business interests, and, most notably on behalf of insurance companies, destroyed public support for President Harry Truman's plan for universal government health care for US citizens.[2] In the 1950s the Simulmatics Corporation brought computing power to the art of influence, advertising, and elections, and nothing has been the same since (Lepore, 2020).

The most notable of this kind of campaign, at least from the number of people who died as a result, is probably the campaign by tobacco companies on behalf of cigarettes. For many decades before they admitted that there were deathly health impacts of smoking, tobacco companies used disinformation campaigns to try to discredit science showing negative effects of smoking—which the internal research of the tobacco companies clearly demonstrated—and thwart investigations into tobacco company practices by offering their own "science" (Howard, 2020). The tobacco companies used this pretend science to help defeat hundreds of lawsuits before finally being held accountable for the devastating health ramifications of their products.

Sometimes corporations do not even bother to generate fake science. When actual scientists discovered that chlorofluorocarbons (CFCs) were destroying the earth's ozone layer, which keeps the sun from literally baking us all, corporations were not happy. CFCs were highly lucrative and present in many forms of spray—hair, paint, deodorant, coolants, and pretty much every other form of aerosol. So, rather than accepting that the uninhibited production and release of CFCs would turn the world into a flaming hellscape, their manufacturers started claiming that the science identifying the harm caused by CFCs was propaganda from the Soviet Union, "orchestrated by the Ministry of Disinformation of the KGB" (Langer, 2020, p. B5). Fortunately, science won, CFCs were banned, and humankind survived long enough to find new ways to cook the planet.

Often advertising is not so much misinformation as unclear information that the advertiser hopes will be interpreted in a certain way, even if that is not quite the truth. A great example comes from an ad campaign in the Washington, D.C., metro region when this book was being written. The local CBS affiliate, WUSA9, wanted everyone to know that the station had "DC's fastest growing morning show." Presumably, station executives hope that people hearing the slogan will think the show has the fastest growing viewership and, therefore, will start watching it too, because everybody else is doing so. However, the ads do not actually say what aspect of the show is growing the fastest; it could be viewership, but it also could be the number of employees, the collective ego of the on-air personalities, or the size of the set. Even if the show actually is the fastest growing in terms of viewership, that still leaves questions about what that really means. If the show previously had two viewers and now has ten, viewership has grown by 500 percent, but it could still be far, far behind a show that had two hundred thousand viewers and added twenty thousand more, reaching only 10 percent growth but still having 219,990 more viewers.

We cannot always blame corporations, governments, and other organizations for commonly held misinformation. Take giraffes, for example. To be clear, we're not blaming giraffes for spreading misinformation; we're talking about misinformation regarding giraffes. As was alluded to earlier, scientists long believed—and virtually all people still seem to—that giraffes have the longest necks in the world for reaching leaves at the tops of trees where there is less competition for the food. There was no evidence for this belief, however. Giraffes clearly bend down to eat, grazing at the same height as other browsers. The necks, in spite of overwhelming popular belief to the contrary, are used for fighting as the animals battle rivals during mating season by using their long necks and thick heads (LaPlante, 2019). Sometimes we just do this to ourselves.

💬 CHAPTER 11 GUIDING QUESTIONS

1. In what ways have governments used the power of disinformation for their own political agendas?
2. How does the media environment impact the practice of information literacy?
3. What benefits does disinformation provide for newspapers (and other traditional media platforms)?
4. In what ways are advertisements similar to disinformation campaigns (and how are they different)?
5. What are some of the historical methods that have been used to counter misinformation? How do they compare to today's methods?

NOTES

1. The staff of the *National Enquirer* were taking notes.
2. Sound vaguely familiar?

Pandemic-Style Disinformation, Misinformation, and Illiteracy

VICTORIAN ANTI-VAX

During the twentieth century, three hundred million people died of smallpox worldwide; now, no one does thanks to widespread use of a preventative vaccine. Smallpox, like many other diseases that were once scourges, are no longer threats. Children are no longer unusually lucky if they survive into adulthood. It seems like vaccines would be universally loved. Yet, for all the enormous success of vaccines, they have been hounded by disinformation campaigns since their invention.

The anti-vaccine movement—often shortened to the zippier anti-vax—began in 1853, when the British government passed the Vaccination Act, mandating that everyone get the smallpox immunization. The arguments of the initial anti-vaccine movement were that vaccines benefited doctors, infringed on people's control of their own bodies, might not work, and would lower the ability of the body to fight other diseases—core anti-vaccine arguments that are still used (Berman, 2020). One anti-vaccine argument that sadly lacks a contemporary parallel was the widespread rumor that the smallpox vaccine would cause the recipient to grow a cow head at the injection site, as was delightfully detailed by National Public Radio (NPR) in 2015. Cows were a much more common element of life for most people at the time, so you would think people would know better. Soon, the UK had the Anti-Compulsory Vaccination League and the US had the Anti-Vaccination Society of America. Claims about vaccines being a tool of government mind control would inevitably follow (St. Jean, Jaeger et al., 2020).

The modern anti-vaccine movement was triggered by a 1998 article in a British medical journal claiming a link between vaccines and autism; the paper was retracted by the journal when it became clear that the data were falsified and that the author, Andrew Wakefield—who lost his medical license for this immoral idiocy—had been paid to show this outcome in a specific group of children for the purpose of lawsuits against drug companies. So that paper achieved almost every possible ethical violation for research, yet anti-vaccine groups still point to it as evidence. Anti-vaccine campaigners in many nations have taken the disinformation from this one discredited paper and turned it into a movement that risks the lives of its adherents and anyone they come into contact with. Some of the disinformation is targeted to specific religious or cultural beliefs (Bailey, 2020). Incredibly, anti-vaccine conspiracy social media accounts numbered 23.1 million in December 2020; across just

Facebook, Instagram, YouTube, and Twitter, these accounts had 59.2 million followers (Dwoskin, 2020a).

As was discussed earlier in the book, the human brain has a number of cognitive and social mechanisms that can lead it to reject correct information in favor of misinformation. Polarization allows people to self-isolate into virtual factions behind filter bubbles, focused on sharing content based on emotion rather than reason (Rosen, 2018). If one already is suspicious of vaccines, confirmation bias will send one to misinformation that reinforces those suspicions. If one belongs to a social circle in which many members are suspicious of vaccines, group polarization will lead all members to be more suspicious. If enough members of that community embrace misinformation about vaccines, that misinformation becomes counterknowledge in the community. Sadly, in many communities—particularly online communities—anti-vaccine disinformation has indeed become counterknowledge.

SOCIAL MEDIA AND DISINFORMATION

The social and cognitive processes that can facilitate disinformation and misinformation are not new. Every new technology, of course, introduces new benefits and new challenges: "To invent the train is to also invent the train wreck" (Nichols, 2019, p. 77). However, social media networks are notable for the enormous extent of their impacts on information in many ways, including loudly amplifying disinformation and facilitating the flow of misinformation. The results of these impacts are readily seen in the blossoming of groups and beliefs based on disinformation, such as the now globally robust—and extremely unhealthy—anti-vaccine movement.

The ways in which people interact with information have been greatly altered by social media, often intentionally by social media companies. Although major social media companies have emphasized that they have policies against disinformation, these efforts have been far less robust than they could be to avoid claims of political bias because the overwhelming majority of disinformation on social media platforms is from conservative sources (Timberg, 2020a). Some conservative social media platforms—like Parler and Gab—intentionally leave what is clearly disinformation on their sites because they support its goals or because it draws traffic, even disinformation identified by law enforcement as being from foreign governments seeking to interfere in US elections (Timberg, 2020b).

The design of social media to spread information—regardless of quality or source, as fast as possible and to as many people as possible—inherently challenges literacy, as does the easy ability to manipulate images, sounds, and video. The speed of information transmission enables social media to serve as extremely effective spreaders of misinformation: "the extent to which systemic features inherent in the design of the sources and channels through which fake news is disseminated ensure[s] its proliferation" (Gelfert, 2018, p. 111). Anyone can create information and try to get it in front of the greatest number of people. Further, more information is encountered than is intentionally sought as newsfeeds push information that the feed identifies as something that the user might like. These newsfeeds, such as Apple News or Facebook, build from user interests and activities to create an algorithmically shaped set of stories that represents not a cross section of information sources or even a collection of vetted information sources but an accumulation of information of varying qualities that fits the information behavior patterns of the user.

Additionally, the technology of social media is so simple to use and so readily available that much disinformation is now created not by an organization, party, or government agency as it typically was in the past, but by individuals at home (Stanley-Becker & Romm, 2019). Once disinformation enters social media, the ideas flow horizontally with no entity in charge, making it easier for the ideas to persist and harder to correct or dismiss them (Serhan, 2019). The algorithms and tools employed by social media platforms can manipulate the ways in which users interact with information through illusion of choice, providing intermittent and variable rewards, constant novelty, and the fear of missing out (L. Diamond, 2019). Viral media really does spread like a virus—the cycle of sharing and promoting emotionally appealing news becomes self-reinforcing and self-replicating online—"which manifests in culture as media confusion, protests in the streets, sleepless nights, and Twitter wars" (Rushkoff, 2018, p. 8).

In this environment, users can be highly influenced by the sociopolitical information, disinformation, or misinformation that they encounter. Sociopolitical information is often viewed as being "sparse, potentially biased, and difficult to obtain," and fact-checking is seen by most voters as a "mind-numbing inconvenience" (O'Hara et al., 2009, pp. 1399–1400). For many, social media fills the void by presenting sociopolitical materials that require little effort. Voters who are less well informed are more likely to be influenced by likes, shares, and comments than by the actual content of the information (McCrummen, 2016). The biggest influence on the amount of sociopolitical materials that will be read is now not the accuracy of the information but how sharable it is (A. Smith, 2011). As one example, the less time British voters spent researching Brexit, the more likely they were to vote in favor of leaving the EU (Singh, 2016).

In contrast, for people who are already better informed and more information literate, social media can be a very effective tool of education and communication. Voters who enjoy collecting and discussing information and put more time into researching political issues are far more likely to be well-informed voters (O'Hara et al., 2009). The level of engagement with information encountered online even impacts perceptions about issues. Active social media use—that is, critically assessing information encountered—results in less support for populists, but passive use or uncivil use of social media leads to increased support for populists (Groshek & Koc-Michalska, 2017).

The way that information flows on social media has also cultivated an entire industry for emotive sociopolitical misinformation. Some brands, like InfoWars, have cultivated the generation of outrage in response into emotive disinformation into major financial success. Lesser known entities promulgate emotive disinformation not to build their own brand but to harvest user information. Hundreds of far right-wing websites that spread wild, emotive disinformation actually exist to harvest and sell information about people who read the articles—several data brokers exist solely to sell information from these sites (Stanley-Becker, 2020).

The rise of social media has coincided with mass distrust and unease due to economic conditions, making users more open to disinformation. Throughout the twenty-first century, most advanced industrial societies have been stuck in economic stagnation, with inflation outpacing wage increases and with climate change and massive waves of migration upsetting social orders (Inglehart, 2016). The great recession, the pandemic, and resulting economic crashes have further heightened a global sense of insecurity and uncertainty even in the most affluent societies. Over the past 150 years, financial crises have created very predictable patterns across democracies—majority parties shrink, far right parties grow, governing becomes more difficult, and polarization and fragmentation rise (Galston, 2018). Against this backdrop, disinformation on social media has found a very, very receptive audience.

In relation to the amount of content that they host, the largest social media companies—such as Facebook and Twitter and Instagram—do very little to directly combat disinformation from infecting their sites. Some take actions like labeling or limiting access to some very specific types of disinformation, removing small amounts of socially damaging content, closing some accounts that are bots, and temporarily limiting access to accounts that prolifically spread misinformation. Smaller but still very successful social media platforms such as LinkedIn, Pinterest, and Nextdoor, in sharp contrast, have been extremely successful at blocking most disinformation from even entering their sites and, when it does get through, removing it with great speed even though they have far fewer staff (Zakrzewski & Lerman, 2020). These sites take the far simpler and far more effective approach of directly blocking misinformation terms and hashtags, having vigilant volunteer moderators who are part of the communities, and creating information centers that provide verified factual information on topics for which much misinformation can be found elsewhere online.

On the global stage, no actor has mastered the use of social media to spread disinformation better than former US president Donald Trump. Avoiding mainstream news media scrutiny by communicating directly with his followers through Twitter, while he still was allowed on Twitter, he found that he can spread disinformation to great impact and no consequence. That it took Twitter until his attempted coup to close his account reveals how meaningless the platform's disinformation policies have been in practice.

Spreading misinformation is far from new, but the frequency and depth have accelerated over the past half century in the US presidency. The steady stream of disinformation about the success of the war in Vietnam during Lyndon Johnson's administration led to the complete embrace of disinformation as a primary tool of governance for Richard Nixon (Perlstein, 2008, 2014). In his first inaugural address, Nixon even made up problems he was going to solve, including a nonexistent rash of public libraries being burned down, which he promised to stop (Jaeger, Gorham, Bertot, & Sarin, 2014). Subsequent administrations employed disinformation more selectively, such as the attempts by the Reagan administration to avoid admitting to the Iran-Contra arms sales.

The big change was the realization that there was little political price to pay for spreading disinformation. Voters, it turns out, are not inclined to vote against a politician who violates democratic norms or principles—such as deliberately spreading disinformation—when they agree with the politics of that politician (Svolik, 2019). Republican politicians discovered during the years of the Barack Obama administration that they could say pretty much anything about his policies, politics, or citizenship status and pay no political price with their supporters (Alterman, 2020). Remember the threats about "death panels" deciding who lives and who dies under the Affordable Care Act?

With no political price for lying, an uneasy electorate because of economic circumstances, and the ease of spreading disinformation through social media, Donald Trump was possible. Once in office, Trump rejoiced in the lack of consequences for lying. He averaged six lies a day in 2017, sixteen in 2018, and twenty-two in 2019, and the total number of lies in 2019 was greater than in 2017 and 2018 combined; by the end of May 2020, he had lied more than nineteen thousand times as president (Kessler, Rizzo, & Kelly, 2020). By the end of his presidency, his average was up to seven hundred a week (Kessler, 2020). The *Washington Post*'s lead fact-checker summarized Trump as "a serial exaggerator without parallel in US politics. He not only consistently makes false claims but repeats them, in some cases hundreds of times, even though they have been proved wrong" (Kessler, 2020, p. A4).

Please be clear that the counting of the lies and the spread of disinformation is not an abstract exercise. Trump's anti-Muslim tweets, as one of many examples, caused spikes in anti-Muslim hate crimes in the US and other countries (Muller & Schwartz, 2018). When Trump blamed China in tweets for his getting the novel coronavirus, the use of racist language against Americans of Asian descent spiked 85 percent in twelve hours on social media, while many online groups and forums featured discourse blaming China or Americans of Asian descent for intentionally infecting him (Dwoskin, 2020b). Unfortunately, this lack of interest in the truth became a very large problem when something very bad happened globally.

THE PANDEMIC

In 2020 about 350,000 Americans were killed by the novel coronavirus. When you read this, the number will be much, much greater. But 350,000 people is a really big number of deaths; the aforementioned Vietnam War that Lyndon Johnson enjoyed lying about resulted in 58,000 American casualties in more than a decade. It is also considerably more Americans than were killed in all of World War II. On just December 9, 2020, 3,124 Americans died of novel coronavirus, more than the 2,403 Americans killed in the Japanese sneak attack on Pearl Harbor on December 7, 1941, or the 2,977 Americans killed in the September 11 terror attacks. With 5 percent of the world's population, the United States shamefully accounted for 20 percent of the pandemic deaths in 2020. The American people, in short, have handled the pandemic worse than any other state, mostly because of the flow of disinformation and the senseless things that people did as a result of embracing information illiteracy. Disinformation can kill many, many people; the pandemic is that story.

When the spring of 2020 dawned across the globe, the world was focusing on the novel coronavirus, a new respiratory virus that quickly became a worldwide pandemic. The novel coronavirus was the fourth significant new respiratory virus to appear this century—following SARS, MERS, and H1N1 swine flu—and the reactions followed an already established pattern. Totalitarian governments tried to suppress information available to their citizens with mixed results, more democratic governments tried to educate their citizens with equally mixed results, and the mainstream media acted as if nothing else was happening on the planet. The difference with this novel coronavirus—beyond the not insignificant fact that it evolved into a global pandemic when the others did not—was that it was the first of these new viruses to appear in a world where social media dominates the information environment.

For many years, disinformation and science have been competing for attention (Dallek, 2020; Mooney, 2005). A right-wing media star of the 1950s named Dan Smoot began the improbable lie that governments put fluoride in the water as a form of mind control, a fabrication that some people still subscribe to. Another movement in the 1950s tried to stop World Health Organization (WHO) efforts to promote awareness and treatment of mental illness, claiming such efforts were intended to promote communism and destroy Christianity. In the 1970s activists pushed for a toxic extract of apricots to be made available as a cancer treatment. Also in the 1970s Ronald Reagan, as governor of California, promoted the war against evolution being taught in schools, which continues today.[1]

The difference between the 1950s or the 1970s and now is the ability of social media to globally broadcast disinformation about science instantly. As the pandemic took hold globally, a lack of information literacy was on prominent display pretty much everywhere. The virus quickly became an opportunity for bad actors and well-meaning but ill-informed actors alike to spread harmful, false claims related to the virus. Through social media platforms, bad actor governments, like Russia and Iran, were working overtime to sow disinformation that the US government had created the virus or, inevitably, that billionaire George Soros had created the virus. Though the virus originated in China, the Chinese government was claiming that the outbreak of the virus originated in several other places, including the US.

Globally, anti-vaccination activists immediately began to claim that the pandemic was engineered as a pretext for an eventual program of mandatory vaccination and state surveillance (Burki, 2020). Populist politicians in the United States and other nations quickly seized on unscientific and incorrect claims that the drugs hydroxychloroquine and azithromycin were effective in curing or preventing infection, creating shortages for people who actually needed those drugs. Retired Microsoft founder Bill Gates was the villain in many of these early disinformation efforts because he famously dedicated much of his wealth to supporting the development and administration of vaccines. In April 2020 disinformation regarding Gates was the most widespread single category of virus misinformation, with the ten most popular YouTube videos spreading the theory being viewed almost five million times in six weeks (Wakabayashi, 2020).

Initially, the right-wing infosphere in the US was somehow simultaneously claiming that the virus was a Chinese bioweapon, that it was no more harmful than the common flu, and that it was only being hyped to hurt then president Trump's reelection efforts. Many state and local politicians in the US, in their official capacities, have asserted that the virus is a hoax or is overhyped and have encouraged ignoring CDC guidance about limiting the spread of the virus. Many US citizens followed the lead of the president and many other politicians and did not wear masks or socially distance or avoid large crowds, making the impact of the disease far worse than it otherwise would have been. The resulting confusion of government responses oddly echoes both of the primary types of responses that governments typically implement in response to pandemics, focusing on either the community or the individual (Fabian, 2020). However, in this situation, some parts of government were focusing on the community and other parts were focusing on the individual. Parallel behaviors by political leaders and citizens were occurring in many other nations as well, though generally not to the same ridiculous extent.

Many people with limited knowledge about viruses were disseminating misinformation that garlic, zinc, nasal spray, vitamin C, colloidal silver, specially-made toothpaste, cocaine, and powdered rhino horn were cures for the virus, as well as admonitions not to eat in Chinese restaurants or open mail sent from China. One particularly surprising assertion was that protective plastic bubble wrap in packages mailed from China somehow contained virulent air that could infect the receiver.

In Iran, the ruling clerics advised drinking camel urine to ward off the virus; in Brazil, the president fired all the leading government health officials and made secret all statistics about the disease in the country. The president of Belarus promoted vodka and saunas as a cure. The leaders of the British government seemed determine to violate their own health orders as ineptly and comically as possible. A conspiracy theory arose that the virus was spread by plutonium falling from orbiting satellites.[2]

One of the wackiest theories took hold in Europe—and provides a great example of information illiteracy: claiming that the real cause of the pandemic was the construction of high-speed 5G wireless data networks, activists tried to burn down or otherwise destroy communications infrastructure to halt the spread of the disease. If you think about it for a moment, the impossibility of a human disease being spread through wireless technology should be screamingly obvious. Perhaps people are confused about what constitutes a "communicable" disease.

As president, Donald Trump promoted several "cures" based on disinformation, none more mind-boggling than encouraging people to ingest disinfectants to stay healthy from the virus, despite very obvious warnings on the packaging not to consume the contents.[3] Keep in mind that injecting bleach into someone was previously discussed only as a means of committing murder.[4] This clearly life-threatening "cure" resulted in a spike in poisonings in the United States after he made this suggestion. He repeatedly said that the virus would simply "disappear" and that it is no worse than the flu, in spite of the global death toll in the millions. He also frequently encouraged protests against public health measures in the pandemic, undermined the messages from federal health officials, and urged people not to follow the guidelines created by the CDC. The frequency of Trump's false and misleading public statements spiked from the onset of the pandemic to the end of his presidency (Kessler, Rizzo, & Kelly, 2020).

The wave of social justice protests that swept the nation during the pandemic in reaction to police brutality toward, and the disproportionate impacts of the pandemic on, communities of color followed a similar pattern of misinformation, starting at the top. Trump and many of his supporters baselessly claimed that the predominantly peaceful and unarmed protestors were domestic terrorists; in contrast, he frequently praised the patriotism of armed protestors who took over the capitols of a number of states to protest pandemic-related public health measures, including some who were later arrested by the FBI for plotting to kidnap the governors of Michigan and Virginia. Many other actors spread huge volumes of disinformation related to the social justice protests through social media, spreading lies about actions of the police and the protestors, trying to demonize, further antagonize, and promote violence.

These claims have included stories that pallets of bricks are being left in cities specifically for protestors to throw at police, while online trolls used misinformation to encourage veterans to show up armed to stop protestors. Republican Party officials promoted stories that the video of George Floyd's death—showing his killing at the hands of Minneapolis police officers—was faked and that the ubiquitous and apparently tireless George Soros was paying the protesters.

Much of the problem with the spread of this kind of false information is that it is heavily spread on social media and on direct messaging services (SMS text, email, WhatsApp, Tik Tok), where much of the false information is being sent as direct messages or as graphical images to avoid being caught by keyword checks. Social media companies, because their algorithms give priority to controversial topics to generate views and thereby revenue (Badia, 2019), were heavily promoting this misinformation even when they intended to stop it. Emotional content is far more memorable to most people than are facts or statistics (Sharot, 2017), and spreading fear about a new virus certainly qualifies as emotive. In their algorithm-fueled filter bubbles (Del Vicario et al., 2016), many users had no idea that they were only receiving misinformation about the virus. Additionally, the politicization of the virus has led to a feeling of two irreconcilable Americas—one that feels the virus is overblown and another that encourages protective measures. There seems to be no room for compromise, empathy, or trials of alternative mitigation strategies.

Even experts in epidemics were getting caught by disinformation, with some of them retweeting materials from Russian disinformation campaigns about the virus (Bellware, 2020). As governments and individuals have become increasingly talented at creating realistic fake news, whole online businesses, like Channel23News, have evolved to allow users to create genuine-looking fake news to populate into social media. "And the bad guys' most powerful weapon? Social media" (M. Sullivan, 2020, p. C1). All told, so much disinformation and misinformation were generated related to the pandemic that the bad information was labeled an *infodemic*.

Social media platforms are now one of the primary sources—if not the primary source— of political and current events information for the majority of Americans, and many individual social media accounts have larger numbers of readers than the major news organizations (Allcott & Gentzkow, 2017; Gottfried & Shearer, 2016). People relying on social media for their political and current events information, unfortunately, do not generally understand the ways in which they receive that information.

A Pew Research study from summer 2020 found that people who rely on social media as their primary or sole pathway to news are far more misinformed—and oddly unconcerned about being misinformed—than those who rely on print media, network television, or news apps. "Even as Americans who primarily turn to social media for political news are less aware and knowledgeable about a wide range of events and issues in the news, they are more likely than other Americans to have heard about a number of false or unproven claims" (quoted in M. Sullivan, 2020, p. C1). Thanks to the mountains of misinformation on social media about vaccines, large numbers of Americans refused to get a novel coronavirus vaccine when it became available.

Although some have argued that the importance of the relationship between democracy and information access for individual citizens has been overrated as a historical concept (Dervin, 1994), recent events would very strongly indicate otherwise. Huge numbers of people are actively choosing to believe what is clearly disinformation to their own detriment. To end as we began: disinformation kills. As does information illiteracy.

The next section of the book explores what can be done to promote information literacy, as well as combat disinformation, misinformation, and information illiteracy, by information professionals and information institutions, ranging from educating our communities to increasing collaboration among information institutions to advocating for policies at all levels of government. These are huge problems, and we have heaps of work to do. It begins with creating a conceptual and practical approach to addressing information literacy as a lifelong issue.

💬 CHAPTER 12 GUIDING QUESTIONS

1. In the concurrent opinion in the 1927 Supreme Court case *Whitney v. California*, Justice Louis Brandeis famously wrote, "If there be time to expose through discussion the falsehoods and fallacies, to avert the evil by the process of education, the remedy to be applied is more speech, not enforced silence." Do you agree? How does this viewpoint fit into today's social media environment?

2. In what ways has the social media disinformation environment contributed to the rise of nationalist, anti-democratic movements in the past decade? Have there been counterexamples (e.g., pro-democratic movements empowered by social media)? How should we balance these costs and benefits of social media?

3. Why has the novel coronavirus been so politically charged? How have mis- and disinformation contributed to this?

4. Why might someone continue to believe misinformation despite being informed otherwise?

5. One casualty of our current information society is the loss of nuance—how can we balance a need to question authority (corporate and government alike) with the conspiratorial nonsense that is being spread by malicious or ignorant actors?

NOTES

1. As does evolution, though not quickly enough.
2. Of course! It all makes sense now.
3. Please do not do this; the warnings on the packaging are telling you the truth.
4. In her classic mystery novel, *Shroud for a Nightingale* (1971), P. D. James begins the story with the murder of a nurse who is killed when she imbibes household disinfectant.

Toward Lifelong
Information Literacy

THE GRAND UNIFICATION THEORY
(OF INFORMATION LITERACY, AT LEAST)

Libraries have long been dedicated to promoting information literacy in the communities that they serve; it is pretty much the defining characteristic of a modern library. From children's storytime to Internet literacy courses to classes teaching undergraduate students about using databases, many of the essential functions of libraries revolve around providing information literacy skills in a multitude of contexts. Although this focus on information literacy has been continuous through the modern era of librarianship, efforts in these areas have snapped into greater focus after the major impacts of online misinformation on the outcome of the 2016 presidential election. In these often distinctly undemocratic times, "we ask ourselves what we as librarians in a democracy can do" (MacLeish, 1940, p. 385).

A great many libraries have created new lists, teaching aids, courses, or interactive learning tools to help patrons understand the qualities of reliable information and valid sources. The Internet is a bouncy castle stuffed with misinformation and lies, and libraries of all types are trying to find ways to empower people to make better decisions when seeking information. A flood of new books related to information literacy have been published in the last several years, many universities have created new courses to promote information literacy (Pashia & Critten, 2019), and many hundreds of new information literacy resources have been created by libraries since 2016 to battle online misinformation (Agosto, 2018).

Promoting information literacy has been one of the longest-running and most socially significant contributions of information professionals. As technologies and methods of communication have evolved, our focus has expanded from literacy in a print world to literacy in an online world and critical literacy to assess the quality of information found. The need to focus our information literacy efforts on the area of policy is becoming increasingly vital. Since the 2016 election, libraries have constructed hundreds of online fake news pathfinders and tools (Agosto, 2018), but the scope of the problem is far larger than pathfinders or other learning aids alone can handle. Additionally, we cannot take for granted information literacy even among members of our profession, the one that exists to teach and promote information literacy to the rest of the population.

As we detailed in earlier chapters, a great deal has been written about information literacy, but primarily in terms of describing specific information literacy programs at individual institutions. Most of these programs are rather constrained in nature. Information literacy instruction in libraries exploded after the introduction of the Internet, especially online catalogs and databases (Leckie et al., 2009). What is taught in college can best be understood as "generic information literacy" because it is taught to supplement course content rather than being the content (Stagg & Kimmins, 2014). Further, one meta-study of information literacy articles found that only 1.5 percent of literacy programs in libraries were evaluated in any way to assess their effectiveness (Crawford & Feldt, 2007). A core problem with focusing information literacy at this population is that students starting college tend to "believe that all library resources are credible" and "that every question has a single answer" (Hinchliffe et al., 2018, p. 9). As a result, most of the programs being written about in the literature are not being assessed as to whether they succeed.

Information literacy programs and tools also primarily exist in isolation. Many, many libraries and related institutions have created many, many programs and tools for information literacy, but not in conjunction with other, similar institutions, much less collaboratively between different kinds of institutions. Efforts, as a result, are perpetually redundant to what other libraries are doing, and expertise is not being shared to create programs and tools that encapsulate the knowledge and expertise of many types of librarians. And, as the last few chapters have explored, disinformation, misinformation, and related topics are central to teaching information literacy but have only recently become a part of considerations of literacy (R. Anderson, 2017; Banks, 2016; Batchelor, 2017; Bluemle, 2018; Burkhardt, 2017; Lor, 2018).

Beyond disinformation and misinformation, there are also unavoidable technological issues that are central to information literacy. Because algorithms, or even the seemingly more objective search engine results, do not necessarily provide the best resources—or even necessarily correct ones—helping users understand that the content that they see can be highly politically motivated, entirely driven by profit motives, or mostly disinformation is an indispensable aspect of teaching information literacy.

To consider ways in which libraries could more effectively collaborate on information literacy, building a bridge between different understandings of information literacy is quite important. As can be seen in the definitions discussed in earlier chapters, library organizations generally tend to present literacy as a definable set of skills that everyone needs and can accomplish as a set of achievable thresholds, whereas researchers, especially those using the terminology of critical literacy, tend to present literacy as a social construct that prepares people either to fully participate in society or, much more pessimistically, to fit into proscribed social roles.

Yet, there are some strong foundational elements from which we can begin to see the way toward lifelong information literacy because information literacy

- has become the foundation for virtually all other types of learning (C. L. Douglass, 2017);
- promotes an emphasis on critical thinking (Sturges & Gastinger, 2010);
- teaches people to ask questions rather than automatically accept what they are told (Burkhardt, 2016);
- helps to "avoid misinformation and disinformation and to ensure that relevant and comprehensible information is available" (Mathiesen, 2014, p. 12);
- encourages the ability to sort information into sensible categories to help deal with large amounts of information (Grabe & Myrick, 2016); and
- is both a right and a responsibility (Carillo, 2019).

Bridging all these insights about information literacy offers the opportunity to construct a comprehensive definition that can serve as the foundation for a comprehensive approach to information literacy that unifies the field into a common purpose and collective action.

LIFELONG INFORMATION LITERACY

When we talk about the process of literacy as a lifelong concept, we are really talking about two things. The first is the need for a comprehensive, consistently used definition for information literacy that treats it as a continual process of learning through an individual's life, and we offered one of those earlier in the book. Second, with such an agreed-upon definition, we can then have a foundation on which to build collaborative education programs and policy initiatives that provide comprehensive lifelong literacy education across information institutions and programs. The current approach of intermittent information literacy trainings that are mostly introductory and brief—and not coordinated across institutions—does not match the overwhelming need for education in information literacy.

To begin defining the process of supporting lifelong information literacy, we should again return to the definition of information literacy that we first suggested chapter 1:

> **Information literacy** is a constantly refined practice of processing, accessing, understanding, critically evaluating, and using information in ways that are relevant to one's life. Information literacy relies on a social structure that promotes the agency of individuals in their communities and in the legal, political, educational, communication, and economic structures in their lives. Practicing information literacy is an iterative learning process that occurs throughout an individual's lifetime.
>
> Information literacy encompasses not only foundational literacies (reading/prose, writing/document, numeracy/quantitative) but also aspects of digital literacy (technology skills and ethics) and media literacy (critical analysis of nontextual content). In many cases, information literacy is closely associated with data, scientific, health, civic, and other context-specific literacies.

And there should be no confusion here—information literacy is an educative function that society needs information professionals to thoroughly embrace and own. That continuous educational nature of information literacy is the process—and professional responsibility—that we are calling lifelong information literacy.

In no small part, the jobs of information professionals have evolved whether or not they admit it yet: because "librarians can no longer compete with the masses of misinformation being circulated on a daily basis, their role is shifting from fact-checker to educator" (De Paor & Heravi, 2020, p. 8). Education for information literacy is not a one-time, or three-time, event. It is a process that requires continual renewal to stay current with perpetually changing technologies that infiltrate more and more spaces of everyday life while tidal waves of information spill froth restlessly.

We have mentioned this before, but it needs repeating. A bigger, coordinated approach to information literacy between types of information institutions is desperately needed. We can only address information literacy as a continuous, lifelong learning process if all information institutions are actively involved in ensuring ongoing information literacy education to all the communities that they serve. The starting point will be establishing a definition for the process of lifelong information literacy that we can all work with.

As earlier chapters have noted, there are a lot of definitions of information literacy floating about and crashing into one another. They come from different professional organizations and different scholars and different fields, but each seems to represent one perspective on a larger topic. It's like having dozens of people each looking at the same mountain, but from their own unique, stationary perspective. Each describes the mountain in terms of what they see, not what everyone sees. This presents an opportunity, however, to build a working definition of the mountain, er, lifelong information literacy, from these divergent perspectives. So, here's our best shot:

> *Lifelong information literacy* is the process by which information professionals foster and support a constantly refined capacity for critical evaluation of information from before one begins school until after one retires. It encompasses teaching foundational literacy (reading/prose, writing/document, and numeracy/quantitative), digital literacy (technology skills and ethics), search literacy (articulating what is being sought), media literacy (critical analysis of nontextual content), sociopolitical literacy (understanding the context), and multimodal literacy (putting it all together and applying it to different types of content) across different information institutions and educational contexts.

Lifelong information literacy is both the point and the goal of literacy education because, by necessity, becoming information literate is a permanent state of existence.

Serving as comprehensive and consistent providers of and educators for lifelong information literacy will require collaboration between information professionals, information professional organizations, information institutions, and information educators. It will require working together so that the process of lifelong information literacy is the programmatic and policy equivalent of omnipresent "Read" posters brought to life.

Getting to lifelong information literacy will necessitate the following:[1]

- Orientation of core and elective courses in library and information science degree programs toward information literacy as the driver of the field and information professionals as information literacy educators as the foundation of professional preparation
- Continuation of this education for information professionals in the field throughout their careers because effectively teaching information literacy will entail staying as current as possible with the information and ICTs that need to be taught
- Collaboration among all types of libraries working together to create teaching programs and tools that build on the specific knowledge of each kind of institution and that all institutions can use with the communities they serve
- Aggregation of tools, programs, assessments, and resources for information literacy in a manner to make them equitably available to all information institutions
- Cooperation among professional organizations to craft field-wide goals, standards, and policy objectives for teaching and promoting information literacy

- Application of teaching programs and tools consistently by all kinds of institutions so that members of all communities receive access to equitable training and resources
- Creation of partnerships with other civic institutions and professional organizations that can be allies and accomplices in the promotion of information literacy in communities
- Education of patrons as an always ongoing process, finding ways to begin engagement with information literacy at the earliest ages possible and continuing that engagement throughout the arc of life
- Promotion of research into approaches to information literacy and of increased funding for research and innovation related to information literacy from agencies such as IMLS and DOE
- Evaluation of teaching programs and tools frequently to measure their effectiveness and iteratively improve them
- Communication about the importance of information literacy by each information institution to the communities that it serves to promote awareness of information literacy and participation in information literacy education programs and tools
- Promotion of better policies related to information literacy at local, state, and national levels and support for information literacy to be addressed and understood by political leaders and decision makers

Yes, this is quite a long and challenging to-do list.[2] However, combating disinformation, misinformation, and information illiteracy in any meaningful way will require ongoing education of ourselves and of the members of the communities that we serve. We need to make people aware of some very complicated issues and help them understand how those issues—and the habits of their own brains—have to be taken into account with any piece of information. The next chapter offers some considerations on how we might try to accomplish this mighty, mighty to-do list.

💬 CHAPTER 13 GUIDING QUESTIONS

1. How does the idea of lifelong information literacy connect with the definitions of IL that we provide in this book (and the other definitions provided by professional organizations and scholars)?
2. What kind of information literacy training do you believe is appropriate for an LIS professional? If you are an MLIS graduate or student, was this (or is this) your experience while getting your degree?
3. What are some potential collaborations or partnerships that you could imagine initiating to establish information literacy programs?
4. What are barriers to the practice of lifelong information literacy? How might those barriers be mitigated?
5. Do you see opportunities for libraries to take a leadership role in developing lifelong information literacy practices? What are some initial steps they could take in addressing some of the to-do items we list in this chapter?

NOTES

1. Each step begins with a rhyming word to help you remember it. We were sadly unable to work in "defenestration," on the basis of it being an excellent word, but we could not determine how throwing people out of windows would ultimately help in this effort, therapeutic as it may sound.
2. You should probably clean out the attic, too.

Advocacy, Activism, and Self-Reflection for Information (Literacy) Professionals

PALACES OF THE PEOPLE DELIVERING BOOKS BY MULE

Libraries have been pithily and alliteratively described as "palaces for the people" (Klinenberg, 2018) because they are open, free, creative, and egalitarian in all the best ways. They are "nonjudgmental, inclusive, and fundamentally kind" (Orlean, 2018, p. 267). Well, most of the time at least; chapter 15 discusses some of the work in this area that libraries still have to do. In many places and situations, they are a bastion of human rights, as well as a profound symbol of those rights. "The idea of the public library is, on the face of it, an improbable one. Only recently in human history has there been a widespread agreement that people have inherent rights deserving universal respect" (Lerner, 2009, p. 125). With more than 320,000 public libraries worldwide, in nations that have libraries that are open and free to members of the public, they are as close to a cross-national symbol of universal human rights as has ever been created.

This unique nature of public libraries is familiar to anyone who has worked in a public library that serves a large number of immigrants. People who immigrate from societies that lack freely accessible public libraries are often hesitant to even enter the library, assuming that they will be excluded. When newcomers learn that they can borrow the materials without cost—which also means returning them, another concept that may need to be explained—the reactions demonstrate what a symbolic revelation a public library truly is.

Libraries also have been exceptionally skilled at becoming whatever their communities most need. As soon as the ability existed to expand community outreach, libraries found ways to do so. The first bookmobile was created in 1905 in Washington County, Maryland; now book bikes, mobile literacy buses, book-delivery drones, vending machines, and little free libraries are among the many ways in which libraries try to reach the communities that need them. One of the most amazing examples of this outreach involved horses and mules in Depression-era America.

The Pack Horse Library Project was established in 1935 as part of the Works Progress Administration (WPA), which was central to Franklin Roosevelt's New Deal to help America out of the Great Depression. Running until 1943, the Pack Horse Library Project was designed to bring literacy, books, and other reading materials into the most isolated areas of Appalachia where there were no libraries, few roads, and few schools. Traveling by horse or mule, these librarians carried reading materials into some of the most inaccessible mountain communities in North America. The WPA provided only a monthly salary; these librarians had to collect all the books as donations, and even drew their own picture books for children and made recipe and cleaning books out of newspaper clippings. These librarians delivered an average of more than 3,500 books and 8,000 magazines a month while serving a population of about 600,000.

This is just one really impressive example, but it is emblematic of what libraries do. It is a profession dedicated to making things better, however possible. We once suggested that the unique contributions of libraries could be summarized in four verbs: belong, provide, create, engage (Jaeger, Gorham, Taylor et al., 2017). Libraries belong to their communities, but they also sustain them. Each library provides a wide range of solutions to community problems. Libraries create educational and community opportunities to meet the individual needs of their specific communities. Engagement is exemplified by the kind of outreach provided by the Pack Horse Library Project.

Information literacy is a part of each of these aspects of library contributions. An information literate populace is essential for the health and inclusiveness of the community, as well as engagement and belonging promoted by the library. Many of the educational and community opportunities created by libraries and many of the resources and services that they provide are intended to promote information literacy for all community members. In summary, "supporting critical information literacy functions, fighting fake news, and advocating for intellectual freedom" are central to the mission of all libraries (Bossaller, 2017, p. 206).

Beyond what we can do in practice to teach, provide, and promote information literacy, our field also can engage in advocacy and activism to make information literacy more available and valued at the individual, community, and societal levels. "Too often, because of our field's resistance to advocacy, we hurt our institutions and our profession by not being louder and prouder about our accomplishments" (Jaeger, Gorham, Taylor et al., 2017, p. 300). Nowhere may this be truer than in the space of information literacy. Libraries and other information institutions have developed many creative and innovative curricula, tools, collaborations, and partnerships focused on information literacy, yet not as consistently and widely and collaboratively as the situation now demands. We are doing much good to improve information literacy, but we need to do more, together.

INFORMATION LITERACY MEETS INFORMATION POLICY

The library and information profession knows more about information literacy than does any other profession, and librarians and information professionals work at the only social institutions dedicated to teaching it. Our perspectives should be central to discussions of policies about information literacy. Instead, not only do we lack a seat at the table for the discussions, the people having the discussions generally do not have a clue about what they are discussing. In a case of irony so sharp that it hurts, many of the problems with information literacy are exacerbated by policy decisions driven by policymakers' lack of literacy about information literacy.

Focusing on the area of information technology tells this story very clearly. The lack of information literacy by US leaders about Internet-related technologies—whether that lack of literacy derives from too little knowledge or uncritical enthusiasm—has significantly shaped the creation of US information policies. As a result, "the government took a primarily hands off approach to avoid curtailing business innovations, with limited regulations or even scrutiny" (Jaeger, 2020, p. 381). These resulting policies have given technology companies great latitude in the ways in which they collect information and share it with users, which has served to forward a lack of information literacy in much of the population as algorithms enhance the existing confirmation biases and filter bubbles of users. This self-reinforcing cycle of information illiteracy has also heavily shaped the online environment in which misinformation has prospered and overridden actual information.

If you think back to chapter 8 ("Literacy Politics and Literacy Policies"), information literacy is having a direct impact on the information policy process in the US in multiple ways:

- At the federal level, a lack of information literacy by many policymakers has led to insufficient policy oversight of Internet-related activities for several decades.
- This insufficient oversight has heavily contributed to the proliferation of misinformation online, driven by bad actors and amoral algorithms.
- The collection of vast amounts of personal information about each user means that online entities have the ability to target information—or misinformation—that will be of most interest to the user.
- Because many members of the public have limited information literacy skills in the online environment, misinformation can quickly become widely believed.
- The widely believed misinformation then can fuel voting habits and the policies supported by the public.

This cycle becomes self-reinforcing, with the lack of policy oversight furthering a lack of public awareness of the need for oversight. At every step of this cycle, failings of information literacy—either by the members of the public or by the policymakers or by both—directly shape the creation and implementation of information policy, or the lack thereof.

The failures of policy and politics to understand information literacy are hardly abstractions, as the pandemic once again reveals. With the US having more cases of and deaths from the pandemic than any other country (Abutaleb & Dawsey, 2020), and misinformation about the virus widespread, the connections between information policy and information literacy are thrown into sharp relief:

- Limited information literacy of many policymakers leads to insufficient information policy oversight of social media.
- Insufficient information policy oversight of social media exacerbates problems of misinformation.
- Limited information literacy among many members of the public leads to widespread belief in misinformation and people acting on those beliefs, including advocating for policies based on the misinformation.
- Some policymakers, again because of limited information literacy, also believe disinformation and enact policies based on the misinformation (Jaeger & Taylor, 2021b).

The result of these connections is the public's and government's failing to respond to the pandemic in a coordinated or coherent manner. Most obviously, the impacts of these failings of information literacy have manifested in the widespread refusal by many Americans to wear masks and socially distance. Although these are time-tested approaches to managing a pandemic—and were key strategies during the last major global pandemic in the 1910s—vast amounts of misinformation online have claimed that these are ineffective or even more likely to make one sick. Many politicians have parroted, and apparently have actually fallen for, this misinformation, furthering its pernicious effects.

We really need to be better engaged in policy discussions related to information literacy at local, state, national, and international levels. We own this topic, and we have to start making people listen to our unique expertise to, it is hoped, shape more sensible policy outcomes and actions by political leaders. And there are actions that we can take in practice, in research, and in advocacy at the intersection of information literacy and information policy.

Since 2016 many libraries, schools, news organizations, and nonpartisan public interest groups have all engaged in campaigns to promote critical information literacy skills and raise awareness about online misinformation. However, these efforts have been primarily uncoordinated, missing the opportunity to build consistent messages for users (Jaeger & Taylor, 2021a, 2021c). Encouraging libraries, schools, news organizations, and nonpartisan public interest groups to work together to collaboratively build consistent messages, educational materials, and reference guides could result in a clearer educational message promoting critical information literacy skills and awareness of online misinformation. These efforts could also try to help users see the broader impacts of online misinformation—that political opinions and policy decisions can be shaped and determined by public support for policies based on misinformation. Perhaps the most difficult aspect of this approach is the need to avoid politicizing the education itself.

Research exploring these connections in more contexts and countries would also help greatly to create a better understanding of the scope of the impacts of connections between information policy and information literacy. More research in this space would help build a knowledge base that demonstrates the range of connections and the different impacts of the global variety of connections. This space could be researched by scholars of information policy and of information literacy, with cross-disciplinary collaborations—or at least with experts in both areas working in collaboration—perhaps being the most likely to identify the full range of issues.

Finally, and most ambitiously, there is a need for education and research in this space to build toward advocacy for improving information literacy among political actors. Voters have not generally been drawn to evaluating candidates based on their capacity to critically assess information, ironically enough. Given the current challenges that the world faces and the growing importance of critical information literacy skills in governing, never has there been a better time to begin an advocacy campaign for political candidates who can demonstrate critical information literacy skills. Perhaps information literacy skills could become a regular part of debates.

In a time of global pandemic, international economic inequity, and renewed focus on issues of social justice around the world, rethinking assumptions in every area of scholarship is needed. For information policy, especially in the world of the IoT, examining the underexplored connections to other aspects of information is vital to ensure that the study of information policy remains relevant and supports the improvement of governance and society. The intersection of information policy and information literacy seems to offer a wealth of opportunities for valuable new contributions and insights. We, however, also need to spend time with our own kind on these issues.

INFORMATION LITERACY MEETS INFORMATION PROFESSIONALS

As a profession—regardless of what we each personally believe—the ideal vision of practice is helping to introduce a patron to a range of valid sources on an issue and ways to assess the quality of those sources, and then letting the patron learn and decide for themselves, as close to honest as possible brokers of information. The idea of our institutions existing to promote a vibrant democracy filled with informed citizens has been a driver for our efforts and self-perceptions for the better part of the past century (some of the best examples of this articulation include Ditzion, 1947; MacLeish, 1940; and Shera, 1949). That "arsenals of democracy" ideal, however, may not always be the case in application.

Libraries intersect with politics and policy processes in a number of long-established and well-known ways (Jaeger & Taylor, 2019). Political and policy decisions, from cutting local taxes to establishing national filtering requirements, can directly shape library operations and services to patrons. Professional organizations advocate in political and policy processes to garner support for libraries and take stands on policy issues, such as ALA officially being against nuclear proliferation. Some librarians tie themselves in knots trying to achieve the absolutely impossible goal of a "neutral" collection so that no one is offended. Community members challenge books in collections because they disagree with them, often for political reasons, and local politicians turn down funding requests for additions to the collection because of their political preferences (see a recent example in Citrus County, Florida, when county commissioners refused to fund a digital subscription to the *New York Times,* decrying it as "fake news"; Carlton, 2019). All of these are extremely complex issues that have received a great deal of attention in the discourse of our field, including by us.

Ultimately, because they exist in all these political contexts, libraries are inherently and unavoidably political institutions (Jaeger & Sarin, 2016a). Politics also cannot be removed from teaching information literacy, at least in certain ways. Because search engine results do not necessarily provide the best resources—or even remotely correct ones—helping users understand that the results can be highly politically motivated and mostly misinformation is a necessary aspect of information literacy.

Neutrality is impossible for a librarian—or anyone in any profession—because each person has their own thoughts, experiences, feelings, and perspectives that shape how they uniquely view the world. Being an automaton clearly does not constitute a realistic professional criterion; even computers cannot achieve neutrality given the human beings that control their data inputs and algorithms. Neutrality is also only a luxury of those who are already privileged, serving to support the existing hegemonies (Branum, 2008). But, under the ethics of our profession, there is an expectation that a librarian should not be leading patrons only to information that solely reflects the beliefs of the librarian. Intentionally steering patrons toward incorrect information is really not good.

Let's say, for example, a librarian believes that the earth is flat. So, if no one can be completely neutral, it is not necessarily a disqualification from being a librarian to hold some views that are emphatically incorrect, like thinking the earth is flat, or shaped like a stellated dodecahedron, for that matter. The problem would be stocking the library with nothing but physical and electronic resources that reflected this opinion and steering all scientific inquiries in their direction.

The simple, uncomfortable truth is that the practice of librarianship involves countless decisions about what information is to be prioritized—what items are ordered, what topics get turned into displays, what events are programmed, what community outreach and engagement activities are planned, whether filters are installed on library computers, what databases are purchased, and so on. During the early years of the public library movement, state libraries often created lists of what books should be in the collection of a library by the size of its service population (Wiegand, 2011). Although there are serious limitations of that approach in terms of tailoring the collection to community needs—to say nothing of opening up the collection to being controlled by the biases of someone at the state level rather than the local level—there really is no contemporary check on how a library handles information.

Writing policies about the use of library space by known hate groups; making choices to highlight potentially controversial books, thereby making them more accessible, instead of burying them in the shelves; producing events that push community standards but make marginalized groups feel welcome, such as drag queen storytimes—these are all political decisions and, for both good and ill, impact the authority of librarians as educators. These are also decisions that are often made by individual librarians and are impacted by their education, personal beliefs, support structure, and personality.

Sadly, though, there appears to be no clean answer to politicization leading to misinformation being spread by some librarians. Our field lacks mechanisms to regularly check on the quality of the information available in a particular institution or the veracity of the service provided by a specific librarian. At this point, colleagues and patrons provide the only system of checks on the work of librarians. In most cases, the previously hypothesized flat-earther librarian would be noticed and mentored by colleagues and eventually lose their job if they persisted in promoting these notions to patrons at work. If the flat-earther was the library director, the situation would be more complicated, though the local government or university officials—depending on the type of library—could probably step in if they learned of it.

It seems deeply unlikely that there would be widespread support for creating a licensing requirement for librarians similar to that for lawyers, doctors, or K–12 teachers, with testing and performance requirements against established standards (although this does exist for school librarians in some states), or for a certification process for libraries along the lines of those for hospitals. Another profession that is information-based but not licensed is journalism. The roles of journalists in spreading misinformation—directly or indirectly—and the potential for personal beliefs to shape reporting have been examined extensively and thoughtfully within the professional and research literature of journalism since 2015 (McDevitt & Ferrucci, 2018; Tandoc, Jenkins, & Craft, 2019; Tandoc, Lim, & Ling, 2018; Waisbord, 2018). Thus far, librarianship has primarily focused on the service implications of polarization rather than the professional implications of polarization.

With few professional licensing requirements and with no applicable legal standards for "information malpractice" or anything similar (R. Diamond & Dragic, 2001; Dragic, 1989; Healey, 1995, 2008), it seems that the most useful response to the issue of the information literacy of librarians is to begin giving it more attention than it currently receives in education and professional development. "Moving from service provider to active educator challenges librarians and library educators to develop new guiding philosophies" (Elmborg, 2006, p. 192). In spite of being teachers of information literacy, "librarians do not typically learn about pedagogy or educational theory in their coursework" (Downey, 2016, p. 53). Information literacy needs to be at the heart of master of library science (MLS) and master of library and information science (MLIS) degree programs, as well as continuing education courses. Simply being an information professional does not exempt someone from being influenced by the unprecedented information inundation of the Internet, nor does being a librarian magically make one an expert in teaching information literacy skills to others.

Along with receiving greater emphasis in LIS and professional education, librarians' information literacy is an issue that needs to be discussed professionally and researched. ACRL published a book entitled *Libraries Promoting Reflective Dialogue in a Time of Political Polarization* (Baer et al., 2019), a collection of essays offering different approaches to promoting information literacy in spite of political divisions, but none of the nearly two dozen essays actually address information literacy gaps in practicing librarians.

Ensuring that information literacy is comprehensively taught to all students wishing to become librarians would be a very important step. Information literacy skills are core to the work of librarians and other information professionals and are required in their jobs not only in their own activities but also in their teaching of others and in their pursuit of institutional and professional missions and goals (Inskip, 2015). However, teaching these skills—and the ability to teach these skills to others—is not a central part of library and information science (LIS) education programs. Students entering LIS programs show no particularly unique capacities or affinities for information literacy (Lamb, 2017). Although LIS students tend to have high levels of confidence in their own skills, the actual skills demonstrate a very wide range (K. Conway, 2011; Hebert, 2018; Pinto & Pascual, 2016; Saunders et al., 2015). There are "indications of discrepancies between perceived and actual information literacy skills" among many LIS students (Hebert, 2018, p. 43), with students having the lowest skills primarily greatly overestimating their skills (Mahmood, 2016).

Some of the avalanche of information literacy resources being created should be focused on professionals in the field, helping librarians continually improve their information literacy teaching skills and become better aware of their own biases and how to not let their own beliefs heavily shape the teaching of information literacy to patrons.

We also need to figure out ways to better evaluate, iteratively, and coordinate information about all types of literacy efforts across the field. As Nicole Cooke (2018) so aptly points out, we have many, many strategies to promote information literacy, but we do not have sufficient data to determine how effective, if at all, these strategies are. We clearly need more research about these efforts. Learning from related research in other fields about the impacts of information literacy on behavior could be very helpful in shaping how we teach and advocate for information literacy. Studies from fields such as mass communication and media studies, as two examples, have determined that Americans are most likely to believe misinformation about political actors (Humprecht, 2019) and are most likely to be influenced by disinformation encountered passively on social media (Groshek & Koc-Michalska, 2017), while research from cognitive sciences could help us better understand the critical thinking errors that people most commonly make when they fall for false information (Levitin, 2017). Such findings could be used to complement and enhance findings from some LIS scholars (e.g., M. C. Sullivan, 2019a, 2019b).

In conjunction, we need to better coordinate all information literacy efforts ongoing across the field. As previously noted, the 2016 election spurred the creation of hundreds of new information tools and programs in libraries, which means that many uncoordinated and heavily redundant efforts occurred in creating all those tools and programs. With more coordination between libraries and library organizations, we could have more consistent and coherent information literacy efforts, greater opportunities to reach a broader array of communities, better chances of collecting useful data about their effectiveness, and more opportunity to evaluate and improve them.

And an important part of these increasing information literacy efforts needs to be a focus on ourselves. Librarians are "the medics of information warfare, rescuing and sustaining the truth without regard for ideological loyalty" (Hartman-Caverly, 2019, p. 167). We need continuing training and tools and methods for the members of our own profession.

Our field has long devoted a great deal of attention and effort to empowering patrons to access and evaluate information to educate themselves. These efforts have admirably, if not totally effectively, increased since the impacts of online misinformation on the democratic process around the world have become glaringly evident. As part of these efforts, though, we cannot neglect that the members of our profession are as open to being influenced by misinformation as is anyone else. Engaging politicians and ourselves about information literacy is necessary for promoting information literacy to promote the health of democracy.

INFORMATION LITERACY MEETS DEMOCRACY

There are several key steps that libraries individually and collectively can take to commit to making information literacy one of our field's key contributions to supporting democracy. The first is the most obvious. All libraries, regardless of their user population, need to find ways to get involved in promoting critical information literacy for their patrons and their communities. Libraries need to make understanding and navigating misinformation a core part of nearly every program they develop (Carillo, 2019). Holding a session on how to work a camera? Incorporate information about how photos can be digitally faked. Developing a user guide for the creation of an email account? Discuss phishing. The opportunities are limitless. Information literacy cannot be confined to school libraries, public library computer courses, and first-year sessions for college students. It is important to keep teaching new information literacy skills to meet changes to information online as a lifelong process.

The next step is to view information literacy as part of services to those currently using the library and find ways to reach beyond the patrons of the individual library. This means collaboration between libraries to extend their reach and share their expertise. Imagine if the hundreds of libraries counted by Denise Agosto (2018) had collaborated and brought together their expertise to build one comprehensive information literacy product instead of making hundreds of separate tools and guides. A search for information literacy guides reveals innumerable options created by different libraries that take very different approaches, but a user would be hard-pressed to identify which ones are better or more appropriate for their individual needs. If standard tools were collaboratively developed and consistently linked by libraries, users would be much more likely to be directed to best practices. Such collaboration depends on direction from a strong professional organization, and support for the American Library Association seems to be at an all-time low.

Collaborative work would also help ensure that insights from a range of libraries with specialized expertise would reach users. Consider a medical library, which typically has a service population of those already working in the areas of health. An increased focus on information literacy in the library's activities would help its current users, but the vast specialized knowledge in health information literacy would not reach beyond its normal user populations. Although some medical libraries are engaged in creative outreach beyond their traditional service populations (St. Jean, Jindal et al., 2020), many are not. Imagine a collaborative effort across the field to build information literacy tools, in which their specialized knowledge for best practices in health information literacy could regularly become more widely available, which would be a benefit to a significant number of non-health-care professionals who are seeking health information.

Overall, information literacy is still regularly written about as a set of skills that school libraries introduce to early learners and that academic libraries reinforce in short courses to new college students. Although fine books are regularly published along these lines, the big picture of information literacy is often avoided in books and other discussions about information literacy. Additionally, the field suffers from a lack of diversity (Vinopal, 2016), hindering the ability of information professionals to understand both the information literacy needs of their communities and how best to reach users not currently in their libraries.

Ironically, one recent exception was published by the Modern Language Association— that is, not librarians. The *MLA Guide to Digital Literacy* (Carillo, 2019) devotes a large portion of the book to the impacts of algorithms, bots, filters, and manipulations and offers multiple sample lesson plans and exercises for teaching students about misinformation. We need to change the LIS focus to a much bigger understanding of what we provide, teach, assess, advocate, and evaluate related to information literacy.

In addition to firming up our own literacy, we must identify how to express the importance of information literacy to our patrons. In other words, the number of guides we create has no meaning if no one cares to look at them. Figuring out how to motivate different groups of users is not a traditional aspect of librarianship, but it is a factor in education and other fields. Perhaps we need to look outside the boundaries of our profession to identify more palatable ways of packaging our expertise. Just as the marketing and sales professions have ways of effectively expressing half-truths, they also have ways of motivating users that we could use to counter negative information actors.

The final key piece of promoting comprehensive lifelong information literacy education is increased research evaluating the different approaches to and practices in teaching critical information literacy, a considerable gap in the current library research literature. The necessity to increase information literacy instruction offers both a need for more research and expanded opportunities for assessing such research.

INFORMATION LITERACY MEETS REALITY

Admittedly, none of these are simple goals, but they are all of great importance. Perhaps the starting point might be the banding together of various library professional organizations to identify best practices and strategies in information literacy instruction across their areas of expertise, maybe even crafting a consistent definition of information literacy across the organizations. From that starting point, each group could be tasked with contributing content, lesson plans, and teaching strategies for their area of expertise. Those materials then could constitute a repository for librarians to draw from as they implement information literacy courses in their libraries. Such materials also could form the content of online information literacy guides that all libraries could point patrons to.

Right now, is there really a more important aspect of information literacy than teaching people how to understand and navigate algorithms, bots, filters, and manipulations as they search for accurate information? These skills are not static; they are critical skills that must be continually cultivated. The topographies of the information landscape of the Internet—and the accompanying threats to accurate information—are constantly changing and evolving. Information literacy is now truly a process of lifelong learning, and not only do libraries need to prioritize teaching critical information literacy for the worst of the online world, they all need to be investing in collaboratively teaching and promoting lifelong information literacy, as detailed in the previous chapter, especially for information-seeking related to politics, health, and current events.

Libraries intersect with politics and policy processes in a number of long-established and well-known ways, primarily in the form of laws and policies that shape access, availability, privacy, and security of information in libraries (Jaeger & Taylor, 2019). Additionally, by their very nature as institutions devoted to education, libraries are inherently and unavoidably political institutions—though we generally do not think of it as such, opening the doors of a learning institution and inviting people inside is a very loud political act in the values of free and widespread education that it states (Jaeger & Sarin, 2016a). Yet, saddled with the long and unhelpful legacy of neutrality, libraries are often afraid of anything that sounds remotely political.

The avoidance of the political, however, will be an enormous hindrance to properly teaching critical information literacy in the current information environment. It is vital to teach people about the political motivations of not only the content creators but the services through which they may be viewing the content.

"At their best, libraries are an expression of the idea that enough of us can reason together about our common world and future" (Cope, 2019, p. vii). This sentiment should not apply just to the users and communities served by libraries; it can also apply to those of us in the library profession. To continue to fulfill our long-standing role as arsenals of democracy, we need to collectively embrace lifelong information literacy education to ensure that we are maximally supporting people in successfully informing themselves about political and current events in ways that foster the health of democratic society.

💬 CHAPTER 14 GUIDING QUESTIONS

1. What are some of the connections between information policy and information literacy?
2. How can libraries better influence information policy—and more specifically, information policy that deals directly with information literacy?
3. Are libraries neutral? Can they be? Should they be?
4. How does the structure of LIS education impact the information literacy practices of librarians? How could it be improved?
5. What are some ways that librarians could better coordinate information literacy education?

CHAPTER 15

The Social Infrastructure for Information Literacy

INFORMATION LITERACY IN SOCIAL CONTEXT

We have offered numerous ways in which the library field can improve upon our information literacy services, but many societal structures impede this work. One key theme that we keep returning to in this book is that the practice of information literacy happens in a sociocultural context. In the US, we live in a deeply racially segregated society (Williams & Emamdjomeh, 2018). Government policies—such as explicit policies banning Black people from buying into certain neighborhoods, the process of redlining, eminent domain being exercised in Black communities, and the design of the highway system to cut through Black neighborhoods—have a long history of serving to disrupt Black communities (Solomon et al., 2019). Simply put, much of the social infrastructure of our society is racist ("Structural racism in America," n.d.), which leads to unequal economic (Solomon et al., 2019), health (Imhoff, 2020), and education outcomes (Chatterji, 2020), among other inequities.

The US is also becoming more politically polarized (Pew Research Center, 2017), which has become particularly concerning because the resulting media silos are quite literally killing people, as evidenced by the increased percentage of pandemic deaths in locations with greater local viewership of Sean Hannity (Bursztyn et al., 2020). Polarization has led to the downplaying of a global pandemic (Tyson, 2020), the rejection of the importance of climate change (Kennedy, 2020), and an ambivalence toward the results of a free and fair election (Kane & Clement, 2020). In this chapter, we take these points—a society built on racial inequalities and a political system that increases polarization—and investigate their role in the practice of information literacy.

In both society in general and the LIS field specifically, these issues have been around for a long time. The US economy was literally built with slave labor (Lockhart, 2019). The very foundations of librarianship in the American context have always rested on uncomfortable beliefs, including racism (Espinal, 2001; Sierpe, 2019). We simply cannot separate libraries from the society in which they are built and operate. As Chris Bourg states in her 2015 talk on libraries and neutrality,

> libraries are not neutral because we exist within societies and systems that are not neutral. But above and beyond that, libraries also contribute to certain kinds of inequalities because of the way in which we exercise influence over the diversity (or lack thereof)

of information we make available to our communities and the methods by which we provide access to that information. (n.p.)

But it's not just LIS that is due a reckoning. Of all the terrible things that came out of 2020, an increased attention to issues of social justice was not one of them. For the practice of information literacy to be relevant to and attainable by everyone, there are aspects of society that simply must change. Until they do, we as librarians will always be working against the system, no matter how much we try to get our own house in order. This chapter attempts to explain the ways that our current sociocultural landscape in the United States represents a barrier to the practice of information literacy. It is not intended to discourage you; rather, it is intended to acknowledge the fact that however many best practices we can work out, we must also work to dismantle those societal structures that produce negative outcomes for information literacy, equity, and social justice.

RACIAL INJUSTICE AND THE IMPACT ON INFORMATION LITERACY

We will begin our exploration of the ways these negative aspects of society impact information literacy with societal racism. In many ways, it is imperfect for us—the authors of this book—to address this. As two white authors, we can only ever see these issues from the outside looking in, and we will always view them through the lens of our racial privilege.

That said, racial injustice has had a terrible impact on the practice of information literacy, so it absolutely should be mentioned here. The inequities brought by this injustice mean that minorities have less access to well-resourced educational institutions (EdBuild, 2019), a reasonable lack of trust in government and other authority figures due to years of abuse and neglect (B. R. Kennedy et al., 2007), and a lack of representation in LIS, the very field purporting to define and teach information literacy (AFL-CIO, 2020; Vinopal, 2016).

WHAT IS A LIBRARY? WHAT IS AN EDUCATION?

We asked the first question in chapter 9 and included several definitions put forward by library associations and scholars. It's worth interrogating those definitions a bit further here, because a library surely means different things to different people. To Black Americans in particular, historically a library is not a straightforward institution. We don't have the space to write a full history of race and racism in the LIS field—and indeed others have done so better than we could (e.g., Fultz, 2006; A. N. Gibson et al., 2017; A. N. Gibson et al., 2020; Knott, 2016; Mattern, 2019; Poole, 2018; Wiegand, 2017)—but it is important to note that until the 1960s, public libraries were not open to Black people across much of the American South. Southern Black librarians were not allowed to join many of their state library chapters. It took the actions of prominent activists in the field, most prominently E. J. Josey, to push ALA to require these library chapters to integrate or risk being barred from ALA entirely (Chancellor, 2020). That's not to say that the South didn't have libraries for Black communities—they just did so without the benefit of the legitimation and support of a national professional body, and often did so without any public funding at all (Du Mont, 1986; Fultz, 2006; Mattern, 2019).

Education has clearly been deeply impacted by racial segregationist policies. Racial disparity in spending is an ongoing legacy—less money is spent on Black students than on white students (EdBuild, 2019). Public libraries too are mostly locally funded, which leads to less money in the form of property taxes for communities with lower home values, disproportionately those where Black Americans live (Perry et al., 2018). Although having access to formal educational institutions and well-resourced libraries isn't always imperative for practicing effective information literacy, it is certainly helpful. These are economic issues, but also inherently racial issues because of historically racist economic policies.

RACISM AND MISTRUST OF AUTHORITY

We talk more in the following political section about the problems associated with defining factual authority in terms of government affiliation, but with the extensive list of lies that historically have been told to minorities by our federal government, it seems important to mention the issue here. The valid mistrust has implications for critical medical issues. There has been much talk in the media about the problems associated with convincing Black Americans to be vaccinated against the coronavirus (Wan, 2020). At alarming rates and disproportionate to the total population, Black Americans are dying from the novel coronavirus (CDC, 2020), and yet many are wary of vaccines that would help protect them. The roots of this mistrust can be traced to medical experimentation on enslaved Black Americans (Washington, 2007), exacerbated by such medical neglect as occurred in the Tuskegee Syphilis Study, wherein Black men were denied medical care in the service of research (CDC, 2009), and further entrenched by current disparities in the health-care system (Scharff et al., 2010). And Black Americans aren't the only minorities who have experienced terrible treatment at the hands of the US government; from lying to American Indians in order to seize their lands (Brinkley, 2003) to forcibly sending Japanese Americans to internment camps during World War II, there are many reasons why racial minority groups wouldn't trust governments and other institutional authorities.

LACK OF BIPOC IN LIS

Librarianship is an overwhelmingly white profession (Vinopal, 2016). In terms of numbers, white librarians represent more than 83 percent of the field, meaning that BIPOC (Black, Indigenous, and people of color) communities are all significantly unrepresented in information professions and institutions (AFL-CIO, 2020). The perpetuation of this imbalanced workforce is enforced by structural racism (Galvan, 2015; Sierpe, 2019). Why does that matter? Well, it impacts scholarship, practice, and perceptions of the field. As Honma (2005) notes, "Historical depictions regarding the public library tend to veer toward the celebratory, touting an egalitarian spirit encapsulated by the public library and its mission within the public sphere" (p. 3). We should note, we are often guilty of that ourselves. Sometimes in our eagerness to celebrate the good things about libraries, we unintentionally prop up hegemonic beliefs; one example is immigrant storytimes in the early twentieth century. Although such programs exemplified libraries as a space for underserved communities, they were also undoubtedly a way to assimilate immigrants into the US economic and social culture—which is one of hierarchical racial privilege. Honma argues this point: these historical depictions ignore "the library's susceptibility in reproducing and perpetuating racist social structures found throughout the rest of society" (p. 2).

So what is the effect of these racial inequities on information literacy? Well, first, if the profession is mostly white, it means those who are implementing information literacy programming, designing information literacy standards, and conducting research on information literacy also are mostly white. We've discussed the rise of LIS scholarship in critical information literacy over the last two decades in past chapters. It seems helpful to return to this now from a perspective focused on issues of race. As Honma (2005) notes, scholarship reinforces the experiences of those doing the research: "If we view the current state of LIS as a local knowledge system, particularly as one that has been dictated through the voice of whiteness, we must do better in finding nonwhite local systems of knowledge that more adequately encompass the populations that have been silenced, marginalized, and overlooked" (p. 16).

Additionally, a lack of BIPOC voices in the field leads to those who are present taking on more than their fair share of the race-related work. Too often it is those most impacted by these acts of racism who are then tasked with educating the rest of us on what we should do about it.

Racism—both past and present—impacts every aspect of our society, so of course the practice of information literacy is no different. To see a truly contextual, relevant, and equitable practice of information literacy for all requires looking at how the LIS field views authority, how it teaches the economy of information, how it treats minorities in the field, and how standards, guidelines, and institutional policies influence the public's perception of what information literacy means. Standards of attribution (J. Anderson & Christen, 2019), the systems that categorize and retrieve information for users (Bourg, 2015; Noble, 2018; Olson, 2013), and the means of using information, such as who gets published (A. N. Gibson & Hughes-Hassell, 2017; Villalpando & Bernal, 2002), are all influenced by legacies of racism. The lack of minority voices in LIS is a detriment to information literacy research and to our users.

Efforts by the field to mitigate this racism in the past, and often still today, have been merely token acknowledgments. If we're going to make an effort to make the field more inclusive, it is important to do so from a real place of wanting to understand and change and not merely as a way to express multiculturalism (an effort that often "merely celebrates differences as exotic"; Peterson, 1995) or superficial diversity (that still requires all involved to replicate whiteness; Hathcock, 2015). Additionally, we need to continue to produce scholarship (Beatty, 2014; Ferretti, 2018; Freeburg, 2017; Rapchak, 2019; Saunders, 2017; Swanson, 2005a) and institute programming and create guides for practitioners (Pashia, 2017; Tewell, 2016; Vangeest & Hawkins, 2016) that interrogate structural information inequalities, address the roots of mistrust of institutions, and work to achieve more anti-racist attitudes in white Americans.

ECONOMIC AND POLITICAL INJUSTICE

Racial injustice is, of course, closely entwined with both political and economic injustice, but neoliberalism has negative ramifications beyond just minority communities, though those are significant. We've outlined many instances of the neoliberal assumptions underlying professional and scholarly definitions of information literacy. In this section we examine how the economic and political structures of US society impact how those who live within them practice information literacy.

If You Can't Sell It, What's the Point?

The direction of public schooling, the media environment, and the development of technology are all profoundly impacted by the capitalist nature of our society. The public sphere is being slowly eroded (Buschman, 2003). Institutions that aren't profit-driven are increasingly denied government attention and funding. The higher education and public school environments described in earlier chapters—and how they subsequently shape the ways that information literacy is conceived—are two examples. Beyond education though, the fact that the media are a largely profit-driven industry has enormous impacts on the news we see. That, of course, in turn impacts the information with which we have to practice information literacy.

Technology and media have become intertwined—over half of people get their news through social media often or some of the time (Shearer & Grieco, 2019). This is despite people having deep concerns about the companies behind these sites and the types of news being produced (Shearer & Grieco, 2019). The influence of social media in news transfer has led some to suggest that social media should be reimagined as a public good (Hanna et al., 2020) or conceived as an active political actor itself (Helberger, 2020). Indeed, public officials have grown so concerned about Facebook's seeming monopoly on social media that the US government along with forty-eight state attorneys general filed an antitrust suit against the company (Romm, 2020).

Perhaps equally concerning to the practice of information literacy as the lack of regulation on social media companies is the mystery of how they work. For example, how exactly are the posts you see when you log in chosen? That algorithm is proprietary information. One impact of the increasingly esoteric and complicated technology infrastructure underlying our everyday lives is that it leads to a loss of control over the data the technology companies use to ensure that their algorithms work and generate profits. A 2019 Pew Research Center report on Americans' views of privacy and their personal information demonstrates that adults struggle with understanding privacy laws and feel that they have very little or no control over the data collected about them by the government or by companies (Auxier et al., 2019, p. 43 and p. 22, respectively). Generally, we have created a society in which certain types of information are prized over others—chiefly those that can make money and those that cannot. Shapiro and Hughes (1996) ask if we can "be information literate if we possess the technical ability to find and evaluate information, but not the human capacity to experience and value it? Can we be committed to an issue if it fails to resonate with anything within us? . . . information literacy requires a more balanced approach to information" (p. 397). To find this balanced approach, though, we must confront the forces that inspire us to create frameworks and practices that encourage only financially and economically associated information.

Information Marginalization

Economic inequality in the US is growing; a 2020 Pew Research Center report on trends in income and wealth inequality determined that "a greater share of the nation's aggregate income is now going to upper-income households and the share going to middle- and lower-income households is falling" and that between 1989 and 2016, the wealth gap between the richest and poorest more than doubled (Horowitz et al., 2020). The economic effects of the coronavirus pandemic have only worsened these inequalities.

Why does this inequality impact information literacy? The concepts of information poverty, information marginalization, and information privilege all help explain the link. Information poverty, as mentioned in earlier chapters, has been referred to as "a persistent lack of information access as experienced by a group or an individual, usually as a result of social factors, embodied by various types of information-related inequalities" (Gibson & Martin, 2019). Much work was done by Chatman (1991, 1996, 1999) and by Chatman and

Pendleton (1995) on examining the resulting behaviors of the so-called information poor. In the years since this work was done, however, there has been a more critical gaze at the structures that produce information inequities. In their research on a group of parents of children with disabilities, Gibson and Martin (2019) move away from the deficit model—what's missing in the person living in poverty—and toward a "theory of information marginalization that describes the systematic, interactive socio-technical processes that can push and hold certain groups of people at social 'margins,' where their needs are persistently ignored or overlooked" (p. 476). The researchers describe this marginalization as a "mismatch of information values and imbalance of power that often exists between marginalized people and the institutions that purport to serve them" (p. 486).

In terms of economic inequality and the oft resulting lack of access to institutions of higher education, we can see the results on the practice of information literacy by a lack of information privilege. Booth (2014) discusses information privilege in the context of academic librarianship and reminds us that a lack of academic information privilege means a lack of access to paywalled research and a lack of opportunities to disseminate work. She suggests that "at their best, libraries are an institutional form of social justice that equalize information availability and provide safe public space for learning and doing. At their worst, they perpetuate inequities and apportion resources among the intellectually sanctioned" (n.p.).

Red and Blue America

If you read the *New York Times* at any point in the past four years, you likely stumbled upon more than one article about why Donald Trump was elected from the perspective of people in middle America (for a good summation, see Wolcott, 2018). Although we think the number of these articles was over the top, the sentiment behind understanding a part of your fellow citizenry with whom you don't regularly interact isn't a bad thing at all. The gist of these articles was that many Americans felt ignored by media and government elites, misunderstood by big urban areas of the country, and left behind by a technology-driven economy. Unspoken, but demonstrated by post-election research, was an undercurrent of racism and xenophobia (Cox et al., 2017).

A recent article in *Time* magazine brought these articles into the conversation of misinformation. The article, about the author's road trip through electoral swing states and her conversations with the people who lived there, reflected not only a deeply divided country but one in which "in the absence of agreed-upon facts, the possibility of consensus itself seemed to be disappearing, and the effect was unsettling" (Alter, 2020, n.p.). The author describes encountering a phenomenon she calls "unlogic . . . not ignorance or stupidity; it is reason distorted by suspicion and misinformation, an Orwellian state of mind that arranges itself around convenient fictions rather than established facts" (n.p.), which was displayed in fake news both big—QAnon conspiracy theories!—and small—Joe Biden is a socialist! Polarization is not only bad for policymaking; it's terrible for information literacy (feel free to return to chapter 12 for many more examples).

INFORMATION LITERACY AND CLIMATE CHANGE

Finally, we want to address maybe the most pressing issue of our time, at least in terms of the continued existence of life on Earth. That is, of course, the issue of climate change. Closely entwined with all the areas just discussed, climate change exacerbates existing economic and racial inequities (Islam & Winkel, 2017). Information literacy has a huge impact on how much effort and resources we are willing to devote to solutions, and the current state of information literacy concerning climate change isn't great. In fact, denial of climate change is perhaps one of the most successful misinformation campaigns of modern times, in the US context at least, which has had terrible implications on the political will of elected officials to craft legislation and enact policies that would help mitigate the effects (Dunlap & McCright, 2010, 2011; Elsasser & Dunlap, 2013; Oreskes & Conway, 2011; Washington, 2013). Van der Linden et al. (2017) suggest that information literacy practice may be one way of addressing the onslaught of information. Klucevsek (2017) suggests that science and information literacy are intertwined and that one limitation of both is the lack of access to published scientific research. That lack, of course, is tied to the economic system of scholarly journals and proprietary databases.

Indeed, the economies of information and technology are deeply entrenched in the climate crisis. Perhaps for economic and political reasons, perhaps merely because of the lack of understanding of technology supply chains (most likely both), we don't really talk about it much. Mirza and Seale (2017) outline several examples of the ways that technology contributes to resource depletion and human suffering, including in the labor of finding resources, assembling devices, performing technical support, and carrying out recycling services. These authors also explicitly label ALA's work on imagining the future library as contributing to the invisibility of these effects of technology.

The issue of climate change is, of course, one that we will all face, belief in it or not. Unfortunately, some will experience the results more negatively than others, regardless of their opinions about current mitigation attempts. Kutner and Armstrong (2012) present their case for the need for a more global understanding of information literacy—or deep information literacy—asking questions about the global world in which we live:

> How is it that the information with which we engage is getting to us? What are the societal and economic forces at work that allow us access to unprecedented amounts of information? As we consider our information environment within the context of globalization, what are the consequences of global information inequality? Who has the greatest and least access to information, and why? What about the majority of the world that does not have ready access to information that would lead to increased quality of life, such as health, agricultural, and environmental information? (p. 28)

Kutner and Armstrong (2012) go on to relate a practice of information literacy like this to climate change—specifically it might lead students to wonder why, when climate change is truly a global issue, are the majority of scholarly articles published in so few places? This type of "deep" information literacy isn't terribly different from what is suggested by a lot of scholarship we've discussed already. What we can do better is to emphasize why such critical thought is so important and tie it directly to such issues as climate change, as well as racism, the wealth gap, and others. We can also push back on the technocratic directions of the LIS field and ensure that the environmental, human, and psychological costs of our information culture are more central to planning and professional values.

CONCLUSION

In this chapter, we have focused on American society because we are most familiar with it, but many of these societal roadblocks to information literacy are present around the world.

In some cases, the barriers to information literacy are even higher. The Council on Foreign Relations describes China as having "one of the world's most restrictive media environments, relying on censorship to control information in the news, online, and on social media" (Xu & Albert, 2017, n.p.). Russia has developed a "disinformation and propaganda ecosystem" that involves state actors and proxy communication channels to spread lies around the world (US Department of State Global Engagement Center, 2020). In other Western democracies, the rise of authoritarianism is a threat to information access (Shahbaz, 2018).

We present this chapter not as a comprehensive overview of how societal injustices make the practice of information literacy hard or impossible. These issues of social infrastructure negatively impact many more populations, and we've only scratched the surface of existing scholarship in these areas. An entire chapter, for example, could have been devoted to the entrenched social barriers and biases faced by disabled people, who have the highest unemployment rate, the lowest level of graduation from high school and college, the lowest level of home Internet access, the lowest level of health insurance coverage, and the largest number of technological barriers to Internet access, among much else, among all populations in the US; all of these, of course, heavily shape information access and literacy for disabled people (Cork, Hoffman et al., 2019; Cork, Jaeger et al., 2016; Jaeger, 2015, 2018).

We intended to present this chapter as an introduction to and overview of some of the lenses through which we think scholarship and practice should view information literacy. As evidenced by the citations referenced, many are already doing this work. We think the field would benefit from a continuation and amplification of voices calling for not only a contextual understanding of information literacy but, where it is necessary, a change to the society within which many of these contexts rest.

Shapiro and Hughes (1996) describe a type of information literacy that is "knowledge that is part of what it means to be a free person in the present historical context of the dawn of the information age" (p. 2). We would add to that—if it's impossible for some in our society to be free even with the practice of information literacy, we need to go beyond teaching. We need to start with asking why and then join the fight to dismantle these underlying structural antecedents of inequality.

As the authors of this textbook, we have a definite point of view on librarianship and what it can be. For example, in general we see the *Core Values of Librarianship* (American Library Association, 2019) as useful ideals. As we've mentioned, even while recognizing that libraries don't currently achieve all the elements of the visions and values outlined earlier, we believed they were worth discussing as a way to consider information literacy because we believe in the potential of librarians to live up to those goals. If not fulfilled, and they most certainly aren't currently, they are at least things to strive for.

Information isn't neutral and neither are libraries (Gibson et al., 2017; Gibson et al., 2020). We put forth these issues as a starting point for you to make your own decisions about how to interpret the practice of information literacy in librarianship, while acknowledging that our own views have shaped the information presented in this book. As Barbara Fister describes in a 2013 blog post, the library profession as an institutional body values

> certain ways of seeking and using evidence. It's important to evaluate your sources and approach research [or] a research question with an open mind. It's not right to seek out only information that supports your viewpoint. It's wrong to appropriate other people's ideas and represent them as your own—and so forth. These are not somehow universal foundational truths. They are beliefs that are rooted historically in a particular way of knowing. We may value them deeply, but they are not the natural order of things, free of

context and controversy. There's nothing wrong with that, so long as we think through what it means, why we promote what we promote, and what really matters to us. (n.p.)

As for our agenda as it is situated with the context just described, we do, by and large, see ways of working within an inherently unequal society, even as we simultaneously believe that the LIS field, and ourselves as individuals, must work to improve that society. Librarianship has plenty of dark history but also a solid values framework that can be (and has been) used for a lot of good. Others feel differently. Sierpe (2019), for example, thinks that by continuing to use the term *librarianship,* the profession is not acknowledging "the many ways the term itself stands as a painful reminder of racist practices, forced assimilation and cultural colonialism and oppression," and the field should reconsider its use entirely (p. 93).

Of course, our point of view is shaped by our whiteness, by our white-collar work, by our acceptance into the professorial class of higher education. We have extraordinary privileges but also a subsequently narrowed perspective on what constitutes truth, authority, and, yes, information literacy. We encourage you to take the ideas we have presented here and engage with them. Cope (2010) asserts:

> A critical theory of IL does not seek to indoctrinate students with an educator's particular viewpoints. Instead, it entails a deep and fundamental embrace of the centrality of questioning in any educative process. To confine one's perspective to that which is strictly measurable diminishes the ability to conceptualize the social whole and the role of specific IL practices within it. A critical theory of IL seeks to engage students as active social subjects charged with interrogating the social world and developing their own capacity for informed questioning. (pp. 24-25)

We agree. Thus: Find opposing viewpoints. Look outside the field of librarianship to consider the ways that information literacy is perceived by non-information professionals. Incorporate (or not) alternate ideas into your programming and your conversations with colleagues. In doing so, we believe the field will be more adept at working within and ultimately changing systems of oppression.

💬 CHAPTER 15 GUIDING QUESTIONS

1. What are some examples of how structural racism contributes to misinformation and disinformation?
2. How might librarians begin to bring together a polarized society (and why is this a responsibility of librarians at all)?
3. In what ways does the lack of diversity within the LIS profession impact our professional information literacy practices?
4. What are some ways that advancements in technology lead to a less information literate society?
5. This chapter suggests that "we can also push back on the technocratic directions of the LIS field and ensure that the environmental, human, and psychological costs of our information culture are more central to planning and professional values." What are some ways we might go about doing this?

The Lifelong Information Literacy Society

DISINFORMATION, CIRCA 1850

In the 1800s, America was full of what were known as *confidence men*, people who used force of personality to gain power and influence in business, religion, politics, and society,[1] perhaps best typified by showman/huckster Phineas Taylor "P. T." Barnum (M. Harvey, 2020). Herman Melville, Mark Twain, Charles Dickens, Nathaniel Hawthorne, and Alexis de Tocqueville were among the major authors of the time who wrote about the odd faith of Americans in people who exuded confidence both before and after the Civil War. The advent of the major social changes and upheaval brought about by wage work, industrialization, and large-scale capitalism left many people searching for answers—even fantastical ones—in the middle of the nineteenth century (E. P. Thompson, 1964). Such fantastical ideas included beliefs that Americans conquering the continent from Atlantic Ocean to Pacific Ocean would lead to the return of Jesus or the creation of a veritable heaven on Earth (Merchant, 2003; C. L. Miller, 1985).

The era of confidence men also coincided with the enormous rise in newspaper production and consumption and the modernization of the post office. The combination of these three things created a golden age of disinformation long before computers or Internets or AI. In 1792 the postal service instituted a policy that created an "exchange paper" network, allowing each printer of a newspaper to send a copy of each edition freely through the USPS to every other printer of a newspaper in the country. By 1843—fifty years after the implementation of the policy—each newspaper in the nation was receiving an average of 364 exchange papers each month, creating a very early information superhighway (Kielbowicz, 1989). The idea was to create "a vast national conversation through the frictionless transmission of voices from equal nodes in an unlimited network" (Nerone, 2011, p. 749).

However, because most newspapers used the network to get news from other parts of the country with little ability to do their own verification of what was printed, confidence men quickly realized that the network was an ideal way to spread disinformation. Like the Internet trolls of today, unscrupulous printers put stories in their papers that would be sufficiently titillating to encourage printers in other parts of the country to repeat the stories, a tactic that was used to try to make money, gain power, or shift public opinion by leaders of religious cults and land speculators—both of which were quite prevalent in nineteenth-century America—as well as by blatant con men like P. T. Barnum (M. Harvey, 2020). This slew of information and disinformation helped create the advent of the first advertising agencies and the coining of the terms *celebrity* and *propaganda* in their modern senses, and make the mid-1800s the golden age of fraudulent elections (Blake, 2008; Lehman, 2013; Summers, 1987). It was also the era in which placing personal ads in newspapers to find love became both commonplace and socially acceptable, another space in which humans have not always been above employing disinformation (Beauman, 2020).

As we have noted more than once in this text, the problems of information literacy and misinformation are not new, but now mobile devices and social media mean that you can have unlimited access to a universe of virtual confidence men and women and bots at all times. About halfway between the age of confidence men and today, Raymond Chandler noted how easy it seems for many people to prefer "the austere simplicity of fiction rather than the tangled woof of fact" (1939, p. 344). Promoting information literacy and combating disinformation will ultimately require more than the dedication and collective effort of librarians and new approaches to advocacy and activism. It will require a societal dedication to building empowerment, education, and agency in individuals, communities, and society as a whole.

THIS IS NOT NEW, BUT IT IS DIFFERENT

This book has already detailed many approaches that our field uses for promoting lifelong information literacy and strategies for better integrating what we do across all institutions in the field and for building support for these efforts through advocacy and engagement. That is not the entire story, however, of what will be required to make real change in information literacy levels in society, because disinformation has clearly persisted for a very, very long time. All our efforts as a field will not make an enormous difference if there is not an accompanying collective desire to seriously prioritize information literacy and combat disinformation, misinformation, and information illiteracy.

Several societal-level challenges seem to loom large. Obviously, all the reasons cataloged earlier that people are drawn to misinformation or incentivized to create disinformation are barriers to information literacy at the individual level. They may also translate upward to the societal level. The entities that benefit from disinformation will work to oppose efforts for large-scale information literacy education. For some of these entities, information literacy represents a direct threat to their ability to recruit and retain members; for other entities, disinformation is the basis of their political power; and for further entities, disinformation is the key to their ability to make money. In many cases, all three of these factors are intertwined. Government agencies that use disinformation to advance the goals of their government would only be concerned about disinformation as a political tool, but, for Fox News or One America News, disinformation is a money-making strategy. For the anti-vaccine movement, disinformation is the lifeblood of their money, political power, and membership. All these entities that benefit so strongly from— or completely owe their existence to—disinformation will vehemently oppose efforts at coordinated information literacy education, inevitably using disinformation to argue against information literacy.

There will also be political resistance to lifelong information literacy in other ways. Not all people in positions of political power in governments might be terribly thrilled by an electorate better able to assess the veracity and quality of the activities of elected officials. Although politicians may not feel it politically opportune to actively declare opposition to information literacy, they might be inclined to inhibit any proposed improvements to funding and policy. Other elected officials, however, may be so frustrated by trying to govern a misinformation-addled populace that they would be very open to improvements in funding and policy to promote lifelong information literacy.

Were political opposition from government officials and other entities to be overcome, there still would be other major obstacles. A large number of individuals seem to have become addicted to disinformation. The people willing to risk their own life and the lives of everyone around them to accept disinformation about the pandemic have already demonstrated a greater commitment to believing misinformation than to continued existence. That's a pretty strong level of commitment, especially when accurate information about the pandemic is so readily available and constantly being reinforced by scientists and public health experts. Although the pandemic and post-2020 election attempts to overturn the popular vote and the Electoral College represent as screamingly obvious a case as possible for increased attention to information literacy as an issue of the highest importance, the fact that such large numbers of people have committed to information illiteracy on these issues also shows the strength with which part of the population will cling to misinformation.

Even for those people not hopped up on misinformation, there will likely still be other barriers to acceptance of information literacy as a major priority. Apathy is likely to be a uniquely difficult challenge. In a time when unemployment, food insecurity, and housing insecurity have become a lived experience for vast numbers of people, information literacy may not seem like a big deal. Even for those people with a greater sense of security in life, issues associated with work, school, and family necessarily dominate attention.

Information literacy not only will have to break through this kind of complacency in general attitudes, it will have additional difficulty because it is an abstract concept. You cannot see or touch information literacy, so it inevitably will seem less tangible and less important to many people. Further, as this book has extensively documented, information literacy is not only an abstract concept, it is also one that is not easy to define concisely and memorably. It is a lot easier to build political capital for something that people can visualize, such as a newly paved road, as opposed to something they cannot visualize, such as information literacy.[2]

As in the era of confidence men, people today are faced with staggering social, political, and economic upheaval, and that was before the pandemic. Whereas in the mid-1800s, the upheaval was tied to the rise of the industrial economy at the expense of the agrarian economy, today the upheaval is driven by the conquest of the Internet economy over the industrial economy. Careers and education are in a state of enormous change, with occupations, educations, and social interactions now flowing heavily through devices rather than interpersonal interaction. Physical places that brought people into shared spaces are disappearing as retail stores, restaurants, and entire shopping centers are depopulated in favor of e-commerce. Many jobs of this new Internet economy are gig work, lacking guaranteed income, hours, or benefits. The outputs of many jobs are now as intangible as information literacy.

In total, people even in industrialized societies have lost the sense that the future was at least somewhat knowable and predictable. Now, employment, education, commerce, and social interaction are simply unanswered questions. This state of roiling constant change also will likely serve as a challenge for greater focus on information literacy. There is so much change and so much distraction that the bandwidth of most people for another major societal issue to tackle will likely be limited, especially one that adds to the distressing sense of change and upheaval.

BUT ON THE OTHER HAND

Just the opposite might be true, as well. The pandemic and the 2020 election—with the anti-mask, anti-vaccine, QAnon, and related groups reveling in misinformation—have certainly made the huge role of misinformation and its direct consequences crystal clear to everyone paying attention. These events seem like they have the possibility to be real drivers of making real the need for a societal emphasis on lifelong information literacy.

Information professionals and information institutions seem better positioned and prepared than any other field to lead the efforts and work together to make tangible positive change, but we must have our eyes wide open about the challenges. Information literacy is a social, political, and economic problem, and it is a human rights problem. It impacts all parts of society and every community and every individual.

Information literacy is also not just the responsibility of information professionals and information institutions. We not only can work together in a much more cohesive and coordinated fashion, we can collaborate with other fields, like education, that are capable of contributing to increasing lifelong information literacy. Through advocacy and outreach, we can rally other partners from nonprofits, corporations, other professions, policymakers, and researchers, among others. Advocacy and outreach efforts will also be vital for building bridges toward legislation and funding to support taking information literacy as seriously as it needs to be taken. The same festival of information illiteracy that has been so obvious in recent events will have deeply affected people in other fields, too. We have to find ways to find them, let them know what we are up to, and invite them to help. If we're going to make a sizable change to improve lifelong information literacy, we will need all the help we can get.

For lifelong information literacy to work across society, we will need to ensure not only that literacy education is occurring but also that it is reaching all the people who will benefit from it. Just as much, we will need to ensure that the social infrastructure is created to support lifelong information literacy. That will mean providing education programs across information institutions, and it will also mean working with other professions to help them integrate information literacy education into their professional certifications and continuing education requirements. Working with institutions of elementary, secondary, and higher education to get consistent information literacy education baked into the curriculum will be another important part of the social infrastructure. Ensuring that continuing information literacy education is central to what all libraries do and is reinforced through schooling and through professions will constitute a very solid scaffolding for information literacy in society.

The more ambitious social infrastructure building will mean working with corporations that provide information online—such as social media companies—to move them beyond thinking of literacy solely in terms of cursory checks for and disclaimers about disinformation and instead to think of it as a responsibility to their users. Modifying our training programs into formats that would be compatible with these providers could lead to required information literacy trainings and refreshers for users built right into the platforms.

Financial and policy support from local, state, and national governments would be the other great goal for building social infrastructure for information literacy. Educating elected officials at all levels of government about the enormous ramifications of information literacy and encouraging positive action would be the path to making the social infrastructure to support lifelong information literacy a permanent feature through improved policy and dedicated funding. The Biden administration has a Special Presidential Envoy for Climate to coordinate federal government efforts in protecting the planet. Given the societal impacts of information literacy, would it not be reasonable to advocate for a Special Presidential Envoy for Information Literacy?

Okay, this sounds like a lot of work, you are probably thinking. You would be correct. But if we collaborate among information institutions and build comprehensive information literacy programs without addressing the social infrastructure, our work will have greatly reduced impact and reach. Admittedly, there are pretty strong headwinds blowing against information literacy right now—fine, it's a flipping Category 5 hurricane—but giving up really is not an acceptable choice. Building the social infrastructure for information literacy is going to be a big project, and there is nobody better for the job than information professionals. We've made big things happen before, and we can make things better in terms of lifelong information literacy as well.

WRITE THIS DOWN

More than thirty years ago, the ALA Presidential Committee on Information Literacy called for more attention on information literacy, stating that "within America's information society, there also exists the potential of addressing many long-standing social and economic inequities. To reap such benefits, people—as individuals and as a nation—must be information literate" (American Library Association, 1989, para. 3). This observation, of course, has become far more poignant since it was written.

By this point in the book, we hope you have taken to heart the centrality of information literacy to information institutions and information professionals, as well as that our field is better prepared than any other to teach and support lifelong information literacy. But, you might be asking, don't we already have enough to do? The struggle against "fake news" alone creates huge tasks for librarians (Buschman, 2019). Adding trying to educate and continue to support information literacy for everyone seems like a lot. And that doesn't even include all the other stuff that has been dumped on libraries, or that we have taken up of our own volition, as other parts of the public sphere have dwindled because of lack of funding.

One of the greatest contributions of our field—most notably of libraries—is a talent for evolution to meet community needs. If there had been any question about this ability, the pandemic put it to rest. Libraries turned their lawns into vegetable gardens and their parking lots into farmers' markets, began delivering books curbside and by drone, blasted the Wi-Fi access to everyone in range of the building, became distribution centers for food and medical supplies, and even turned into virus testing centers, among much, much else (Jaeger, Taylor, Gorham, & Kettnich, 2021). And all this on top of the seemingly innumerable other things that libraries do to promote education and equity and inclusion in their communities (Jaeger, Taylor, & Gorham, 2015).

So, yes, information professionals and information institutions are already expected to do much more than they should. But the answer is not to give up; rather, it is to be clear about our skills and contributions and work to get the acknowledgment and support we need to fulfill all of these roles. It not only means taking on the additional work of providing greatly increased support for information literacy, it also means creating messages to explain these programs to communities and advocating for changes in policies and increased funding to support lifelong information literacy programs.

As we have discussed earlier in the book, once people believe misinformation, it is very hard to dislodge it, and being presented with the correct information often serves to harden belief in the disinformation. As the first line of instructors of information literacy at every level of education, librarians have the opportunity to impart and reinforce the information literacy skills to limit the ability of disinformation to take root in the first place. That may be the best way to disarm disinformation.

Evolving to meet the challenges to information literacy presented by social, technological, and political change is simply the next iteration of the evolution of our field. Lifelong information literacy, in addition, is the best response to anyone who claims that there is no longer a need for libraries and other community-focused information institutions: a search engine gives you an infinite number of options; an information professional teaches you the skills needed to figure out which option provides the information that you need.

GOOD TROUBLE, NECESSARY TROUBLE

Recently departed civil rights icon and conscience of Congress, John Lewis, often spoke of the importance of good trouble and necessary trouble. It was an exceptionally poetic and easy to understand way of saying that needed change usually does not come easily. We freely admit that emphasizing lifelong information literacy will not be easy and that it will likely be a great deal of trouble, but it sure is necessary.

Information literacy is an essential human right, perhaps the most essential human right, because education, employment, civic engagement, interpersonal interactions, and most everyday tasks are intermediated by information and ICTs. Limitations of information literacy stand as barriers to inclusion and equitable participation in much of life. The move to mostly virtual education during the pandemic has demonstrated the profound impacts on educational participation and success caused by differences in information literacy. Information professionals and information institutions are engines of human rights and social justice in the communities that they serve, and educating for and promoting lifelong information literacy is vital to helping individuals and communities protect and sustain their rights and continue to strive for justice.

Individuals, communities, and society as a whole admittedly ask heaps from information institutions, especially libraries, but focusing on and improving the problem of lifelong information literacy will not just contribute to rights and justice in communities. It will, in turn, help address a large number of major problems. Expanding information literacy education will never eliminate disinformation, misinformation, and information illiteracy, but more information literacy will definitely mitigate and reduce their impacts. And the past few years have shown how enormous those impacts can be. We won't be able to save the entire world, but we absolutely can make it a lot less rotten.

More than a century ago, Fredrick Douglass implored fellow Americans to "accept the inspiration of hope" (1894, p. 629). Hope may seem to be in short supply at the moment for many reasons.[3] Hope also has been the inspiration for just about everything positive that our profession has done for a very long time. And, yes, though we did focus on the need to address the negative aspects of the history of the field, we have also done some very good things in the past. Some relevant examples from library history:

- Libraries regularly began serving patrons with print disabilities more than a hundred years before the US government granted disabled people civil rights.

- In many big cities, the public libraries were the first government agencies to adopt inventions, such as air conditioning, that improved health and sanitation for those using their buildings.
- Censorship of reading materials—those in library collections and those sold in bookstores—was common in communities around the United States until librarians directly challenged these practices and publicly codified their anti-censorship stance with the 1939 Library Bill of Rights.
- During the Jim Crow era, "freedom libraries" were created in many segregated communities to ensure that nonwhite community members still had access to resources when they were not allowed access to the public library.
- When the George W. Bush administration launched the War on Terror after September 11, the only profession that collectively stood up to the ensuing infringements on freedoms of expression and access were librarians.
(Jaeger, 2021, p. xv)

If we learn from both the positive and negative aspects of our history, we can harness lessons of "creativity and determination in trying to make the communities we serve more equitable and more inclusive" (Jaeger, 2021, p. xvi).

When you pull away all the terminology and practice of information professions and institutions, the underlying reality is that we are here to teach literacy, whether that literacy is for language, content, software, or hardware. Information literacy is why we are here, and it is our responsibility to the individuals and communities that we serve and to the democracy that we are here to support.

TO LEAD OUT

The word *educate* is derived from a Latin word that meant "to lead out." If it seems too, too much to conceive of all the things that need to be done to build information literacy and combat disinformation, then perhaps it might be more manageable to imagine our professional role as leading people from one place to another, a bad place to a good one. Teaching information literacy is truly leading people out of the realm of misinformation. A field of information professionals committed to working together to promote and sustain lifelong information literacy will be able to help a great many people in their practice of information literacy and in avoiding falling for disinformation.

As this book has explored, the LIS field has had some important accomplishments with information literacy but has neglected, or needs to pay more attention to, some major concerns. Fortunately, we know what we need to do better and how to work to bring "light to the areas that our past failed to reach" (Jaeger, Taylor, Gorham, & Kettnich, 2021, p. 1). For information professionals and information institutions, this is a monumental point in time. Being uniquely positioned to teach others about information literacy and possessing unique knowledge, skills, and social standing, librarians can educate, can lead out of this mess. Lifelong information literacy is our opportunity to restore health to the information environment and improve the lives of the individuals and communities that we serve.

🗨 CHAPTER 16 GUIDING QUESTIONS

1. What are some of the allures of mis- and disinformation? Why might they be preferable to truth?
2. How can the library profession demonstrate to lawmakers that information literacy should be a policy priority? What type of resistance might we meet?
3. In what ways could information literacy education be woven into the way that society meets more immediately apparent needs, such as the procurement of food and shelter? Is there a way to ensure that those short on time or resources or both can still practice effective information literacy?
4. How do modern changes in economic and political structures lead to less effective information literacy practices?
5. After reading this book, how would you define information literacy? Has your definition changed? If so, how and why?

NOTES

1. Sound vaguely familiar?
2. Maybe we need an adorable information literacy mascot? Leela the Leaping Lemur of Literacy?
3. The lizard people being one reason.

REFERENCES

Abilock, D. (2004). Information literacy from prehistory to K-20: A new definition. *Knowledge Quest, 32*(4), 9-11.

Abutaleb, Y., & Dawsey, J. (2020, September 1). Trump medical adviser pushes "herd immunity." *The Washington Post*, A1, A8.

ACRL RBMS-SAA Joint Task Force on the Development of Guidelines for Primary Source Literacy. (2018). *Guidelines for primary source literacy*. https://www2.archivists.org/sites/all/files/Guidelines%20 for%20Primary%20Souce%20Literacy%20-%2018%20January%202018%20Revision.pdf

Adams, N. E. (2014). A comparison of evidence-based practice and the ACRL information literacy standards: Implications for information literacy practice. *College and Research Libraries, 75*(2), 232-248.

Addison, C., & Meyers, E. (2013). Perspectives on information literacy: A framework for conceptual understanding. *Information Research: An International Electronic Journal, 18*(3), n3.

AFL-CIO. (2020). *2020 fact sheet*. Department for Professional Employees, AFL-CIO. https://static1 .squarespace.com/static/5d10ef48024ce300010f0f0c/t/5f3d859bc7bd79018e9160f3/1597867420016/ Library+Workers+Facts+%26+Figures+2020.pdf

Agosto, D. (2018). *Information literacy and libraries in the age of fake news*. Libraries Unlimited.

Aharony, N., Julien, H., & Nadel-Kritz, N. (2020). Survey of information literacy instructional practices in academic libraries. *Journal of Librarianship and Information Science, 52*(4), 964-971.

Alexander, J. (2020). Tumblr is rolling out an Internet literacy initiative to help combat misinformation and cyberbullying. *The Verge*, January 6. https://www.theverge.com/2020/1/6/21048134/tumblr -misinformation-2020-election-cyberbullying-digital-literacy

Allcott, H., & Gentzkow, M. (2017). Social media and fake news in the 2016 election. *Journal of Economic Perspectives, 31*(2), 211-236.

Allport, G. (1954). *The nature of prejudice*. Addison-Wesley.

Alter, C. (2020, October 8). How a road trip through America's battlegrounds revealed a nation plagued by misinformation. *Time*. https://time.com/5897887/swing-states-2020-election/

Alterman, E. (2020). *Lying in state: Why presidents lie—and why Trump is worse*. Basic Books.

American Association of Law Libraries. (2019). *Strategic plan*. https://www.aallnet.org/about-us/what-we -do/strategic-plan/

American Association of Law Libraries. (2020). *Principles and standards for legal research competency*. https://www.aallnet.org

American Association of Law Libraries Law Student Research Competency Standards Task Force. (2011). *Report for the AALL executive spring board meeting*. https://www.aallnet.org/wp-content/ uploads/2017/11/2010-2011-CommFR-Law-Student-Research-Competency-Standards-Task-Force.pdf

American Association of School Librarians. (2007). *Standards for the 21st century learner*. American Library Association.

American Association of School Librarians. (2017). *National school library standards for learners, school librarians, and school libraries*. American Library Association.

American Association of School Librarians. (2018). "How do I read the Standards?" https://standards.aasl .org/wp-content/uploads/2017/11/AASL_ReadingtheStandards_OnePager_2017.pdf

American Association of School Librarians & Association for Educational Communications and Technology. (1988). *Information power: Guidelines for school library media programs; A discussion guide.* American Library Association. https://archive.org/details/ERIC_ED315029/page/n5/mode/2up

American Association of School Librarians & Association for Educational Communications and Technology. (1998a). *Information literacy standards for student learning.* https://www.ala.org/ala/aasl/aaslproftools/informationpower/InformationLiteracyStandards_final.pdf

American Association of School Librarians & Association for Educational Communications and Technology. (1998b). *Information power: Building partnerships for learning.* American Library Association.

American Library Association. (1989). *Presidential Committee on Information Literacy: Final report.* http://www.ala.org/acrl/publications/whitepapers/presidential

American Library Association. (1998). *A progress report on information literacy: An update on the American Library Association Presidential Committee on Information Literacy Final Report.* Association of College and Research Libraries. http://www.ala.org/acrl/publications/whitepapers/progressreport

American Library Association. (2017). *Strategic directions.* http://www.ala.org/aboutala/sites/ala.org.aboutala/files/content/governance/StrategicPlan/Strategic%20Directions%202017_Update.pdf

American Library Association. (2019). *Core values of librarianship.* http://www.ala.org/advocacy/intfreedom/corevalues

American Library Association. (2020). *The State of America's Libraries 2020.* http://www.ala.org/news/state-americas-libraries-report-2020

Andersen, H. C. (1847/2006). The emperor's new clothes. In *Fairy Tales* (pp. 211-216) (M. H. Hult, trans.). Barnes & Noble.

Andersen, J. (2005). The public sphere and discursive activities: Information literacy as sociopolitical skills. *Journal of Documentation, 62*(2), 213-228.

Anderson, B. (1991). *Imagined communities: Reflections on the origins and spread of nationalism.* Verso.

Anderson, J., & Christen, K. (2019). Decolonizing attribution. *Journal of Radical Librarianship, 5,* 113-152.

Anderson, R. (2017). Fake news and alternative facts: Five challenges for academic libraries. *Insights: The UKSG Journal, 30*(2), 4-9.

Andrews, T. M. (2020, October 17). QAnon is tearing families apart. *The Washington Post,* B1-B2.

Applebaum, A. (2018). A warning from Europe: The worst is yet to come. *The Atlantic.* http://www.theatlantic.com

Asheim, L. (1953). Not censorship but selection. *Wilson Library Bulletin, 28*(1), 63-67.

Association of College and Research Libraries. (2000). *Information literacy competency standards for higher education.* http://www.ala.org/acrl/standards/highereducation

Association of College and Research Libraries. (2011). *Information literacy competency standards for journalism students and professionals.* http://www.ala.org/acrl/sites/ala.org.acrl/files/content/standards/il_journalism.pdf

Association of College and Research Libraries. (2013). *Information literacy competency standards for nursing.* http://www.ala.org/acrl/standards/nursing

Association of College and Research Libraries. (2015). *Framework for information literacy for higher education.* http://www.ala.org/acrl/sites/ala.org.acrl/files/content/issues/infolit/framework1.pdf

Association of College and Research Libraries. (2019a). *ACRL plan for excellence.* http://www.ala.org/acrl/aboutacrl/strategicplan/stratplan

Association of College and Research Libraries. (2019b). *Characteristics of programs of information literacy that illustrate best practices: A guideline.* http://www.ala.org/acrl/standards/characteristics

Association of College and Research Libraries Education and Behavioral Sciences Section (EBSS) Social Work Committee. (2020). *Social work: Companion document to the ACRL Framework.* https://acrl.libguides.com/sw/about

Association of Specialized, Government and Cooperative Library Agencies. (2020, July 31). "ASGCLA transitions 2020." https://www.asgcladirect.org/2020/07/asgcla-transitions-2020/

Aufderheide, P. (1992). *Media literacy: A report of the National Leadership Conference on Media Literacy.* Aspen Institute.

Auxier, B., Rainie, L., Anderson, M., Perrin, A., Kumar, M., & Turner, E. (2019). *Americans and privacy: Concerned, confused and feeling lack of control over their personal information.* Pew Research Center. https://www.pewresearch.org/Internet/wp-content/uploads/sites/9/2019/11/Pew-Research-Center _PI_2019.11.15_Privacy_FINAL.pdf

Azzarito, A. (2020). *The elements of a home: Curious histories behind everyday household objects, from pillows to forks.* Chronicle.

Babalhavaeji, F., Isfandyari-Moghaddam, A., Aqili, S., & Shakooii, A. (2009). Quality assessment of academic library performance: The case of an Iranian academic library. *Malaysian Journal of Library and Information Science, 14*(2), 51–81.

Badia, A. (2019). *The information manifold: Why computers can't solve algorithmic bias and fake news.* MIT Press.

Badke, W. (2011). Why information literacy is invisible. *Communications in Information Literacy, 4*(2), 2.

Baer, A. (2018). It's all relative? Post-truth rhetoric, relativism, and teaching on "Authority as Constructed and Contextual." *College and Research Library News, 79*(2), 72–75, 97.

Baer, A., Cahoy, A. S., & Schroeder, R. (Eds.). (2019). *Libraries promoting reflective dialogue in a time of political polarization.* Association of College and Research Libraries.

Bailey, S. P. (2020, October 9). Orthodox Jewish leaders sue to block virus restrictions. *The Washington Post,* A11.

Baker, K. (2013). *Information literacy and cultural heritage: Developing a model for lifelong learning.* Elsevier.

Balingit, M. (2019, December 31). Book-burning reveals how fraught the topics of race, class are on campus. *The Washington Post,* A3.

Bandura, A. (1999). Moral disengagement in the perpetration of inhumanities. *Personality and Social Psychology Review, 3*(3), 193–209.

Bandura, A. (2002). Selective moral disengagement in the exercise of moral agency. *Journal of Moral Education, 31*(2), 101–119.

Banks, M. (2016, December 27). Fighting fake news: How libraries can lead the way on media literacy. *American Libraries Magazine.* https://americanlibrariesmagzine.org/2016/12/27/fighting-fake-news/

Barber, B. R. (2003). *Strong democracy: Participatory politics for a new age.* University of California Press.

Barclay, D. A. (2017). The challenge facing libraries in an era of fake news. https://theconversation.com/the-challenge-facing-libraries-in-an-era-of-fake-news-70828

Barnett, S. (2020). Why teens are falling for TikTok conspiracy theories. *Wired Magazine.* https://www.pew research.org/politics/2019/07/22/trust-and-distrust-in-america/

Barth, V. (2014). The formation of global news agencies, 1859–1914. In W. B. Rayward (Ed.), *Information beyond borders: International cultural and intellectual exchange in the Belle Époque* (pp. 35–48). Ashgate.

Batchelor, O. (2017). Getting out the truth: The role of libraries in the fight against fake news. *Reference Services Review, 45*(2), 143–148.

Bates, M. J. (2006). Fundamental forms of information. *Journal of the American Society for Information Science and Technology, 57*(8), 1033–1045.

Bates, M. J. (2010). Information. In M. J. Bates & M. N. Maack (Eds.), *Encyclopedia of library and information sciences* (3rd ed., Vol. 3, pp. 2347–2360). CRC Press. https://pages.gseis.ucla.edu/faculty/bates/articles/information.html

Battles, M. (2015). *Palimpsest: A history of the written word.* Norton.

Bauman, S. (2020). *Political cyberbullying: Perpetrators and targets of a new digital aggression.* Praeger.

Baumeister, R., Bratavsky, E., Finkenauer, C., & Vohs, K. D. (2001). Bad is stronger than good. *General Review of Psychology, 5*(4), 323–370.

Bawden, D. (2001). Information and digital literacies: A review of concepts. *Journal of Documentation, 57*(2), 218–259.

Bawden, D. (2008). Origins and concepts of digital literacy. In C. Lankshear and M. Knobel (Eds.), *Digital literacies: Concepts, policies and practices* (pp. 17–32). Peter Lang.

Beal, G. (1975). *Playing cards and their story*. Arco.

Bearak, M. (2019, January 21). Despite leaked data, Congo court upholds election result. *The Washington Post*, A7.

Beatty, J. F. (2014). Locating information literacy within institutional oppression. *In the Library with the Lead Pipe*. http://www.inthelibrarywiththeleadpipe.org/2014/locating-information-literacy-within-institutional-oppression/

Beauman, F. (2020). *Matrimony, Inc.: From personal ads to swiping right, a story of America looking for love*. Pegasus.

Becker, B. W. (2016). The librarian's information war. *Behavioral and Social Sciences Librarian, 35*(4), 188–191.

Becker, C. H., Jr. (2012). Student values and research: Are millennials really changing the future of reference and research? *Journal of Library Administration, 52*(6–7), 474–497.

Behrens, S. J. (1994). A conceptual analysis and historical overview of information literacy. *College and Research Libraries, 55*(4), 309–322.

Beilin, I. G. (2015). Beyond the threshold: Conformity, resistance, and the ACRL information literacy framework for higher education. *In the Library with the Lead Pipe*. http://www.inthelibrarywiththeleadpipe.org/2015/beyond-the-threshold-conformity-resistance-and-the-aclr-information-literacy-framework-for-higher-education/

Beisel, N. (1997). *Imperiled innocents: Anthony Comstock and family reproduction in Victorian America*. Princeton University Press.

Bell, S. J. (2013). Rethinking ACRL's information literacy standards: The process begins. *ACRL Insider*. https://acrl-ala-org.ezproxy.lib.usf.edu/acrlinsider/archives/7329

Bellware, K. (2020, February 12). Experts cite "insidious confusion" as misinformation about virus spreads. *The Washington Post*, A12.

Berg, C., Malvey, D., & Donohue, M. (2018). Without foundations, we can't build: Information literacy and the need for strong school library programs. *In the Library with the Lead Pipe*. http://www.inthelibrarywiththeleadpipe.org/2018/strong-school-library-programs/

Bergmeier, H. J. P., & Lotz, R. E. (1997). *Hitler's airwaves: The inside story of Nazi radio broadcasting and propaganda swing*. Yale University Press.

Berlin, I. (1996). *The sense of reality: Studies in ideas and their history*. Farrar, Strauss and Giroux.

Berliner, D. C., & Biddle, B. J. (1995). *The manufactured crisis: Myths, fraud, and the attack on America's public schools*. Addison-Wesley Publishing.

Berman, J. M. (2020). *Anti-vaxxers: How to challenge a misinformed movement*. MIT Press.

Berns, G. (2017). *What it's like to be a dog: And other adventures in animal neuroscience*. Basic Books.

Bertot, J. C. (2003). The multiple dimensions of the digital divide: More than technology "haves" and "have nots." *Government Information Quarterly, 20*, 185–191.

Bertot, J. C., Gorham, U., Jaeger, P. T., & Sarin, L. C. (2014). Big data, libraries, and the information policies of the Obama administration. In D. Bogart (Ed.), *Library and book trade almanac* (pp. 5–23). Information Today.

Bertot, J. C., Gorham, U., Jaeger, P. T., Sarin, L. C., & Choi, H. (2014). Big data, open government, and e-government: Issues, policies, and recommendations. *Information Polity, 19*(1–2), 5–16.

Bertot, J. C., Jaeger, P. T., Langa, L. A., & McClure, C. R. (2006). Public access computing and Internet access in public libraries: The role of public libraries in e-government and emergency situations. *First Monday, 11*(9). http://www.firstmonday.org/issues/issue11_9/bertot/index.html

Bimber, B. (2003). *Information and American democracy: Technology in the evaluation of political power*. Cambridge University Press.

Bingham, T. J., Wirjapranata, J., & Chinnery, S. A. (2016). Merging information literacy and evidence-based practice for social work students. *New Library World, 117*(3/4), 201-213.

Blake, D. (2008). *Walt Whitman and the culture of American celebrity.* Yale University Press.

Blakeslee, S. (2004). The CRAAP test. *Loex Quarterly, 31*(3), 4.

Blau, J. R., & Moncada, A. (2006). *Justice in the United States: Human rights and the US Constitution.* Rowman & Littlefield.

Blevens, C. L. (2012). Catching up with information literacy assessment: Resources for program evaluation. *College & Research Libraries News, 73*(4), 202-206.

Bluemle, S. R. (2018). Post-facts: Information literacy and authority after the 2016 election. *portal: Libraries and the Academy, 18*(2), 265-282.

Boden, E. (2017, November 15). *Keeping up with . . . Debiasing and fake news.* American Library Association. http://www.ala.org/acrl/publications/keeping_up_with/debiasing

Bombaro, C. (2016). The framework is elitist. *Reference Services Review, 44*(4), 552-563.

Bond, S. (2020, October 27). Facebook stops new political ads to try to limit misinformation. *NPR.* https://www.npr.org/2020/10/27/928120956/facebook-stops-new-political-ads-to-try-to-limit-misinformation

Booth, C. (2014). On information privilege. *Info-mational* (blog). https://infomational.com/2014/12/01/on-information-privilege/

Borgmann, A. (1999). *Holding on to reality: The nature of information at the turn of the millennium.* University of Chicago Press.

Bossaller, J. (2017). Alternatives to apathy and indifference: Civic education in public libraries. *Library Quarterly, 87,* 195-210.

Bourg, C. (2015). *Never neutral: Libraries, technology, and inclusion.* OLITA Spotlight Talk, 2015 Ontario Library Association Super Conference. https://chrisbourg.wordpress.com/2015/01/28/never-neutral-libraries-technology-and-inclusion/

Bousquet, M., & Wills, K. (Eds.). (2003). *The politics of information: The electronic mediation of social change.* Alt-X Press.

boyd, d. (2018, March 9). You think you want media literacy . . . Do you? *Data & Society: Points* (blog). https://points.datasociety.net/you-think-you-want-media-literacy-do-you-7cad6af18ec2

Boyer, E. L. (1997). *Scholarship reconsidered: Priorities of the professoriate.* Carnegie Foundation for the Advancement of Teaching.

Boyles, J. L., & Meisinger, J. (2020). Automation and adaptation: Reshaping journalistic labor in the newsroom library. *Convergence, 26*(1), 178-192.

Bradley, C. (2013). Information literacy in the programmatic university accreditation standards of select professions in Canada, the United States, the United Kingdom and Australia. *Journal of Information Literacy, 7*(1), 44-68.

Brandt, D. (2001). *Literacy in American lives.* Cambridge University Press.

Branum, C. (2008). The myth of library neutrality. *Humanities Commons, Modern Language Association, 5.*

Breakstone, J., Smith, M., Wineburg, S., Rapaport, A., Carle, J., Garland, M., & Saavedra, A. (2019). *Students' civic online reasoning: A national portrait.* Stanford History Education Group; Gibson Consulting. https://purl.stanford.edu/gf151tb4868

Bregman, R. (2019). *Humankind: A hopeful history.* Little, Brown.

Breivik, P. S., & Gee, E. G. (2006). *Higher education in the Internet age: Libraries creating a strategic edge.* Greenwood Publishing Group.

Brennan, E. A., Ogawa, R. S., Thormodson, K., & von Isenburg, M. (2020). Introducing a health information literacy competencies map: Connecting the Association of American Medical Colleges Core Entrustable Professional Activities and Accreditation Council for Graduate Medical Education Common Program Requirements to the Association of College and Research Libraries Framework. *Journal of the Medical Library Association: JMLA, 108*(3), 420.

Brinkley, J. (2003, January 7). American Indians say documents show government has cheated them out of billions. *The New York Times.* https://www.nytimes.com/2003/01/07/us/american-indians-say-documents-show-government-has-cheated-them-out-of-billions.html

Brosh, A. (2020). *Solutions and other problems.* Gallery Books.

Brown, J. A. (1998). Media literacy perspectives. *Journal of Communication, 48*(1), 44–57.

Brown, J. S., & Duguid, P. (2002). *The social life of information.* Harvard Business School.

Bruce, C. (1997). *The seven faces of information literacy.* Aus-lib Press, Adelaide.

Bruce, C., Edwards, S., & Lupton, M. (2006). Six frames for information literacy education: A conceptual framework for interpreting the relationships between theory and practice. *Innovation in Teaching and Learning in Information and Computer Sciences, 5*(1), 1–18.

Bruce, C., Candy, P. C., & Klaus, H. (Eds.). (2000). *Information literacy around the world: Advances in programs and research* (Vol. 1). Centre for Information Studies, Charles Sturt University.

Buckland, M. K. (1991). Information as thing. *Journal of the American Society for Information Science, 42,* 351–360.

Buckland, M. K. (1997). What is a "document"? *Journal of the American Society for Information Science, 48,* 804–809.

Burchinal, L. G. (1976). The communications revolution: America's third century challenge. In *The Future of Organizing Knowledge: Papers Presented at the Texas A&M University Library's Centennial Academic Assembly,* September 24, 1976, Texas A&M University Library.

Burkhardt, J. M. (2016). *Teaching information literacy reframed.* Neal-Schuman.

Burkhardt, J. M. (2017). Combating fake news in the digital age. *Library Technology Reports, 53*(8), 5–9.

Burki, T. (2020). The online anti-vaccine movement in the age of COVID-19. *The Lancet.* https://www.thelancet.com/journals/landig/article/PIIS2589-7500(20)30227-2/fulltext

Burnett, G., & Jaeger, P. T. (2008). Small worlds, lifeworlds, and information: The ramifications of the information behaviors of social groups in public policy and the public sphere. *Information Research, 13*(2), paper 346. http://InformationR.net/ir/13-2/paper346.html

Burnett, G., Jaeger, P. T., & Thompson, K. M. (2008). The social aspects of information access: The viewpoint of normative theory of information behavior. *Library and Information Science Research, 30,* 56–66.

Burns, E., Gross, M., & Latham, D. (2019). The information literacy continuum: Mapping the ACRL Framework to the AASL School Library Standards. *School Libraries Worldwide, 25*(1), 1–20.

Burns, E. (2020). AASL National School Library Standards: Progress toward implementation. *School Libraries Worldwide, 26*(1), 1–12.

Bursztyn, L., Rao, A., Roth, C., & Yanagizawa-Drott, D. (2020). *Misinformation during a pandemic* [Working paper]. Becker Friedman Institute for Economics at the University of Chicago, September. https://bfi.uchicago.edu/wp-content/uploads/BFI_WP_202044.pdf

Buschman, J. (2003). *Dismantling the public sphere: Situating and sustaining librarianship in the age of the new public philosophy.* Libraries Unlimited.

Buschman, J. (2009). Information literacy, "new" literacies, and literacy. *The Library Quarterly, 79*(1), 95–118.

Buschman, J. (2012). *Libraries, classrooms, and the interests of democracy: Marking the limits of neoliberalism.* Scarecrow.

Buschman, J. (2017). The library in the life of the public: Implications of a neoliberal age. *The Library Quarterly, 87*(1), 55–70.

Buschman, J. (2019). Good news, bad news, and fake news. *Journal of Documentation, 75,* 213–228.

Cabello, M., & Butler, S. M. (2017, March 30). *How public libraries help build healthy communities.* The Brookings Institution. https://www.brookings.edu/blog/up-front/2017/03/30/how-public-libraries-help-build-healthy-communities/

Calhoun, C. (2007). *Nations matter: Culture, history and the cosmopolitan dream.* Routledge.

Campbell, B. (1990). What is literacy? Acquiring and using literacy skills. *Australasian Public Libraries and Information Services, 3*(3), 149.

Caplin, A., Dean, M., & Martin, D. (2011). Search and satisficing. *American Economic Review, 101*(7), 2899-2922.

Carey, J. O. (2003). Michael Eisenberg and Robert Berkowitz's Big6™ information problem-solving model. *School Library Media Activities Monthly, 19*(5), 24.

Carillo, E. C. (2019). *MLA guide to digital literacy.* Modern Language Association of America.

Carini, P. (2016). Information literacy for archives and special collections: Defining outcomes. *portal: Libraries and the Academy, 16*(1), 191-206.

Carlton, S. (2019, November 8). Dissing access to the "New York Times," Citrus County commissioners embarrass Florida. *Tampa Bay Times.* https://www.tampabay.com/florida-politics/2019/11/08/dissing-access-to-the-new-york-times-citrus-county-commissioners-embarrass-florida/

Carr, M. (2006). *The infernal machine: A history of terrorism.* New Press.

Carr, N. (2011). *The shallows: What the Internet is doing to our brains.* Norton.

Case, D. O. (2002). *Looking for information: A survey of research on information seeking, needs and behavior.* Academic Press.

Centers for Disease Control and Prevention. (2009). *How Tuskegee changed research practice.* http://www.cdc.gov/tuskegee/after.htm

Centers for Disease Control and Prevention. (2020). *Health equity considerations and racial and ethnic minority groups.* https://www.cdc.gov/coronavirus/2019-ncov/community/health-equity/race-ethnicity.html?CDC_AA_refVal=https%3A%2F%2Fwww.cdc.gov%2Fcoronavirus%2F2019-ncov%2Fneed-extra-precautions%2Fracial-ethnic-minorities.html

Chancellor, R. L. (2020). *E. J. Josey: Transformational leader of the modern library profession.* Rowman & Littlefield Publishers.

Chandler, R. (1939/2018). *The big sleep, annotated edition* (O. Hill, P. Jackson, & A. D. Rizzuto, Eds.). Vintage Crime/Black Lizard.

Chatfield, T. (2019). *Why we believe fake news.* BBC. www.bbc.com

Chatman, E. A. (1991). Life in a small world: Applicability of gratification theory to information-seeking behavior. *Journal of the American Society for Information Science, 42*(6), 438-449.

Chatman, E. A. (1996). The impoverished life-world of outsiders. *Journal of the American Society for Information Science, 47*(3), 83-92.

Chatman, E. A. (1999). A theory of life in the round. *Journal of the American Society for Information Science, 50*(3), 207-217.

Chatman, E. A., & Pendleton, V. E. (1995). Knowledge gap, information-seeking and the poor. *The Reference Librarian, 49-50,* 135-145.

Chatterji, R. (2020, July 8). *Fighting systemic racism in K-12 education: Helping allies move from the keyboard to the school board.* Center for American Progress. https://www.americanprogress.org/issues/education-k-12/news/2020/07/08/487386/fighting-systemic-racism-k-12-education-helping-allies-move-keyboard-school-board/

Childers, T., & Post, J. A. (1975). *The information-poor in America.* Scarecrow.

Children's Internet Protection Act, Pub. L. No.106-554 (2001).

Christakis, N. A., & Fowler, J. H. (2011). *Connected: The surprising power of our social networks and how they shape our lives—how your friends' friends' friends affect everything you think, feel, and do.* Back Bay Books.

Christenson, D. P., Kreps, S. E., & Kriner, D. L. (2020). Contemporary presidency: Going public in an era of social media; Tweets, corrections, and public opinion. *Presidential Studies Quarterly.*

Church, A. P., Dickinson, G. K., Everhart, N., & Howard, J. K. (2012). Competing standards in the education of school librarians. *Journal of Education for Library and Information Science,* 208-217.

Cisco Systems. (2020, March 9). *Cisco annual Internet report (2018-2023) white paper*. https://www.cisco .com/c/en/us/solutions/collateral/executive-perspectives/annual-Internet-report/white-paper -c11-741490.html

Clark, C. (2010). Linking school libraries and literacy: Young people's reading habits and attitudes to their school library, and an exploration of the relationship between school library use and school attainment. *National Literacy Trust*. https://files.eric.ed.gov/fulltext/ED513438.pdf

Clarke, K. E. & Radcliff, C. (2018). Information literacy assessment for instruction and improvement and demonstration of library value: Comparing locally grown and commercially created tests. *Libraries*, 161. https://commons.lib.jmu.edu/letfspubs/16

Clayton, K., Blair, S., Busam, J. A., Forstner, S., Glance, J., Green, G., . . . Sandhu, M. (2019). Real solutions for fake news? Measuring the effectiveness of general warnings and fact-check tags in reducing belief in false stories on social media. *Political Behavior, 42*(2), 1-23.

Cohen, H. (2020, June 2). Bringing fact check information to Google Images. *Google: The Keyword* (blog). https://www.blog.google/products/search/bringing-fact-check-information-google-images/

Coleman, J. S. (1972). The children have outgrown the schools. *Psychology Today, 5*, 72-75.

Communications Act of 1934. 48 Stat. 1064.

Conger, K. (2019, October 30). Twitter will ban all political ads, C.E.O. Jack Dorsey says. *The New York Times*. https://www.nytimes.com/2019/10/30/technology/twitter-political-ads-ban.html

Congressional Research Service. (n.d.). *About this collection*. https://crsreports.congress.gov/Home/About

Conway, K. (2011). How prepared are students for postgraduate study? A comparison of the information literacy skills of commencing undergraduate and postgraduate studies students at Curtin University. *Australian Academic and Research Libraries, 42*(2), 121-135.

Conway, M. (2002). Reality bytes: Cyber terrorism and terrorist "use" of the Internet. *First Monday, 7*(11). http://www.firstmonday.org

Cooke, N. (2017). Posttruth, truthiness, and alternative facts: Information behavior and critical information consumption for a new age. *Library Quarterly, 87*, 211-221.

Cooke, N. (2018). *Fake news and alternative facts: Information literacy in a post-truth era*. ALA Neal-Shuman.

Cooper, J. (2007). *Cognitive dissonance: 50 years of a classic theory*. Sage.

Cope, J. (2010). Information literacy and social power. In E. Drabinski, A. Kumbier, & M. Accardi (Eds.). *Critical library instruction: Theories and methods* (pp. 13-28). Library Juice Press.

Cope, J. (2019). Foreword. In A. Baer, A. S. Cahoy, & R. Schroeder (Eds.), *Libraries promoting reflective dialogue in a time of political polarization* (pp. v-xi). Association of College and Research Libraries.

"CORA study examines students' ability to critically assess information from the Internet and from social media." (2020, April 14). Johannes Gutenberg University Mainz. https://www.uni-mainz.de/presse/ aktuell/11197_ENG_HTML.php

Cork, S. J., Hoffman, K., Douthirt-Cohen, B., Jaeger, P. T., & Strausser, A. (2019). Beyond random acts of diversity: Ableism, academia, and institutional sites of resistance. In M. Berghs, T. Chataika, Y. El-Lahib, & K. Dube (Eds.), *Routledge handbook of disability activism* (pp. 299-314). Routledge.

Cork, S. J., Jaeger, P. T., Jette, S., & Ebrahimoff, S. (2016). The politics of (dis)information: "Crippled America," the twenty-fifth anniversary of the Americans with Disabilities Act (ADA), and the 2016 United States presidential campaign. *International Journal of Information, Diversity, and Inclusion, 1*(1). http://jps.library.utoronto.ca/index.php/ijidi

Cornelius, I. (1996). Information and interpretation. In *CoLIS 2: Second international conference on conceptions of library science; Integration in perspective, Copenhague, October 13-16, 1996* (pp. 11-21).

Corner, J. (1995). *Television form and public address*. Edward Arnold.

Costello, R. (2019, October 24). Twitter builds partnership with UNESCO on media and information literacy. *Twitter* (blog). https://blog.twitter.com/en_us/topics/company/2019/twitter-launches-new -media-literacy-handbook-for-schools.html

Council for Basic Education. (1961). *Tomorrow's illiterates: The state of reading today.* Council for Basic Education.

Council on Communications and Media. (2016). Media use in school-aged children and adolescents. *Pediatrics, 138*(5), e20162592.

Courtney, I. (2017). In an era of fake news, information literacy has a role to play in journalism education in Ireland. *Irish Communication Review, 16*(1), Article 3.

Cox, D., Lienesch, R., & Jones, R. P. (2017, May 9). Beyond economics: Fears of cultural displacement pushed the white working class to Trump. PRRI/*The Atlantic.* https://www.prri.org/research/white-working -class-attitudes-economy-trade-immigration-election-donald-trump/

Crawford, G. A., & Feldt, J. (2007). An analysis of the literature on instruction in academic libraries. *Reference & User Services Quarterly, 46*(3), 77-88.

Crocco, M. S., Segall, A., Halvorsen, A. L., Stamm, A., & Jacobsen, R. (2020). "It's not like they're selling your data to dangerous people": Internet privacy, teens, and (non-) controversial public issues. *The Journal of Social Studies Research, 44*(1), 21-33.

DaCosta, J. (2010). *Is there an information literacy skills gap to be bridged? An examination of faculty perceptions and activities relating to information literacy in the United States and England.* http://derby .openrepository.com

Dallek, M. (2020, October 11). The GOP's long history of ignoring science. *The Washington Post,* B1, B4.

Daly, C. B. (2012) *Covering America: A narrative history of a nation's journalism.* University of Massachusetts Press.

Daniels, H. A. (1983). *Famous last words: The American language crisis reconsidered.* Southern Illinois University Press.

Davies, D. W. (1974). *Public libraries as culture and social centers: The origin of the concept.* Scarecrow.

Davis, H. (2010). Critical literacy? Information! *In the Library with the Lead Pipe.* http://www.inthelibrary withtheleadpipe.org/2010/critical-literacy-information/

Davis, P. (2012). Libraries receiving a shrinking piece of the university pie. *The Scholarly Kitchen.* https://scholarlykitchen.sspnet.org/2012/02/15/a-shrinking-piece-of-the-university-pie/

Day, R. E. (2017). Before information literacy [Or, Who Am I, as a subject-of-(information)-need?]. *Proceedings of the Association for Information Science and Technology, 54*(1), 57-70.

Deibert, R. J. (2015). Authoritarianism goes global: Cyberspace under siege. *Journal of Democracy, 26*(3), 64-78.

Deibert, R. J. (2019). The road to digital unfreedom: Three painful truths about social media. *Journal of Democracy, 30*(1), 25-39.

De Jager, K., & Nassimbeni, M. (2007). Information literacy in practice: Engaging public library workers in rural South Africa. *IFLA Journal, 33*(4), 313-322.

DelGuidice, M. (2012). Snooki, whale sperm, and Google: The unfortunate extinction of librarians when they are needed most. *In the Library with the Lead Pipe.* http://www.inthelibrarywiththeleadpipe.org/ 2012/snooki-whale-sperm-and-google-the-unfortunate-extinction-of-librarians-when-they-are -needed-most/

Del Vicario, M., Bessi, A., Zollo, F., Petroni, F., Scala, A., Caldarelli, G., Stanley, H. E., & Quattrociocchi, W. (2016). The spreading of misinformation online. *Proceedings of the National Academy of Sciences, 113*(3), 554-559.

Demasson, A., Partridge, H., & Bruce, C. (2019). How do public librarians constitute information literacy? *Journal of Librarianship and Information Science, 51*(2), 473-487.

Dempsey, K. (2017, May 6). What's behind fake news and what you can do about it. *Information Today.*

De Paor, S., & Heravi, B. (2020). Information literacy and fake news: How the field of librarianship can help combat the epidemic of fake news. *The Journal of Academic Librarianship, 46*(5), 102218.

Dervin, B. (1977). Useful theory for librarianship: Communication, not information. *Drexel Library Quarterly, 13*(3), 16-32.

Dervin, B. (1994). Information and democracy: An examination of underlying assumptions. *Journal of the American Society for Information Science, 45*(6), 369-385.

Diamond, L. (2019). The road to digital unfreedom: The threat of postmodern totalitarianism. *Journal of Democracy, 30*(1), 20-24.

Diamond, R., & Dragic, M. (2001). Professionalism in librarianship: Shifting focus from malpractice to good practice. *Library Trends, 50,* 395-414.

Ditzion, S. H. (1939). Social reform, education and the library. *Library Quarterly, 9,* 156-184.

Ditzion, S. H. (1947). *Arsenals of a democratic culture.* American Library Association.

Dollinger, A. (2017). Can librarians save us from fake news? *VICE,* March 21. https://www.vice.com/en_us/article/can-librarians-save-us-from-fake-news

Dou, E., & Harwell, D. (2020, December 13). Huawei worked on several systems to identify ethnicity. *The Washington Post,* A19.

Douglass, C. L. (2017). *A house of brick: Using the ACRL framework to [re]build a stronger, more sustainable democracy through a stand-alone, information literacy course* [Master's thesis, University of Maryland].

Douglass, C. L., Gorham, U., Hill, R. F., Hoffman, K., Jaeger, P. T., Jindal, G., & St. Jean, B. (2017). Information access and information literacy under siege: The potentially devastating impacts of the proposed 2017 White House budget on already-marginalized populations in the United States. *First Monday, 22*(10). http://firstmonday.org/ojs/index.php/fm/article/view/8088/6554

Douglass, F. (1845/2003). *Narrative of the life of Fredrick Douglass, an American slave.* Barnes and Noble Classics.

Douglass, F. (1894). The blessings of liberty and education. *Fredrick Douglass Papers, 5,* 629.

Downey, A. (2016). *Critical information literacy: Foundations, inspiration, and ideas.* Library Juice Press.

Doyle, C. S. (1992). *Outcome measures for information literacy within the National Education Goals of 1990. Final report to National Forum on Information Literacy. Summary of findings.* https://files.eric.ed.gov/fulltext/ED351033.pdf

Doyle, C. S. (1994). *Information literacy in an information society: A concept for the information age.* Diane Publishing.

Dragic, M. (1989). Information malpractice: Some thoughts on the potential liability of information professionals. *Information Technology and Libraries, 8,* 265-272.

Dretske, F. (1981). *Knowledge and the flow of information.* MIT Press.

Duffy, T. M. (2001). Museums of "human suffering" and the struggle for human rights. *Museum International, 53*(1), 10-16.

Du Mont, R. R. (1986). Race in American librarianship: Attitudes of the library profession. *Journal of Library History, 21,* 488-509.

Dunlap, R. E., & McCright, A. M. (2010). Climate change denial: Sources, actors and strategies. In C. Lever-Tracy (Ed.), *Routledge handbook of climate change and society* (pp. 240-260). Routledge.

Dunlap, R. E., & McCright, A. M. (2011). Organized climate change denial. In J. S. Dryzek, R. B. Norgaard, & D. Schlosberg (Eds.), *The Oxford handbook of climate change and society* (pp. 144-160). Oxford University Press.

Dwoskin, E. (2020a, August 20). Report: Health misinformation far outpacing Facebook's efforts against it. *The Washington Post,* A18.

Dwoskin, E. (2020b, October 10). New spike seen in anti-Asian sentiment. *The Washington Post,* A19.

Dwoskin, E., & Romm, T. (2019, June 27). Twitter adds labels for tweets that break its rules—A move with potentially stark implications for Trump's account. *The Washington Post.* https://www.washingtonpost.com/technology/2019/06/27/twitter-adds-labels-tweets-that-break-its-rules-putting-president-trump-companys-crosshairs/

EdBuild. (2019). $23 billion. https://edbuild.org/content/23-billion/full-report.pdf

Eisenberg, M. B. (2008). Information literacy: Essential skills for the information age. *DESIDOC Journal of Library and Information Technology, 28*(2), 39-47.

Eisenberg, M. B., & Berkowitz, R. E. (1988). *Curriculum initiative: An agenda and strategy for library media programs*. Ablex Publishing.

Eisenberg, M. B., Lowe, C. A., & Spitzer, K. L. (2004). *Information literacy: Essential skills for the information age*. Libraries Unlimited.

Eisenstein, E. (1993). *The printing revolution in early modern Europe*. Cambridge University Press.

Ellenwood, D. (2020). "Information has value": The political economy of information capitalism. *In the Library with the Lead Pipe*. http://www.inthelibrarywiththeleadpipe.org/2020/information-has-value-the-political-economy-of-information-capitalism/

Elmborg, J. (2006). Critical information literacy: Implications for instructional practice. *Journal of Academic Librarianship, 32*, 192-199.

Elmborg, J. (2016). Foreword. In N. Piagowsky & K. McElroy (Eds.), *Critical library pedagogy: Essays and workbook activities: Vol. 1* (pp. vii-xiii). Association of College and Research Libraries.

Elsasser, S. W., & Dunlap, R. E. (2013). Leading voices in the denier choir: Conservative columnists' dismissal of global warming and denigration of climate science. *American Behavioral Scientist, 57*(6), 754-776.

Emmanuel, I., & Stanier, C. (2016). Defining big data. In *Proceedings of the International Conference on Big Data and Advanced Wireless Technologies* (pp. 1-6).

Enis, M. (2018). *LJ* study: Electronic resources continue steady gains in academic libraries. *Library Journal*. https://www.libraryjournal.com/?detailStory=lj-study-electronic-resources-continue-steady-gains

Epstein, A. S. (2008). An early start on thinking. *Educational Leadership, 65*(5), 38-42.

Eslami, M., Rickman, A., Vaccaro, K., Aleyasen, A., Vuong, A., Karahalios, K., . . . Sandvig, C. (2015). "I always assumed that I wasn't really that close to [her]": Reasoning about invisible algorithms in news feeds. *Proceedings of the 33rd Annual ACM Conference on Human Factors in Computing Systems* (pp. 153-162). ACM.

Espinal, I. (2001). A new vocabulary for inclusive librarianship: Applying whiteness theory to our profession. In L. Castillo-Speed (Ed.), *The Power of Language/El Poder de la Palabra* (pp. 131-149). Libraries Unlimited.

Espinosa, L. L., Turk, J. M., Taylor, M., & Chessman, H. M. (2019). *Race and ethnicity in higher education: A status report*. American Council on Education.

Ettinger, D. (2008). The triumph of expediency: The impact of Google Scholar on library instruction. *Journal of Library Administration, 46*(3-4), 65-72.

Fabian, J. (2020). *American contagions: Epidemics and the law from smallpox to Covid-19*. Yale University Press.

Fahim, K., Kim, M. J., & Hendrix, S. (2020, May 3). Uneasy tolerance as surveillance keeps expanding. *The Washington Post*, A1, A16.

Farmer, L. S. (2013). How AASL learning standards inform ACRL information literacy standards. *Communications in Information Literacy, 7*(2), 171-176.

Federal Library and Information Center Committee Education Working Group. (2014). *The handbook of federal librarianship* (3rd ed). Library of Congress FEDLINK. http://www.loc.gov/flicc/publications/LibHandbook2014/HandbookforFedLib2014final2.pdf

Feekery, A., & Jeffrey, C. (2019). A uniquely Aotearoa-informed approach to evaluating information using the Rauru Whakarare Evaluation Framework. *Set: Research Information for Teachers, 2*, 3-10.

Feinstein, N. (2011). Salvaging science literacy. *Science Education, 95*(1), 168-185.

Feldstein, S. (2019). The road to digital unfreedom: How artificial intelligence is reshaping repression. *Journal of Democracy, 30*(1), 40-52.

Ferretti, J. A. (2018). *Neutrality is polite oppression: How critical librarianship and pedagogy principles counter neutral narratives and benefit the profession* [Keynote presentation]. Critical Librarianship and Pedagogy Symposium, November 15-16, 2018, The University of Arizona, Tucson, AZ.

Festinger, L. (1962). Cognitive dissonance. *Scientific American, 207*(4), 93-106.

Fister, B. (2013, August 29). Admitting our agendas. *Library Babel Fish* (blog). *Inside Higher Ed.* https://www.insidehighered.com/blogs/library-babel-fish/admitting-our-agendas

Fister, B. (2019, February 14). Information literacy's third wave. *Library Babel Fish* (blog). *Inside Higher Ed.* https://www.insidehighered.com/blogs/library-babel-fish/information-literacy%E2%80%99s-third-wave

Flanders, J. (2017). *Christmas: A biography.* Thomas Dunne Books.

Flesch, R. (1955). *Why Johnny can't read, and what you can do about it.* Harper and Brothers.

Floridi, L. (2010). *Information: A very short introduction.* Oxford University Press.

Foa, R. S. (2018). Modernization and authoritarianism. *Journal of Democracy, 29*(3), 129-140.

Foasberg, N. (2015). From standards to frameworks for IL: How the ACRL Framework addresses critiques of the Standards. *portal: Libraries and the Academy 15*(4), 702.

Ford, E., Izumi, B., Lottes, J., & Richardson, D. (2015). Badge it! *Reference Services Review, 43*(1), 31-44.

Ford, H. (1921). *The international Jew.* Dearborn, MI: Dearborn Publishing Company.

Fortier, A., & Burkell, J. (2014). Influence of need for cognition and need for cognitive closure on three information behavior orientations. *Proceedings of the American Society for Information Science and Technology, 51*(1).

Foster, S. (1993, April). Information literacy: Some misgivings. *American Libraries, 24.*

Fowler, G. (2020, November 9). Twitter and Facebook warning labels aren't enough to save democracy. *The Washington Post.* https://www.washingtonpost.com/technology/2020/11/09/facebook-twitter-election-misinformation-labels/

Fox, C. (1983). *Information and misinformation: An investigation of the notions of information, misinformation, informing, and misinforming.* Greenwood.

"Framework." (n.d.). *National Assessment of Adult Literacy (NAAL).* National Center for Education Statistics. https://nces.ed.gov/naal/framework.asp

Freeburg, D. (2017). A knowledge lens for information literacy: Conceptual framework and case study. *Journal of Documentation, 73*(5), 974-991.

Freedom House. (2019). Democracy in retreat: Freedom in the world 2019. *Freedom House.* http://www.freedomhouse.org

Fultz, M. (2006). Black public libraries in the South in the era of de jure segregation. *Libraries and the Cultural Record, 41*, 337-359.

Furner, J. (2004). Information studies without information. *Library Trends, 52*(3), 427-446.

Gaines, B. J., Kulinski, J. H., Quirk, P. J., Peyton, B., & Verkuilen, J. (2007). Same facts, different interpretations: Partisan motivation and opinion in Iraq. *Journal of Politics, 62*, 957-974.

Galvan, A. (2015). Soliciting performance, hiding bias: Whiteness and librarianship. *In the Library with the Lead Pipe.* http://www.inthelibrarywiththeleadpipe.org/2015/soliciting-performance-hiding-bias-whiteness-and-librarianship/

Galston, W. A. (2018). The populist challenge to liberal democracy. *Journal of Democracy, 29*(2), 5-19.

Gardner, A. (2020, December 21). The forging of a lie. *The Washington Post,* A1, A8-A9.

Geiger, A. W. (2017). *Most Americans—especially Millennials—say libraries can help them find reliable, trustworthy information.* Pew Research Center. https://www.pewresearch.org/fact-tank/2017/08/30/most-americans-especially-millennials-say-libraries-can-help-them-find-reliable-trustworthy-information/

Gelfert, A. (2018). Fake news: A definition. *Informal Logic, 38*(1), 84-117.

Gibson, A. N., Chancellor, R. L., Cooke, N. A., Dahlen, S. P., Lee, S. A., & Shorish, Y. L. (2017). Libraries on the frontlines: Neutrality and social justice. *Equality, Diversity and Inclusion: An International Journal, 36*(8), 751-766.

Gibson, A. N., Chancellor, R. L., Cooke, N. A., Dahlen, S. P., Patin, B., & Shorish, Y. L. (2020). Struggling to breathe: COVID-19, protest and the LIS response. *Equality, Diversity and Inclusion: An International Journal.*

Gibson, A. N., & Hughes-Hassell, S. (2017). We will not be silent: Amplifying marginalized voices in LIS education and research. *The Library Quarterly, 87*(4), 317–329.

Gibson, A. N., & Martin, J. D., III. (2019). Re-situating information poverty: Information marginalization and parents of individuals with disabilities. *Journal of the Association for Information Science and Technology, 70*(5), 476–487.

Gibson, C., & Jacobson, T. E. (2018). Habits of mind in an uncertain information world. *Reference and User Services Quarterly, 57*(3), 183–192. http://dx.doi.org/10.5860/rusq.57.3.6603

Gilster, P. (1997). *Digital literacy.* John Wiley.

Gire, J. (2010). Information literacy plans: Does your law library need one? *AALL Spectrum.*

Glendon, M. A. (2002). *A world made new: Eleanor Roosevelt and the Universal Declaration of Human Rights.* Random House.

Goguen, J. (1997). Toward a social, ethical theory of information. In G. C. Bowker, S. L. Star, W. Turner, & L. Gasser (Eds.), *Social science, technical systems and cooperative work: Beyond the great divide* (pp. 27–56). Psychology Press.

Golden, H. (2019, September 4). The decline and evolution of the school librarian. *Bloomberg CityLab.* https://www.bloomberg.com/news/articles/2019-09-04/school-librarian-jobs-face-an-uncertain-future

Golten, E. (2019). *Public libraries as place and space—new services, new visibility* [Paper presentation]. IFLA WLIC 2019, Libraries: Dialogue for change, Athens, Greece, in Session S09, Recruiting and managing the new generation of employees to attract new markets and create new services, Management and Marketing, 22–23 August 2019, Pythagoreion, Samos, Greece.

Gorham, U., Taylor, N. G., & Jaeger, P. T. (2016). *Perspectives on libraries as institutions of human rights and social justice.* Emerald.

Gottfried, J., & Grieco, E. (2018). *Younger Americans are better than older Americans at telling factual news statements from opinions.* Pew Research Center. Retrieved from https://pewrsr.ch/2NXnRgI

Gottfried, J., & Shearer, E. (2016). *News use across social media platforms 2016.* Pew Research Center, Journalism and Media. Retrieved from http://www.journalism.org

Gottfried, J., Stocking, G., & Grieco, E. (2018, September 25). *Partisans remain sharply divided in their attitudes about the news media.* Pew Research Center. https://www.journalism.org/2018/09/25/partisans-remain-sharply-divided-in-their-attitudes-about-the-news-media/

Gottschalk, F. (2019). Impacts of technology use on children: Exploring literature on the brain, cognition and well-being. *Organisation for Economic Co-operation and Development (OECD) Education Working Paper No. 195.*

Goulding, A. (2001). Information poverty or overload? *Journal of Librarianship and Information Science, 33*(3), 109–111.

Goulding, A. (2009). Engaging with community engagement: Public libraries and citizen involvement. *New Library World, 110*(1/2), 37–51.

Government Libraries Section of the International Federation of Library Associations and Institutions. (2011). Mission and/or vision statements of government libraries worldwide. https://www.ifla.org/publications/mission-andor-vision-statements-of-government-libraries-worldwide?og=45

Grabe, M. E., & Myrick, J. (2016). Informed citizenship in a media-centric way of life. *Journal of Communication, 66*, 215–235.

Graff, H. J. (Ed.). (2017). *Literacy myths, legacies, and lessons: New studies on literacy.* Routledge.

Grafstein, A. (2002). A discipline-based approach to information literacy. *The Journal of Academic Librarianship, 28*(4), 197–204.

Gramsci, A. (1971). *Prison notebooks.* Lawrence and Wishart.

Gratch-Lindauer, B. (2002). Comparing regional accreditation standards: Outcomes assessment and other trends. *Journal of Academic Librarianship, 28*, 14–25.

Gregory, L., & Higgins, S. (2013). Introduction. In L. Gregory & S. Higgins (Eds.), *Information literacy and social justice: Radical professional praxis* (pp. 1–11). Library Juice Press.

Grey, W. S. (1956). *The teaching of reading and writing*. Paris: UNESCO.

Grey Ellis, E. (2020, June 17). How to spot phony images and online propaganda. *Wired Magazine*. https://www.wired.com/story/how-to-spot-fake-images/

Grimes, J. M., Jaeger, P. T., & Fleischmann, K. R. (2008). Obfuscatocracy: Contractual frameworks in the governance of virtual worlds. *First Monday, 13*(9). http://firstmonday.org/ojs/fm/article/view/2153/2029

Grinberg, N., Joseph, K., Friedland, L., Swire-Thompson, B., & Lazer, D. (2019). Fake news on Twitter during the 2016 U.S. presidential election. *Science, 363*(6425), 374–378.

Groshek, J., & Koc-Michalska, K. (2017). Helping populism win? Social media use, filter bubbles, and support for populist presidential candidates in the 2016 US election campaign. *Information, Communication and Society, 20*, 1389–1407.

Gross, M., Latham, D., & Julien, H. (2018). What the framework means to me: Attitudes of academic librarians toward the ACRL framework for information literacy for higher education. *Library and Information Science Research, 40*(3–4), 262–268.

Guess, A. M., Lerner, M., Lyons, B., Montgomery, J. M., Nyhan, B., Reifler, J., & Sircar, N. (2020). A digital media literacy intervention increases discernment between mainstream and false news in the United States and India. *Proceedings of the National Academy of Sciences, 117*(27), 15536–15545.

Guess, A. M., Nagler, J., & Tucker, J. (2019). Less than you think: Prevalence and predictors of fake news dissemination on Facebook. *Science Advances, 5*(1), eaau4586.

Guo, Y. R., & Goh, D. H. L. (2016). Library Escape: User-centered design of an information literacy game. *The Library Quarterly, 86*(3), 330–355.

Gureckis, T. M., & Goldstone, R. L. (2009). *How you named your child: Understanding the relationship between individual decision making and collective outcomes*. Cognitive Science Society.

Guyatt, G., Rennie, D., Meade, M., & Cooke, D. J. (2011). *Users' guides to the medical literature: A manual for evidence-based clinical practice* (2nd ed.). McGraw-Hill.

Habermas, J. (1989). *The structural transformations of the public sphere: An inquiry into a category of bourgeois society*. Cambridge: Polity.

Hachman, M. (2020, June 12). Facebook now says it won't even try to block 2020 election misinformation. *PCWorld*. https://www.pcworld.com/article/3562477/facebook-now-says-it-wont-even-try-to-block-2020-election-disinformation.html

Haigh, M., & Haigh, T. (2020). Fighting and framing fake news. In P. Baines, N. O'Shaughnessy, & N. Snow (Eds.), *The SAGE handbook of propaganda* (pp. 303–323). Los Angeles: SAGE Reference.

Haigh, M., Haigh, T., & Kozak, N. I. (2018). Stopping fake news: The work practices of peer-to-peer counterpropaganda. *Journalism Studies, 19*(14), 2062–2087.

Hales, S. (2016, April 19). *SLA takes fresh look at skills used for information work* [Press release]. Special Libraries Association. https://www.sla.org/about-sla/media-room/press-releases/sla-takes-fresh-look-at-skills-used-for-information-work/

Hall, R. (2010). Public praxis: A vision for critical information literacy in public libraries. *Public Library Quarterly, 29*(2), 162–175.

Halpin, E. F., Hick, S., & Hoskins, E. (2000). Introduction. In S. Hick, E. F. Halpin, & E. Hoskins (Eds.), *Human rights and the Internet* (pp. 3–15). St. Martin's Press.

Hamelink, C. (1976). An alternative to news. *Journal of Communication, 20*, 120–123.

Hanna, T., Lawrence, M., & Peters, N. (2020). A common platform: Reimagining data and platforms. *Common Wealth*. https://www.common-wealth.co.uk/reports/common-platform-tech-utility-antitrust

Hansen, K., Paul, N., & Neibergall, B. (2003). Survey of large newspapers studies information practices. *Newspaper Research Journal, 24*(4), 36–48.

Hansen, K. & Paul, N. (2015). Newspaper archives reveal major gaps in digital age. *Newspaper Research Journal, 36*(3), 290–298.

Hanson, E. C. (2008). *The information revolution and world politics*. Rowman & Littlefield.

Harding, J. (2008). Information literacy and the public library: We've talked the talk, but are we walking the walk? *Australian Library Journal 57(3)*, 274–294.

Hare, S., & Evanson, C. (2018). Information privilege outreach for undergraduate students. *College and Research Libraries, 79(6)*, 726.

Harris, B. R. (2008). Communities as necessity in information literacy development: Challenging the standards. *The Journal of Academic Librarianship, 34(3)*, 248–255.

Hartman-Caverly, S. (2019). TRUTH always wins: Dispatches from the information war. In A. Baer, A. S. Cahoy, & R. Schroeder (Eds.), *Libraries promoting reflective dialogue in a time of political polarization* (pp. 167–233). Association of College and Research Libraries.

Harvey, M. (2020). *The king of confidence: A tale of utopian dreamers, frontier schemers, true believers, false prophets, and the murder of an American monarch.* Little, Brown.

Harvey, R. (2015). Australasia. In P. S. Richards, W. A. Wiegand, & M. Diabello (Eds.), *A history of modern librarianship: Constructing the heritage of Western cultures* (pp. 179–204). Libraries Unlimited.

Harwell, D. (2019, January 1). "Deepfake" porn becomes a high-tech tool of harassment. *The Washington Post*, A1–A2.

Harwell, D. (2020, January 14). Doctored images have become a fact of life for political campaigns. When they're disproved, believers "just don't care." *The Washington Post*. https://www.washingtonpost.com/technology/2020/01/14/doctored-political-images/

Harwell, D., & Dou, E. (2020, December 9). Huawei tested AI software that could recognize Uighur minorities and alert police, report says. *The Washington Post*, A24.

Hathcock, A. (2015). White librarianship in blackface: Diversity initiatives in LIS. *In the Library with the Lead Pipe.* http://www.inthelibrarywiththeleadpipe.org/2015/lis-diversity/

Haupt, A. (2020, October 22). Don't fall for a conspiracy theory: Here's how to protect yourself. *The Washington Post*, 11.

Hawkey, E. (2019). Media use in childhood: Evidence-based recommendations for caregivers. *American Psychological Association.* https://www.apa.org/pi/families/resources/newsletter/2019/05/media-use-childhood

Head, A. J. (2007). Beyond Google: How do students conduct academic research? *First Monday, 12(8)*. https://doi.org/10.5210/fm.v12i8.1998

Healey, P. D. (1995). Chicken Little at the reference desk: The myth of librarian liability. *Law Library Journal, 87*, 515–533.

Healey, P. D. (2008). *Professional liability issues for librarians and information professionals.* Neal-Schuman.

Hebert, A. (2018). Information literacy skills of first-year library and information science graduate students: An exploratory study. *Evidence Based Library and Information Practice, 13*.

Heider, K. (2009, March). Information literacy: The missing link in early childhood education. In *Society for Information Technology & Teacher Education International Conference* (pp. 3263–3269). Association for the Advancement of Computing in Education (AACE).

Helberger, N. (2020). The political power of platforms: How current attempts to regulate misinformation amplify opinion power. *Digital Journalism, 8(6)*, 842–854.

Hernon, P. (1995). Disinformation and misinformation through the Internet: Findings of an exploratory study. *Government Information Quarterly, 12(2)*, 133–139.

Hibbing, J. R., & Smith, K. B. (2013). *Predisposed: Liberals, conservatives, and the biology of political difference.* Routledge.

Hicks, A. (2020). Privacy and surveillance in the classroom: Responding to new information literacy challenges. *Information Literacy Group Blog.* https://infolit.org.uk/privacy-and-surveillance-in-the-classroom-responding-to-new-information-literacy-challenges/

Hicks, A. E. (2018). Making the case for a sociocultural perspective on information literacy. In K. P. Nicholson & M. Seale (Eds.), *The politics of theory and the practice of critical librarianship* (pp. 69–85). Library Juice Press.

Hinchliffe, L. J., Rand, A., & Collier, J. (2018). Predictable information literacy misconceptions of first-year college students. *Communications in Information Literacy, 12*(1), 4–18.

Hoare, P. (2015). Europe. In P. S. Richards, W. A. Wiegand, & M. Diabello (Eds.), *A history of modern librarianship: Constructing the heritage of Western cultures* (pp. 1–68). Libraries Unlimited.

Hobbs, R., & Jensen, A. (2009). The past, present, and future of media literacy education. *Journal of Media Literacy Education, 1*(1), 1.

Hoffman, M. (2001). Developing the electronic collection: The University of Minnesota Human Rights Library. *Legal Reference Services Quarterly, 19*, 143–155.

Holan, A. D. (2016). 2016 lie of the year: Fake news. *PolitiFact.* Retrieved from http://www.politifact.com

Honma, T. (2005). Trippin' over the color line: The invisibility of race in library and information studies. *Interactions: UCLA Journal of Education and Information Studies, 1*(2), 1–27. https://escholarship.org/uc/item/4nj0w1mp

Hornaday, A. (2018, November 2). Eliminating FilmStruck would be the cruelest cut. *The Washington Post,* C1–C2.

Horowitz, J. M., Igielnik, R., & Kochhar, R. (2020, January 9). *Trends in income and wealth inequality.* Pew Research Center. https://www.pewsocialtrends.org/2020/01/09/trends-in-income-and-wealth-inequality/

Horrigan, J. B. (2016). *Libraries 2016.* Pew Research Center. http://www.pewInternet.org/2016/09/09/2016/Libraries-2016/

Horton, F. W. (Ed.). (1982). *Understanding US information policy: The infostructure handbook, Vols. 1–4.* Information Industry Association.

Howard, P. N. (2020). *Lie machines: How to save democracy from troll armies, deceitful robots, junk news operations, and political operatives.* Yale.

Howe, D. W. (2007). *What hath God wrought: The transformation of America, 1815–1848.* Oxford University Press.

Hughes, J. (2018, September 4). Federal, armed forces, specialized and cooperative libraries merge to form new division of ALA [Press release]. *ALA Member News.* http://www.ala.org/news/member-news/2018/09/federal-armed-forces-specialized-cooperative-libraries-merge-form-new-division

Humprecht, E. (2019). Where "fake news" flourishes: A comparison tour across four Western democracies. *Information, Communication and Society, 22*, 1973–1988.

Hurd, P. D. (1958). Science literacy: Its meaning for American schools. *Educational Leadership, 16*(1), 13–16.

Ignatieff, M. (2005). Introduction. In M. Ignatieff (Ed.), *American exceptionalism and human rights* (pp. 1–26). Princeton University Press.

Illeris, K. (2002). *The three dimensions of learning.* Roskilde University Press.

Imhoff, J. (2020, June 3). Health inequality actually is a "black and white issue," research says. *University of Michigan Health.* https://healthblog.uofmhealth.org/lifestyle/health-inequality-actually-a-black-and-white-issue-research-says

Inglehart, R. F. (2016). The danger of deconsolidation: How much should we worry? *Journal of Democracy, 27*(3), 18–23.

Inskip, C. (2015). Information literacy in LIS education: Exploring the student view. *Journal of Information Literacy, 9*(2), 94–110.

International Federation of Library Associations and Institutions. (2011). *IFLA media and information literacy recommendations.* http://www.ifla.org/en/publications/ifla-media-and-information-literacy-recommendations

International Federation of Library Associations and Institutions. (2019). *IFLA strategy 2019-2024.* https://www.ifla.org/files/assets/hq/gb/strategic-plan/ifla-strategy-2019-2024-en.pdf

International Society for Technology in Education. (2016). *ISTE standards for students.* https://www.iste.org/standards/for-students

Ireland, S. (2018). Fake news alerts: Teaching news literacy skills in a meme world. *Reference Librarian*.

Isaac, M. (2020, September 3). Facebook moves to limit election chaos in November. *The New York Times*. https://www.nytimes.com/2020/09/03/technology/facebook-election-chaos-november.html

Islam, S. N., & Winkel, J. (2017). *Climate change and social inequality*. United Nations Department of Economic and Social Affairs Working Paper No. 152. https://www.un.org/esa/desa/papers/2017/wp152_2017.pdf

Jackson, B., & Jamieson, K. H. (2007). *unSpun: Finding facts in a world of disinformation*. Random House.

Jacobs, H. L. (2010). Posing the Wikipedia "problem": Information literacy and the praxis of problem-posing in library instruction. In M. T. Accardi (Ed.), *Critical library instruction: Theories and methods* (pp. 179-197). Library Juice Press.

Jacobs, H. L. (2014). Pedagogies of possibility within the disciplines: Critical information literacy and literatures in English. *Communications in Information Literacy, 8*(2), 192-207.

Jacobs, H. L., & Berg, S. (2011). Reconnecting information literacy policy with the core values of librarianship. *Library Trends, 60*(2), 383-394.

Jacobsen, M. (2017). Fantasy football, information literacy, and the library. *Public Libraries, 56*(4), 21-23.

Jacobson, T. E., & Gibson, C. (2015). First thoughts on implementing the framework for information literacy. *Communications in Information Literacy, 9*(2), 102-110.

Jaeger, P. T. (2003). The endless wire: E-government as global phenomenon. *Government Information Quarterly, 20*(4), 323-331.

Jaeger, P. T. (2015). Disability, human rights, and social justice: The ongoing struggle for online accessibility and equality. *First Monday, 20*(9). http://firstmonday.org/ojs.php/fm/article/view/6164/4898

Jaeger, P. T. (2018). Designing for diversity and designing for disability: New opportunities for libraries to expand their support and advocacy for people with disabilities. *International Journal of Information, Diversity, and Inclusion, 2*(1/2). http://jps.library.utoronto.ca/index.php/ijidi

Jaeger, P. T. (2020). Arsenic and information policy, or, how the Net was won and where it got us. *Library Quarterly, 90*, 380-386.

Jaeger, P. T. (2021). Foreword: Hope and the past, present, and future of libraries. In R. F. Hill (Ed.), *Hope and a future: Perspectives on the impact that librarians and libraries have on our world* (pp. xv-xvii). Emerald.

Jaeger, P. T., & Bertot, J. C. (2009). E-government education in public libraries: New service roles and expanding social responsibilities. *Journal of Education for Library and Information Science*, 39-49.

Jaeger, P. T., & Bertot, J. C. (2011). Responsibility rolls down: Public libraries and the social and policy obligations of ensuring access to e-government and government information. *Public Library Quarterly, 30*, 91-116.

Jaeger, P. T., Bertot, J. C., & Gorham, U. (2013). Wake up the nation: Public libraries, policy-making, and political discourse. *Library Quarterly, 83*, 61-72.

Jaeger, P. T., Bertot, J. C., Thompson, K. M., Katz, S. M., & DeCoster, E. J. (2012). Digital divides, digital literacy, digital inclusion, and public libraries: The intersection of public policy and public access. *Public Library Quarterly, 31*(1), 1-20.

Jaeger, P. T., & Burnett, G. (2010). *Information worlds: Social context, technology, & information behavior in the age of the Internet*. Routledge.

Jaeger, P. T., & Fleischmann, K. R. (2007). Public libraries, values, trust, and e-government. *Information Technology and Libraries, 26*(4), 35-43.

Jaeger, P. T., Gorham, U., Bertot, J. C., & Sarin, L. C. (2013). Democracy, neutrality, and value demonstration in the age of austerity. *The Library Quarterly, 83*(4), 368-382.

Jaeger, P. T., Gorham, U., Bertot, J. C., & Sarin, L. C. (2014). *Public libraries, public policies, and political processes: Serving and transforming communities in times of economic and political constraint*. Rowman & Littlefield.

Jaeger, P. T., Gorham, U., Taylor, N. G., Sarin, L. C., & Kettnich, K. (2017). Aftermath part 2: In spite of the way it may seem, all is not lost for libraries and librarianship. *Library Quarterly, 87,* 295-302.

Jaeger, P. T., McClure, C. R., & Bertot, J. C. (2005). The E-rate program and libraries and library consortia, 2000-2004: Trends and issues. *Information Technology and Libraries, 24*(2), 57-67.

Jaeger, P. T., Paquette, S., & Simmons, S. N. (2010). Information policy in national political campaigns: A comparison of the 2008 campaigns for president of the United States and prime minister of Canada. *Journal of Information Technology and Politics, 7,* 1-16.

Jaeger, P. T., & Sarin, L. C. (2016a). All librarianship is political: Educate accordingly. *Political Librarian, 2*(1), 17-27. http://openscholarship.wustl.edu/polib/vol2/iss1/8/

Jaeger, P. T., & Sarin, L. C. (2016b). The politically engaged public library: Admitting and embracing the political nature of libraries and their goals. *Public Library Quarterly, 35,* 325-330.

Jaeger, P. T., & Taylor, N. G. (2019). *Foundations of information policy.* American Library Association.

Jaeger, P. T., & Taylor, N. G. (2021a). Arsenals of lifelong information literacy: Educating users to navigate political and current events information in a world of ever-evolving misinformation. *Library Quarterly, 91*(1), 19-31.

Jaeger, P. T., & Taylor, N. G. (2021b). The intertwined futures of information policy and information literacy. In A. Duff (Ed.), *Research handbook on information policy.* Edward Elgar Publishing.

Jaeger, P. T., & Taylor, N. G. (2021c). Raking the forests: Information literacy, political polarization, fake news, and the educational roles of librarians. In N. G. Taylor, K. M. Kettnich, U. Gorham, & P. T. Jaeger (Eds.), *Libraries and the global retreat of democracy.* Emerald.

Jaeger, P. T., Taylor, N. G., & Gorham, U. (2015). *Libraries, human rights, and social justice: Enabling access and promoting inclusion.* Rowman & Littlefield.

Jaeger, P. T., Taylor, N. G., Gorham, U., & Kettnich, K. M. (2021). The light, of course, in the library: Pandemics, protests, and being what the community needs most. *Library Quarterly, 91,* 1-4.

Jaeger, P. T., & Thompson, K. M. (2003). E-government around the world: Lessons, challenges, and new directions. *Government Information Quarterly, 20*(4), 389-394.

Jaeger, P. T., & Thompson, K. M. (2004). Social information behavior and the democratic process: Information poverty, normative behavior, and electronic government in the United States. *Library and Information Science Research, 26*(1), 94-107.

Jaeger, P. T., & Yan, Z. (2009). One law with two outcomes: Comparing the implementation of CIPA in public libraries and schools. *Information Technology and Libraries, 28*(1), 6-14.

James, P. D. (1971). *Shroud for a nightingale.* Scribner.

James, W. (1910, August). The moral equivalent of war. *McClure's Magazine,* 463-468.

Jamison, P. (2018, April 19). DC lawmaker who says Jews control the weather visits Holocaust Museum, but leaves early. *The Washington Post.* http://www.washingtonpost.com

Jamison, P., & Strauss, V. (2018, March 18). DC lawmaker says recent snowfall caused by "Rothschilds controlling the climate." *The Washington Post,* http://www.washingtonpost.com

Jeffreys-Jones, R. (1989). *The CIA and American democracy.* Yale University Press.

Johnson, B. (2017). Information literacy is dead: The role of librarians in a post-truth world. *Computers in Libraries, 37*(2), 12-15.

Jones, B. J. (2013). *Jim Henson: The biography.* Ballentine Books.

Jones-Jang, S. M., Mortensen, T., & Liu, J. (2021). Does media literacy help identification of fake news? Information literacy helps, but other literacies don't. *American Behavioral Scientist, 65*(2), 371-388.

Julien, H. (2005). Education for information literacy instruction: A global perspective. *Journal of Education for Library and Information Science, 46,* 210-216.

Julien, H., & Barker, S. (2009). How high-school students find and evaluate scientific information: A basis for information literacy skills development. *Library and Information Science Research, 31*(1), 12-17.

Julien, H., Gross, M., & Latham, D. (2018). Survey of information literacy instructional practices in US academic libraries. *College and Research Libraries, 79*(2), 179.

Julien, H., & Hoffman, C. (2008). Information literacy training in Canada's public libraries. *The Library Quarterly, 78*(1), 19–41.

Julien, H., & Williamson, K. (2011). Discourse and practice in information literacy and information seeking: Gaps and opportunities. *Information Research, 16*(1). http://InformationR.net/ir/16-1

Juskiewicz, S., & Cote, C. (2015). Teaching information literacy to undergraduate students: Reflecting on the past, present and future of library instruction. *Pacific Northwest Library Association Quarterly, 79*(1).

Kahan, D. M., Peters, E., Wittlin, M., & Slovic, P. (2012). The polarizing impact of science literacy and numeracy on perceived climate change risks. *Nature Climate Change, 2,* 732–735.

Kamenetz, A. (2017, October 31). *Learning to spot fake news: Start with a gut check.* NPR. https://www.npr .org/sections/ed/2017/10/31/559571970/learning-to-spot-fake-news-start-with-a-gut-check

Kane, P., & Clement, S. (2020, December 5). Just 27 congressional Republicans acknowledge Biden's win, *Washington Post* survey finds. *The Washington Post.* https://www.washingtonpost.com/politics/survey-who -won-election-republicans-congress/2020/12/04/1a1011f6-3650-11eb-8d38-6aea1adb3839_story.html

Kaplan, A., & Haenlein, M. (2010). Users of the world, unite: The challenges and opportunities of social media. *Business Horizons, 53,* 59–68.

Karlova, N. A., & Lee, J. H. (2011). Notes from the underground city of disinformation: A conceptual investigation. *Proceedings of the American Society for Information Science and Technology, 48,* 1–9.

Katz, I. R. (2007). Testing information literacy in digital environments: ETS's iSkills assessment. *Information Technology and Libraries, 26*(3), 3–12.

Kawashima-Ginsberg, K. (2014). *National Civics Teacher Survey: Information literacy in high school civics* [Fact sheet]. Center for Information and Research on Civic Learning and Engagement (CIRCLE).

Keefe, E. B., & Copeland, S. R. (2011). What is literacy? The power of a definition. *Research and Practice for Persons with Severe Disabilities, 36*(3–4), 92–99.

Keeling, M. (2017, November 1). Rewriting the standards. *American Libraries.* https://americanlibraries magazine.org/2017/11/01/rewriting-standards-aasl/

Keller, K., LeBeau, C., Malafi, E., & Spackman, A. (2014). *Financial literacy education in libraries: Guidelines and best practices for service.* Reference and User Services Association (RUSA). http://www.ala.org/ rusa/sites/ala.org.rusa/files/content/FLEGuidelines_Final_September_2014.pdf

Kelley, S., Jr. (1956). *Professional public relations and political power.* Johns Hopkins University Press.

Kennedy, B. (2020, April 6). *U.S. concern about climate change is rising, but mainly among Democrats.* Pew Research Center. https://www.pewresearch.org/fact-tank/2020/04/16/u-s-concern-about-climate -change-is-rising-but-mainly-among-democrats/

Kennedy, B. R., Mathis, C. C., & Woods, A. K. (2007). African Americans and their distrust of the health care system: Healthcare for diverse populations. *Journal of Cultural Diversity, 14*(2), 56–60.

Kessler, G. (2020, December 20). By more than a nose, biggest Pinocchios of the year relate to Covid-19 and the election. *The Washington Post,* A4.

Kessler, G., Rizzo, S., & Kelly, M. (2020, June 7). Trump's false claims are accelerating. *The Washington Post,* B1, B4.

Key, V. O. (1966). *The responsible electorate.* Harvard University Press.

Kielbowicz, R. B. (1989). *News in the mail: The press, post office, and public information, 1700–1860.* Greenwood Press.

Kim, E. M., & Yang, S. (2016). Internet literacy and digital natives' civic engagement: Internet skill literacy or Internet information literacy? *Journal of Youth Studies, 19*(4), 438–456.

Kim-Prieto, D. (2011). The road not yet taken: How law student information literacy standards address identified issues in legal research education and training. *Law Library Journal, 103,* 605–630.

Kindig, D. A., Panzer, A. M., & Nielsen Bohlman, L. (Eds.). (2004). *Health literacy: A prescription to end confusion.* National Academies Press.

Kintgen, E. R., Kroll, B. M., & Rose, M. (Eds.). (1988). *Perspectives on literacy.* Southern Illinois University Press.

Klinenberg, E. (2018). *Palaces for the people: How social infrastructure can help fight inequality, polarization, and the decline of civic life*. Broadway Books.

Klinenberg, E. (2020, September 3). How libraries can save the 2020 election. *The New York Times*. https://www.nytimes.com/2020/09/03/opinion/mail-voting-trump-libraries.html

Klotz, R. J. (2004). *The politics of Internet communication*. Rowman & Littlefield.

Klucevsek, K. M. (2017). The intersection of information and science literacy. *Communications in Information Literacy, 11*(2), 354-365.

Knoblauch, C. H. (1990). Literacy and the politics of education. In A. A. Lumsford, H. Moglen, & J. Slevin (Eds.), *The right to literacy* (pp. 74-80). The Modern Language Association of America.

Knott, C. (2016). *Not free, not for all: Public libraries in the age of Jim Crow*. University of Massachusetts Press.

Knuth, R. (2003). *Libricide: The regime-sponsored destruction of books and libraries in the twentieth century*. Praeger.

Koh, J., Kim, Y. G., Butler, B., & Bock, G. W. (2007). Encouraging participation in virtual communities. *Communications of the ACM, 50*(2), 68-73.

Koltay, T. (2011). The media and the literacies: Media literacy, information literacy, digital literacy. *Media, Culture and Society, 33*(2), 211-221.

Kranich, N. (2004). Why filters won't protect children or adults. *Library Leadership and Management, 18*(1), 14.

Kuhlthau, C. C. (1991). Inside the search process: Information seeking from the user's perspective. *Journal of the American Society for Information Science, 42*(5), 361-371.

Kuhlthau, C. C. (1993). *Seeking meaning: A process approach to library and information services*. Greenwood.

Kulinski, J. H., Quirk, P. J., Jerit, J., Schweider, D., & Rich, R. F. (2003). Misinformation and the currency of democratic citizenship. *Journal of Politics, 62*, 790-816.

Kundu, D. K. (2017). Models of information seeking behaviour: A comparative study. *Methodology, 7*, 4.

Kutner, L., & Armstrong, A. (2012). Rethinking information literacy in a globalized world. *Communications in Information Literacy, 6*(1), 24-33.

Lamb, A. (2017). Debunking the librarian "gene": Designing online information literacy instruction for incoming library science students. *Journal of Education for Library and Information Science, 58*(1), 15-26.

Langer, E. (2020, October 15). Nobel laureate revealed CFC's threat to Earth's protective ozone layer. *The Washington Post*, B5.

Lanier, J. (2018). *Ten arguments for deleting your social media accounts right now*. Henry Holt.

Lankes, R. D. (2016a). *Expect more: Demanding better libraries for today's complex world* (2nd ed.). Riland Publishing.

Lankes, R. D. (2016b). *The new librarianship field guide*. MIT Press.

Lankes, R. D. (2019). *Library as movement*. Victoria Libraries 2019 Planning Summit, Kalorama, Victoria, Australia (video conference). https://davidlankes.org/library-as-movement/#Script

LaPlante, M. D. (2019). *Superlative: The biology of extremes*. BenBella.

Lau, J. (2006). *Guidelines on information literacy for lifelong learning*. International Federation of Library Associations and Institutions, Boca del Río, Veracruz, Mexico. https://www.ifla.org/files/assets/information-literacy/publications/ifla-guidelines-en.pdf

Lawless, J., Toronto, C. E., & Grammatica, G. L. (2016). Health literacy and information literacy: A concept comparison. *Reference Services Review, 44*(2), 144-162.

Lawton, C., & Ackrill, R. (2016, July 8). Hard evidence: How areas with low immigration voted mainly for Brexit. *The Conversation*.

Lazer, D., Baum, M., Grinberg, N., Friedland, L., Joseph, K., Hobbs, W., & Mattsson, C. (2017). *Combating fake news: An agenda for research and action*. Harvard University; Northeastern University. https://

shorensteincenter.org/wp-content/uploads/2017/05/Combating-Fake-News-Agenda-for-Research
-1.pdf

Leaning, M. (2019). An approach to digital literacy through the integration of media and information literacy. *Media and Communication, 7*(2), 4–13.

Leckie, G. J., Given, L., & Campbell, G. (2009). Technologies of social regulation: An examination of library OPACs and web portals. In G. J. Leckie & J. E. Buschman (Eds.), *Information technology in librarianship: New critical approaches* (pp. 221–260). Libraries Unlimited.

Leckie, G. J., & Hopkins, J. (2002). The public place of central libraries: Findings from Toronto and Vancouver. *The Library Quarterly, 72*(3), 326–372.

Lee, M. Y. H., & Narayanswamy, A. (2020, December 4). Trump raises $207.5 million post-election with flurry of misleading appeals. *The Washington Post*, A8.

Lehman, E. D. (2013). *Becoming Tom Thumb: Charles Stratton, P. T. Barnum, and the dawn of American celebrity*. Wesleyan University Press.

Lenker, M. (2016). Motivated reasoning, political information, and information literacy education. *portal: Libraries and the Academy, 16*(3), 511–528.

Lepore, J. (2018). *These truths: A history of the United States*. W. W. Norton & Company.

Lepore, J. (2020). *If then: How the Simulmatics Corporation invented the future*. Liveright.

Lerman, R. (2020, July 21). Facebook labels Trump, Biden posts on voting. *The Washington Post*. https://www.washingtonpost.com/technology/2020/07/21/facebook-labels-trump-voting/

Lerman, R., & Timberg, C. (2020, June 27). Bowing to pressure, Facebook will start labeling violating posts from politicians. But critics say it's not enough. *The Washington Post*. https://www.washingtonpost.com/technology/2020/06/26/facebook-hate-speech-policies/

Lerner, F. (2009). *The story of libraries: From the invention of writing to the computer age*. Continuum.

Levitin, D. J. (2017). *Weaponized lies: How to think critically in the post-truth era*. Dutton.

Library of Congress. (2015). *Library of Congress strategic plan, FY2016–FY2020*. https://www.loc.gov/static/portals/about/documents/library_congress_stratplan_2016-2020.pdf

Library of Congress. (2020). *Foundations: Information literacy and primary sources* [Event notice]. https://www.loc.gov/item/webcast-9469/

Lim, S. (2020). Academic library guides for tackling fake news: A content analysis. *Journal of Academic Librarianship, 46*(5), 102195.

Limberg, L., & Sundin, O. (2006). Teaching information seeking: Relating information literacy education to theories of information behaviour. *Information Research: An International Electronic Journal, 12*(1), n1.

Lin, P., Cheng, H., Liao, W., & Yen, Y. (2012). A study of the mobile technology literacy indicators in Taiwan. *Proceedings of the International Conference on Emerging Computation and Information Technologies for Education (ECICE 2012)*.

Lindstrom, M. (2011). *Brandwashed: Tricks companies use to manipulate our minds and persuade us to buy*. Crown Business.

"Literacy." (n.d.). UNESCO. https://en.unesco.org/themes/literacy

Lloyd, A. (2005). Information literacy: Different contexts, different concepts, different truths? *Journal of Librarianship and Information Science, 37*(2), 82–88.

Lloyd, A. (2010a). Framing information literacy as information practice: Site ontology and practice theory. *Journal of Documentation, 66*(2), 245–258.

Lloyd, A. (2010b). *Information literacy landscapes: Information literacy in education, workplace and everyday contexts*. Elsevier.

Lloyd, A. (2012). Information literacy as a socially enacted practice. *Journal of Documentation, 68*(6), 772–783.

Lockhart, P. R. (2019, August 16). How slavery became America's first big business. *Vox*. https://www.vox.com/identities/2019/8/16/20806069/slavery-economy-capitalism-violence-cotton-edward-baptist

Loertscher, D. (2008). Information literacy: 20 years later. *Teacher Librarian, 35*(5), 42.

Loertscher, D. V. (2018). National School Library Standards for Learners, School Librarians, and School Libraries. *Teacher Librarian, 45*(3), 36-71.

Loertscher, D. V., & Woolls, B. (2002). *Information literacy: A review of the research.* Hi Willow Research and Publishing.

Lomas, N. (2019, September 13). This game uses troll tactics to teach critical thinking. *TechCrunch.* https://techcrunch.com/2019/09/13/this-game-uses-troll-tactics-to-teach-critical-thinking/

Long, E. (1992). Textual interpretation as collective action. In J. Boyarin (Ed.), *The ethnography of reading* (pp. 180-211). University of California Press.

Long, H., & Douglas-Gabriel, D. (2020, September 18). Low-income students are in a dropout crisis. *The Washington Post,* A1, A16.

Lor, P. J. (2018). Democracy, information, and libraries in a time of post-truth discourse. *Library Management, 39,* 307-321.

Losee, R. M. (1997). A discipline independent definition of information. *Journal of the American Society for Information Science, 48*(3), 254-269.

Lowrie, R., & Truslow, H. (2017). *Caught in the maelstrom: How two academic librarians were pulled into the dangerous undercurrents of disinformation* [Paper presentation]. Media in the Post-Truth World: The New Marketplace of (Dis)information, November 2-4, Prague.

Lumpkin, L. (2020, December 7). A crisis for community colleges. *The Washington Post,* B1, B5.

Luo, L. (2010). Web 2.0 integration in information literacy instruction: An overview. *The Journal of Academic Librarianship, 36*(1), 32-40.

Lyons, M. (2010). *A history of reading and writing: In the Western world.* Palgrave Macmillan.

Macaraeg, P. (2019, December 7). CrowdTangle rolls out new, better search tool for fact checkers. Rappler. https://www.rappler.com/technology/crowdtangle-rolls-out-new-better-search-tool-fact-checkers

Mackey, T. P., & Jacobson, T. E. (2011). Reframing information literacy as a metaliteracy. *College and Research Libraries, 72*(1), 62-78.

Macklin, A. S., & Culp, F. B. (2008). Information literacy instruction: Competencies, caveats, and a call to action. *Science and Technology Libraries, 28*(1-2), 45-61.

MacLeish, A. (1940). Public libraries and the democratic process. *ALA Bulletin, 34*(6), 385-388, 421-422.

MacMillan, M. E. (2014). Fostering the integration of information literacy and journalism practice: A long-term study of journalism students. *Journal of Information Literacy, 8*(2), 3-22.

Macrotrends. (2020). *Amazon—23-year stock price history.* http://macrotrends.net

Madden, M., Lenhart, A., Cortesi, S., Gasser, U., Duggan, M., Smith, A., & Beaton, M. (2013). *Teens, social media, and privacy.* Pew Research Center and The Berkman Center for Internet and Society. https://www.pewresearch.org/Internet/2013/05/21/teens-social-media-and-privacy/

Madison, J., Jr. (1840/1987). *Notes of debates in the federal convention of 1787* (bicentennial edition). Norton.

Mahmood, K. (2016). Do people overestimate their information literacy skills? A systematic review of empirical evidence on the Dunning-Kruger Effect. *Communications in Information Literacy, 10*(2), 199-213.

Manguel, A. (1996). *A history of reading.* Viking.

Martin, J. (2013). Refreshing information literacy: Learning from recent British information literacy models. *Communications in Information Literacy, 7*(2), 6.

Masyada, S., & Washington, E. Y. (2019). Creating the citizen: Critical literacy, civics, and the C3 Framework in Social Studies. In *Critical Literacy Initiatives for Civic Engagement* (pp. 94-122). IGI Global.

Mathiesen, K. (2013). The human right to a public library. *Journal of Information Ethics, 22,* 60-79.

Mathiesen, K. (2014). Human rights for the digital age. *Journal of Mass Media Ethics, 29,* 2-18.

Mathiesen, K. (2015). Human rights as a topic and guide for LIS research and practice. *Journal of the Association for Information Science and Technology, 66,* 1305-1322.

Mattern, S. (2019, October). Fugitive libraries. *Places Journal*. https://placesjournal.org/article/fugitive-libraries/?cn-reloaded=1

Matteson, M. L., & Gersch, B. (2020). Information literacy instruction in public libraries. *Journal of Information Literacy, 14*(2), 71-95.

Mauldin, A. (2019, August 22). 466 Tbps: The global Internet continues to expand. *Telegeography Blog*. https://blog.telegeography.com/466-tbps-the-global-Internet-continues-to-expand

Mayer, H. (1998). *All on fire: William Lloyd Garrison and the abolition of slavery*. St. Martin's Griffin.

McCook, K. d. l. P., & Bossaller, J. (2018). *Introduction to public librarianship* (3rd ed.). ALA Editions.

McCook, K. d. l. P., & Phenix, K. J. (2006). Public libraries and human rights. *Public Library Quarterly, 25*, 57-73.

McCrummen, S. (2016, October 1). Finally, someone who thinks like me. *The Washington Post*.

McCulley, C. (2009). Mixing and matching: Assessing information literacy. *Communications in Information Literacy, 3*(2), 171-180.

McDevitt, M., & Ferrucci, P. (2018). Populism, journalism, and the limits of reflexivity: The case of Donald J. Trump. *Journalism Studies, 19*, 512-526.

McGowan, B. S., Cantwell, L. P., Conklin, J. L., Raszewski, R., Wolf, J. P., Slebodnik, M., . . . Johnson, S. (2020). Evaluating nursing faculty's approach to information literacy instruction: A multi-institutional study. *Journal of the Medical Library Association: JMLA, 108*(3), 378.

McKenna, S. (2018). Here are five signs that universities are turning into corporations. *The Conversation*. https://theconversation.com/here-are-five-signs-that-universities-are-turning-into-corporations-93100

McKenzie, L. (2020). Libraries brace for budget cuts. *Inside Higher Ed*. https://www.insidehighered.com/news/2020/04/17/college-librarians-prepare-looming-budget-cuts-and-journal-subscriptions-could-be

McKenzie, P. J. (2003). A model of information practices in accounts of everyday-life information seeking. *Journal of Documentation, 59*(1), 19-40.

McTavish, M. (2009). "I get my facts from the Internet": A case study of the teaching and learning of information literacy in in-school and out-of-school programs. *Journal of Early Childhood Literacy, 9*(1), 3-28.

Meckler, L., & Natanson, H. (2020, December 7). Remote learning widens equity gap. *The Washington Post*, A1, A16-A17.

Medical Library Association. (2017). *MLA competencies for lifelong learning and professional success*. https://www.mlanet.org/p/cm/ld/fid=1217

Meek, M. (1991). *On being literate*. Random House.

Meleady, R., Seger, C., & Vermue, M. (2017). Examining the role of positive and negative intergroup contact and anti-immigrant prejudice in Brexit. *British Journal of Social Psychology, 56*(4), 799-808.

Merchant, C. (2003). *Reinventing Eden: The fate of nature in Western culture*. Routledge.

Mesler, B., & Cleaves, H. J., II. (2016). *A brief history of creation: Science and the search for the origin of life*. Norton.

Metzger, M. J., Flanagin, A. J., & Zwarun, L. (2003). College student web use, perceptions of information credibility, and verification behavior. *Computers and Education, 41*(3), 271-290.

Mihalcik, C. (2020, July 16). Facebook to label posts about voting from political candidates. *CNET*. https://www.cnet.com/news/facebook-to-label-posts-about-voting-from-political-candidates/

Milham, W. I. (1918). *Meteorology: A text-book for the weather, the causes of its changes, and weather forecasting for the student and the general reader*. Macmillan.

Miller, C. L. (1985). *Prophetic worlds: Indians and whites on the Columbia Plateau*. University of Washington Press.

Miller, J. (2014, August 7). "Britons spend more time on tech than asleep, study suggests." BBC News. www.bbc.com

Mirza, R., & Seale, M. (2017). Who killed the world? White masculinity and the technocratic library of the future. In G. Schlesselman-Tarango (Ed.), *Topographies of whiteness: Mapping whiteness in library and information science* (pp. 175–201). Library Juice Press.

Mitchell, A., Gottfried, J., Stocking, G., Walker, M., & Fedeli, S. (2019). *Many Americans say made-up news is a critical problem that needs to be fixed.* Pew Research Center. https://www.journalism.org/2019/06/05/many-americans-say-made-up-news-is-a-critical-problem-that-needs-to-be-fixed/

Mokhtar, I. A., & Majid, S. (2008). Information literacy standards, guidelines and their implementation: An analysis. *DESIDOC Journal of Library and Information Technology, 28*(2).

Mooney, C. (2005). *The Republican war on science.* Basic Books.

Moore, P. (2005). An analysis of information literacy education worldwide. *School Libraries Worldwide, 11*(2), 1–23.

Morgan, P. K. (2015). Pausing at the threshold. *portal: Libraries and the Academy, 15*(1), 183–195.

Muller, K., & Schwartz, C. (2018). *Fanning the flames of hate: Social media and hate crime.* Centre for Competitive Advantage in the Global Economy.

National Academies of Sciences, Engineering, and Medicine. (2016). *Science literacy: Concepts, contexts, and consequences.* The National Academies Press.

National Committee on Excellence in Education. (1983). *A nation at risk: The imperative for education reform.* Government Printing Office.

National Council of Teachers of English. (2019). *Definition of literacy in a digital age.* https://ncte.org/statement/nctes-definition-literacy-digital-age/

National Library of Medicine. (n.d.). "Digital health literacy." *All of Us.* https://nnlm.gov/all-of-us/resources/digitalhealthliteracy

National Library of Medicine. (2021). *An introduction to health literacy.* https://new.nnlm.gov/guides/intro-health-literacy

National Public Radio. (2015, January 7). "A cow head will not erupt from your body if you get a smallpox vaccine." *Goats and Soda.* https://www.npr.org/sections/goatsandsoda/2015/01/07/375598652/a-cow-head-will-not-erupt-from-your-body-if-you-get-a-smallpox-vaccine

Nerone, J. (2011). Representing public opinion: US newspapers and the news system in the long nineteenth century. *History Compass, 9*(9), 743–759.

Neuman, D. (2011). *Learning in information-rich environments: I-LEARN and the construction of knowledge in the 21st century.* Springer.

Neuman, D., Teece DeCarlo, M. J., Lee, V. J., Greenwell, S., & Grant, A. (2019). *Learning in information-rich environments: I-LEARN and the construction of knowledge from information* (2nd ed.). Springer.

Newhouse, A. (2020, November 27). Parler is bringing together mainstream conservatives, anti-Semites and white supremacists as the social media platform attracts millions of Trump supporters. *The Conversation.* https://theconversation.com/parler-is-bringing-together-mainstream-conservatives-anti-semites-and-white-supremacists-as-the-social-media-platform-attracts-millions-of-trump-supporters-150439

Nichols, J. L. (2019). *Suzanne and Gertrude.* Pushcart Press.

Nickerson, R. S. (1998). Confirmation bias: A ubiquitous phenomenon in many guises. *Review of General Psychology, 2*(2), 175.

Nielsen, B. G., & Borlund, P. (2013, October). Information literacy and the public library: Danish librarians' views on information literacy. In *European Conference on Information Literacy* (pp. 632–638). Springer, Cham.

Noble, S. U. (2018). *Algorithms of oppression: How search engines reinforce racism.* NYU Press.

No Child Left Behind Act, Pub. L. No. 107-110 (2001).

NodeGraph. (2020). How much data is on the Internet? The big data facts update 2020. https://www.nodegraph.se/how-much-data-is-on-the-Internet/

Nowlain, L. (2020). Information literacy for parents in comics. *ALSC Blog*. https://www.alsc.ala.org/blog/2020/04/information-literacy-for-parents/

Nunberg, G. (1996). *The future of the book*. University of California Press.

Nutbeam, D. (2008). The evolving concept of health literacy. *Social Science and Medicine, 67*(12), 2072-2078.

Nyhan, B., & Reifler, J. (2010). When corrections fail: The persistence of political misperceptions. *Political Behavior, 32*, 303-330.

Oakleaf, M. (2008). Dangers and opportunities: A conceptual map of information literacy assessment approaches. *portal: Libraries and the Academy, 8*(3), 233-253.

Oakleaf, M., & Kaske, N. (2009). Guiding questions for assessing information literacy in higher education. *portal: Libraries and the Academy, 9*(2), 273-286.

Obama, B. H. (2009). *National Information Literacy Awareness Month proclamation*. White House Office of Communications.

Obama, B. H. (2020). *A promised land*. Crown.

O'Hara, R. E., Walter, M. I., & Christopher, A. N. (2009). Need for cognition and conscientiousness as predictors of political interest and voting strategy. *Journal of Applied Psychology, 39*, 1397-1416.

Ohlheiser, A. (2020, June 2). How to protect yourself online from misinformation right now. *MIT Technology Review*. https://www.technologyreview.com/2020/06/02/1002505/black-lives-matter-protest-misinformation-advice/

Olden, A. (2015). Africa. In P. S. Richards, W. A. Wiegand, & M. Diabello (Eds.), *A history of modern librarianship: Constructing the heritage of Western cultures* (pp. 143-178). Libraries Unlimited.

Oliemat, E., Ihmeideh, F., & Alkhawaldeh, M. (2018). The use of touch-screen tablets in early childhood: Children's knowledge, skills, and attitudes towards tablet technology. *Children and Youth Services Review, 88*, 591-597.

Olivarez-Giles, N. (2011, June 3). United Nations report: Internet access is a human right. *Los Angeles Times*, June 3. Retrieved from http://www.latimes.com/business/technology

Olson, H. A. (2013). *The power to name: Locating the limits of subject representation in libraries*. Springer Science and Business Media.

Oreskes, N., & Conway, E. M. (2011). *Merchants of doubt: How a handful of scientists obscured the truth on issues from tobacco smoke to global warming*. Bloomsbury Publishing USA.

Orlean, S. (2018). *The library book*. Simon and Schuster.

O'Sullivan, C. (2002). Is information literacy relevant in the real world? *Reference Services Review, 30*(1), 7-14.

Owusu-Ansah, E. K. (2005). Debating definitions of information literacy: Enough is enough! *Library Review, 54*(6), 366-374.

Oxenham, J. (1980). *Literacy, writing, reading and social organisation*. Routledge.

Paine, T. (1776). *Common sense*. J. P. Lippincott & Company.

Pariser, E. (2011). *The filter bubble: How the new personalized web is changing what we read and how we think*. Penguin.

Pashia, A. (2017). Examining structural oppression as a component of information literacy: A call for librarians to support #BlackLivesMatter through our teaching. *Journal of Information Literacy, 11*(2), 86-104.

Pashia, A., & Critten, J. (Eds.). (2019). *Critical approaches to credit-bearing information literacy courses*. Association of College and Research Libraries.

Paul, N. (1997). *Information strategy in newsrooms: New emphasis on traditional roles for news librarians*. Poynter Institute.

Paul, N., & Hansen, K. (2002). Reclaiming news libraries. *Library Journal, 127*(6), 44-46.

Pawley, C. (2003). Information literacy: A contradictory coupling. *The Library Quarterly, 73*(4), 422-452.

Perez, S. (2019, October 3). TikTok explains its ban on political advertising. *TechCrunch*. https://techcrunch.com/2019/10/03/tiktok-explains-its-ban-on-political-advertising/

Perlstein, R. (2008). *Nixonland: The rise of a president and the fracturing of America.* Scribner.

Perlstein, R. (2014). *The invisible bridge: The fall of Nixon and the rise of Reagan.* Scribner.

Perry, A. M., Rothwell, J., & Harshbarger, D. (2018, November 27). *The devaluation of assets in Black neighborhoods.* The Brookings Institution. https://www.brookings.edu/research/devaluation-of-assets -in-black-neighborhoods/

Peter, J., Leichner, N., Mayer, A. K., & Krampen, G. (2017). Making information literacy instruction more efficient by providing individual feedback. *Studies in Higher Education, 42*(6), 1110-1125.

Peterson, L. (1995). Multiculturalism: Affirmative or negative action? *Library Journal, 120*(July), 30-33.

Petronzio, M. (2014, March 5). US adults spend 11 hours a day with digital media. *Mashable.* www.mashable .com

Petrov, C. (2019, June 16). Big data statistics 2020. *TechJury* (originally published March 22). https://techjury.net/stats-about/big-data-statistics

Pettigrew, T. F. (2017). Social psychological perspectives on Trump supporters. *Journal of Social and Political Psychology, 5*(1), 107-116.

Pew Research Center. (2017, October). *The partisan divide on political values grows even wider.* https://www.pewresearch.org

Phenix, K. J., & McCook, K. d. l. P. (2005). Human rights and librarians. *Reference and User Services Quarterly, 45,* 23-26.

Pilerot, O. (2016). Connections between research and practice in the information literacy narrative: A mapping of the literature and some propositions. *Journal of Librarianship and Information Science, 48*(4), 313-321.

Pilerot, O., & Lindberg, J. (2011). The concept of information literacy in policy-making texts: An imperialistic project? *Library Trends, 60*(2), 338-360.

Pinker, S. (2011). *The better angels of our nature: Why violence has declined.* Vintage.

Pinto, M., & Pascual, R. F. (2016). Exploring LIS students' beliefs in importance and self-efficacy of core information literacy competencies. *College and Research Libraries, 77*(6), 703-726.

Polger, M. A., & Okamoto, K. (2010). "Can't anyone be a teacher anyway?": Student perceptions of librarians as teachers. *Library Philosophy and Practice.* http://www.webpages.uidaho.edu/~mbolin/polger -okamoto.htm

Polkinghorne, S., & Julien, H. (2019). Survey of information literacy instructional practices in Canadian academic libraries. *Canadian Journal of Information and Library Science 42*(1/2): 69-93.

Pool, I. d. S. (1990). *Technologies with boundaries.* Harvard University Press.

Poole, A. H. (2018). "Could my dark hands break through the dark shadow?": Gender, Jim Crow, and librarianship during the long freedom struggle, 1935-1955. *The Library Quarterly, 88*(4), 348-374.

Poynter Institute. (2018, March 20). Poynter receives $3 million from Google to lead program teaching teens to tell fact from fiction online [News release]. https://www.poynter.org/news-release/2018/poynter -receives-3-million-from-google-to-lead-program-teaching-teens-to-tell-fact-from-fiction-online/

Prado, J. C., & Marzal, M. Á. (2013). Incorporating data literacy into information literacy programs: Core competencies and contents. *Libri, 63*(2), 123-134.

Pratt, A. D. (1977). The information of the image. *Libri, 27*(3), 204-220.

Prensky, M. (2001). Digital natives, digital immigrants. *On the Horizon, 9*(5), 1-6.

Proferes, N. (2017). Information flow solipsism in an exploratory study of beliefs about Twitter. *Social Media + Society, 3*(1), doi:2056305117698493.

Protecting Children in the 21st Century Act, 15 U.S.C. § 6552-53 (2008).

Qiang, Y. (2019). The road to digital unfreedom: President Xi's surveillance state. *Journal of Democracy, 30*(1), 53-67.

Rader, E., & Gray, R. (2015). Understanding user beliefs about algorithmic curation in the Facebook news feed. *Proceedings of the 33rd Annual ACM Conference on Human Factors in Computing Systems* (pp. 173-182). ACM.

Rader, H. B. (2002). Information literacy 1973-2002: A selected literature review. *Library Trends, 51*(2), 242-259.

Rader, H. B., & Coons, W. (1992). Information literacy: One response to the new decade. In B. Baker & M. E. Litzinger (Eds.), *The educational mission of the library* (pp. 118-128). American Library Association.

Rahula, E., & Morris, L. (2020, November 14). QAnon at loss in US after election but is vibrant abroad. *The Washington Post*, A13.

Rainie, L., Keeter, S., & Perrin, A. (2019). *Trust and distrust in America*. Pew Research Center. https://www.pewresearch.org/politics/2019/07/22/trust-and-distrust-in-america/

Ramsey, E., & Aagard, M. C. (2018). Academic libraries as active contributors to student wellness. *College and Undergraduate Libraries, 25*(4), 328-334.

Ranganathan, S. R. (1931). *The five laws of library science*. Madras Library Association; Edward Goldston.

Rapchak, M. (2019). That which cannot be named: The absence of race in the Framework for Information Literacy for Higher Education. *Journal of Radical Librarianship, 5*, 173-196.

Raphael, D. D. (1967). *Political theory and the rights of man*. Macmillan.

Redi, F. (1687). *Esperienze intorno a diverse cose naturali, e particolarmente a quelle, che ci son portate dall'Indie*. Giacomo Raillard.

Richards, P. S. (2001). Cold War librarianship: Soviet and American activities in support of national foreign policy, 1946-1991. *Libraries and the Cultural Record, 36*, 183-203.

Rieh, S. Y. (2010). Credibility and cognitive authority of information. In M. J. Bates & M. N. Maack (Eds.), *Encyclopedia of library and information sciences* (pp. 1337-1344). Taylor and Francis.

Ritzhaupt, A. D., Liu, F., Dawson, K., & Barron, A. E. (2013). Differences in student information and communication technology literacy based on socio-economic status, ethnicity, and gender: Evidence of a digital divide in Florida schools. *Journal of Research on Technology in Education, 45*(4), 291-307.

Robb, A. (2017). Anatomy of a fake news scandal. *Rolling Stone*. https://www.rollingstone.com

Robbins, L. S. (1996). *Censorship and the American library: The American Library Association's response to threats to intellectual freedom*. Greenwood.

Roberts-Mahoney, H., Means, A. J., & Garrison, M. J. (2016). Netflixing human capital development: Personalized learning technology and the corporatization of K-12 education. *Journal of Education Policy, 31*(4), 405-420.

Romm, T. (2020, December 9). U.S., states sue Facebook as an illegal monopoly, setting stage for potential breakup. *The Washington Post*. https://www.washingtonpost.com/technology/2020/12/09/facebook-antitrust-lawsuit/

Roose, K. (2020, September 1). What is QAnon, the viral pro-Trump conspiracy theory? *The New York Times*. https://www.nytimes.com/article/what-is-qanon.html

Roosevelt, E. (2019). *What are we for? The words and ideals of Eleanor Roosevelt*. Harper Perennial.

Rosen, J. (2018). Madison v. the mob. *The Atlantic*. http://www.theatlantic.com

Rosoff, M. (2019, November 20). Google is taking the middle ground between Facebook and Twitter on political advertising. *CNBC*. https://www.cnbc.com/2019/11/20/google-wont-allow-false-info-or-microtargeting-in-political-ads.html

Rubin, A. (1998). Media literacy. *Journal of Communication, 48*(1), 3-5.

Rubin, V. L. (2010). On deception and deception detection: Content analysis of computer-mediated stated beliefs. *Proceedings of the American Society for Information Science and Technology, 47*, 1-10.

Rushkoff, M. (2018). Why Donald Trump is a media virus. *Digital Trends*. http://www.digitaltrends.com

Samek, T. (1996). The Library Bill of Rights in the 1960s: One profession, one ethic. *Library Trends, 45*(1), 50-60.

Sample, A. (2020). Historical development of definitions of information literacy: A literature review of selected resources. *The Journal of Academic Librarianship*, 102-116.

Sardarizadeh, S. (2020, May 12). Coronavirus: Twitter will label Covid-19 fake news. *BBC News*. https://www.bbc.com/news/technology-52632909

Saunders, L. (2017). Connecting information literacy and social justice: Why and how. *Communications in Information Literacy, 11*(1), 55–75.

Saunders, L., Kurbanoglu, S., Boustany, J., Dogan, G., Becker, P., Blumer, E., . . . Terra, A. L. (2015). Information behaviors and information literacy skills of LIS students: An international perspective. *Journal of Education for Library and Information Science, 56,* S80–S99.

Schardt, C. (2011). Health information literacy meets evidence-based practice. *Journal of the Medical Library Association: JMLA, 99*(1), 1.

Scharff, D. P., Mathews, K. J., Jackson, P., Hoffsuemmer, J., Martin, E., & Edwards, D. (2010). More than Tuskegee: Understanding mistrust about research participation. *Journal of Health Care for the Poor and Underserved, 21*(3), 879–897.

Schield, M. (2005). Information literacy, statistical literacy, data literacy. *IASSIST Quarterly, 28*(2–3), 6–6.

Schloman, B. F. (2019). Reflecting on TRAILS. *Information Literacy Assessment,* Carrick Enterprises, Inc. https://www.informationliteracyassessment.com/?p=1714

Schmuck, D., & von Sikorski, C. (2020). Perceived threats from social bots: The media's role in supporting literacy. *Computers in Human Behavior, 113,* 106507.

Schudson, M. (1978). *Discovering the news: A social history of American newspapers.* Basic Books.

Schultz, P. W., Nolan, J. M., Cialdini, R. B., Goldstein, N. J., & Griskevicius, V. (2007). The constructive, destructive, and reconstructive power of social norms. *Psychological Science, 18*(5), 429–434.

Schutz, A. (1964). *Collected papers II. Studies in social theory* (A. Brodersen, Ed.). Martinus Nijhoff.

Scott, J. C. (2017). *Against the grain: A deep history of the earliest states.* Yale University Press.

Scott, S. (2020a, June 23). Hearts and minds: Misinformation, polarization, and resistance to fact-checking. *Medium.* https://medium.com/dfrlab/hearts-and-minds-misinformation-polarization-and-resistance-to-fact-checking-8868c355d1f1

Scott, S. (2020b, November 12). Georgia State University Library to lead new public interest data literacy initiative. *Georgia State University Library Blog.* https://blog.library.gsu.edu/2020/11/12/georgia-state-university-library-to-lead-new-public-interest-data-literacy-initiative/

Seale, M. (2013). The neoliberal library. In L. Gregory & S. Higgins (Eds.), *Information literacy and social justice: Radical professional praxis* (pp. 39–61). Library Juice Press.

Seale, M. (2016). Enlightenment, neoliberalism, and information literacy. *Canadian Journal of Academic Librarianship, 1,* 80–91.

Searing, S. E. (2007). Integrating assessment into recurring information literacy instruction: A case study from LIS education. *Public Services Quarterly, 3*(1–2), 191–220.

Sellars, K. (2002). *The rise and rise of human rights.* Sutton.

Serhan, Y. (2019). How long can leaderless movements last? *The Atlantic.* http://www.theatlantic.com

Series of tubes. (2021, June 17). In *Wikipedia.* https://en.wikipedia.org/wiki/Series_of_Tubes

Shafer, R. G. (2019, November 29). A president turned up the heat after a tale about a turkey. *The Washington Post,* B2.

Shahbaz, A. (2018, October). Freedom on the net 2018: The rise of digital authoritarianism. *Freedom House.* https://freedomhouse.org/sites/default/files/2020-02/10192018_FOTN_2018_Final_Booklet.pdf

Shahbaz, A., & Funk, A. (2019). The crisis of social media. *Freedom House.* http://www.freedomhouse.org

Shannon, C. E., & Weaver, W. (1964). *The mathematical theory of communication.* University of Illinois Press.

Shapiro, J. J., & Hughes, S. K. (1996). Information literacy as a liberal art? *Educom Review, 31,* 31–35.

Sharot, T. (2017). *The influential mind: What the brain reveals about our power to change others.* Henry Holt.

Shearer, E., & Grieco, E. (2019, October 2). *Americans are wary of the role social media sites play in delivering the news.* Pew Research Center. https://www.journalism.org/2019/10/02/americans-are-wary-of-the-role-social-media-sites-play-in-delivering-the-news/

Shelby, T. (2003). Ideology, racism, and critical social theory. *The Philosophical Forum, 34*(2), 153–188.

Shera, J. (1949). *Foundations of the public library: The origins of the public library movement in New England, 1629–1855.* Shoestring Press.

Sierpe, E. (2019). Confronting librarianship and its function in the structure of white supremacy and the ethno state. *Journal of Radical Librarianship, 5*, 84–102.

Silver, N. (2012). *The signal and the noise: Why so many predictions fail—but some don't.* Penguin Press.

Silverman, C., & Singer-Vine, J. (2016). Most Americans who see fake news believe it, new survey says. *Buzzfeed.* http://www.buzzfeed.com

Singh, R. (2016, July 4). Brexit referendum: Voting analysis. *Parliament Magazine.* https://www.the parliamentmagazine.eu/articles/news/brexit-referendum-voting-analysis

Slater, J. (2020, November 27). Indian leaders promise to combat interfaith marriages. *The Washington Post,* A9.

Smith, A. (2011). *Social media and politics in the 2010 campaign.* Pew Internet and American Life Project. http://www.pewInternet.org

Smith, L. N. (2016). Information literacy as a tool to support political participation. *Library and Information Research, 40*(123), 14–23.

Snavely, L., & Cooper, N. (1997). The information literacy debate. *The Journal of Academic Librarianship, 23*(1), 9–14.

"The social media fact-check farce." (2020, November 27). *The Wall Street Journal.* https://www.wsj.com/articles/the-social-media-fact-check-farce-11606519380

Society of American Archivists. (n.d.) "Information literacy." *Dictionary of Archives Terminology.* https://dictionary.archivists.org/entry/information-literacy.html

Society of American Archivists. (2020). *SAA core values statement and code of ethics.* https://www2.archivists.org/statements/saa-core-values-statement-and-code-of-ethics#core_values

Society of College, National and University Libraries (SCONUL) Working Group on Information Literacy. (1999). *Information skills in higher education.* https://www.sconul.ac.uk/sites/default/files/documents/Seven_pillars2.pdf

Society of College, National and University Libraries (SCONUL) Working Group on Information Literacy. (2011). *The SCONUL seven pillars of information literacy: Core model for higher education.* https://www.sconul.ac.uk/sites/default/files/documents/coremodel.pdf

Solomon, D., Maxwell, C., & Castro, A. (2019). *Systemic inequality: Displacement, exclusion, and segregation.* Center for American Progress. https://www.americanprogress.org/issues/race/reports/2019/08/07/472617/systemic-inequality-displacement-exclusion-segregation/

Special Libraries Association. (2016). *Competencies for information professionals.* https://www.sla.org/about-sla/competencies/

Stagg, A., & Kimmins, L. (2014). First year in higher education (FYHE) and the coursework post-graduate student. *Journal of Academic Librarianship, 40*, 142–151.

Stanley-Becker, I. (2020, August 12). By harvesting email addresses, sites turn conservative outrage into cash. *The Washington Post,* A22.

Stanley-Becker, I., & Romm, T. (2019, November 29). Homespun disinformation campaigns on social media represent rising threat. *The Washington Post,* A6.

Stapleton, A. C. (2016). "No, you can't vote by text message." CNN. https://www.cnn.com/2016/11/07/politics/vote-by-text-message-fake-news/index.html

Stauffer, S. M. (2005). Polygamy and the public library: The establishment of public libraries in Utah before 1910. *Library Quarterly, 75*, 346–370.

Stein, P. (2020). When e-learning is a struggle. *The Washington Post.* http://www.washingtonpost.com

Stewart, E. (2019, November 27). Why everybody is freaking out about political ads on Facebook and Google. *Vox.* https://www.vox.com/recode/2019/11/27/20977988/google-facebook-political-ads-targeting-twitter-disinformation

Stinnett, G. (2009). Archival landscape: Archives and human rights. *Progressive Librarian, 32*, 10–20.

St. Jean, B., Jaeger, P. T., Jindal, G., & Liao, Y. (2020). Introduction: Libraries and librarians as agents of health information justice. In B. St. Jean, G. Jindal, Y. Liao, & P. T. Jaeger (Eds.), *Roles and responsibilities of libraries in increasing consumer health literacy and reducing health disparities* (pp. 3-19). Emerald.

St. Jean, B., Jindal, G., Jaeger, P. T., Liao, Y., & Barnett, B. (2020). Libraries and librarians as agents of health information justice: Concluding thoughts. In B. St. Jean, G. Jindal, Y. Liao, & P. T. Jaeger (Eds.), *Roles and responsibilities of libraries in increasing consumer health literacy and reducing health disparities* (pp. 287-296). Emerald.

Strauss, V. (2020, April 28). Three doctored Covid-19 protest photos—and other lessons on fake news. *The Washington Post.* https://www.washingtonpost.com/education/2020/04/28/three-doctored-covid-19-protest-photos-other-lessons-fake-news/

Street, B. (1984). *Literacy in theory and practice.* Cambridge University Press.

Strittmatter, K. (2020). *We have been harmonized: Life in China's surveillance state.* Custom House.

Strover, S. (2003). Remapping the digital divide. *Information Society, 19,* 275-277.

Strover, S., Chapman, G., & Waters, J. (2004). Beyond community networking and CTCs: Access, development, and public policy. *Telecommunications Policy, 28,* 465-485.

"Structural racism in America." (n.d.). Urban Institute. https://www.urban.org/features/structural-racism-america

Sturges, P., & Gastinger, A. (2010). Information literacy as a human right. *Libri, 60,* 195-202.

Suarez, D. (2007). Education professionals and the construction of human rights education. *Comparative Education Review, 51*(1), 48-70.

Sullivan, M. (2020, July 31). This was the week America lost the war on misinformation. *The Washington Post,* C1, C3.

Sullivan, M. C. (2019a). Leveraging library trust to combat misinformation on social media. *Library and Information Science Research, 41*(1), 2-10.

Sullivan, M. C. (2019b). Libraries and fake news: What's the problem? What's the plan? *Communications in Information Literacy 13*(1).

Sullivan, M. C. (2019c). Why librarians can't fight fake news. *Journal of Librarianship and Information Science, 51*(4), 1146-1156.

Summers, M. W. (1987). *The plundering generation: Corruption and the crisis of the Union, 1849-1861.* Oxford University Press.

Sunstein, C. R. (2004). We need to reclaim the Second Bill of Rights. *Chronicle of Higher Education, 50*(40).

Sunstein, C. R. (2005). *Laws of fear: Beyond the precautionary principle.* Cambridge University Press.

Sunstein, C. R. (2009). *On rumors: How falsehoods spread, why we believe them, what can be done.* Farrar, Straus and Giroux.

Svendsen, G. L. H. (2013). Public libraries as breeding grounds for bonding, bridging and institutional social capital: The case of branch libraries in rural Denmark. *Sociologia Ruralis, 53*(1), 52-73.

Svenonius, E. (2000). *The intellectual foundation of information organization.* MIT Press.

Svolik, M. W. (2019). Polarization versus democracy. *Journal of Democracy, 30*(3), 20-32.

Swanson, T. A. (2005a). Applying a critical pedagogical perspective to information literacy standards. *Community and Junior College Libraries, 12*(4), 65-77.

Swanson, T. A. (2005b). Teaching students about information: Information literacy and cognitive authority. *Research Strategies, 20*(4), 322-333.

Sweeny, K., Melnyk, D., Miller, W., & Shepperd, J. A. (2010). Information avoidance: Who, what, when, and why. *Review of General Psychology, 14*(4), 340-353.

Tallack, M. (2017). *The undiscovered islands: An archipelago of myths and mysteries, phantoms and fakes.* Picador.

Tandoc, E. C., Jr., Jenkins, J., & Craft, S. (2019). Fake news as a critical incident in journalism. *Journalism Practice, 13,* 673-689.

Tandoc, E. C., Jr., Lim, Z. W., & Ling, R. (2018). Defining "fake news": A typology of scholarly definitions. *Digital Journalism, 6,* 137-153.

Taylor, N. G. (2015). *Information at the nexus: Young people's perceptions of government and government websites* [Doctoral dissertation, University of Maryland].

Telecommunications Act of 1996, 47 USC 225 et seq. (1996).

Tewell, E. (2015). A decade of critical information literacy: A review of the literature. *Communications in Information Literacy, 9*(1), 24–43.

Tewell, E. (2016). Putting critical information literacy into context: How and why librarians adopt critical practices in their teaching. *In the Library with the Lead Pipe.* http://www.inthelibrarywiththeleadpipe.org/2016/putting-critical-information-literacy-into-context-how-and-why-librarians-adopt-critical-practices-in-their-teaching/

Tewell, E. C. (2018). The practice and promise of critical information literacy: Academic librarians' involvement in critical library instruction. *College and Research Libraries, 79*(1). http://crl.acrl.org

Thompson, D. (2008). *Counterknowledge: How we surrendered to conspiracy theories, quack medicine, bogus science, and fake history.* W. W. Norton.

Thompson, E. P. (1964). *The making of the English working class.* Pantheon.

Thompson, F. B. (1968). The organization is the information. *American Documentation (pre-1986), 19*(3), 305.

Thompson, K. M. (2007). Furthering understanding of information literacy through the social study of information poverty. *The Canadian Journal of Information and Library Science, 31*(1), 87–115.

Thompson, K. M., Jaeger, P. T., Taylor, N. G., Subramaniam, M., & Bertot, J. C. (2014). *Digital literacy and digital inclusion: Information policy and the public library.* Rowman & Littlefield.

Timberg, C. (2020a, February 21). How conservatives secured friendly Facebook policies. *The Washington Post*, A1, A 14–A15.

Timberg, C. (2020b, October 8). Conservative social media sites yet to remove alleged Russian accounts. *The Washington Post*, A20.

Timberg, C., & Dwoskin, E. (2020, October 2). For years, Facebook and Twitter missed QAnon threads. *The Washington Post*, A1, A21.

Timberg, C., Dwoskin, E., Romm, T., & Tran, A. B. (2018, December 11). Despite YouTube's efforts, it's still a "vortex" of hate. *The Washington Post*, A1, A16.

Timberg, C., & Stanley-Becker, I. (2020). QAnon learns to survive—even thrive—amid Silicon Valley's crackdown. *The Washington Post*, A7.

Trust Project. (2018, October 8). Major effort to increase trust in news achieves widespread adoption [Press release]. https://thetrustproject.org/2018/10/08/news18/

"The Trust Project explained." (2020). The Trust Project. https://thetrustproject.org/faq/

Tuominen, K., Savolainen, R., & Talja, S. (2005). Information literacy as a sociotechnical practice. *The Library Quarterly, 75*(3), 329–345.

Tyson, A. (2020, July 22). *Republicans remain far less likely than Democrats to view COVID-19 as a major threat to public health.* Pew Research Center. https://www.pewresearch.org/fact-tank/2020/07/22/republicans-remain-far-less-likely-than-democrats-to-view-covid-19-as-a-major-threat-to-public-health/

United Nations. (1948). *Universal declaration of human rights.* https://www.un.org/en/about-us/universal-declaration-of-human-rights

UNESCO/IFLA/NFIL United Nations Educational, Scientific and Cultural Organization, International Federation of Library Associations and Institutions, & National Forum on Information Literacy. (2006). *Beacons of the information society: The Alexandria Proclamation on Information Literacy and Lifelong Learning.* http://portal.unesco.org

UNESCO/NCLIS/NFIL United Nations Educational, Scientific and Cultural Organization, National Commission on Libraries and Information Science, & National Forum on Information Literacy. (2003). *The Prague Declaration: Towards an information literate society.* Information Literacy Meeting of Experts, September 20–23, Prague, Czech Republic. http://www.unesco.org/new/fileadmin/MULTIMEDIA/HQ_/CI/CI/pdf/PragueDeclaration.pdf

UN Human Rights Council. (2011). *Report of the Special Rapporteur on the promotion and protection of the right to freedom of opinion and expression, Frank La Rue.* United Nations General Assembly.

US Department of Education, Office of Educational Technology. (2017). *National educational technology plan.*

US Department of Health and Human Services, Office of Disease Prevention and Health Promotion. (2021). *Health literacy in Healthy People 2030.* https://health.gov/our-work/national-health-initiatives/healthy-people/healthy-people-2030/health-literacy-healthy-people-2030

US Department of State Global Engagement Center. (2020). "Pillars of Russia's disinformation and propaganda ecosystem." https://www.state.gov/wp-content/uploads/2020/08/Pillars-of-Russia%E2%80%99s-Disinformation-and-Propaganda-Ecosystem_08-04-20.pdf

Vaidhyanathan, S. (2004). *The anarchist in the library: How the clash between freedom and control is hacking the real world and crashing the system.* Basic Books.

Vaidhyanathan, S. (2018). *Anti-social media: How Facebook disconnects us and undermines democracy.* Oxford University Press.

Valtin, R., Bird, V., Brooks, G., Brozo, B., Clement, C., Ehmig, S., Garbe, C., de Greef, M., Hanemann, U., Hammink, K., Mallows, D., Nascimbeni, F., Sulkunen, S., & Tamburlini, G. (2016). *European declaration of the right to literacy.* European Literacy Policy Network.

Van der Linden, S., Leiserowitz, A., Rosenthal, S., & Maibach, E. (2017). Inoculating the public against misinformation about climate change. *Global Challenges, 1*(2), 1600008.

Vangeest, J., & Hawkins, B. (2016). How to be a #critlib: Reflections on implementing critical theory in practice. *See Also: The University of British Columbia iSchool Student Journal, 2*(1).

Vårheim, A. (2014). Trust in libraries and trust in most people: Social capital creation in the public library. *The Library Quarterly, 84*(3), 258–277.

Varlejs, J., & Stec, E. (2014). Factors affecting students' information literacy as they transition from high school to college. *School Library Research, 17.*

Villalpando, O., & Bernal, D. D. (2002). A critical race theory analysis of the barriers that impede the success of faculty of color. In W. A. Smith, P. Altbach, & K. Lomotey (Eds.), *The Racial Crisis in American Higher Education* (pp.135–148). SUNY Press.

Vinopal, J. (2016). The quest for diversity in library staffing: From awareness to action. *In the Library with the Lead Pipe.* http://www.inthelibrarywiththeleadpipe.org/2016/quest-for-diversity/

Wade, A. C., Lysenko, L., & Abrami, P. C. (2020). Developing information literacy skills in elementary students using the web-based Inquiry Strategies for the Information Society of the Twenty-First Century (ISIS-21). *Journal of Information Literacy, 14*(2), 96–127.

Waisbord, S. (2018). Truth is what happens to news: On journalism, fake news, and post-truth. *Journalism Studies, 19,* 1866–1878.

Wakabayashi, D. A. (2020, April 17). Bill Gates, at odds with Trump on virus, becomes a right-wing target. *The New York Times.* https://www.nytimes.com/2020/04/17/technology/bill-gates-virus-conspiracy-theories.html

Wan, W. (2020, November 23). Coronavirus vaccines face trust gap in Black and Latino communities, study finds. *The Washington Post.* https://www.washingtonpost.com/health/2020/11/23/covid-vaccine-hesitancy/

Ward, D. (2006). Revisioning information literacy for lifelong meaning. *The Journal of Academic Librarianship, 32*(4), 396–402.

Wardle, C., & Derakhshan, H. (2017). Information disorder: Toward an interdisciplinary framework for research and policy making (Council of Europe Report DGI(2017)09). Council of Europe.

Wardle, C., & Derakhshan, H. (2018). Thinking about "information disorder": Formats of misinformation, disinformation, and mal-information. In *Journalism, "Fake News" and Disinformation* (pp. 43–54). UNESCO.

Washington, H. (2013). *Climate change denial: Heads in the sand.* Routledge.

Washington, H. A. (2007). *Medical apartheid: The dark history of medical experimentation on Black Americans from colonial times to the present.* Doubleday.

Watson, P. D. (1994). Founding mothers: The contribution of women's organizations to public library development in the United States. *Library Quarterly, 64,* 233-269.

Webber, S., & Johnston, B. (2000). Conceptions of information literacy: New perspectives and implications. *Journal of Information Science, 26*(6), 381-397.

Webber, S., & Johnston, B. (2017). Information literacy: Conceptions, context and the formation of a discipline. *Journal of Information Literacy, 11*(1) 156-183.

Webster, F. (2014). *Theories of the information society.* Routledge.

Weems, M. L. (1806/1858). *Life of George Washington: With curious anecdotes, equally honorable to himself and exemplary to his young countrymen.* J. P. Lippincott & Company.

Weiner, S. A. (2012). Institutionalizing information literacy. *The Journal of Academic Librarianship, 38*(5), 287-293.

Wellington, S. (2013). Information literacy and cultural heritage: Developing a model for lifelong learning. *Library Review, 62*(8/9), 619-620.

"What Is PIACC?" National Center for Education Statistics. https://nces.ed.gov/surveys/piaac/index.asp

Whelan, D. J. (2010). *Indivisible human rights: A history.* University of Pennsylvania Press.

White, H. S. (1992). Bibliographic instruction, information literacy and information empowerment. *Library Journal, 117*(1), 76-78.

White, S., & Dillow, S. (2005). *Key concepts and features of the 2003 National Assessment of Adult Literacy* (NCES 2006-471). National Center for Education Statistics.

Whitworth, A. (2014). *Radical information literacy: Reclaiming the political heart of the IL movement.* Elsevier.

Whitworth, A. (2020). The discourses of power, information and literacy. In S. Goldstein (Ed.), *Informed societies: Why information literacy matters for citizenship.* Facet.

Wiegand, W. A. (1989). *An active instrument for propaganda: The American public library during World War I.* Greenwood.

Wiegand, W. A. (2011). *Main street public library: Community places and reading spaces in the rural heartland, 1876-1956.* University of Iowa Press.

Wiegand, W. A. (2017). "Any ideas?": The American Library Association and the desegregation of public libraries in the American South. *Libraries: Culture, History, and Society, 1*(1), 1-22.

Williams, A., & Emamdjomeh, A. (2018, May 10). America is more diverse than ever—but still segregated. *The Washington Post.*

Williamson, K. (1998). Discovered by chance: the role of incidental information acquisition in an ecological model of information use. *Library and Information Science Research, 20*(1), 23-40.

Williamson, K., & Asla, T. (2009). Information behavior of people in the fourth age: Implications for the conceptualization of information literacy. *Library and Information Science Research, 31*(2), 76-83.

Willson, G., & Angell, K. (2017). Mapping the Association of College and Research Libraries information literacy framework and nursing professional standards onto an assessment rubric. *Journal of the Medical Library Association: JMLA, 105*(2), 150.

Wilson, P. (1977). *Public knowledge, private ignorance.* Greenwood.

Winchester, S. (2021). *Land: How the hunger for ownership shaped the modern world.* Harper.

Wineburg, S., & McGrew, S. (2019). Lateral reading and the nature of expertise: Reading less and learning more when evaluating digital information. *Teachers College Record, 121*(11), n11.

Wineburg, S., McGrew, S., Breakstone, J., & Ortega, T. (2016). Evaluating information: The cornerstone of civic reasoning. *Stanford Digital Repository.* Retrieved from https://sheg.stanford.edu

Winstanley, W. (1669). *The flying serpent, or strange news out of Essex.* London. www.henham.org/FlyingSerpent

Wolcott, J. (2018, September 7). The "left behind" Trump voter has nothing more to tell us. *Vanity Fair*.
https://www.vanityfair.com/news/2018/09/the-left-behind-trump-voter-has-nothing-more-to-tell-us

Wolf, M. (2007). *Proust and the squid: The story and science of the reading brain*. Harper.

Wolf, M. (2018). *Reader, come home: The reading brain in a digital world*. Harper.

Wollstonecraft, M. (1792). *A vindication of the rights of woman: With Strictures on political and moral subjects*. J. Johnson.

Wong, J. C. (2020, June 25). Down the rabbit hole: How QAnon conspiracies thrive on Facebook. *The Guardian*. http://www.guardian.uk

Woodiwiss, A. (2005). *Human rights*. Routledge.

Woolf, V. (1929/1989). *A room of one's own*. Harvest.

Xu, B., & Albert, E. (2017, February 17). *Media censorship in China*. Council on Foreign Relations.
https://www.cfr.org/backgrounder/media-censorship-china

Yakel, E., & Torres, D. (2003). AI: Archival intelligence and user expertise. *The American Archivist, 66*(1), 51–78.

Yee, A. (2020, August 22). Recognize misinformation on the Internet. *The New York Times*.
https://www.nytimes.com/2020/08/22/at-home/recognize-misinformation-Internet.html

Young, L. M., & Hinton, E. G. (Eds.). (2019). *Framing health care instruction: An information literacy handbook for the health sciences*. Rowman & Littlefield; Medical Library Association.

Yurieff, K. (2020, November 5). How Twitter, Facebook and YouTube are handling election misinformation. *CNN*. https://www.cnn.com/2020/11/04/tech/social-media-election-misinformation/index.html

Zakrzewski, C., & Lerman, R. (2020, November 9). LinkedIn, Pinterest and Nextdoor take a different take to fight election misinformation. *The Washington Post*, A31.

Zannettou, S., Sirivianos, M., Blackburn, J., & Kourtellis, N. (2019). The web of false information: Rumors, fake news, hoaxes, clickbait, and various other shenanigans. *Journal of Data and Information Quality, 11*(3), 1–37.

Zelenika, I., & Pierce, J. M. (2013). The Internet and other ICTs as tools and catalysts for sustainable development innovation for the 21st century. *Information Development, 29*(3), 217–232.

Zhou, L., & Zhang, D. (2007). An ontology-supported misinformation model: Toward a digital misinformation library. *IEEE Transactions on Systems, Man, and Cybernetics–Part A: Systems and Humans, 37*(5), 804–813.

Zimmer, M. (2014). Librarians' attitudes regarding information and Internet privacy. *The Library Quarterly, 84*(2), 123–151.

Zittrain, J., & Palfrey, J. (2008). Internet filtering: The politics and mechanisms of control. In R. Deibert, J. Palfrey, R. Rohozinsky, & J. Zittrain (Eds.), *Access denied: The practice and policy of global Internet filtering* (pp. 29–56). MIT Press.

Zurkowski, P. G. (1974). "The information service environment relationships and priorities" (ED No. 100391). ERIC Clearinghouse on Information Resources, National Commission on Libraries and Information Science. https://eric.ed.gov/?id=ED100391

ABOUT THE AUTHORS

NATALIE GREENE TAYLOR, PhD, MLS, is an associate professor and program director of the Master of Library and Information Science (MLIS) at the School of Information of the University of South Florida. Dr. Taylor's research focuses on youth information literacy, information intermediaries, and information policy as it affects youth information access. She has published articles in more than two dozen scholarly journals, her research has appeared in *American Libraries* and other professional journals, and she has coauthored and coedited five books: *Digital Literacy and Digital Inclusion: Information Policy and the Public Library; Libraries, Human Rights, and Social Justice: Enabling Access and Promoting Inclusion; Foundations of Information Policy; Libraries and the Global Retreat of Democracy: Confronting Polarization, Misinformation, and Suppression;* and this book. She is coeditor of *Library Quarterly*.

PAUL T. JAEGER, PhD, MLS, JD, MEd, is a professor at the College of Information Studies and codirector of the Museum Scholarship and Material Culture program at the University of Maryland. He studies the impacts of law and policy on information access, accessibility, and literacy, with a primary focus on human rights and civil rights. He is the author of about 200 journal articles and book chapters, as well as twenty books. His research has been funded by the Institute of Museum and Library Services, the National Science Foundation, the American Library Association, the Smithsonian Institution, and the Bill & Melinda Gates Foundation, among others. He is coeditor of *The Library Quarterly*. In 2014 he received the *Library Journal/ALISE* Excellence in Teaching Award. A 2019 study published in *Public Library Quarterly* named him one of the two most influential scholars of public library research in the past thirty-five years (it was a tie).

INDEX

A

Aagard, M. C., 110

AALL (American Association of Law Libraries), 69-70

AASL

    See American Association of School Librarians

Abilock, D., 54

academic libraries

    Framework for Information Literacy for Higher Education, 49-53

    information literacy in, 45-46

    mission of, 102

    questions about, 59

    Standards, years of, 46-49

    trust of, 110

access

    information/misinformation access, 127-128

    to online learning, 78-79

    open access, 40

    See also Internet access

Accreditation Council for Graduate Medical Education, 72

Ackrill, R., 123

ACRL

    See Association of College and Research Libraries

acronyms, 55

activism, 154

Adams, N. E., 71

addiction, 175

Addison, C., 49

advertising

    disinformation in, 133-135

    first advertising agencies, 174

    user data collection and, 90

advocacy

    for archives, 73

    for information literacy, 113, 156, 174

    for information literacy among political actors, 156

    information literacy assessments for, 48

    by libraries for information literacy, 154, 157

    for lifelong information literacy, 176

AECT

    See Association for Educational Communications and Technology

affective information behaviors, 30

AFL-CIO, 164, 165

agency

    in information literacy definition, 29

    social structure for enabling, 39-40

Agosto, D.

    on fact-checking, 119

    libraries counted by, 160

    on library fake news pathfinders, 147

Aharony, N., 51

AI (artificial intelligence), 91-92

ALA

    See American Library Association

Albert, E., 170

Alexander, J., 101

Alexandria Proclamation on Information Literacy and Lifelong Learning (UNESCO, IFLA, & NFIL)

    declarations of, 21-22

    on information literacy as human right, 82

    link between information literacy/democracy, 104

algorithms

    content provided by, 162

    disinformation on social media, 138-139

    disinformation/misinformation produced by, 118

    lack of regulation on social media companies, 167

    pandemic disinformation and, 143

    user lack of control of information, 124

Allcott, H., 123, 144

Allport, G., 123

Alter, C., 168

Alterman, E., 140

alternative facts, 122

Amazon, 89, 99

American Association of Law Libraries (AALL), 69-70

American Association of School Librarians (AASL)
Information Literacy Standards for Student Learning, 20, 53-54, 56
Information Power: Building Partnerships for Learning, 20-21, 46, 53-54
Information Power: Guidelines for School Media Programs, 17, 20, 26-27
Standards for the 21st-Century Learner, 56-57
Standards Framework for Learners, 26-27
American Library Association (ALA)
ALA Federal and Armed Forces Libraries Round Table, 65
ALA Presidential Committee on Information Literacy, 46, 96, 177
climate change, information literacy and, 168-169
on funding for school libraries, 53
information as human right, 81
on information illiteracy, 121
information literacy, call for more attention on, 177
information literacy definition by, 17-18
information literacy report in 1998, 21
library integration, 164
on mission of library, 102
standards on information literacy, 45
support for, 160
American Revolution, 79
Andersen, Hans Christian, 124-125
Andersen, J., 24, 39
Anderson, B., 95
Anderson, J., 166
Anderson, R., 148
Andrews, T. M., 120
Angell, K., 72
Anti-Compulsory Vaccination League, 137
Anti-Vaccination Society of America, 137
anti-vaccine movement
disinformation during pandemic and, 142-144
modern, 137-138
Victorian, 137
apathy, 175
Apple, 89, 99
Applebaum, A., 92
archives
archival practices, 68
information literacy as human right, 82
information literacy instruction in, 72-74
archivists, 72-73
Armstrong, A., 169
Article 19, UDHR, 81, 82
artificial intelligence (AI), 91-92

ASGCLA (Association of Specialized, Government and Cooperative Library Agencies), 65
Asheim, L., 88
Asla, T., 104
assessment, 47-48
Association for Educational Communications and Technology (AECT)
Framework for Information Literacy for Higher Education, 25-27
Information Literacy Standards for Student Learning, 54
Information Power: Guidelines for School Media Programs, 17
Association of American Medical Colleges, 72
Association of College and Research Libraries (ACRL)
Characteristics of Programs of Information Literacy That Illustrate Best Practices: A Guideline, 51-52
Education and Behavioral Sciences Section (EBSS) Social Work Committee, 72
Framework for Information Literacy for Higher Education, 49-51, 57-58, 72
Health Sciences Interest Group, 72
Information Literacy Competency Standards for Higher Education, 19-20, 25, 46-47
Information Literacy Competency Standards for Higher Education Task Force, 50
Information Literacy Competency Standards for Journalism Students and Professionals, 68
information literacy standards, development of, 45
Libraries Promoting Reflective Dialogue in a Time of Political Polarization, 159
Rare Book and Manuscript Section, 73-74
on role of academic libraries, 102
Association of Specialized, Government and Cooperative Library Agencies (ASGCLA), 65
attribution, 166
Aufderheide, P., 34
Australia
conspiracy theories in, 120
information literacy role of public librarians, 61
information literacy standards in, 47
Australian and New Zealand Information Literacy Framework (Australian and New Zealand Institute for Information Literacy), 47
authoritarianism
lack of information literacy and, 37-38
online, 91-93
rise of, 170
authority, 165

autism, 137
Auxier, B., 167
Azzarito, A., 85

B

Babalhavaeji, F., 20
Badia, A., 143
Badke, W., 48
Baer, A., 159
Bailey, Nathaniel, 86
Bailey, S. P., 137
Baker, K., 73
Balingit, M., 88
Bandura, A., 125
Banks, M.
    on fake news, 52
    on information literacy instruction, 148
    on "Storytellers without Borders" program,
        107-108
Barber, B. R., 89
Barclay, D. A., 46
Barker, S., 53
Barnett, S., 53
Barnum, Phineas Taylor "P. T.", 173
Barth, V., 133
Batchelor, O., 148
Bates, Marcia, 11-13
Battles, M., 77
Bauman, S., 125
Baumeister, R., 125
Bawden, D.
    on digital literacy, 33
    on information literacy as lifelong practice,
        38
    on information literacy term, 16
    on literacy, 14
    social structures for agency, 39
Beal, G., 85
Bearak, M., 92
Beatty. J. F.
    on access to information, 40
    Framework, criticism of, 51
    on structural information inequities,
        166
Beauman, F., 174
Becker, C. H., 46
behavior
    See information behavior
Behrens, S. J., 16
Beilin, I. G., 26, 51
Beisel, N., 87-88

belief
    anti-vaccine movement and, 137-138
    cognitive dissonance, 124-125
    confirmation bias, 90-91, 126
    in disinformation/conspiracy theories, 124
    in dragons, 1-2
    in misinformation/disinformation, 127-128,
        159
    misinformation/information literacy and, 2-3
Bell, S. J., 49-50
Bellware, K., 143
Berg, C.
    on AASL *Framework*, 27
    questions for young people, 58
    on role of school libraries, 109
Berg, S.
    on information literacy as problem, 112
    on information literacy/democracy link, 104
    on mission of libraries, 102-103
Bergmeier, H. J. P., 131
Berkowitz, R. E., 20, 55
Berkowitz model
    See Big6 model
Berlin, I., 86
Berliner, D. C., 96
Berman, J. M., 137
Bernal, D. D., 166
Berns, G., 78
Bertot, J. C.
    on civic literacy, 36
    on digital literacy, 33
    on information literacy as human right, 82
    on Internet, 98
    on library for help with government
        information, 111
    on policies for information literacy, 97
    on presidential use of disinformation, 140
    on public libraries, 63
bias
    confirmation bias, 30, 90, 109, 125, 126
    negativity bias, 125
    recognition of, 54
Biddle, B. J., 96
Biden, Joe, 176-177
Big6 model
    limitations of, 40
    school library information literacy instruction,
        54-55
    stages of, 20
bigotry, 121
Bill of Rights, 95
Bimber, B., 133

Bingham, T. J., 71
Black, Indigenous, and people of color (BIPOC)
    lack of in LIS, 165-166
    mistrust of authority, 165
    racial injustice, impact on information literacy,
      164
    racially segregated society in US, 163
Blake, D., 174
Blakeslee, Sarah, 55
Blau, J. R., 80
Blevens, C. L., 47
Bloom's Taxonomy, 55
Bluemle, S. R., 148
Bombaro, C., 26
Bond, S., 106
book burnings, 88-89
bookmobile, 153
books
    control of printed materials, 86-87
    information literacy/library's role, 8
    printing press, invention of, 85-86
Booth, C., 168
Borgmann, A., 13
Borlund, P., 61
Bossaller, J., 63, 154
Boston Liberator (newspaper), 132
botnets, 118
bots, 118
Bourg, C., 163-164, 166
Bousquet, M., 89
boyd, d., 109
Boyer, E. L., 8, 79
Boyles, J. L., 68
Bradbury, Ray, 37-38
Bradley, C., 47, 72
Brandt, D., 89
Branum, C., 157
Brazil, 142
Breakstone, J., 53
Bregman, R., 90
Breivik, P. S., 17
Brennan, E. A., 72
Brexit, 123
Brinkley, J., 165
Brosh, Allie, 78
Brown, J. A., 34
Brown, J. S., 13, 95
Bruce, C., 47, 48-49
Buckland, Michael, 13
Burchinal, L. G., 16, 22
Burkell, J., 32
Burkhardt, J. M.

on belief in information, 124
    on information illiteracy, 123, 148
Burki, T., 142
Burnett, G.
    control of printed materials, 86-87
    on information, 13
    on information access stages, 128
    on lifeworld, 31
Burns, E., 57-58
Bursztyn, L, 163
Buschman, J.
    on corporate funding for schools, 53
    on erosion of public sphere, 166-167
    on fake news, 177
    on roles of library, 109
    on state of public spaces, 110
Bush, George H. W., 120
Bush, George W., 179
Butler, S. M., 111

C

Cabello, M., 111
Calhoun, C., 79
Cambridge Dictionary, 31
Campaigns, Inc., 133-134
Campbell, B., 14
Canada
    conspiracy theories in, 120
    information literacy role of public librarians,
      61
    public libraries as hubs in, 111
Canadian Social Sciences and Humanities
    Research Council (SSHRC), 47
Caplin, A., 32
Carey, J. O., 55
Carillo, E. C.
    on information literacy, 148
    on misinformation/disinformation, 118,
      160
Carini, P., 73
Carlton, S., 157
Carnegie, Andrew, 87
Carr, M., 131
Carr, N., 78
Carrick Enterprises, 56
Case, D. O., 31
Catholic Church, 88
Cawdrey's Table Alphabetical, 86
CDC
    See Centers for Disease Control and Prevention
celebrity, 174

censorship
    challenges of by libraries, 179
    in China, 170
    of information, history of, 87-89
Centers for Disease Control and Prevention (CDC)
    on coronavirus vaccine, 165
    pandemic guidance from, 142, 143
Chancellor, R. L., 164
Chandler, Raymond, 174
Channel23News, 141-144
*Characteristics of Programs of Information Literacy
    That Illustrate Best Practices: A Guideline*
    (ACRL), 51-52
Chatfield, T., 124
Chatman, E. A., 31, 167-168
Chatterji, R., 163
cheap fakes, 118
Chicago Defender (newspaper), 133
Childers, T., 32
children, 53
Children's Internet Protection Act (CIPA), 53, 91
China
    authoritarianism online, 91-93
    book burning in, 88
    media environment of, 170
chlorofluorocarbons (CFCs), 134
Choi, H., 98
Christakis, N. A., 125
Christen, K., 166
Christenson, D. P., 108
Church, A. P., 58
CIPA (Children's Internet Protection Act), 53, 91
Cisco Systems, 4-5
citizenship scores, 92
civic literacy, 36
civic participation, 83
civil rights, 80-81
    See also human rights
Clark, C., 110
Clayton, K., 108
Cleaves, H. J., II., 2
Clement, S., 163
climate change
    information literacy and, 169
    political polarization and, 163
Clinton, Hillary, 119, 122
cognitive dissonance
    description of, 124-125
    misinformation and, 108
Cohen, H., 101
Cold War, 88
Coleman, J. S., 32

collaborate, 26, 57
collaboration
    for consistent information literacy messages,
        156
    of libraries for information literacy, 148, 160
    for lifelong information literacy, 149-150
Comet Ping Pong, 119
Common Core, 58
Common Program Requirements (Accreditation
    Council for Graduate Medical Education),
    72
Common Sense (Paine), 95
communication
    about importance of information literacy, 151
    communicatory understanding of information,
        11
    corporate control of information literacy,
        89-91
    media literacy, 34
Communications Act of 1934, 97
community
    libraries' contributions to, 154
    libraries' service to during pandemic, 177
    outreach by libraries, 153
    practice of information literacy and, 49
    trust/relationship with communities, 110
community technology centers (CTCs), 97
community-based educators, 7
competencies
    of literacy, 14-15
    in *National School Library Standards*, 57
Competencies for Information Professionals (SLA),
    64-65
computer, 17
Comstock, Anthony, 87-88
confidence men, 173, 174
confirmation bias
    anti-vaccine misinformation and, 138
    changing, 126
    corporate control of information literacy and,
        90-91
    description of, 30, 125
    example of, 126-127
    misinformation solutions and, 109
Conger, K., 106
Congo, 92
Congressional Research Service (CRS), 66
conservative sources, 138
conspiracy theories
    coronavirus pandemic disinformation, 141-144
    flat earth conspiracy theory, 93
    government use of, 92

conspiracy theories *(cont.)*
    information retrieval and, 40
    Phantom Time Theory, 93
    Pizzagate, 119, 127
    QAnon conspiracy theory, 119-121
    War on Christmas, 92
    young people and, 53
content, 23
context
    college students, context of, 45
    contextual information literacy instruction, 52
    critical information literacy and, 23
    information worlds/landscapes and, 31-32
    social structure for enabling agency, 39
Conway, E. M., 169
Conway, K., 159
Conway, M., 89
Cooke, N.
    on assessment of information literacy, 159
    on disinformation, 117
    on fake news, 116
    Fake News and Alternative Facts: Information Literacy in a Post-Truth Era, 30
    on information as human right, 81
    on misinformation, 109, 118
    on psychology/information literacy, 123
Coons, W., 38
Cooper, J., 124
Cooper, N., 19, 33
cooperation, 149-150
Cope, J.
    on critical theory of IL, 171
    on libraries, 157, 162
Copeland, S. R., 14
CORA (Critical Online Reasoning Assessment), 46
Core Entrustable Professional Activities (Association of American Medical Colleges), 72
Core Values of Librarianship (American Library Association), 170
Cork, S. J., 170
Cornelius, I., 12
Corner, J., 31, 87
coronavirus (COVID-19) pandemic
    disinformation, addiction to, 175
    information policies, failures of, 155-156
    Internet access, importance of, 78-79
    libraries serving communities during, 177
    misinformation/disinformation during, 6, 7-8, 141-144
    political polarization and, 163
    proposed medical cures for, 3
    virtual education during, 178

corporations
    advertising/misinformation, 133-135
    corporatization of schools, 53
    Senate hearing, 2020, 99
Costello, R., 106
Cote, C., 46
Council for Basic Education, 96
Council of Australian University Librarians, 47
Council on Communications and Media, 53
Council on Foreign Relations, 170
counterknowledge, 126, 138
Courtney, I., 68
COVID-19
    See coronavirus (COVID-19) pandemic
Cox, D., 168
CRAAP (Currency, Relevance, Authority, Accuracy, and Purpose) test, 55
Craft, S., 117, 158
Crawford, G. A., 148
critical information literacy
    ACRL *Framework for Information Literacy for Higher Education*, 25-27
    definition of, 23-24
    digital divide and, 24-25
    library promotion of, 160
    library support of, 154, 156
    for lifelong information literacy, 161-162
    race and, 166
    reflection in, 37
    scholarship on, 22-24
critical literacy, 148
Critical Online Reasoning Assessment (CORA), 46
critical thinking, 41, 64
Critten, J., 147
Crocco, M. S., 53
CrowdTangle, 105
Crown Dependencies, 115
CRS (Congressional Research Service), 66
Crucet, Jennine Capó, 88
CTCs (community technology centers), 97
Cuba, 91
Culp, F. B., 47
cultural heritage institutions, 82
culture
    as criterion of literacy, 14
    cultural contexts of information literacy, 24-25
    cultural heritage, 73
curate, 26, 57
currency, myth of, 116

D

DaCosta, J., 48
Dallas Public Library (DPL), 107-108
Dallek, M., 141
Daly, C. B., 133
Daniels, H. A., 96
data
    literacy, 34-35
    privacy of, 167
    user data collected by corporations, 89-91
    user data harvesting, 139
Davies, D. W., 87
Davis, H., 48
Davis, P., 45
Day, R. E., 39
De Jager, K., 62
De Paor, S., 149
"Debating Definitions of Information Literacy:
        Enough Is Enough!" (Owusu-Ansah), 112
"A Decade of Critical Information Literacy: A
        Review of the Literature" (Tewell), 24
Declaration of Independence, 79
deconstructionism, 13
deep fakes, 118
Deibert, R. J., 92, 126
Del Vicario, M.
    on belief in information, 124
    on pandemic disinformation, 143
    on psychology/information literacy, 123
Delaware, 116
DelGuidice, M., 110
Demasson, A., 61
democracy
    civic literacy and, 36
    information access and, 144
    information literacy and, 104, 160-161
    Internet's impact on, 93
    libraries as arsenals of, 157
Democrats, 106
Dempsey, K., 105
Derakhshan, H., 117-118
Dervin, B., 12, 144
Diamond, L., 139
Diamond, R., 158
Dickens, Charles, 173
dictionaries, 86
Dictionary of Archives Terminology (Society of
        American Archivists), 73
digital assistants, 89-90
digital divide
    critical information literacy and, 24-25
    in history of information literacy, 17

information poverty, 32
practice of information literacy, context of,
        43-44
digital literacy
    in information literacy definition, 29
    overview of, 33-34
    search on term, 4
DigitalLiteracy.gov, 97-98
Dillow, S., 15
disabled people, 170
disinformation
    addressing, 101, 102
    anti-vaccine movement, 137-138
    consequences of, 7-8
    conspiracy theories, 119-121
    definition of, 117
    description of, 117-118
    history of advertising/propaganda, 131-135
    information illiteracy and, 121-123
    information literacy and, 6, 148
    libraries' role in disarming, 177-178
    in newspapers, 132
    during pandemic, 141-144
    psychology/information literacy, 123-127
    Russian government operative scenario,
        118-119
    social media and, 138-141
    societal-level challenges to information
        literacy, 174-175
    types of, 118
    in US in 1800s, 173-174
dispositions, of literacy, 14-15
Ditzion, S. H., 87, 157
divine rights, 131
document literacy, 4
DOE (US Department of Education), 4, 98
Dollinger, A., 52
Dou, E., 91
Douglas-Gabriel, D., 79
Douglass, C. L., 92, 148
Douglass, Fredrick
    Boston Liberator and, 132
    inspiration of hope, 178
    quest for literacy, 77
Downey, A., 8, 158
Doyle, C. S., 16, 19
Dragic, M., 158
dragons, belief in, 1-2
Dretske, F., 12
Duffy, T. M., 82
Duguid, P., 13, 95
Du Mont, R. R., 164

Dunlap, R. E., 169
Dwoskin, E.
    on anti-vaccine conspiracy social media
        accounts, 137-138
    on disinformation by Donald Trump, 140-141
    on QAnon, 120
    on technology companies/misinformation, 105

E

Earth
    climate change, information literacy and,
        169
    flat earth conspiracy theory, 93, 157, 158
EBP (evidence-based practice), 71
echo chamber
    description of, 31
    psychology/information literacy, 123
economic injustice, 166-168
economic participation, 83
economic rights, 81
economy
    social media disinformation and, 139
    social structure for enabling agency, 39
EdBuild, 164
educate, 179
education
    academic libraries, information literacy in,
        45-53
    information literacy as human right, 82
    information literacy responsibility of librarian,
        8
    for lifelong information literacy, 149-151, 176
    media-led literacy instruction, 106-108
    partnerships for information literacy
        education, 112
    racial disparity in spending on, 164-165
    virtual, during pandemic, 178
educational participation, 83
educational rate (E-rate) program, 97
Educational Testing Service (ETS) iSkills
    assessment, 56
Eisenberg, M. B.
    Big6 model of, 20, 40, 54-55
    information literacy term, origins of, 16
Eisenstein, E., 85
elections
    fake news, presidential election and, 117
    golden age of fraudulent elections, 174
    Internet as tool for, 98
    libraries used as polling places, 111
    political polarization and, 163

    US presidential election of 2016, 3, 122, 123,
        147, 159
    US presidential election of 2020, 105, 175, 176
electronic information, 3
electronic media, 4-5
Ellenwood, D., 52
Elmborg, J.
    on critical information literacy, 24
    on critical theory, 22
    on information literacy, 99, 158
Elsasser, S. W., 169
Emamdjomeh, A., 163
Emmanuel, I., 34
emotional content, 143
emotions, 30
"The Emperor's New Clothes" (Andersen), 124-125
Encyclopedia of Library and Information Sciences
    (Bates), 11
engage, 26, 57
Enis, M., 45
Enlightenment, 79
environment, 30, 169
Eslami, M., 124
Espinal, I., 163
Espinosa, L. L., 45
Ettinger, D., 47
Europe, 87
European Declaration of the Right to Literacy
    (European Literacy Policy Network), 15
European Literacy Policy Network, 15
Evanson, C., 52
everyday life, 44
everyday-life information seeking, 40-41
evidence-based practice (EBP), 71
"exchange paper" network, 173-174
experience, of libraries, 109-110
explore, 26, 57

F

Fabian, J., 142
Facebook
    antitrust suit against, 167
    corporate control of information literacy,
        89
    disinformation, actions to combat, 140
    disinformation, spread of, 127
    political ads on, 105-106
    QAnon conspiracy theory on, 120
    Senate hearing, 2020, 99
    "Tips to Spot False News," 106
    Trust Project, work with, 107

fact-checking
    for Google Image searches/YouTube, 101
    by librarians, 158
    misinformation, 119
    tools for, 105
facts
    polarization in US and, 168
    preference for fiction over, 174
    relativism of postmodernism, 46
FAFLRT (ALA Federal and Armed Forces Libraries
    Round Table), 65
Fahim, K., 92
fake news
    academic librarians and, 52
    early uses of, 116
    embrace of, 117
    librarians' struggle against, 177
    libraries for information literacy instruction,
        111-113
    media's responsibility for solution to,
        106-108
    misinformation/disinformation, 117-119
    pandemic disinformation, 141-144
    Pizzagate, 119, 127
    social media's proliferation of, 138
    spread of, 105
Fake News and Alternative Facts: Information
    Literacy in a Post-Truth Era (Cooke), 30
false information
    information illiteracy and, 121-123
    libraries for information literacy instruction,
        111-113
    measures to address, 101-102
    media's responsibility for solution to, 106-108
    technology companies and, 105-106
    See also disinformation; misinformation
Farmer, L. S., 56
federal libraries, 65-66
Federal Library and Information Center
    Committee Education Working Group,
    64-65
Feekery, A., 52
feelings, 30
Feinstein, N., 35
Feldstein, S., 91
Feldt, J., 148
Ferretti, J. A., 166
Ferrucci, P., 121, 158
Festinger, L., 108
field guide to incorrect information
    conspiracy theories, 119-121
    fake news, 116-117

information access/misinformation access,
    127-128
information illiteracy, 121-123
misinformation/disinformation, 117-119
myth of currency, 115-116
psychology/information literacy,
    123-127
questions about, 129
filter bubbles
    description of, 30-31
    group polarization from, 126
    pandemic disinformation on social media,
    143
    psychology/information literacy, 123
filtering
    disinformation/misinformation produced by,
    118
    of Internet access by authoritarian states,
    91-93
financial support, 176-177
Finnish Public Broadcasting Company, 107
Fister, Barbara, 45-46, 170-171
5G wireless data networks, 142
Flanders, J., 87
flat earth conspiracy theory
    as easily disproved, 93
    librarian belief in, scenario about, 157, 158
Flat Earth Wiki, 93
Fleischmann, K. R., 97
Flesch, R., 96
Floridi, L., 90
Floyd, George, 143
The Flying Serpent, or Strange News Out of Essex
    (Winstanley), 1
Foa, R. S., 91
Foasberg, N., 25
Foote, Shelby, 45
Ford, E., 52
Ford, Henry, 92
Fortier, A., 32
Foster, S., 19
Foucault, M., 32
foundational literacies
    definition of, 14
    in information literacy definition, 5, 29
    pre-Internet, 4
"Four Freedoms," 80
Fowler, Geoffrey, 101
Fowler, J. H., 125
Fox, C., 12, 117
Fox News, 174
frames, 50

Framework for Information Literacy for Higher Education (ACRL)
  development of, 49-50
  information literacy, definition of, 25-27
  National School Library Standards vs., 57-58
  nursing professional standards mapped to, 72
  operationalization of, 51-52
  reactions to, 50-51
Framework for Literacy in a Digital Age (NCTE), 14-15
Frazzledrip conspiracy theory, 119
Freeburg, D., 166
freedom, 79-80
Freedom House, 93
"freedom libraries," 179
French Revolution, 79
Fultz, M., 164
funding, 53
Funk, A., 92
Furner, Jonathan, 13

G

Gab, 138
Gaines, B. J., 126
Galilei, Galileo, 2
Galston, W. A., 139
Galvan, A., 165
games, 107-108
Gardner, A., 122
Garrison, William Lloyd, 132
Gastinger, A., 148
Gates, Bill, 142
Gee, E. G., 17
Geiger, A. W., 110
Gelfert, A., 138
Gentzkow, M., 123, 144
Georgia Southern University, 88
Germany, 115, 120
Gersch, B., 62-63
Gibson, A. N.
  on information poverty, 167
  on information/neutrality, 170
  on racism in LIS, 166
Gibson, C., 50
Gilster, Paul, 33
giraffes, 126, 135
Gire, J., 70
Glendon, M. A., 80
global learning community, 27
Goethe University Frankfurt, 46
Goguen, J., 12

Goh, D. H. L., 52
Golden, H., 53
Goldstone, R. L., 125
Golten, E., 111
Google
  corporate control of information literacy, 89
  fact-checking for Google Image searches/ YouTube, 101
  filter bubbles and, 30-31
  political ads on, 106
Gore, Al, 98
Gorham, U.
  on contributions of libraries, 154
  on information as human right, 81
  on information literacy as human right, 3, 6, 82
  on libraries serving communities during pandemic, 177
  on lifelong information literacy, 179
  on Obama's embrace of technology, 98
  on presidential use of disinformation, 140
Gottfried, J.
  on fake news, 117
  on lack of trust in media, 109
  on psychology/information literacy, 123
  on social media readers, 144
Gottschalk, F., 53
Gouges, Olympe de, 79
Goulding, A.
  on experience of libraries, 110
  on information poverty, 32
  on satisficing behavior, 32
government
  authoritarianism online, 91-93
  civic literacy, 36
  information literacy as human right, 83
  information policies and, 154-156
  library for access to government information, 63, 111
  political resistance to lifelong information literacy, 174-175
  politics of information literacy, 95-99
  propaganda, history of, 131-135
  racial policies of, 163
  racism/mistrust of, 165
  responses to coronavirus pandemic, 141
government libraries, 65-66
Grabe, M. E., 148
Graff, H. J., 14
Grafstein, A., 49
Gramsci, A., 22
Gratch-Lindauer, B., 48
Gray, R., 124

Great Depression, 153-154
Great Firewall of China, 91, 92
Gregory, L., 23-24
Grey, W. S., 14
Grey Ellis, E., 107
Grieco, E., 117, 167
Grimes, J. M., 90
Grinberg, N., 127
Groshek, J., 139, 159
Gross, M., 51
group polarization, 126
Guess, A. M., 127
Guidelines on Information Literacy for Lifelong Learning (IFLA), 62
Guo, Y. R., 52
Gureckis, T. M., 125
Guyatt, G., 71

H

Habermas, J., 31, 87
Hachman, M., 106
Haenlein, M., 100
Haigh, M., 117
Haigh, T., 117
Hales, S., 64
Hall, R., 61
Halpin, E. F., 80
Hamelink, C., 16, 22-23
Handbook of Federal Librarianship (Federal Library and Information Center Committee Education Working Group), 64-65
Hanna, T., 167
Hannity, Sean, 163
Hansen, K., 67, 68
Hanson, E. C., 87, 91
Harding, J., 61
Hare, S., 52
Hartman-Caverly, S., 160
Harvey, M., 132, 173
Harvey, R., 87
Harwell, D., 91, 118
Hathcock, A., 166
Haupt, A., 124
Hawkey, E., 53
Hawkins, B., 166
Hawthorne, Nathaniel, 173
Head, A. J., 46
Healey, P. D., 158
health literacy
    information literacy and, 71-72
    overview of, 35-36

Healthy People 2030 Initiative, 71
Hearst, William Randolph, 133
Hebert, A., 159
Heider, K., 104
Helberger, N., 167
Hemings, Sally, 132
Heravi, B., 149
Hernon, P., 117, 118
HHS (US Department of Health and Human Services), 71
Hibbing, J. R., 125
Hicks, A. E., 25-26, 52
Higgins, S., 23-24
High-Level Colloquium on Information Literacy and Lifelong Learning, 21-22
Hinchliffe, L. J., 148
Hinton, E. G., 72
Hoare, P., 88
Hobbs, R., 34
Hoffman, C., 61, 82
Hoffman, K., 170
Holland, 61
Honma, T., 165
hope, 178
Hopkins, J., 111
Hornaday, A., 89-90
Horowitz, J. M., 167
Horrigan, J. B., 110
Howard, P. N., 133, 134
Howe, D. W., 91
Hughes, J., 65
Hughes, S. K.
    on balanced approach to information literacy, 167
    on information literacy, 37, 170
Hughes-Hassell, S., 166
human rights
    foundations of, 79-80
    information and, 80-82
    information literacy as basic right, 24
    information literacy as essential right, 178
    information literacy as foundational human right, 82-84
    information literacy as fundamental right, 3, 6
    information literacy, shaping of, 7
    literacy as living, 77-79
    questions about, 84
Humprecht, E., 118, 159
Hurd, P. D., 35
Hypatia, 2
hypotheses, 30

I

IAL (Innovative Approaches to Literacy) program, 92

ICTs (information and communications technologies), 91, 97

IFLA
   See International Federation of Library Associations and Institutions

Ignatieff, M., 80

IIA (Information Industry Association), 17

Illeris, Knud, 30

illiteracy
   See information illiteracy

Imhoff, J., 163

immigrants, 153

inanimate objects, 78

include, 26, 57

income, 167

incorrect information
   See field guide to incorrect information

The Index of Forbidden Books (Catholic Church), 88

India, 83, 121

infodemic, 143

information
   access, 127, 128
   censorship of, 87–89
   definition of, 11–12
   in echo chamber, 31
   expansion of with technology, 78
   as human right, 79, 81
   human rights and, 80–82
   in information literacy definition, 25
   meaning of, 16

information access
   presumption about, 127
   stages of, 128

Information and Misinformation: An Investigation of the Notions of Information, Misinformation, Informing, and Misinforming (Fox), 117

information avoidance, 33

information behavior
   confirmation bias, 30
   filter bubble/echo chamber, 30–31
   information avoidance, 33
   information poverty, 32
   information seeking, 30
   information worlds/landscapes, 31–32
   satisficing, 32
   societal factors of, 32–33
   theories of, 29–33

information empowerment, 39

information illiteracy

consequences of, 7–8, 122–123
description of, 121–122
information illiterates, 16
information literacy in relation to, 6
social consequences of, 3

Information Industry Association (IIA), 17

information landscapes, 31–32

information literacy
   author definition of, 29, 41–42
   authoritarianism online, 91–93
   book's coverage of, 6–7
   climate change and, 169
   corporate control of, 89–91
   critical information literacy, 22–27
   critics of libraries' information literacy roles, 111–112
   definitions of, 5, 16–22, 38, 149
   democracy and, 160–161
   digital literacy *vs.*, 33–34
   economic/political injustice and, 166–168
   failure to practice, 37–38
   as foundational human right, 82–84
   Framework's definition of, 50
   information, definitions of, 11–13
   information policy and, 154–156
   information professionals and, 157–160
   in larger contexts, 6
   libraries' mission of teaching/providing/ promoting, 154
   libraries' missions, relationship to, 102–104
   libraries' role in, 104–105, 112–113
   library efforts to battle misinformation, 147–148
   lifelong, process of supporting, 149–151
   as lifelong concept, 5
   as lifelong learning practice, 38–39
   literacy, definition of, 14–16
   literacy, meaning of, 3–5
   media literacy *vs.*, 34
   misinformation and, 2–3
   politics of, 95–99
   politics of, 2020-style, 99–100
   as prime function of librarian, 8
   psychology and, 123–127
   questions about, 9
   racial injustice's impact on, 164
   reality and, 161–162
   in social context, 163–164
   social infrastructure for, 163–171
   social structure for enabling agency, 39–40
   societal-level challenges to, 174–175
   structure of book, 5–8

as unifying concept, 6
See also human rights
Information Literacy Competency Standards for Higher Education (ACRL)
    assessment of information literacy instruction, 47–48
    criticisms of, 49
    development of, 46–47
    Framework for Information Literacy for Higher Education and, 25–26
    on information literate person, 19
Information Literacy Competency Standards for Journalism Students and Professionals (ACRL), 68
Information Literacy Competency Standards for Nursing (ACRL), 71–72
information literacy, controlling
    authoritarianism online, 91–93
    censorship, history of, 87–89
    history of efforts to control literacy, 85–87
    Internet and, 89–91
    questions about, 93
information literacy education
    ideal location for, 22–23
    information literacy as metaliteracy, 36–37
    information literacy standards and, 46–49
    by librarian, 8
    as lifelong, 7
    practice of information literacy, context of, 43–44
Information Literacy Guidelines (Singapore), 54
information literacy, in practice
    failure to practice information literacy, 37–38
    information behavior, theories of, 29–33
    information literacy definition, 41–42
    information retrieval, nature of, 40–41
    as iterative lifelong practice, 38–39
    literacies, types of, 33–36
    metaliteracy, 36–37
    misinformation and, 41
    power of, 29
    questions about, 42
    social structure for enabling agency, 39–40
"Information Literacy Is Dead: The Role of Librarians in a Post-Truth World" (Johnson), 105
Information Literacy Meeting of Experts, 2003, 24–25
information literacy, operationalization of
    academic libraries, 45–53
    archives, 72–74
    conclusion about, 74–75
    early information literacy, 43–44

libraries, promotion of information literacy, 44–45
    public libraries, 61–64
    questions about, 59, 75
    school libraries, 53–58
    special libraries, 64–72
Information Literacy Standards (Council of Australian University Librarians), 47
Information Literacy Standards for Student Learning (AASL), 20, 53–54, 56
information literates
    meaning of, 16
    skills of, 18–19
    standards for, 19
information marginalization, 167–168
information overload, 32
information policy, 154–156
information poverty, 32, 167
Information Power: Building Partnerships for Learning (AASL)
    ACRL *Standards*, development of, 46
    Information Literacy Standards for Student Learning in, 54
    revision of, 20–21
Information Power: Guidelines for School Media Programs (AASL)
    emphasis on information literacy, 26–27
    goals of, 17
    revision of, 20
information privilege, 168
information professionals
    BIPOC, lack of in LIS, 165–166
    as community-based educators, 7
    information literacy as human right, 82
    information literacy as unifying concept, 6
    information literacy of, 157–160
    leadership for information literacy, 179
    lifelong information literacy and, 176
    See also librarians
information retrieval, 40–41
information search process
    affective information behaviors, 30
    limitations of, 40
information seeking
    everyday-life information seeking, 40–41
    information literacy and, 30
    satisficing behavior, 32
Information Skills in Higher Education (SCONUL), 21
information technologies
    information literacy, continuous need for, 4
    information literacy for, 3

information technologies (cont.)
    in information literacy history, 16–17
    information literacy promotion and, 21
    information policies for, 154–155
    See also technology
information worlds, 31–32
InfoWars, 119, 139
Inglehart, R. F., 139
Innovative Approaches to Literacy (IAL) program, 92
inquire, 26, 57
Inskip, C., 159
Instagram, 140
intellectual access, 128
intellectual contributions, 39
International Bill of Human Rights, 80–81
international community
    conspiracy theories in, 120
    information literacy role of public librarians, 61
International Covenant on Civil and Political Rights, 80
International Covenant on Economic, Social, and Cultural Rights, 80
International Federation of Library Associations and Institutions (IFLA)
    Alexandria Proclamation on Information Literacy and Lifelong Learning, 21–22
    Government Libraries Section, 66
    Guidelines on Information Literacy for Lifelong Learning, 62
    information as human right, 81
    information literacy programs in Southeast Asia, 54
    Lyons Declaration on Access to Information and Development, 82
    media/information literacy recommendations of, 24
    on purpose of libraries, 102
international human rights, 79–80
The International Jew (Ford), 92
International Society for Technology in Education (ISTE), 58
international standards, 47, 54
Internet
    authoritarianism online, 91–93
    conspiracy theories on, 119–121
    corporate control of information literacy, 89–91
    echo chambers on social media, 123
    fake news on, 117–119
    filter bubbles on, 30–31
    information illiteracy and, 121–123

    information literacy after adoption of, 4–5
    information literacy as human right and, 82–83
    information literacy, controlling, 89–91
    information literacy, improvement of, 6
    information policy, failures of, 154–156
    lifelong information literacy and, 161–162
    misinformation, addressing, 101–102
    online information assessment by college students, 46
    policies, failure of, 99–100
    policies for information literacy and, 97–99
Internet access
    authoritarianism online, 91–93
    as human right, 82
    lack of, 78–79
Internet of things (IoT), 89–91, 156
Internet-enabled devices, 89–91
Introduction to Public Librarianship (McCook & Bossaller), 63
IOM (US Institute of Medicine), 35
Iran, 141–142
Iraq, 126–127
Ireland, 21
Isaac, M., 105
Islam, S. N., 168–169
ISTE (International Society for Technology in Education), 58
Italy, 115

J

Jackson, B., 126
Jacobs, H. L.
    on critical information literacy, 24
    on information literacy as problem, 112
    on information literacy instruction, 47
    on information literacy/democracy link, 104
    on mission of libraries, 102–103
Jacobsen, M., 61–62
Jacobson, T. E., 37, 50
Jaeger, P. T.
    on Al Gore and Internet, 98
    on anti-vaccine arguments, 137
    on authoritarianism online, 91
    on censorship in US, 87
    on civic literacy, 36
    on contributions of libraries, 154
    on control of printed materials, 86–87
    on digital literacy, 33
    on disabled people, 170
    on Donald Trump/Internet policy, 99
    on funding for school libraries, 53

on government information at public libraries, 63
information, discussion of, 13
on information access stages, 128
on information as human right, 81
on information literacy as human right, 3, 6, 82, 83
on information literacy as lifelong concept, 5
on information literacy, libraries and, 4
on information policy, 154–155, 156
on lack of digital literacy, 98
on learning from history, 179
on libraries serving communities during pandemic, 177
on libraries/politics, 157, 162
on library for help with government information, 111
on lifeworld, 31
on policies for information literacy, 96, 97
on presidential use of disinformation, 140
on user data, 90
James, William, 128
Jamieson, K. H., 126
Jamison, P., 93
Jefferson, Thomas, 127, 132
Jeffrey, C., 52
Jeffreys-Jones, R., 131
Jenkins, J., 117, 158
Jensen, A., 34
Jim Crow era, 133, 179
Jindal, G., 160
Johannes Gutenberg University Mainz, 46
John Birch Society, 92
Johnson, B., 105, 111
Johnson, Lyndon, 140, 141
Johnston, B., 47, 105
Jones, Alex, 119
Jones-Jang, S. M., 109
Josey, E. J., 164
journalism
    disinformation/propaganda in, 132–133
    misinformation, roles in spreading, 158
    See also media
journalists
    information literacy instruction for, 68–69
    news libraries, information literacy and, 67
    solution to misinformation, 106–108
Julien, H.
    on *Framework for Information Literacy for Higher Education*, 51
    on information literacy among children, 53
    on information literacy instruction, 47

on information literacy role of public librarians, 61
on information seeking/information literacy, 30
Juskiewicz, S., 46

K
Kahan, D. M., 127
Kamenetz, A., 108
Kane, P., 163
Kaplan, A., 100
Karlova, N. A., 117
Kashmir, 92
Kaske, N., 47, 48
Katz, I. R., 56
Kawashima-Ginsberg, K., 36
Keefe, E. B., 14
Keeling, Mary, 57
Keller, K., 63
Kelly, M., 140, 143
Kennedy, B., 163
Kennedy, B. R., 164
Kennedy, John F., Jr., 120
Kent State University, 47, 55–56
Kessler, G., 140, 143
Kettnich, K. M., 177, 179
Key, V. O., 31
Key Concepts and Features of the 2003 National Assessment of Adult Literacy (White & Dillow), 15
Kielbowicz, R. B., 173
Kim, E. M., 104
Kimmins, L., 148
Kim-Prieto, Dennis C., 70
Kindig, D. A., 35
King Abdulaziz City for Science and Technology (KACST), 91
Kintgen, E. R., 14
Klinenberg, E., 111, 153
Klotz, R. J., 91
Klucevsek, K. M., 169
Knoblauch, C. H., 16
knowledge
    for archives work, 73
    printing press and, 85
    social structures for, 39
    in *Standards for the 21st-Century Learner*, 56
Knuth, R., 88
Koc-Michalska, K., 139, 159
Koh, J., 110
Koltay, T., 34

Kranich, N., 53
Kuhlthau, C. C.
    information search process, 30, 40
    on misinformation, 41
    on objective of library/information services,
        103
Kulinski, J. H., 126
Kundu, D. K., 40
Kutner, L., 169

L

labels, on social media posts, 105
Lamb, A., 159
Langer, E., 134
language, 14
Lanier, J., 90
Lankes, R. D., 103
LaPlante, M. D.
    on giraffes, 135
    on megalith species, 2
    on myth of spinach, 133
Lau, J., 62
law librarians, 69-70
law libraries, 69-70
"Law Student Information Literacy Standards"
        (AALL Law Student Research Competency
        Standards Task Force), 70
Lawless, J., 71
Lawton, C., 123
Lazer, D., 108
leadership, 179
Leaning, M., 33
learners, 26-27
    See also students
learning
    affective information behaviors, 30
    information literacy as lifelong learning
        practice, 38-39
    information literacy as metaliteracy, 37
    in information literacy definition, 22
    lifelong information literacy, process of
        supporting, 149-151
    practice of information literacy, 43-44
    See also education
Leckie, G. J., 111, 148
Lee, J. H., 117
Lee, M. Y. H., 121
Lehman, E. D., 174
Lehrman, Sally, 107
Lenker, M., 104, 108
Lepore, J., 134

Lerman, R., 105, 140
Lerner, F.
    on attacks on libraries, 89
    on censorship of information, 87
    on early writings, 77
    on human rights, 153
    on misinformation/tech companies, 106
    on printing press, 85
Levitin, D. J., 124, 159
Lewis, John, 178
librarians
    BIPOC, lack of in LIS, 165-166
    as community-based educators, 7
    Competencies for Information Professionals,
        64-65
    critical information literacy and, 23-24
    experience of, 109-110
    good trouble/necessary trouble, 178-179
    information literacy meets information policy,
        154-156
    information literacy of, 157-160
    information literacy role of public librarians,
        61-64
    information literacy, serving, 8
    leadership for information literacy, 179
    lifelong information literacy and, 176-177
    lifelong information literacy, process of
        supporting, 149-151
    practice of information literacy, 170-171
    roles of, 103
libraries
    academic libraries, 45-53
    arguments against libraries' role in information
        literacy, 104-105
    censorship of information in, 87-89
    critics of libraries' information literacy roles,
        111-112
    democracy, information literacy and, 160-161
    experience of, 109-110
    false news, 108
    good trouble/necessary trouble, 178-179
    information literacy as human right, 82-84
    information literacy as lifelong learning
        practice, 39
    in information literacy history, 17
    information literacy, promotion of, 3-4, 44-45,
        147-149
    information literacy role of, 112-113
    information literacy, work towards improving,
        6
    information literacy/information policy,
        154-156

information literacy/information professionals, 157–160

lifelong information literacy, supporting, 149–151

lifelong information literacy, work towards, 177–178

lifelong literacy, to-do list for, 150–151

media/misinformation, 106–108

misinformation problems, addressing, 101–102

misinformation solutions, limitations of, 108–109

missions of, 102–104

physical spaces of, 110–111

questions about libraries/information literacy, 113

school libraries, 53–58

social context, information literacy in, 163–164

technology companies, misinformation and, 105–106

trust/relationship with communities, 110

Libraries and the Search for Academic Excellence (Breivik & Gee), 17

Libraries Promoting Reflective Dialogue in a Time of Political Polarization (Baer et al.), 159

library, meaning of, 164–165

library and information science (LIS)

BIPOC, lack of in, 164, 165–166

information literacy education in, 159, 161

information literacy, research/practice gap, 74

neutrality and, 163–164

Library Bill of Rights, 88

"Library Escape" game, 52

Library of Congress (LOC)

creation of, 127

information literacy training of, 66

on mission of, 102

licensing, 158

lies, 140

See also disinformation; misinformation

Life of George Washington: With Curious Anecdotes, Equally Honorable to Himself and Exemplary to His Young Countrymen (Weems), 116

lifelong information literacy

arguments for, 38–39

definition of, 150

to-do list for, 150–151

information literacy role of public libraries, 62

library mission for information literacy, 103–104

process of supporting, 149–151

reality of, 161–162

visionary model of, 112–113

lifelong information literacy society

disinformation, circa 1850, 173–174

good trouble/necessary trouble, 178–179

leadership for, 179

libraries' role in, 177–178

questions about, 180

social infrastructure for, 176–177

societal-level challenges to, 174–175

lifeworld, 31–32

Lim, S., 52

Lim, Z. W., 116, 158

Lin, P., 20

Lindberg, J., 23, 24

Lindstrom, M., 125

Ling, R., 116, 158

LinkedIn, 140

Linnaeus, 1

LIS

See library and information science

literacies

civic literacy, 36

data/scientific literacies, 34–35

digital literacy, 33–34

health literacy, 35–36

information literacy as metaliteracy, 37

media literacy, 34

in *Standards for the 21st-Century Learner*, 56

types of, 33–36

literacy

censorship of information, 87–89

corporate control of, 89–91

definition of, 14–16

as freedom, 77–78

history of efforts to control, 85–87

as living, 77–79

meaning of, 3–5

politics of, 95–99

See also information literacy

lizard people story, 120, 122

Lloyd, A.

on critical information literacy, 24

on information literacy, 31–32, 39

LOC

See Library of Congress

Locke, John, 79

Lockhart, P. R., 163

Loertscher, D., 56–57

Loertscher, D. V., 27

Lomas, N., 107

Long, E., 98

Long, H., 79

Lor, P. J., 148

Losee, R. M., 11–12, 117
Lotz, R. E., 131
"love jihad" conspiracy theory, 121
Lumpkin, L., 79
Luo, L., 47
Lyons, M., 85
*Lyons Declaration on Access to Information and
Development* (IFLA), 82

M
Macaraeg, P., 105
Mackey, T. P., 37
Macklin, A. S., 47
MacLeish, A., 147, 157
MacMillan, M. E., 68–69
Macrotrends, 99
Madden, M., 53
Madison, James, 95
Magna Carta, 79
Mahmood, K., 159
Majid, S., 47, 54
Malaysia, 91
malinformation, 117–118
Manguel, A.
    on censorship, 88
    on control of literacy, 85
    on reading, 78
    on troubadours, 86
manipulated content, 118
Martin, J., 49
Martin, J. D., III., 168
Marzal, M. Á., 34
masks, 142, 156
Masyada, S., 36
Mathiesen, K., 82, 148
Mattern, S., 164
Matteson, M. L., 62–63
Mauldin, A., 5
McCain, John, 120
McCarthy era, 88
McClure, C. R., 97
McCook, Kathleen de la Peña, 63, 82
McCright, A. M., 169
McCrummen, S., 139
McCulley, C., 47
McDevitt, M., 121, 158
McGowan, B. S., 72
McGrew, S., 108
McKenna, S., 45
McKenzie, L., 45
McKenzie, P. J., 40–41

McTavish, M., 96, 104
meaning, 11–12
Meckler, L., 78–79
media
    disinformation as money-making strategy, 174
    lack of trust in, 109
    misinformation solution, responsibility for,
        106–108
    news libraries, 66–69
    political polarization/media silos, 163
    as profit-driven industry, 167
media literacy
    fake news and, 117
    in information literacy definition, 29
    lack of trust in media and, 109
    media's responsibility for misinformation
        solution, 106–108
    overview of, 34
media production, 34
medical librarians, 70–72
medical libraries
    collaboration for information literacy, 160–161
    information literacy in, 70–72
Medical Library Association (MLA), 70–71
Meek, M., 14
Meisinger, J., 68
Meleady, R., 123
Melville, Herman, 173
Merchant, C., 173
Mesler, B., 2
metaliteracy, 36–37, 50
Metzger, M. J., 46
Meyers, E., 49
Microsoft, 89, 99
Mihalcik, C., 101
Milham, W. I., 77
Miller, C. L., 173
Miller, J., 4
Ministry of Propaganda, 131
minorities
    See Black, Indigenous, and people of color
Mirza, R., 169
misinformation
    academic librarians and, 52
    access and, 127–128
    anti-vaccine movement, 137–138
    characteristics of, 117
    on climate change, 169
    consequences of, 7–8
    conspiracy theories, 119–121
    definition of, 117
    fake news, 116–117

history of advertising/propaganda, 131-135
in human history, 1-3
information definition and, 12
information illiteracy and, 121-123
information literacy and, 6, 41, 148
information literacy as human right, 83
information policy, lack of, 155, 156
information/misinformation access, 127-128
librarians' information literacy and, 157-160
libraries for information literacy instruction,
    111-113
library efforts to battle, 147-148
library's role in information literacy
    instruction, 104-105
media's responsibility for solution to, 106-108
during pandemic, 141-144
polarization in US and, 168
problems, addressing, 101-102
psychology/information literacy, 123-127
Russian government operative scenario,
    118-119
scholarship about, 108
social media and, 138-141
societal-level challenges to information
    literacy, 174-175
solutions, limitations of, 108-109
technology companies and, 105-106
types of, 118
mission, library, 102-104
MIT Technology Review, 107
Mitchell, A., 106
MLA (Medical Library Association), 70-71
*MLA Competencies for Lifelong Learning and
    Professional Success* (Medical Library
    Association), 70-71
MLA Guide to Digital Literacy (Carillo), 161
modeling, 125
Modern Language Association, 161
Mokhtar, I. A., 47, 54
Moncada, A., 80
money
    disinformation and, 174
    information marginalization and, 167-168
    media as profit-driven industry, 167
    monetization of disinformation, 120-121
    myth of currency, 116
Mooney, C., 141
Moore, P., 54
"The Moral Equivalent of War" (James), 128
Morgan, P. K., 51
Morris, L., 120
motivation, 33

Muller, K., 123, 140-141
museums, 82
Myrick, J., 148
myth of currency, 116
mythical creatures, 1-2

N

NAAL (National Assessment of Adult Literacy)
    (NCES), 15
Nagler, J., 127
Narayanswamy, A., 121
*Narrative of the Life of Fredrick Douglass, An
    American Slave* (Douglass), 77, 132
Nassimbeni, M., 62
Natanson, H., 78-79
*A Nation at Risk: The Imperative for Education
    Reform* (National Committee on Excellence
    in Education), 96
National Academies of Sciences, Engineering, and
    Medicine's Committee on Science Literacy
    and Public Perception of Science, 35
National Assessment of Adult Literacy (NAAL)
    (NCES), 15
national borders, 115-116
National Center for Education Statistics (NCES),
    15
National Commission on Libraries and
    Information Science (NCLIS)
    information literacy report, 1974, 16
    Prague Declaration on information literacy,
        24-25, 81-82
National Committee on Excellence in Education,
    96
National Council of Teachers of English (NCTE),
    14-15
National Education Goals, 19
National Educational Technology Plan (DOE's Office
    of Educational Technology), 98
National Forum on Information Literacy (NFIL)
    ACRL *Standards*, development of, 46
    *Alexandria Proclamation on Information
        Literacy and Lifelong Learning*, 21-22
    creation of, 96
    growth of, 21
    information literacy studies, 18-19
    Prague Declaration, 24-25, 81-82
National Information Literacy Awareness Month,
    96-97
National Library of Medicine (NLM), 66, 71
National Park Service, 122
National Public Radio (NPR), 137

National School Library Standards for Learners, School Librarians, and School Libraries (AASL)
adoption of, 57–58
critique of, 27
National Telecommunications and Information Administration (NTIA), 97
Natural History (Pliny the Elder), 1
Nazis, 88, 131
NCES (National Center for Education Statistics), 15
NCLIS
See National Commission on Libraries and Information Science
NCTE (National Council of Teachers of English), 14–15
negativity bias, 125
neoliberalism, 51, 166
Nerone, J., 173
Neuman, D., 55
neutrality, 157, 163–164
New Deal, 80, 153–154
New York Journal, 133
New York Sun, 132
New York Times
article on fake news, 107
articles on election of Donald Trump, 168
digital subscription to, 157
New Zealand, 120
Newhouse, A., 108
news
newsfeeds of social media channels, 138
reliance on social media for, 143–144
from social media, 167
See also fake news; journalism; media
news librarians, 67–68
news libraries, 66–69
Newsmax, 121
newspaper archives, 68
newspapers
in American Revolution time, 95
disinformation in, 116, 132–133
"exchange paper" network, 173–174
literacy and, 86, 87
news libraries and, 67–68
Nextdoor, 140
NFIL
See National Forum on Information Literacy
NGOs (nongovernmental organizations), 96
Nichols, J. L., 138

Nickerson, R. S.
on belief in misinformation, 108
on confirmation bias, 30, 125
Nielsen, B. G., 61
Nixon, Richard, 140
NLM (National Library of Medicine), 66, 71
No Child Left Behind Act, 18
Noble, S. U., 166
NodeGraph, 5
nongovernmental organizations (NGOs), 96
North Carolina Libraries, 45
Norway, 111
novel coronavirus
See coronavirus (COVID-19) pandemic
Nowlain, Lisa, 55
NPR (National Public Radio), 137
NTIA (National Telecommunications and Information Administration), 97
Nunberg, G., 13
nursing, 71–72
Nutbeam, D., 35–36
Nyhan, B., 126

O
Oakleaf, M., 47, 48
Obama, Barack
disinformation about, 140
inauguration of, 122
Internet campaign of, 98–99
National Information Literacy Awareness Month, 96–97
Occam's razor, 83
OECD (Organisation for Economic Co-operation and Development), 15–16
O'Hara, R. E., 139
Ohlheiser, A., 107
Oliemat, E., 53
Olivarez-Giles, N., 82
Olson, H. A., 166
One America News, 174
online assessment tools, 55–56
online learning, 78–79
open access, 40
Oreskes, N., 169
Organisation for Economic Co-operation and Development (OECD), 15–16
Orlean, S., 89, 153
O'Sullivan, C., 39
outreach, 176
Owusu-Ansah, E. K., 112
Oxenham, J., 14

P

Pack Horse Library Project, 153–154

Paine, Thomas, 95

Palfrey, J., 91

pandemic

    See coronavirus (COVID-19) pandemic

Paquette, S., 96, 98

Parler, 108, 138

partnerships

    for information literacy education, 112

    for lifelong information literacy, 151

    See also collaboration

Pascual, R. F., 159

Pashia, A., 147, 166

paternalism, 23

pattern recognition, 124

Paul, N., 67, 68

Pawley, C., 23

Pendleton, V. E., 167–168

penny press, 132

Perez, S., 106

Perlstein, R., 140

Perry, A. M., 165

Perry, Katy, 119

Peter, J., 52

Peterson, L., 166

Petronzio, M., 4

Petrov, C., 5

Pettigrew, T. F., 123

Pew Research Center

    on Americans' views of privacy, 167

    on false news, 106

    on income/wealth inequality trends, 167

    on media literacy, 117

    on political polarization in US, 163

    on public libraries, 109–110

    on social media for news, 144

Phantom Time Theory, 93

Phenix, K. J., 82

physical access, 128

physical spaces, 110–111

PIAAC (Program for the International Assessment of Adult Competencies), 15–16

Pierce, J. M., 82

Pilerot, O., 23, 24

Pinker, S., 86

Pinterest, 140

Pinto, M., 159

pixie dust, 125–126

Pizzagate, 119, 127

PLA (Public Library Association), 61

Plain Language Action and Information Network (PLAIN), 66

plain language movement, 66

plants, 77

PLG (Progressive Librarians Guild), 81

Pliny the Elder, 1

polarization

    anti-vaccine movement and, 138

    political polarization in US, 163

policies

    for information literacy, 151

    information literacy efforts on, 147

    information literacy meets information policy, 154–156

    information literacy meets politicians, 99–100

    libraries, intersection with, 162

    libraries' advocacy role, 157, 158

    support for lifelong information literacy, 176–177

    US policies for information literacy, 96–99

political ads

    ban of on social media sites, 105–106

    social media ad policy changes, 109

political consulting firm, 133–134

political injustice, 166–168

political rights, 80–81

political science, 108

politicians

    advocacy for information literacy, 156

    coronavirus pandemic disinformation, 142

    spin by, 131

politics

    authoritarianism online, 91–93

    civic literacy, 36

    climate change and, 169

    disinformation in advertising, 134

    disinformation in newspapers, 132

    disinformation on social media, 139

    echo chamber and, 31

    filter bubbles on social media, 123

    of information literacy, 95–99

    of information literacy, 2020-style, 99–100

    information literacy meets politicians, 99–100

    information literacy in practice, power of, 29

    libraries, intersection with, 157–158, 162

    misinformation, media's responsibility for, 106

    political resistance to lifelong information literacy, 174–175

    questions about literacy policies, 100

    red and blue America, 168

polling places, libraries as, 111

Pool, I. d. S, 86

Popeye (comic strip), 133
Post, J. A., 32
postmodernism, 46
power
    of disinformation, 128, 174
    of information literacy, 29, 85
    structures, 32
Poynter Institute, 106
practice
    See information literacy, in practice
Prado, J. C., 34
Prague Declaration (UNESCO, NFIL, & NCLIS),
    24-25, 81-82
Pratt, A. D., 12
prejudice, 123
    See also racism
Prensky, M., 53
*The Presidential Commission on Information
    Literacy: Final Report* (ALA Presidential
    Commission on Information Literacy),
    96
presidential elections
    See elections
primary source literacy, 73-74
*Principles and Standards for Legal Research
    Competency* (AALL), 69
printed materials, 86-87
printing press
    control of printed materials, 86-87
    information availability with, 85-86
privacy
    Americans' views of, 167
    politics of information literacy, 95
    young people and, 53
process, 11, 12
Proferes, N., 124
professional organizations, 157
profit, 167
Program for the International Assessment of Adult
    Competencies (PIAAC), 15-16
Progressive Librarians Guild (PLG), 81
Project SAILS (Standardized Assessment of
    Information Literacy Skills), 47
propaganda
    coining of term, 174
    fake news term and, 116, 117
    history of, 131-133
    online, spotting, 107
prose literacy, 4
Protecting Children in the 21st Century Act,
    53
protests, social justice, 143

psychology
    information literacy and, 123-127
    misinformation, reasons for believing, 108
public librarians, 61-64
public libraries
    censorship of information, 87-89
    good actions by, historical examples of, 178-179
    information literacy instruction in, 61-64
    information literacy role of, 109-110
    local funding of, 164-165
    Pack Horse Library Project, 153-154
    trust/relationship with communities, 110
Public Library Association (PLA), 61
public library movement, 87
Pulitzer, Joseph, 133

Q
QAnon conspiracy theory, 119-121
QAnon products, 120-121
Qiang, Y., 91
Qin Shi Huange (Emperor of China), 88
quantitative literacy, 4
questions
    about advertising/propaganda, 135
    about advocacy, activism, self-reflection, 162
    about control of information literacy, 93
    about disinformation/misinformation, 144
    about field guide to incorrect information, 129
    about information literacy, 9, 27
    about information literacy as human right, 84
    about information literacy in practice, 42
    about information literacy, operationalization
        of, 59, 75
    about information literacy politics/policies,
        100
    about information literacy/information
        behavior, 42
    about libraries/information literacy, 113
    about lifelong information literacy, 151
    about social infrastructure, 171

R
race
    BIPOC, lack of in LIS, 165-166
    racial injustice, 164
    racially segregated society in US, 163
racism
    BIPOC, lack of in LIS, 165-166
    disinformation by Donald Trump, 140-141
    in LISS history, 164-165

mistrust of authority and, 165
racial injustice, 164
Rader, E., 124
Rader, H. B., 38
Radical Information Literacy (Whitworth), 16, 21
Rahula, E., 120
Rainie, L., 53
Ramsey, E., 110
Ranganathan, S. R., 103
Rapchak, M., 166
Raphael, D. D., 80
Rapid Estimate of Adult Literacy in Medicine
    (REALM), 35
Rappler, 105
Rauru Whakarare Evaluation Framework (Feekery
    & Jeffrey), 52
reading, 77-78
Reagan, Ronald, 141
REALM (Rapid Estimate of Adult Literacy in
    Medicine), 35
Redi, Francesco, 2-3
Reference and User Services Association (RUSA),
    63
reflection
    in critical information literacy, 37
    in practice of information literacy, 41
    in SCONUL model, 47
regulations, 167
Reifler, J., 126
relationships, 110
relevance, 35
religions, 85-86
Republic of Ireland, 115
Republicans, 106
research
    for information literacy assessment, 159
    on information policy/information literacy, 156
    models for school library information literacy,
        54-55
Richards, P. S., 88
Rieh, S. Y., 123
Ritzhaupt, A. D., 104
Rizzo, S., 140, 143
Robbins, L. S., 88
Roberts-Mahoney, H., 53
Roman Empire, 88
Romm, T.
    on disinformation on social media, 138-139
    on Facebook's monopoly, 167
    on technology companies/misinformation, 105
A Room of One's Own (Woolf), 77
Roose, K., 120

Roosevelt, Eleanor, 80, 82
Roosevelt, Franklin Delano
    on book burning, 88-89
    Pack Horse Library Project, 153-154
    social programs of, 80
Roosevelt, Theodore, 133
Rosen, J., 138
Rosoff, M., 106
royal dynasties, 131
Rubin, A., 34
Rubin, V. L., 117
RUSA (Reference and User Services Association),
    63
Rushkoff, M., 139
Russia
    disinformation on social media during
        pandemic, 141-142
    disinformation/propaganda in, 170

S
SAA
    See Society of American Archivists
Samek, T., 88
Sardarizadeh, S., 101
Sarin, L. C.
    on censorship in US, 87
    on libraries/politics, 157, 162
    on Obama's embrace of technology, 98
    on presidential use of disinformation, 140
satisficing, 32
Saudi Arabia, 91
Saunders, L., 52, 159, 166
Schardt, C., 71
Scharff, D. P., 165
Schield, M., 34
Schmuck, D., 107
school librarians
    information literacy instruction by, 55-56
    information literacy standards and, 57-58
school libraries
    *Framework for Information Literacy for Higher
        Education*, development of, 49-53
    information literacy at, 45-46
    information literacy instruction at, 58
    information literacy role of, 109
    information power, 53-56
    *National School Library Standards for Learners,
        School Librarians, and School Libraries*,
        57-58
    overview of state of, 53
    questions about, 59

school libraries *(cont.)*
>   *Standards*, years of, 46–49
>   *Standards for the 21st-Century Learner*, 56–57
Schudson, M., 132–133
Schultz, P. W., 31, 125
Schwartz, C., 123, 140–141
science
>   climate change, information literacy and,
>   169
>   disinformation and, 141–142
>   fake science, 134
scientific literacy, 34–35
SCONUL
>   *See* Society of College, National and University
>   Libraries
The SCONUL Seven Pillars of Information Literacy:
>   *Core Model for Higher Education* (SCONUL),
>   21, 38
Scott, J. C., 85
Scott, S., 52
screen time, 53
Seale, M.
>   on climate change, 169
>   criticism of information literacy concepts, 49
>   *Framework*, criticism of, 51
>   on information literacy, 21
search, 30–31
Searing, S. E., 48
self-empowerment, 83
Sellars, K., 79, 80
Senegal, 89
Serhan, Y., 139
Shafer, R. G., 133
Shahbaz, A., 92, 170
Shannon, C. E., 11, 13
Shapiro, J. J.
>   on balanced approach to information literacy,
>   167
>   on information literacy, 37, 170
Shared Foundations, 57
Sharot, T., 143
Shearer, E.
>   on news from social media, 167
>   on psychology/information literacy, 123
>   on social media readers, 144
Shelby, T., 123
Shera, J., 157
Sierpe, E.
>   information literacy in social context, 163
>   on lack of BIPOC in LIS, 165
>   on librarianship, 171
Silver, N., 86, 124

Silverman, C., 117
Simmons, S. N., 96, 98
Simulmatics Corporation, 134
Singapore, 54
Singer-Vine, J., 117
Singh, R., 139
skills
>   of information literacy, 22
>   of literacy, 14–15
>   skills-based approach, 54
SLA (Special Libraries Association), 64–65
Slater, J., 121
slavery
>   control of information literacy and, 85
>   Fredrick Douglas's autobiography, 77
>   journalism and, 132
>   literacy, restrictions on, 85
>   in US Constitution, 79
>   US economy built on, 163
small worlds, 31–32
smallpox, 137
Smith, A., 139
Smith, K. B., 125
Smith, L. N., 36
Smoot, Dan, 141
Snavely, L., 19, 33
social access, 128
social bots, 107
social contagion, 125–126
social distancing, 142, 156
social element, of learning processes, 30
social groups, 31–32
social infrastructure
>   BIPOC, lack of in LIS, 165–166
>   climate change, information literacy and, 169
>   conclusion about, 169–171
>   economic/political injustice, 166–168
>   information literacy in social context, 163–164
>   for information literacy support, 7
>   library, meaning of, 164–165
>   lifelong information literacy and, 176–177
>   questions about, 171
>   racial injustice, impact on information literacy,
>   164
>   racism/mistrust of authority, 165
>   societal roadblocks to information literacy,
>   169–170
social justice protests, 143
The Social Life of Information (Brown & Duguid), 13
social media
>   anti-vaccine conspiracy social media accounts,
>   137–138

coronavirus pandemic and, 141-144
corporate control of information literacy, 89-91
disinformation and, 138-141
Donald Trump's use of, 99
fake news, spread of, 105
filter bubbles on, 30-31
as government tool of control, 92
information illiteracy and, 122
information policies, failures of, 155
lifelong information literacy and, 176
misinformation, addressing, 101-102
misinformation solutions, limitations of,
    108-109
misinformation/disinformation on, 118
misinformation/technology companies and,
    105-106
news from/lack of regulation of, 167
psychology/information literacy, 123-127
QAnon conspiracy theory and, 119-121
for US presidential campaign, 98
"The Social Media Fact-Check Farce" (*Wall Street
    Journal*), 108
social norming, 125
social participation, 83
social practice, 26
social structure
    for enabling agency, 39-40
    in information literacy definition, 29
*Social Work: Companion Document to the ACRL
    Framework* (ACRL), 72
societal racism, 164
society
    as context to literacy, 98-99
    failure to practice information literacy, 37-38
    information worlds/landscapes, 31-32
    lack of information literacy, consequences of, 7
    societal factors of information behavior, 32-33
    societal roadblocks to information literacy,
        169-170
    societal-level challenges to information
        literacy, 174-175
Society of American Archivists (SAA)
    Core Values Statement, 72-73
    on information literacy, 73-74
Society of College, National and University
    Libraries (SCONUL)
    on information literacy standards, 47
    Information Skills in Higher Education, 21
    *The SCONUL Seven Pillars of Information
        Literacy: Core Model for Higher Education*,
        21, 38
sociopolitical information, 139

Solomon, D., 163
Soros, George, 142, 143
South Africa
    information literacy role of public librarians
        in, 62
    information literacy standards in, 54
Southeast Asia, 54
special libraries
    Competencies for Information Professionals
        (SLA), 64-65
    government libraries, 65-66
    information literacy education in, 64-72
    law libraries, 69-70
    medical libraries, 70-72
    news libraries, 66-69
Special Libraries Association (SLA), 64-65
spin, 132
St. Jean, B., 137, 160
Stagg, A., 148
standardized tests, 55-56
standards
    assessment of information literacy instruction,
        47-48
    frames of information literacy instruction,
        48-49
    for information literacy, 45
    *Information Literacy Competency Standards for
        Higher Education* (ACRL), 46-47
    *Information Literacy Competency Standards
        for Journalism Students and Professionals*
        (ACRL), 68
    *Information Literacy Competency Standards for
        Nursing*, 71-72
    *Information Literacy Standards for Student
        Learning* (AASL), 54
    international information literacy standards,
        47
    *National School Library Standards for Learners,
        School Librarians, and School Libraries*
        (AASL), 57-58
    *Principles and Standards for Legal Research
        Competency* (AALL), 69
    Standards for Students (ISTE), 58
    Standards for the 21st-Century Learner (AASL),
        56-57
    Standards Framework for Learners (AASL),
        26-27
Stanier, C., 34
Stanley-Becker, I., 120, 138-139
Stapleton, A. C., 122
states, borders of, 115-116
statistics, 34-35

Stauffer, S. M., 87
Stec, E., 53
Stevens, Ted, 98
Stewart, E., 109
Stinnett, G., 82
"Storytellers without Borders" program (Dallas Public Library), 107-108
Strauss, V., 93, 107
Street, B., 14
Strittmatter, K., 92
Strover, S., 97
Struve, Fredrich von, 93
students
    college students, context of, 45-46
    media literacy of, 117
    online learning, Internet access for, 78-79
    school libraries, information literacy at, 53-58
Sturges, P., 148
Suarez, D., 82
Sullivan, M., 143, 144
Sullivan, M. C.
    on cognitive dissonance, 108
    criticism of information literacy instruction, 104, 105
    criticism of lifelong information literacy, 112-113
    on fake news/misinformation, 111
    on misinformation, 52
    on trust of public libraries, 110
Summers, M. W., 174
Sunstein, C. R.
    on control of information, 86
    on correcting political misinformation, 127
    on group polarization, 126
    on "Second Bill of Rights," 80
surveillance, 91-92
Svendsen, G. L. H., 110
Svenonius, E., 13
Svolik, M. W., 140
Swanson, T. A., 47, 166
Sweeny, K., 33
Systema Natura (Linnaeus), 1

T
tags, on tweets, 101
Tallack, M., 1
Tandoc, E. C., Jr.
    on fake news, 116, 117
    on journalism's roles in spreading misinformation, 158

tasks
    in Big6 model, 20
    in information search process, 40
    literacy for performing, 15
TATIL (Threshold Achievement Test for Information Literacy), 47-48
Taylor, N. G.
    on civic literacy, 36
    on contributions of libraries, 154
    on Donald Trump/Internet policy, 99
    on funding for school libraries, 53
    on information as human right, 81
    on information literacy as human right, 3, 6
    on information literacy, libraries and, 4
    on information policy, 156
    on libraries serving communities during pandemic, 177
    on libraries/politics, 157, 162
    on lifelong information literacy, 5, 179
    on politics of information literacy, 98
    on user data, 90
technology
    climate change and, 169
    digital literacy, 33-34
    information as human right, 81
    information literacy as human right, 82-84
    Internet economy/industrial economy, 175
    policies for information literacy and, 97
    as profit-driven industry, 167
    See also information technologies
technology companies
    information policy, lack of, 155
    misinformation, addressing, 105-106
    partnerships for information literacy education, 112
Telecommunications Act of 1996, 97
telegraph
    government control with, 91
    newspapers' use of, 133
terms of service agreements, 90
tests, 55-56
Tewell, E., 23-24, 166
Thirty Years' War, 86
Thompson, D., 126
Thompson, E. P., 173
Thompson, F. B., 12
Thompson, K. M.
    on digital literacy, 33
    on information access stages, 128
    on information literacy as human right, 82, 83
    on information poverty, 32
    on Internet access, 89

on lack of digital literacy, 98
on lack of online access, 78
on policies for information literacy, 97, 98-99
Thoreau, Henry David, 132
Threshold Achievement Test for Information
  Literacy (TATIL), 47-48
threshold concepts
  criticism of, 51
  definition of, 25
  of *Framework*, 51
  Framework's definition of, 50
  information literacy instruction and, 49
TikTok, 106
Timberg, C.
  on conspiracy theories, 120
  on disinformation on social media, 138
  on Frazzledrip, 119
  on technology companies/misinformation, 105
Time magazine, 168
TMIA (Tripartite Model of Information Access),
  128
tobacco companies, 134
Tocqueville, Alexis de, 173
Tomorrow's Illiterates (Council for Basic
  Education), 96
Torres, D., 73
TRAILS (Tool for Real-Time Assessment of
  Information Literacy Skills) trails, 55-56
training, 97-98
Tripartite Model of Information Access (TMIA),
  128
troubadours, 86
trouble, 178-179
Truman, Harry, 134
Trump, Donald
  coronavirus pandemic disinformation and,
    142-143
  crowd size, alternative facts about, 122
  disinformation, monetization of, 121
  disinformation on Twitter, spread of, 127
  fake news before 2016 election, 117
  fake news, use of term, 116
  funding cuts for information literacy, 92
  information illiteracy and, 122
  Internet, relationship to, 99
  misinformation spread by, 3
  New York Times articles about, 168
  pixie dust phenomenon and, 126
  QAnon conspiracy theory and, 119-121
  social media, use of, 140
  supporters of, 123
  tweets with warning labels, 101

trust
  lack of trust in media, 109
  mistrust of authority, 165
  in public libraries, 110-111
  racial injustice and, 164
  social media and, 108
  trust/relationship with communities, 110
Trust Indicators, 107
Trust Project, 107
truth
  assessment of validity of information, 119
  conspiracy theories and, 92
  doubt and, 2
  information literacy and, 8, 13
  Occam's razor, 83
  point of view and, 171
  relativism of postmodernism, 46
Truth, Sojourner, 132
Tucker, J., 127
Tuominen, K., 24
Turkey, 91
Tuskegee Syphilis Study, 165
Twain, Mark, 173
Twitter
  corporate control of information literacy, 89
  disinformation, actions to combat, 140
  disinformation, spread of, 127
  Donald Trump's use of, 99, 140-141
  misinformation prevention by, 106
  QAnon conspiracy theory on, 120
  social media ad policy changes, 109
  warning labels on Donald Trump's tweets,
    101
Tyson, A., 163

U
UDHR (Universal Declaration of Human Rights),
  80-82
UN Human Rights Council, 82
United Kingdom
  Brexit support, 123
  Brexit vote in, 3
  disinformation in, 118
  information literacy in, 21
  information literacy standards in, 47
  journalism students in, 68-69
  Magna Carta, 79
  public libraries in, 87
  states/borders of, 115
  Victorian anti-vaccine movement in, 137
United Nations, 80

United Nations Educational, Scientific and
Cultural Organization (UNESCO)
*Alexandria Proclamation on Information
Literacy and Lifelong Learning*, 21-22
definition of literacy, 15
information as human right, 81
information literacy programs in Southeast
Asia, 54
Prague Declaration, 24-25, 81-82
United States
censorship of information in, 87-89
coronavirus pandemic in, 141-144
disinformation in, 118
foundations of human rights in, 79-80
founding myths/borders of, 115-116
misinformation in presidential election, 3
politics of information literacy, 95-99
racism/political polarization in, 163
Universal Declaration of Human Rights (UDHR),
80-82
Universal Etymological English Dictionary (Bailey),
86
universal rights, 79-80
University of Illinois at Urbana-Champaign, 48
unlogic phenomenon, 168
US Committee on Public Information, 133
US Constitution
human rights included in, 79
information issues in, 95
UDHR and, 80
US Department of Education (DOE), 4, 98
US Department of Health and Human Services
(HHS), 71
US Department of State Global Engagement
Center, 170
US Institute of Medicine (IOM), 35
US Postal Service (USPS), 173
US presidential election of 2008, 98
US presidential election of 2016
disinformation during, 122
filter bubbles on social media, 123
information literacy efforts after, 159
misinformation and, 3, 147
US presidential election of 2020
attempts to overturn popular vote/Electoral
college, 175
misinformation and, 176
political ads on social media, 105
user data, 139, 167
users
corporate control of information literacy,
89-91

information literacy, motivating users about,
161
USPS (US Postal Service), 173

V
Vaccination Act, 137
vaccine
anti-vaccine movement, modern, 137-138
anti-vaccine movement, Victorian, 137
counterknowledge about, 126
disinformation during pandemic and, 142-144
mistrust of, 165
Vaidhyanathan, S., 90, 91
Valtin, R., 15
vampirism, 119
Van der Linden, S., 169
Vangeest, J., 166
Vårheim, A., 110
Varlejs, J., 53
Vienna World Conference on Human Rights, 1993,
81
Vietnam War, 141
Villalpando, O., 166
A Vindication of the Rights of Woman
(Wollstonecraft), 79
Vinopal, J., 161, 165
von Sikorski, C., 107
voters, 140

W
Wade, A. C., 55
Waisbord, S.
on disinformation, 132
on government control of information, 92
on misinformation, 158
Wakabayashi, D. A., 142
Wakefield, Andrew, 137
Wall Street Journal, 108
war
disinformation in journalism and, 133
religious wars after printing press, 85-86
William James on, 128
The War of the Worlds (Wells), 97
War on Christmas, 92
War on Terror, 179
Ward, D., 64
Wardle, C., 117-118
warnings, on social media posts, 105
Washington, E. Y., 36
Washington, George, 116

Washington, H., 169
Washington, H. A., 165
Washington Post, 140
Watson, P. D., 87
Wayles, Martha, 132
wealth inequality, 167
weapons of mass destruction (WMDs), 126–127
Weaver, W., 13
Webber, S., 47, 105
Weems, Mason Locke, 116
Weiner, S. A., 48
Wellington, S., 73
Wells, H. G., 97
West Virginia, 116
Whelan, D. J., 81
White, H. S., 39
White, S., 15
White House, 127
Whitworth, A.
    on ACRL's information literacy standards, 20
    on civic literacy, 36
    on critical information literacy, 22–23
    on information, 13
    on information in small worlds, 31
    on information literacy, 17
    on information literacy standards in US, 21
    on misinformation, 41
    on power structures/information poverty, 32
    Radical Information Literacy, 16
WHO (World Health Organization), 141
Why Johnny Can't Read (Flesch), 96
Wiegand, W. A.
    on censorship, 87, 88
    on library book lists, 158
William of Occam, 83
Williams, A., 163
Williamson, C., 30
Williamson, K., 31, 104
Wills, K., 89
Willson, G., 72
Wilson, P., 40
Winchester, S., 93
Wineburg, S., 108, 117
Winkel, J., 168–169
Wired Magazine, 107
Wisconsin Health Literacy, 66
WMDs (weapons of mass destruction), 126–127
Wolcott, J., 168
Wolf, M., 78
Wollstonecraft, M., 79
women, rights of, 79
Wong, J. C., 120

Woodiwiss, A., 80
Woolf, Virginia, 77
Works Progress Administration (WPA), 153–154
World Health Organization (WHO), 141
World War I
    censorship of information in, 88
    disinformation in journalism and, 133
World War II
    American casualties in, 141
    censorship of information in, 88–89
    fake news during, 116
    prejudice during, 123
WPA (Works Progress Administration), 153–154
writing
    early human writing, 77
    human adoption of, 78
WUSA9 (television station), 134

X
Xu, B., 170

Y
Yakel, E., 73
Yan, Z., 91, 97
Yang, S., 104
Yee, A., 107
Young, L. M., 72
YouTube, 101, 109
Yurieff, K., 105

Z
Zakrzewski, C., 140
Zang, D., 117
Zannettou, S., 118
Zelenika, I., 82
Zhou, L., 117
Zimmer, M., 82
Zittrain, J., 91
Zurkowski, P. G.
    on information illiteracy, 121
    on information literacy, 22
    information literacy groundwork by, 16